GEORGE H. CALLCOTT

A History of the
University of Maryland

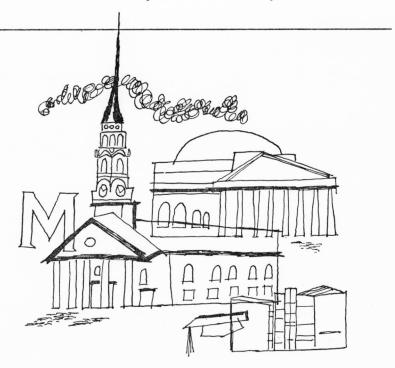

MARYLAND HISTORICAL SOCIETY
BALTIMORE, MARYLAND

Foreword

The Maryland Historical Society, from time to time, publishes works which its Publications Committee and its Council deem to be of value to the history of the State. The Society believes that *A History of the University of Maryland* by Professor George H. Callcott is such a work. The book deals with the largest educational institution of the State—an institution which has grown from a small professional school into one of the dozen largest state universities in the country, with activities reaching far beyond the borders of Maryland and, indeed, of the United States. Its history is the story of an unusual growth, in that the development of the great undergraduate school has followed, rather than preceded, the establishment and development of several professional schools which were brought together in 1920 with a then small undergraduate college.

In presenting this history, Professor Callcott has not confined himself to a mere recital of chronological events or statistics. He has undertaken to picture the development of the institution through its more than 150 years and the people who have played prominent parts, some of them quite recently, in that development. Such a work necessarily involves the expression of many appraisals or evaluations of persons and events. These are, of course, those of the author and are not intended to be or to be taken as expressions of opinions of the Society. As Professor Callcott makes clear in his Preface, the book does not purport to be an official history of the University.

The book is written with affection for the University, with sympathetic understanding of and for those who strove to advance its cause and to enhance its stature, and with an understanding of the academic problems which confront a university; and it is enlivened with touches of humor. We consider it a valuable and scholarly addition to works on Maryland history.

FREDERICK W. BRUNE, *President*
Maryland Historical Society

November 29, 1965

HAMILTON OWENS
For the Publications Committee

Preface

The history of the University of Maryland is in some ways a history of all large modern universities. It is a story of eighteenth century educational theories which slowly developed, of nineteenth century classical colleges and professional schools which merged with the land-grant movement, and of twentieth century technology and affluence which have made universities a part of the life and hope of all society. I have tried to tell the story in these broad terms. I have tried to emphasize the traditions, the ideas and the social forces which have shaped the modern university.

The University of Maryland also has a distinct life and personality of its own. Its youth was unusually long and hard, its adolescence sometimes bumptious, but today it seems to be in the summer of its maturity as one of the oldest and largest educational institutions in the United States. Although this book is not primarily a memorial to individual efforts, nor a record of anecdotes about favorite professors, I have tried to capture the University's unique personality. It has been a humbling experience for me to sit in judgment. Thousands of men and women have given their careers to the institution; over 120,000 have received degrees from it; and probably millions have felt its influence. Surely it is for me to dedicate this volume to all of them.

Six years ago the University's History Department recommended that this book be undertaken by a member of the faculty who would be given free access to University records and a completely free hand in interpreting the material. The Department recommended the creation of a faculty committee to offer advice, but emphasized that the author must be solely responsible for the book that would finally result. President Elkins and the board of regents accepted these recommendations, and I was asked to undertake the project. For three years I received partial relief from teaching duties, and for two summers I received research grants from the General Research Board. Th University always made plain that this assistance was aid to an individual on a private research project. For this assistance, and for this freedom, I am grateful. The book is in no way an "official" history, and has in no way been "approved" by the administration or the board of regents. I am alone responsible for all factual statements and for all interpretations drawn from them.

Many people have aided me. I am indebted to Professors Verne E. Chatelain, Paul K. Conkin, Aubrey C. Land, David S. Sparks and Roland Stromberg, all of the History Department, and to Professor Owen Aldridge of the English Department for serving as an advisory committee. I obtained especially valuable interviews and suggestions from Dr. H. C. Byrd, Dr. W. H. Elkins, Mr. George Fogg, Dean Adele Stamp, Mrs. John L. Whitehurst and Professor A. E. Zucker. Mr. Howard Rovelstad and Mrs. Isabella M. Hayes, Miss Elizabeth Litzinger, Mrs. Ida M. Robinson and Dr. Morris L. Radoff and their staffs at the McKeldin Library, the Enoch Pratt Library, the Health Sciences Library and the Hall of Records have all been of assistance. Dean Charles Manning of the College of Arts and Sciences, and Professor Frank Gatell of the University of California, Los Angeles, provided aid and encouragement. Mr. Carl P. Lewis and Mr. Frank Waselewski served ably as graduate assistants. The picture of H. C. Byrd before the legislature is reproduced through courtesy of the Baltimore *Sunpapers,* and the picture of Charles Benedict Calvert is reproduced through the courtesy of his great-granddaughter, Mrs. David Randolph Ray of Fayetteville, North Carolina. The Maryland Historical Society has generously supported the publication of this volume. To Mr. Harold R. Manakee, Director of the Society, I am especially indebted for his painstaking editorial assistance. Finally, thanks are due my parents, Professor and Mrs. W. H. Callcott, and to my wife, Peggy.

College Park   GEORGE H. CALLCOTT
November, 1965

Table of Contents

A History of the
University of Maryland

First the forests, then the huts, then the villages,
then the cities, and finally the academies.

VICO

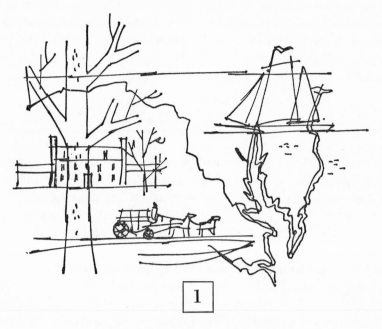

The Idea of a University

Almost from the time men heard of America they were planning its universities. The virgin land inspired practical men to dream of gold and glory, oppressed men to dream of freedom and philosophical men to conceive of new institutions springing up in the wilderness to create a new and nobler society. The Puritans established Harvard in 1636, only six years after they landed; the Virginia settlers opened William and Mary in 1693; and when George Washington became president in 1789 the little frontier American nation boasted twenty institutions of higher learning, each ambitiously building its own version of a more perfect society.

In Maryland as elsewhere the idea of a university flourished. Before the first settlers arrived, and while great philosophers like Sir Francis Bacon and Sir Thomas More talked grandly of utopian universities, an eccentric English gentleman actually purchased an island within the present boundaries of the state to build a university which would be awaiting the first settlers. Of course the scheme failed, but the Maryland colonial legislature spent so much time considering other plans that, according to one historian, it devoted more time to debating education than to any other subject.[1] In any case, of the twenty colleges in America in 1789, two of the most promising were on opposite shores of the Chesapeake Bay, combined, according to their charter, as the University of Maryland.

The Yearning for a University

The man who spent his fortune trying to found the first university in the English colonies was a peculiar idealist, Edward Palmer. Little is known of him except that he was a wealthy art collector and that two of his associates chose the word "curious" to describe him. He attended Oxford University but never graduated. Perhaps his experiences there impelled him to create his own college which, to say the least, would be unhampered by tradition.[2]

Palmer's scheme began about 1616, eighteen years before the permanent Maryland settlement appeared at St. Mary's. At that time the Virginia Company owned the territory of Maryland, and Palmer purchased from it an island in the mouth of the Susquehanna River near the present town of Havre de Grace. The land cost Palmer about one hundred pounds, but since he was "at many *thousand* pounds expense" in his scheme for a college his plans must have gone further. In 1622 an English trading vessel reported about a hundred settlers and fur traders on the island, and several years later another vessel found there a deserted village and a small abandoned library. Palmer himself may have led the group to America, or perhaps he employed agents with professed interests in higher education. It may have been that they attempted to trade with the Indians to make a profit for the college or for themselves. Whatever happened, the enterprise failed. We have left only Palmer's cryptic remark that he had been "betrayed" by dishonest agents.[3]

[1] Bernard C. Steiner, *History of Education in Maryland* (Washington, 1894), 20.

[2] William Camden, *Britannia; or, A Chronological Description of Great Britain and Ireland* . . . [first edition 1590], 2 vols. (London, 1753), I, 283; Thomas Fuller, *History of the Worthies of England* [first edition 1662], 2 vols. (London, 1811), I, 387. See also Anthony A. Wood, *Athenea Oxoniensis, An Extant History of All the Writers and Bishops Who Have Had Their Education in the University of Oxford*, 2 vols. (London, 1815), II, 28.

[3] Susan Myra Kingsbury (ed.), *Records of the Virginia Company of London*, 4 vols. (Washington, 1906-1935), I, 421 and *passim;* II, 77, 90; III, 549; Fuller, *History of the Worthies of England*, I, 387; William Hand Brown *et al.* (eds.), *Archives of Maryland*, 68 vols. (Baltimore, 1883-1959), III, 76.

The most complete information about the college occurs in Palmer's will written in 1624 just before he died. Hoping that someone would revive his design, he briefly sketched the plan to which he had devoted his life and fortune:

All the aforesaid Castles Lande Tenements and Heriditaments in Virginia and new England aforesaid shall be and remaine for the foundinge and maintenance of an Universitie and such schooles in Virginia as shall be there erected and shall be called Academia Virginiensis et Oxoniensis and shall be divided into severall streets or Alleyes of Twenty foot broade. And further my will is that the Schollers of the said Universitye for avoydinge of idleness at their hours of recreation shall have two paynters the one for oyle Coullers and the other for water Coullers which shall be admitted fellows in the same college to the end and intent that the said Schollers shall or may learne the arte of paynting. And further my mind and will is that two grinders the one for oyle Coullers and [the] other for water Coullers and also Coullers oyle and gumme waters shall be provided from tyme to tyme at the Costs and Charges of the said Colledge.[4]

Palmer's college and art institute soon were forgotten. Yet even in this quixotic episode certain prophetic implications seem to appear for American education. For one thing, it seemed to point to an extraordinary faith in frontier colleges as a means of setting the world straight and improving men. Within a few decades of settlement the English colonists could boast the highest proportion of college graduates to total population of any society in history. By attempting to underwrite the cost of higher education, Palmer seemed to point toward the relatively inexpensive education which would become available in the new land. Above all, his initiative in founding a college and outlining its function was prophetic. Instead of growing up largely on their own around a guild of scholars as most European institutions had done, American colleges usually were founded and controlled by outside philanthropists, religious denominations or state appointed trustees. Such outside control meant strong college administrations, emphasis on teaching rather than scholarship and relatively low status for the employed faculty members, all of which marked the development of American higher education.

When settlement finally came, the Maryland pioneers were almost as visionary as Palmer in their endless planning for the college which

[4]Palmer's will is registered PCC 114 Byrde, Somerset House, London, England. Photostatic copy, McKeldin Library, University of Maryland.

seemed so necessary. In 1671, for example, when there were less than 8,000 people, including slaves, scattered over the colony, the legislative assembly launched a long debate over establishing a "Colledge within this Province for the Education of Youth in Learning and Virtue."[5] A few years later, when there was still no village of as many as 200 souls, Governor Francis Nicholson became so disturbed about the lack of higher education that he offered a personal endowment of fifty pounds if the assembly would charter a university. The legislature claimed to share the governor's enthusiasm, and as individuals they pledged 45,400 pounds of tobacco and a guinea of gold as their contribution to the project. The promise far exceeded the original endowment of Harvard, but legislation never materialized.[6]

The plans for a college multiplied, always outdistancing the possibilities for realization. A prominent planter, Augustine Herrman, in 1684 left three estates to his sons, providing that if the line ever died out the lands should revert to the general assembly to endow a university. One of his stipulations was that the institution should offer "free alms and . . . hospitality" to anyone lost or in need of shelter.[7]

The general assembly, in 1732, considered a plan to import scholars from England for a university which would teach not only the traditional subjects, but also "Diversions and Amusements . . . Diet, Washing, Lodging, etc." Graduates were then to disseminate this higher learning by employment in a vast public school system. One reason for the enthusiasm for higher education was the assumption that learning percolated down instead of up and that teachers had to be trained before students. The emphasis on colleges rather than on public schools helps to explain the disappointing growth of many colonial colleges, since they seldom found a sufficient number of qualified applicants.[8]

By the end of the eighteenth century, the most ambitious discussion in American educational circles concerned the possibilities of a national school system capped by a national university, and when such grandiose plans were discussed Maryland always seemed in the

[5]Brown et al., Archives of Maryland, II, 262-264.
[6]Ibid., XIX, 36, 49.
[7]Steiner, Education in Maryland, 18.
[8]Brown et al., Archives of Maryland, XXXVIII, 456-458; L, 473-482; LVIII, 259, 377-381, 393-394, 402-404; Maryland Gazette (Annapolis), 4 November 1773.

forefront. A Presbyterian minister and educational propogandist in Baltimore, Samuel Knox, drew up a detailed plan which he presented in 1799 to the general assembly. According to his plan, a free elementary school should be available in every village in the country; the best students should then be allowed to attend a free high school which should be established in each county. The best high school graduates would go on to a state college, and the best college graduates would proceed to a free national university which would be established, of course, in Maryland.

Knox's national university, designed for the elite of the nation, would serve as the apex of American culture. Devoted exclusively to graduate work, it would offer a three-year master's degree to the future leaders of the nation. Knox envisioned a lovely campus with neat quadrangles, a model which may have influenced Thomas Jefferson's plans for the University of Virginia. Around the quadrangles would be professors' homes, with servant quarters in the rear, and with a wing attached to each house to serve as classrooms and laboratories. Nearby would be dormitories, auditoriums, chapels, art galleries and book stalls. A university press would disseminate those ideas which the students or professors felt worthwhile.[9]

For at least twenty years various plans for a national university were debated. Washington and Jefferson both corresponded with Knox, and both presented similar plans to the United States Congress. Washington became so enthusiastic over the idea that he left a bequest of almost $100,000 to found a national university. What happened to this money is a minor unsolved riddle of American history, for certainly Congress never used it for the designated purpose. State rights, sectional jealousy, hatred of taxation and fear of government influence in education all conspired against the plan. The idea of a national cultural and intellectual center has so fascinated dreamers, however, that even today there are occasional flurries of interest in the possibilities of a national university.[10]

[9]Samuel Knox, *Essay on the Best System of Liberal Education . . . To Which Is Prefixed, An Address to the Legislature of Maryland on That Subject* (Baltimore, 1799). The legislature liked the plan and took 500 pounds from Washington College as a start toward establishing Knox's public schools. William Kilty, *Laws of Maryland . . .*, 2 vols. (Annapolis, 1799-1800), II, 1798, Chap. 107.

[10]John S. Brubacher and Willis Rudy, *Higher Education in Transition; An American History: 1636-1956* (New York, 1958), 217-218; Edgar B. Wesley, *Proposed: The University of the United States* (Minneapolis, 1936).

Although Maryland fully shared the colonial passion for colleges, and if anything planned too grandly, there were also powerful forces which conspired against higher education within the colony. For at least a century after settlement the chief problem in Maryland was the sparseness of population, or more particularly the wide separation of settlers from each other. In the northern colonies, where eight of the first nine successful colleges were established, men settled in towns, but in Maryland they lived far apart on plantations. A hundred years after the settlement at St. Mary's there was still no town of more than 500 people in the entire colony, and few roads connected the tiny villages that existed.[11]

Another problem, greater than in some other colonies, was Maryland's dependence upon the culture and the cultural institutions of England. Prosperous planters who lived along the tidewater streams that flowed into the Chesapeake generally sold directly to England from their own tobacco landings, and directly imported necessities for their families and other dependents, so that in many ways their contacts with London were closer than their contacts with Annapolis or Chestertown. Despite their lip-service enthusiasm for American culture and education, in fact they looked to England which they called "home" even to the fourth and fifth generation. Each year at least a dozen and sometimes more than a score of the planters' sons went to learn Latin and the social graces at Oxford, Cambridge or Edinburgh. Each year three or four Maryland planters sent their sons south to William and Mary or north to Pennsylvania or Princeton.

As population slowly increased, a graver problem appeared in the rivalry between residents of the eastern and western shores of the Chesapeake. The jealousy must be illustrated rather than explained, for it was generally easier to travel across the Bay than across an equivalent number of land miles, and the economic and political differences between the shores was hardly as great as those between the northern and southern counties of the colony. Still, the rivalry became more intense throughout the eighteenth century until even a marriage could evoke feelings worthy of Montagues and Capulets. The general assembly noted in 1782 that every recent plan for a college "hath been retarded . . . chiefly by the great difficulty of

[11]Arthur Eli Karinen, "Numerical and Distributional Aspects of Maryland Population, 1631-1840" (Ph.D. dissertation, University of Maryland, 1958), 104, 158 and *passim*.

fixing a situation on either shore of this state."[12] Two years later when Washington College finally was established at Chestertown, St. John's College had to be established at Annapolis; and with state support thus divided, neither college fulfilled expectations.

Religion was also a problem. Most of the original thirteen colonies possessed a religious homogeneity so that denominational fervor and educational enthusiasm combined to procure state support for colleges to train ministers. Each of the first nine successful colleges in America involved an alliance between church and state. In Maryland, on the other hand, the population was more or less evenly divided between Roman Catholics and Protestants, most of whom were Anglicans. Neither group could hope to obtain state support for a college.[13] Religious diversity made the state the most tolerant of the English colonies so that Maryland's famous Toleration Act of 1649 may have been the first official act of its kind in the history of Christendom, but toleration did not make colleges. Marylanders also wanted denominational institutions, and by 1860 eleven church-supported colleges were established; but all struggled along without state support and without the success achieved by similar colleges in other colonies.[14]

Finally, by the end of the eighteenth century the most powerful opposition to a state university came from the proponents of public schools who believed elementary education should come before higher education. Essentially the struggle was between the rich and the poor. Since the upper classes ordinarily hired tutors for their sons' education, they did not want to be taxed for a public school system, but they did want state-supported colleges. The poorer classes, meanwhile, felt a need for public schools, but had no desire to be taxed for a system of higher education. In the colonies and states north of Maryland class distinctions were relatively slight so that public schools and public colleges tended to emerge simultaneously. In the colonies and states south of Maryland, the upper classes were strong enough to override opposition and establish state

[12]Kilty, *Laws of Maryland*, I, 1782, Chap. 8; II, 1784, Chap. 37.

[13]*Maryland Gazette*, 16 May 1754; 29 September 1785; 30 May 1793; Leo Joseph McCormick, *Church-State Relationships in Education in Maryland* (Washington, 1942), 33-37.

[14]Cokesbury (Methodist) 1784; St. Mary's (Catholic) 1806; Mount St. Mary's (Catholic) 1808; Asbury (Methodist) 1816; St. Charles (Catholic) 1829; New Windson (Presbyterian) 1843; St. James (Episcopalian) 1843; Loyola (Catholic) 1856; Borroneo (Catholic) 1860. Most lasted only a year or two; St. Mary's, Mount St. Mary's and Loyola exist today.

universities without concern for public schools. But Maryland was the middle ground where the upper and lower classes checkmated each other, so that the state was handicapped in building either public schools or colleges.[15]

And yet the obstacles were going to be surmounted. By the 1780's the state was prosperous and population was soaring. Independence from England was making the development of American educational institutions a practical necessity as well as an idealistic dream. With the tacit agreement that a state university must be nondenominational, Maryland began laying a secular base for education which promised more in the long run than the traditional theological base. Problems of state sectionalism and of lower class opposition to a university both continued to be substantial, and they would plague the future university of Maryland for many years; but they were chiefly a matter of prejudice that could be overcome by a convincing spokesman. Here, in fact, may have been the most fundamental problem, and one that frequently recurred. Maryland needed a practical leader who could maintain idealistic aims and at the same time defend the values of a university against the arguments of its opponents. By 1782 such a man had appeared, and as long as he was in the state prospects for a university looked bright.

The First University of Maryland

Of all Maryland's early educational leaders William Smith was at once the most idealistic and the most ruthlessly realistic. Almost singlehandedly in 1782 he created Washington College at Chestertown, and three years later he founded St. John's College in Annapolis, combining them under state control as the University of Maryland. The colleges remain, the two oldest in the State. If Smith had remained they might have provided the base for the permanent state university he intended.

William Smith was a big, contentious Scotsman who arrived in America in 1751, fresh from the University of Aberdeen and full of ideas for founding new colleges of his own. Outlining his concept of an ideal institution in a remarkable pamphlet entitled *A General*

[15]*Maryland Gazette,* 21 April 1785; 22 December 1785; 12 March 1795; 10 March 1803.

Idea for the College of Mirania, he immediately became one of the most influential men in the history of American higher education.[16] As he hoped, the pamphlet caught the attention of Benjamin Franklin, and Smith was invited to join the faculty of the academy in Philadelphia which Franklin was trying to convert into a university. Fully intending to take over as its first provost, a title which he invented to distinguish himself from ordinary college presidents, the 26-year-old Smith was only momentarily put off by the disdain of Philadelphians for his brashness and youth. To attain the requisite dignity, off he sailed to England to return a year later wearing the vestments of an Anglican clergyman. In 1755 he wrote the charter for, and became provost of, the University of Pennsylvania which he proceeded to mold into his Miranian ideal. Although the University flourished, the irascible provost was soon in trouble. Within three years he had talked his way into jail by opposing too violently the colony's Indian policy. During the Revolution he was again jailed for his loyalist views, and this time was discharged from the University.[17]

William Smith then came to Maryland. The ex-college president arrived humbly in Chestertown in 1780, accepting a position as parish minister for an annual salary of 600 bushels of wheat. Almost immediately he was teaching private classes for boys, and a few months later when Kent Academy needed a principal it seemed natural that Smith should have the post. The university builder was on his way again. When he became principal the little academy had about 30 students, but within two years it was bursting with 144. Smith was ready to make it into a college and into a state university.[18]

Mirania and the colleges which Smith launched were distinguished by the breadth of their aims, for he believed that higher education, more than any other agency in society, was capable of producing virtuous men and a flourishing civilization. Colleges would not only preserve the learning of the past, provide justification for moral conduct and train for the learned professions, but also would fun-

---

[16]Brubacher and Rudy, *Higher Education in Transition,* 13-21.

[17]Harris Elwood Starr, "William Smith," Allen Johnson and Dumas Malone (eds.), *Dictionary of American Biography,* 22 vols. (New York, 1946), XVII, 353-357; Gilbert W. Mead, "William Smith, Founder of Colleges," *Association of American Colleges Bulletin,* XXVII (May, 1941), 270-280; Edward Potts Cheyney, *History of the University of Pennsylvania, 1740-1840* (Philadelphia, 1940), 61-170.

[18]Horace Wemyss Smith, *Life and Correspondence of Rev. William Smith, D.D.,* 2 vols. (Philadelphia, 1880), II, 34-35, 64.

damentally broaden the moral and intellectual capacity of men. Designed to improve society rather than sustain it, to perfect men
rather than hold them in check, Smith's aims for a college have been
called the first "not deriving from medieval tradition nor designed to
serve a religious purpose." He combined the traditional American
desire to straighten out the world with the eighteenth century belief
in the perfectability of man. Smith launched the American colleges
on their quest to impart knowledge as well as character, truth as well
as virtue, and intellectual and social happiness as well as the means of
earning a livelihood.[19]

But with philosophical ideas Smith had only begun. Quickly he
displayed the kind of practical, aggressive leadership that Maryland
had never seen in its previous educational planners. Pupils, congre-
gations, legislators and total strangers were dunned to help him
obtain a college charter for his academy. In May, 1782, the general
assembly reluctantly acceded, providing that if 5,000 pounds sterling
could be raised as a private endowment within five years, then Kent
Academy might become a college.[20] Pity the Marylander in the path
of William Smith! On horseback he appeared at almost every village
and farm, postmen carried his letters and circulars, trembling par-
ishioners bought their way out of hell with contributions, and the
well-intentioned who defaulted on their pledges found themselves
headed for jail.[21] George Washington, after whom the college was
named, was persuaded to contribute over 50 pounds and humbly
apologized for not giving more.[22] One historian estimated that
Smith collected five percent of the circulating money in the entire
state.[23] In any case, within five months instead of the five years
allotted by the legislature, Smith easily exceeded the required 5,000
pounds, and Washington College received its official charter.

Aware of the problems that university builders had faced before
him, Smith met them forthrightly. To allay rivalry between the
shores—and possibly also to enlarge his sphere of operation—he

[19]William Smith, *A General Idea of the College of Mirania* (New York, 1753), 3-17
and *passim;* Guy E. Snavely, "The College of Mirania," *Association of American
Colleges Bulletin,* XXVII (May, 1941), 281-285; Frederick Rudolph, *The American
College and University: A History* (New York, 1962), 32 and *passim.*

[20]Kilty, *Laws of Maryland,* I, 1782, Chap. 8.

[21]Warrant for arrest of Thomas Craddock, 10 February 1795; and for Adam Gantz,
12 March 1796. MS. scrap, University of Maryland Papers, McKeldin Library, University of Maryland.

[22]Smith, *Life of Smith,* II, 85-86.

[23]McCormick, *Church-State Relationships,* 49.

covered all his efforts for an eastern shore college with assurances that a sister institution would be established on the western shore. Two years after Washington College was chartered, he began collecting money for St. John's College in Annapolis, and while that school did not begin college level instruction until 1789, Smith dominated its opening ceremonies.[24]

To guarantee that the two colleges prosper as a single state-supported institution, Smith persuaded the legislature, in 1784, to make plain in a long act of incorporation that Washington and St. John's were "declared to be one university by the name of the University of Maryland," combined under "one supreme legislative and visitational jurisdiction." A single body of trustees, elected from each county that had contributed at least 500 pounds to one of the schools, coordinated the two branches, made faculty appointments, governed curricula and established academic procedures. The governor of the state served as chancellor of the University, which meant that he also served as chairman of the trustees, and the heads of the two colleges alternated as vice-chancellor, or provost, of the combined University. The act also provided that Washington and St. John's receive state appropriations of 1,250 and 1,750 pounds respectively, promised "annually and for ever hereafter." Typical of Smith's operations with the legislature was a provision inserted by him exempting both faculty and students from military service and state taxation.[25]

To meet possible religious objections to the University, the Anglican clergyman moved cautiously in an effort to make the institution appear both pious and nondenominational. As a balance to his position as provost of Washington College, he saw to it that the Roman Catholic Archbishop John Carroll was a member of the trustees and arranged that he preside at the first meeting. Other members of the faculty and trustees were chosen to give proportionate weight to the various other denominations. Although the curriculum was highly secular by the standards of the day, Smith emphasized the institution's dedication to moral ends and included a special course on the "Evidences of Christianity."[26]

To secure the support of the lower classes, the astute Scotsman

[24]Kilty, *Laws of Maryland*, II, 1784, Chap. 37; *Maryland Gazette*, 3 December 1789.
[25]Kilty, *Laws of Maryland*, II, 1784, Chap. 37.
[26]William Smith, *Account of Washington College in the State of Maryland* (Philadelphia, 1784), 14-20; *Maryland Gazette*, 31 March 1785; 7 April 1785.

concentrated his greatest effort. Assuming the support of the wealthy, he directed his appeal for a university to the poor. On a philosophical plane he argued that democracy, not aristocracy, depended on education; on a practical plane he saw to it that taxes levied to support the institution were largely upon luxury items. He showed how money left the state when its citizens went abroad for an education, and how only the wealthy could afford to send their sons out of the state. Finally, he continued elementary training at both of his colleges and provided free scholarships for needy students. His curriculum, moreover, was designed to appeal to the people as a practical and hence a democratic type of education. Except for a similar curriculum at Pennsylvania, Smith's plan for the University of Maryland was the most forward-looking course of studies yet offered in an American college.[27]

For both Washington and St. John's Smith outlined two distinct programs. The first was a relatively traditional course, designed for students who intended to become clergymen, lawyers, doctors, politicians or gentlemen—the only kinds of students who had been considered in the earlier colonial colleges. For these students Latin and Greek still comprised the core of the curriculum, requiring about 60 percent of their time. According to the Renaissance-humanist tradition which had found its way into English and colonial colleges, the classical languages were not only essential living languages in which learned men of the day expressed their thoughts, but also the literature of those languages provided the best possible source material on the human condition. Through the classical authors students broadened their experience, finding through countless examples what had produced virtue and prosperity in the most important age of the past. While in the older colleges the classics, along with a smattering of philosophy and mathematics, had occupied students almost exclusively, Smith devoted almost 40 percent of his curriculum to English literature and grammar, modern languages, logic, history, mathematics, chemistry, botany and rhetoric. Through this extraordinary emphasis, he expressed his belief that the modern world, as well as the ancient one, had valuable lessons to provide, and his more radical belief that college might provide knowledge which reached beyond the moral sphere into the daily affairs of men. For

[27]Kilty, Laws of Maryland, I, 1782, Chap. 8; II, 1784, Chap. 7, 37; Smith, Account of Washington College, 14; Maryland Gazette, 21 April 1785.

the first half of the nineteenth century, most American colleges would be catching up with these curriculum changes which Smith considered modest.[28]

His second course of studies, even more radical than the first, was drawn up for students who expected to become merchants, farmers, artisans and mechanics, a group for which college had never been intended in the past. This program, influenced by Benjamin Franklin as well as by Smith, was designed to help men earn a living rather than to discover truth, and to create good citizens rather than wise leaders. Although this was the philosophy behind the Morrill Land Grant College Act of 1862, it was not widely accepted in higher education until near the end of the nineteenth century. In such a program, both classics and philosophy were almost eliminated on the grounds that the masses did not have time to discover examples of virtuous behavior in the ancients and would only be shown how virtue could be discovered. Instead, students concentrated on reading and appreciating the examples of virtue available in the English language. They studied history, modern languages, mathematics and science. To prepare them for making a livelihood, Smith established courses in English composition, accounting, economics, geography, surveying, navigation and architecture, plus a course in agriculture which apparently never materialized.[29]

Although this second course of studies probably never went into operation at St. John's, it seems to have enrolled at least half of the Washington College students. At any rate, under Smith's inspiration both institutions prospered. The first commencement of Washington College in May, 1783, was a gala two-day affair with public examinations, parades, cannon salutes, and dramas and orations in a multitude of languages. With the ubiquitous Smith dominating the proceedings, the governor laid the cornerstone for a new building. Even more pomp and pageantry came the following year when George Washington received an honorary degree from the college named in his honor.[30] By 1806 about 50 students had earned degrees from Washington College. St. John's did not hold its first commencement until 1793, but under an able faculty headed by Dr. John McDowell it grew even faster. By 1806 it had graduated 105 students, including 4 future state governors, 6 United States senators

[28]Smith, *Account of Washington College*, 15-20, 42-43.
[29]*Ibid.*, 20-25, 42-43.
[30]Smith, *Life of Smith*, II, 87-89, 248; *Maryland Gazette*, 8 July 1783.

and congressmen, 6 judges, 21 members of the state legislature, and Francis Scott Key.[31]

Once both colleges were launched and going well, however, their great leader resigned, dashing hopes that the two institutions would in fact develop as a real state university. Apparently William Smith enjoyed administering churches as much as universities, for in 1789 he left the academic world in expectation of becoming the first bishop of the American Episcopal Church. The Maryland clergy supported his bid for the new office, but in other circles his haughty manner, his Tory politics and his reputation for strong langauge and strong drink had antagonized too many, and someone else gained the post. For a time Smith dabbled again with the University of Pennsylvania; then he retired to New York to write his memoirs, speculate in western lands and drink all he pleased.[32]

Many devoted faculty members remained at Washington and St. John's, but the vision of a state university was gone. With Smith's departure the central administration broke down, for records remain of only two additional, perfunctory meetings of the trustees. The two colleges became rivals instead of partners, the once-popular term "University of Maryland" went out of fashion, and as the professional educators transformed the curriculum along more traditional lines the people of the state grew hostile. Observers began to describe the institutions as "aristocratic," existing only for "the rich and extravagant."[33] The year after Smith left the legislature began to pare down the appropriations that had been promised "for ever," and in 1805 it ended the last remnant of state support by declaring void the act that had created the University of Maryland.[34] The interest of the legislature turned to the creation of public schools and the support of private academies. While Washington and St. John's continued as struggling private institutions, the first University of Maryland had failed.

By the early nineteenth century the people of Maryland seem to have turned from grand schemes for higher education as if in frus-

[31]Steiner, History of Education in Maryland, 81-82; Philip Randall Voorhees, Address on the One Hundreth Anniversary of St. John's College . . . (Baltimore, 1889), 23; Terch Francis Tilghman, "The Founding of St. John's College, 1784-1789," Maryland Historical Magazine, XLIV (June, 1959), 75-92.

[32]Starr, "William Smith," 356; Smith, Life of Smith, II, 89 and ff.; W. S. Perry, History of the American Episcopal Church, 2 vols. (New York, 1885), II, 29.

[33]Joseph Scott, Geographical Description of the State of Maryland and Delaware . . . (Philadelphia, 1807), 59.

[34]Laws of Maryland . . . 1805 (Annapolis, 1805), Chap. 85.

tration at their early failure. Elsewhere the state university movement was beginning to bear fruit. But Marylanders, who had provided the other states with important ideas and examples, turned to the practical matter of earning a living.

The present University of Maryland evolved out of this concern with practical matters. While the state continued to fall behind in the development of an outstanding undergraduate college, it assumed national leadership in the creation of professional schools which helped men vocationally. During the early nineteenth century, Maryland was to give birth to the sixth medical college in the country, the fourth college of pharmacy, the third college of agriculture, one of the earliest effective colleges of law and the first college of dentistry in the world.

2

Doctors Create a University

Young America had two university traditions on which to draw. The first was the English tradition of Oxford and Cambridge, designed primarily to develop the student's moral character, secondarily to develop his capacity to learn, but hardly to provide knowledge which would be useful in life. Located in the country, the English colleges were residential, maintaining a spartan discipline, a strong religious orientation, and an inflexible undergraduate curriculum. With minor exceptions, such as the modifications by William Smith, this tradition was the starting point for all of the successful colonial experiments in higher education. The other tradition stemmed from the Scottish and Continental universities which were designed primarily to develop intellectual capacity and to provide specific knowledge. Located in cities where the student lived freely among the townspeople, these universities were oriented toward the professions.

The present University of Maryland was born in the latter tradition and became one of the most important American experiments in nonresident, basically professional education. Chartered as a medical college in 1807, its founders were interested more in organizing and improving the medical profession than in creating a university. The College of Medicine was so successful, however, that in 1812 it was re-chartered as the University of Maryland, authorized to add other professional schools and an undergraduate college. Generally the professional schools flourished, but the undergraduate college, combining a Scottish academic structure with English aims and curriculum, was not very successful.

The Medical College of Maryland

Baltimore has been a medical center ever since 36-year-old Charles F. Wiesenthal arrived from Prussia in 1755. As physician to Frederick the Great, he already had proved himself one of the ablest medical men in Europe, and no one knows why he left the glitter of court life for the hardships of a village still on the frontier. At the time of his arrival, Baltimore had a population of only 800 and parties of hostile Indians were murdering isolated settlers within 50 miles of the town. But here he settled, becoming surgeon general of Maryland during the Revolution, organizer of the Maryland medical profession and founder of a little school which foreshadowed the University of Maryland.

When Wiesenthal arrived there were no medical colleges in America, and few students could afford European training. Doctors passed on their knowledge to apprentices, and the current medical lore occasionally was refreshed by someone like Wiesenthal. As established physicians and apprentices flocked to the newcomer, his instruction gradually took the form of a school. Sometime in the 1760's, probably in 1769, he built behind his house on Gay Street a small two-story brick laboratory to provide better facilities for his students. Each winter about 15 or 20 of them paid $10 each for the privilege of using the laboratory, hearing occasional lectures and consulting the learned doctor on their reading and practice.[1]

[1]Eugene Fauntleroy Cordell, "Charles Frederick Wiesenthal, Medicinae Practicus...," *Johns Hopkins Hospital Bulletin*, No. 113 (August, 1900), 170-182; Eugene Fauntleroy Cordell, *Medical Annals of Maryland, 1700-1899* (Baltimore, 1903), 11-20. A series of lengthy and beautiful letters between Wiesenthal and his son, Andrew, are preserved in manuscript in the archieves of the Medical and Chirurgical Faculty of Maryland, Baltimore.

Like the best eighteenth century physicians in Europe, Wiesenthal believed that medical education should be based on the study of human anatomy, and here lay the seeds of trouble. Even abroad human dissection was frowned upon, and the idea terrified Americans. Nevertheless, Wiesenthal and his colleagues quitely secured corpses and pursued their investigations without publicity, and as the little school prospered inevitably the populace began to gossip about what went on behind its locked doors. On a late December afternoon in 1788, when Wiesenthal and his students were working on the body of a murderer whose corpse they had purchased from the public executioner, an angry mob burst into the school, destroyed the furnishings and dragged the body through the streets.[2]

More than superstition and fear lay behind the raid. For the first time in Maryland the little medical school was creating a clear distinction between trained physicians and uneducated charlatans who practiced without restrictions. Only a few weeks before the mob action, Wiesenthal had organized the reputable Baltimore physicians to promote some form of medical licensing, and this organization may have frightened the charlatans themselves into leading the raid. In addition, many poor people looked upon medical education and organization as efforts by the physicians to create monopoly, raise fees and deprive them of inexpensive cures. Said one poor farmer:

> The Doctors have established their Medital Societyes . . . by which they have so nearly enielated Quackery of all kinds, that a poor man cant git so grate cures of them for a ginna, as he could 50 years ago of an old Squaw for halfe a pint of Rhum. The bisiness of a Midwife could be purformed 50 years ago for halfe a dollar & now it costs a poor man 5 hole ones.[3]

Instead of retarding medical education in Maryland, however, the invasion of Wiesenthal's school actually promoted it. Although Wiesenthal died a few months after the raid, the mob action impelled the reputable doctors of the state to band together, obtain legal recognition and suppress quackery. Laying aside their professional jealousies, they formally organized, and in 1799 obtained incorporation as the Medical and Chirurgical Society of Maryland. The general assembly empowered the group to grant licenses to

[2]Thomas Waters Griffith, *Annals of Baltimore* (Baltimore, 1824) , 124-127.
[3]William Manning, *The Key of Libberty* . . ., Samuel Eliot Morison, ed. (Billerica, Mass., 1922) , 26.

qualified physicians and to prosecute in the courts anyone practicing without a license.[4]

Several able doctors, meanwhile, assumed the apprentice instruction which Wiesenthal had organized so well. His son, Andrew Wiesenthal, returned from his studies at Edinburgh to inherit his father's school, and elsewhere in the city George Buchanan, a former pupil of the elder Wiesenthal, also offered lectures. At first the two men lectured on midwifery and the theory of medicine, but as the public memory of dissection began to fade and as the medical society grew stronger, they began to work on cadavers. More ambitious than their mentor, the young doctors talked of combining their efforts to transform their informal apprentice instruction into a full-scale medical college, such as the recently established College of Philadelphia. From time to time during the 1790's Buchanan and young Wiesenthal tried to interest the medical society in sponsoring such a scheme, and in 1801 the general assembly narrowly rejected a bill to recognize the Baltimore schools by an act of incorporation. Launched by the elder Wiesenthal and propelled by the needs of reputable medical men for a formal medical education, a movement was under way. It lacked only a leader to crystallize it into a college.[5]

Into this atmosphere shy, stolid John Beale Davidge, the true founder of the University of Maryland, came to Baltimore to practice medicine. Diligently going his way unperturbed and unpretentious, Davidge did not look like the leader of a movement and never thought of himself as one. Quietly he wrote his books and taught his classes, shrinking from the limelight, but providing the knowledge and the stability around which ambitious men would rally. Born in Annapolis, the son of a British officer who disappeared when the Revolution began, Davidge received his A.B. and M.A. degrees from newly opened St. John's College. Working his way to Europe, he attended lectures at renowned Edinburgh Uni-

---

[4]*Baltimore Advertiser,* 21 November 1785; 21 February 1786; 5 December 1788; 11 December 1788; 26 December 1788; 22 June to 16 July 1790. Also Cordell, *Medical Annals,* 13-22. William Kilty, *Laws of Maryland . . .,* 2 vols. (Annapolis, 1800), II, 1798, Chap. 105.

[5]*Baltimore Advertiser,* 2 July 1790; 16 June 1802; *Baltimore Evening Post,* 16 December 1801; *Baltimore Federal Gazette,* 11 October 1797; 16 June 1802; 3 December 1802; Griffith, *Annals of Baltimore,* 127; J. Thomas Scharf, *History of Baltimore City and County . . .* (Philadelphia, 1881), 731-735; Cordell, *Medical Annals,* 16-22. A ticket to Andrew Wiesenthal's lectures is preserved in the James M. Taylor Papers, Maryland Historical Society, Baltimore.

versity, but took his M.D. degree from Glasgow because it was less expensive. He arrived in Baltimore in 1797, and by 1802 he had enough apprentices to offer regular lectures on midwifery. Cautiously he added classes in anatomy and surgery, and by 1807 he was generally recognized as unofficial heir to the Wiesenthal school.[6]

Attracted to that school were two young doctors who provided exactly the complements which Davidge needed for the next step forward. The first was James Cocke of Virginia a businesslike organizer, a practical man who could influence legislators, newspapers and philanthropists. Wealthy in his own right, educated in London and Philadelphia, the 25-year-old Cocke arrived in Baltimore in 1805 and associated himself with Davidge to offer lectures in physiology and anatomy.[7] The other colleague was James Shaw, a romantic idealist full of ambitious schemes to reform the world. From Annapolis and educated at St. John's, Shaw had no medical degree, but on a hit-or-miss basis had attended medical lectures in various parts of the world. He wrote poetry, had been a surgeon in the United States Navy, American consul in Tunis and a colonizer in Canada. Arriving in Baltimore early in 1807 at the age of 29, he joined Davidge and Cocke to teach chemistry to the half-dozen apprentices, and immediately began dreaming of founding a great medical college.[8] In 1807 the three doctors, at their own expense, built a two-story brick medical laboratory behind Davidge's house on Saratoga Street, much like the one that Wiesenthal had built many years before.[9]

Several times in October, 1807, modest announcements appeared in the Baltimore newspapers stating that Davidge's building was almost complete, and that on November 2, classes would begin. The announcements emphasized that "the course on Anatomy

[6]*Federal Gazette*, 3 December 1802; Eugene Fauntleroy Cordell, *University of Maryland . . .*, 2 vols. (New York, 1907), I, 175-180. Professor Cordell received his M.D. from the University in 1868, and was professor of the history of medicine and librarian from 1903 to 1913. He devoted a large portion of his life to his massive history of the University. To modern readers the work may lack a certain breadth, and much of it is devoted to biographical sketches of professors and alumni. It is, however, thorough and accurate, and I acknowledge a great debt to Professor Cordell. His work has been a point of departure for much of this study.

[7]Nathaniel Potter, *Some Account of the Rise and Progress of the University of Maryland* (Baltimore, 1838), 5-9; Cordell, *University*, I, 134-137.

[8]John E. Hall (ed.), *Poems by the Late Doctor John Shaw, To Which Is Prefixed a Biographical Sketch of the Author* (Baltimore, 1810), 85-99.

[9]*Federal Gazette*, 21 October 1807; *Baltimore American*, 28 November 1807; Potter, *Some Account*, 5; Scharf, *History of Baltimore*, 735.

will be rendered more full and complete, by a series of prelections, on the functions of some of the most important organs of the body."[10] In the awkward language of the advertisement, students caught the implication that instruction would include more than lectures. Indeed, subsequent developments may not have been so unprovoked as the doctors pretended, because they had grown bold since the creation of the medical society. They asked too few questions when a ruffian offered them a corpse. Gossip had it that anyone could collect up to $20 by robbing a fresh grave, and even a murderer's victim was unrecognizable after the students had worked on his body. Unfortunately for the professors, other people also saw implications in the advertisements.

Classes began on schedule, and late at night on November 17, when only Dr. Cocke was in the laboratory, a shadowy sort of man knocked on the door. Few words were spoken as he brought in a corpse and laid it on the table. "The price demanded was paid," confessed Dr. Cocke later. As to the man who brought the body he stated, "I had never seen him before; I have never seen him since; nor do I know his name." The incident occurred on Tuesday, and for the rest of the week the classes were plagued by boys climbing on the roof and by "impertinent men asking questions."[11]

On Saturday, November 21, Cocke again was alone in the laboratory when suddenly he was startled to see the face of a woman peering down at him through the skylight. When he angrily went outside to confront her, she calmly replied that she wanted only to see the body of her dead husband. No doubt the doctor was taken aback. He thought of offering her a bribe to go away and vehemently denied that the corpse could possibly be that of her husband. He described the darkness of the room and added that if she entered it she would have to go in alone. Cocke must have been pleased with his strategy, for the woman declined, and hastily he went inside and bolted the door. Soon, however, a small crowd collected, jeering and throwing stones. Cocke returned outside to order the people to disperse, but discerning their angry temper he decided to leave in search of the police.[12]

The mob grew, and the arrival of the police seemed to excite the

[10]*Federal Gazette*, 21 October 1807.
[11]*Ibid.*, 28 November 1807. This is a long account written by Cocke.
[12]*Ibid.*; *Baltimore American*, 28 November 1807; *Baltimore Evening Post*, 25 November 1807.

ruffians. Suddenly the crowd, now numbering hundreds, stormed the building and demolished its interior, even ripping the wood frames from the windows. Shouting, cursing, they bore the corpse through the streets and finally deposited it on the steps of Davidge's home. The doctors denied to the end that the cadaver had been the late husband of the woman peering through the window, but they never suggested who it might have been. Certainly the crowd had not treated it reverently.[13]

Now it was the doctors' turn for action. The medical society convened to offer its unanimous support for an act of incorporation which would provide legal recognition and official approval of the school. Letters appeared in the newspapers berating the rabble for standing in the way of scientific progress. The most powerful physicians in the city—venerable George Brown, Thomas Emerson Brown, and William Donaldson—agreed that their names might be used as future faculty members in the request for incorporation. Colonel John Eager Howard, Revolutionary hero and a former governor of the state, offered a plot of ground on which the school might be rebuilt and lent his name to a city-wide request for funds.[14]

By a remarkably curious coincidence, a bill to incorporate the medical school had been presented to the general assembly the day on which the raid occurred. Drafted by Dr. Shaw and introduced by a delegate from Baltimore, Thomas E. Dorsey, it was similar to the requests for incorporation which had been tabled in the past. Now, however, with violence apparent and with the support of the most substantial elements in the state, the legislature perceived the need for formal recognition of medical training. For Davidge, Cocke and Shaw the raid had occurred at precisely the right time. Just as the violence in 1788 had impelled the medical profession into organization and licensing, the violence of 1807 impelled it to the creation of a medical college. Years later the participants remembered only the raid as the prime factor in the origin of the college; they never mentioned that the charter already had been drawn.[15]

On December 18, 1807, less than a month after the raid, the assembly finally approved a charter incorporating the College of Medicine

[13]*Federal Gazette*, 28 November 1807.

[14]*Baltimore American*, 3 December 1807; *Federal Gazette*, 7 December 1807; *Baltimore American*, 31 December 1807; "The College of Anatomy and Medicine," *Observer and Repository of Original and Selected Essays*, II (12 December 1807), 376-378.

[15]*Votes and Proceedings of the House of Delegates of Maryland, November Session, 1807* (Annapolis, 1807), 26; Potter, *Some Account*, 6.

of Maryland. Only the mildest token opposition appeared, apparently from those who feared monopoly. The physicians requested no money, only the rights to own property and to grant degrees. No issues of religion, state sectionalism or class interest were at stake. One provision, borrowed from the act that had incorporated the defunct University of Maryland, exempted both the students and faculty from taxation. That section was struck out, but otherwise the bill passed by voice vote with no debate.[16]

The charter was an ordinary act of private incorporation, with the faculty of the College and the licensing committee of the state medical society making up the corporation, or the board of regents as they called themselves. Davidge, Cocke, Shaw, Brown, Bond and Donaldson were named as the six members of the original faculty. Since the licensing committee had twelve members, the medical society was in a position to control the College, but friction between the two groups never occurred. In practice, members of the committee seldom attended board meetings, and the faculty established requirements, elected new staff members, and generally governed the affairs of the institution as it pleased. The College of Medicine of Maryland was the sixth such college in the country and the first south of Pennsylvania. The College of Philadelphia, later the University of Pennsylvania School of Medicine, opened in 1765, after which came Columbia, Harvard, Dartmouth, and New York.[17]

At the regents' organizational meeting held immediately after incorporation, Brown, Bond and Donaldson resigned, for they had only lent their names to aid the passage of the charter. Davidge took the chair of surgery and was named dean of the College. Cocke assumed the chair of anatomy and physiology—which meant dissection—and Shaw took the chair of chemistry. To the fourth chair, the theory and practice of medicine, concerning the identification and cure of diseases, the faculty named slow, old-fashioned Nathaniel Potter, a hard-working giant of a man who was to make the College his entire life for the next 36 years. The chair of pharmacy, then called *Materia Medica*, remained vacant for two years until the faculty elected Samuel Baker, a brilliant lecturer who probably was the most fashionable physician in Baltimore. The final chair, ob-

[16]*Votes and Proceedings, 1807*, 50, 66.
[17]*Laws of Maryland . . . 1807* (Annapolis, 1808), Chap. 53; William Frederick Norwood, *Medical Education in the United States before the Civil War* (Philadelphia, 1944), 430 and *passim*.

stetrics, was the most difficult to fill, and perhaps the faculty made a mistake in its choice. Briefly Davidge filled the position, and then the faculty named Richard Wilmot Hall as temporary "adjunct professor." Temporary appointments have a way of becoming permanent, and although Hall's teaching was poor and his personality irritating, he outlasted all his colleagues, withstanding insult and impeachment for 40 years. Nevertheless he loved the school, and like Davidge and Potter, he may have provided an element of stability which never was sufficiently appreciated.[18]

Six professors constituted the usual number of faculty members even at the great European universities, and by any standards those of the new College were respectable if not outstanding. All were young and their training sound. Davidge, at 39, was the oldest, and four of the men were still in their twenties. Davidge had been trained at Edinburgh and Glasgow; Cocke, Potter, Baker and Hall had their medical degrees from Philadelphia where the famous Benjamin Rush dominated American medical education; Shaw joked that he was a doctor "by act of the Assembly," the title given him by a mistake in the act of incorporation.[19]

During the excitement of organizing the College, Davidge remained characteristically in the background, quietly moving his tiny class of seven students into his home and continuing his instruction in surgery and obstetrics as if nothing had happened. Cocke and Shaw also, when they had time, continued to meet their classes of anatomy and chemistry in their homes. It seemed unwise to obtain more cadavers that term, and Cocke provided lectures instead of demonstrations. He also arranged with the city poorhouse to care for the destitute in exchange for the right to deliver there a few clinical lectures to his students. In March, 1808, after slightly more than four months of instruction, the first year of classes came to a ragged end.[20]

The second year, with only 10 students enrolled in the College, was almost as difficult. The chief problem was to find a building, for both the students and faculty disliked meeting in private homes in various parts of the city, and faculty wives may have felt that the

[18]*Federal Gazette,* 30 December 1807; Potter, *Some Account,* 6-7; Cordell, *University,* I, 97, 193-194, 213-214, 219; *Baltimore American,* 31 December 1807; 26 July 1811; *Baltimore Medical and Philosophical Lyceum,* I (October, 1811), 414-415.

[19]Hall, *Poems of Shaw,* 96.

[20]Potter, *Some Account,* 7; *Baltimore Medical and Physical Register,* I (1809), 53-54.

presence of dissected corpses hindered orderly housekeeping. At some time during the second year the doctors acquired an abandoned schoolhouse on Fayette Street. They boarded up the windows and tried to fix the roof, but rain still came through cracks in the walls. They stumbled in holes in the floor, and there was no heat. The winter was particularly cold, and in the mornings the professors shoveled snow from the floor, frightened rats from the cadavers and poured hot water over the chemical apparatus to thaw it. About mid-term Cocke and Potter could take no more. They arranged with a local hotel to use a ballroom for lectures from noon until two o'clock each afternoon. Davidge contracted pleurisy which interrupted his lectures for almost a month. The faculty and students especially remembered the martyrdom that winter of Dr. Shaw, delicate and tubercular as the dreamer is so often depicted, laboring with his chemical experiments in the cold shack, his arms immersed in freezing water. He, too, contracted pleurisy. Upon the insistence of his colleagues he canceled his course and sailed for Bermuda; but it was too late, for in January he died.

During the third year classes met in the shack and in the borrowed ballroom for the last time. Everything seemed to go better, if for no other reason than the fact that the winter was milder. Students numbered 18, and the faculty also had grown. In addition to Davidge at surgery, Cocke at anatomy and Potter at theory and practice, Baker was beginning at pharmacy, and Hall at obstetrics. To replace Shaw at chemistry came the shy Elisha DeButts, fresh from his degree at Philadelphia, a meticulous, poetic soul like his predecessor.[21]

According to Professor Potter, writing twenty years later, five students received degrees at the end of that third year, in March, 1810, and ten others in 1811. Certainly it is reasonable to suppose that some students would have completed the two-year course by those dates, but there is no record of the first two commencements in the faculty minutes, in the newspapers of the period or in the obituaries of Maryland physicians who received licenses to practice in those years. Thus, it may have been 1812, at the end of the fifth year of instruction, when Maryland conferred its first five M.D. degrees.[22]

From the beginning the professors had ambitious plans for a

[21]Potter, *Some Account*, 8; Hall, *Poems of Shaw*, 96-99.
[22]Potter, *Some Account*, 8; *Baltimore Medical and Philosophical Lyceum*, I (October, 1811), 415; *Baltimore American*, 7 May 1812; Cordell, *University*, 24.

campus, and in part the pitiful condition of the shack was their sacrifice for the future. During the first years they accepted no salaries, but spent student fees for the purchase of equipment, and even supplemented those sums with their private funds and personal credit.[23] Some of them may have thought vaguely of their sacrifices as an investment, for if the College grew they stood to profit from larger tuition fees. Yet certainly they also were motivated by a sincere devotion to the medical profession and to the public. The fact that, for many decades, they continued to invest most of their fees in better facilities lends a ring of sincerity to their talk of serving society. Professor Hall claimed, after 30 years of service, that he had spent over $28,000 on the University;[24] another professor, Maxwell McDowell, reported the expenditure of $10,000 of personal funds; and when Professor Potter died, after 35 years of teaching and conducting a large medical practice, his colleagues had to take up a collection to pay for his funeral. The professors never faltered in their obligations, and their devotion made a deep impression on bankers and the public as well.[25]

In the excitement following the raid on Davidge's laboratory, Colonel John Eager Howard, a noted philanthropist, had offered the physicians a lot at the corner of Lombard and Greene Streets, the present location of the College of Medicine. It was then on the outskirts of town, with the surrounding bare fields affording a clear view to the Patapsco River. True to his promise and asking no security or time limit for payment, Howard offered the lot for $10,000, considerably below its market value. When the professors accepted, the colonel made the first $1,000 payment. Further efforts to obtain substantial contributions failed.[26]

The chief method of financing the infant school was by lottery, a favorite means of raising revenue in the early nineteenth century which even the federal government occasionally employed. In Maryland, where some of the best lotteries were conducted, the general

[23]Potter, *Some Account*, 8. The State recognized and eventually paid over $30,000 in debts assumed by individual faculty members. See *Report of the Joint Committee [of the General Assembly] on the Memorial of the Regents of the University of Maryland* (Annapolis, 1839), 5-8.

[24]Minutes of the Faculty, 9 October 1843; these minutes are in manuscript, preserved in the archives of the medical school, Baltimore.

[25]Cordell, *University*, I, 97, 190, 214.

[26]*Baltimore American*, 3 December 1807; 5 December 1807; *Federal Gazette*, 19 October 1821; Potter, *Some Account*, 9. For a complete list of gifts see Faculty Minutes, inserted note, 1826.

assembly licensed the drawings carefully, designating each for a specific cause, such as financing a courthouse, a fire company, a canal, a school or even a church. In 1808 the assembly granted the College of Medicine permission to conduct such a drawing. The professors were not sufficiently promotion-minded for such an enterprise, however, and as much as they needed the money they put it off for four years. Finally, in 1811, the legislature amended the act, granting the faculty the unusual permission to hire professionals to manage the lottery for them.[27]

The lottery was well-publicized and successful, with about 35,000 tickets sold at $10 each. Almost 12,000 prizes ranged from $50,000 to $12, with the total prize money equaling the ticket sales, and the profit to the College coming from a 15 percent tax on each prize. Daily for 55 days the drawings took place while excitement mounted over the state. After all expenses of the lottery were paid, the College realized slightly over $18,000.[28]

Long before the money was in the faculty was planning for the new building, inviting two of the finest architects in the country to submit designs. One set of plans came from Maximilian Godefroy, father of the Gothic revival in America, and the other came from Robert Carey Long, a proponent of the popular classic style. The faculty chose Long's design which was modeled after the Pantheon in Rome, and consisted of an upright dome-topped barrel surrounded by a square box. The barrel, divided into two floors, provided two great amphitheatres each capable of seating over 500 students, while the surrounding box was divided into three floors of offices and laboratories. The design required strangely curving halls, triangular closets and dark winding stairs which, according to student legend, were designed as means of escape from mobs protesting dissection. Construction of the $45,000 structure began in May, 1812, with John Eager Howard laying the cornerstone.[29] That fall classes began in the building, still far from complete, but infinitely finer than the old shack. The following year, at the beginning of the

[27]*Laws of Maryland . . . 1807* (Annapolis, 1808), Chap. 111; *Laws of Maryland . . . 1808* (Annapolis, 1809), Chap. 96; *Laws of Maryland . . . 1811* (Annapolis, 1812), Chap. 132.

[28]*Baltimore Evening Post,* 20 January 1808; *Baltimore American,* 15 February 1812; 6 May 1812.

[29]*Baltimore Weekly Register,* 17 October 1812; *Baltimore American,* 23 August 1813; 25 October 1820; Benjamin Latrobe to Maximillian Godefroy, 28 April 1812, Latrobe Papers, Maryland Historical Society, Baltimore; Griffith, *Annals of Baltimore,* 187-188; Potter, *Some Account,* 9.

term in October, 1813, James Cocke was supposed to deliver the dedicatory address. A few days before the ceremony, however, he became ill, and as commencement orators in that romantic generation liked to recall, he died at the moment his address was to have begun. But the building did not lack rhapsodists. Not only was it one of the finest structures in the little city, but also it was probably the finest medical school building in the world.[30]

Even more than the act of incorporation the new building gave permanence to the College of Medicine, attracting for the first time a large number of students from other states. The War of 1812 served only to increase enrollment. On that morning, late in the war, when Francis Scott Key peered toward Baltimore to see if the flag were still there, at least 50 students were attending classes at the corner of Lombard and Greene Streets. The term had just been lengthened to five months and the professors had ready even bigger plans.[31]

The University of Maryland

So many schemes for establishing a state university had collapsed that no one paid much attention when in 1812 the general assembly authorized the College of Medicine of Maryland to become the University of Maryland. No one definitely knows who drew up the charter, the assembly never debated the act and few newspapers mentioned its passage. Convinced that other subjects could be taught like medicine in the Scottish-Continental tradition without administrative apparatus and with tuition paid directly to the professors, the faculty members again were asking for no money, only for the rights to call themselves a university and to offer an assortment of degrees. The charter was scarcely more than another act of private incorporation for a well-intentioned organization with a slightly pretentious name.

[30]*Federal Gazette,* 27 October 1813; 18 October 1822; 10 February 1824; Potter, *Some Account,* 9; *Baltimore American,* 23 August 1813; 26 October 1813; 25 October 1820; John B. Davidge, *Physical Sketches,* 3 vols. (Baltimore, 1814-1823), III, 12.

[31]Richard Wilmot Hall, *An Oration Delivered by Appointment before the Medical and Surgical Faculty* . . . (Baltimore, 1815), 3; *Baltimore American,* 23 August 1813; 20 July 1816; *Journal of the House of Delegates of Maryland* . . . *1825* (Annapolis, 1826), 309.

The medical faculty had much to gain from expansion. University association meant added prestige, larger enrollments and greater potential profits for the professors. More important for some of the faculty, however, university association provided a means of raising medical standards by requiring an undergraduate college education for all entering medical students. Already the medical school offered reduced tuitions to college graduates and provided prizes to its most literate students in an effort to encourage pre-medical study.[32] The requirement of a college degree for entrance was an ideal not to be realized for more than a century, but for the doctors it was a fundamental reason for establishing a university. Finally, creating a university was a genuine community service on the part of the physicians. Aware of the Scottish-Continental university tradition and of the failure of the English university tradition in the state, they saw in the founding of a University of Maryland infinite possibilities for the improvement of society and the progress of the state.

Talk of making the Medical College into a university began after the raid on Davidge's laboratory in 1807, when a member of the general assembly suggested a merger with St. Mary's College in Baltimore. St. Mary's, however, was a struggling Roman Catholic institution, more an academy than a college, and the suggestion did not appeal to the doctors.[33] The next public mention of university status came in the lottery advertisements of 1812 which suggested that other colleges "may hereafter be engrafted" on the Medical College, "and thus an University may be constituted."[34]

The University charter, possibly written by Professor Cocke, was introduced to the assembly in 1812, a week before Christmas. It was not a charter for a state university despite the name, for it established no state responsibility and did not even call for an annual report to the legislature. It simply authorized the medical faculty to annex three other "faculties," one for arts and sciences, another for divinity and a third for law. The assembly forbade any "religious or civil test" for admittance, required that all final examinations be made public and established a minimum of two annual terms of four months each for all degrees. Beyond these provisions

[32]*Baltimore American*, 26 August 1812.
[33]*Votes and Proceedings . . . 1807*, 50.
[34]*Baltimore American*, 15 February 1812.

the professors were free to govern themselves and award degrees as they thought proper.

According to the charter each of the four colleges—medicine, arts and sciences, divinity and law—should have seven professors. To gain a semblance of conventionality the total of 28 professors was called a board of regents, but in fact outside government, such as had become standard for American educational institutions, did not exist. The professors governed themselves by majority vote, appropriated student fees for facilities and salaries, filled vacancies and established academic rules. Annually each college elected a dean from its own members, and also annually the entire group selected a provost for the whole University. Perils lay ahead for an institution owned and operated by its faculty, but for the present it offered unparalleled academic dignity and made easy the recruitment of outstanding professors.[35]

The new University of Maryland faculty included many prominent Baltimore citizens. The college of arts and sciences attracted the most outstanding teachers and gentlemen-scholars of the city, each honored with the title of professor; the divinity school included the best clergymen; and the law school obtained the outstanding lawyers. The new professors expected to follow the example of those in the medical school, selling tickets of admission for each course, offering one or two courses the first term and expanding as demand required. Perhaps, in flights of imagination, they dreamed of students flocking to their classes, of giving up their other interests and of becoming rich and famous for their scholarship. If so, they dreamed too much. Their very prominence in daily affairs left them too little time for university building, and some of them were soon arguing that the legislature never intended them to build a real university, but merely to provide miscellaneous lectures for the improvement of the local citizenry and the advancement of the medical school.

The perils of faculty autonomy and a spare-time approach to building a university became apparent at the first general faculty meeting in January, 1813, for no one was empowered to assume active leadership and no one knew quite what to do next. Presiding at the meeting, for lack of anyone else, was elderly Dr. Charles

[35]Votes and Proceedings . . . 1812 (Annapolis, 1813), 56, 74, 86, 105; Laws of Maryland . . . 1812 (Annapolis, 1813), Chap. 159.

Warfield, chairman of the licensing committee of the medical society. Actually the society had never exercised control over the faculty, and once the University charter of 1812 had been gained, association between the two groups ended. The medical faculty "proceeded to annex to itself the other three faculties," and amid embarrassed inactivity the group adjourned for three months.[36]

The more ambitious medical professors recognized the need for strong leadership, however, and in April they called a second meeting to urge the election of a provost who would serve without salary but would take over active guidance of the University. To encourage the other schools the physicians did not nominate a member of their own faculty, proposing instead the most prominent clergyman in the state, Roman Catholic Archbishop John Carroll, a widely respected and successful administrator who had been active in William Smith's University of Maryland. The all-Protestant faculty was pleased enough with the nomination, but the Archbishop was more aware than the professors of the difficulties in launching a university and politely declined.[37]

The faculty turned next to Robert Smith, a famous name but a poor choice for the first president. A Marylander educated at Princeton, Smith had served as Jefferson's Secretary of the Navy and as Madison's Secretary of State. Even more than the faculty, he viewed his position as an honorary one involving the laying of cornerstones, presiding at commencements and lending his name to an institution left to grow by its own devices. In April, 1813, he attended his first faculty meeting to accept the appointment, and in May, 1815, he came to his second to tender his resignation.[38]

Smith's interpretation of the position of provost set a tragic precedent for the University of Maryland. As his successor, the combined faculties, or the regents, elected James Kemp, the pious and modest Episcopal Bishop of Maryland who followed the example of his predecessor until his retirement in 1826, presiding at commencements, calling occasional faculty meetings, standing for all of the right things, but never venturing to provide leadership. The remarkable fact is how far the faculty moved on its own.[39]

[36]Faculty Minutes, 6 January 1813; 28 September 1821; 29 October 1821.

[37]Ibid., 22 April 1813; Griffith, Annals of Baltimore, 207; Annabelle M. Melville, John Carroll of Baltimore . . . (New York, 1955), 152.

[38]Faculty Minutes, 22 April 1813; 4 December 1813; 25 March 1814; 13 May 1815; 29 May 1815.

[39]Ibid., 29 May 1815.

A college of arts and sciences is the heart of any university and the most difficult to launch in the informal, under-administered Continental tradition. Whatever the reason, American undergraduates have tended to be immature and unable to educate themselves without an organized system of campus discipline. Medical and law students were in some ways already professional men, refining their skills in courses they needed and paid for, but undergraduates apparently needed the guidance of full-time teachers wielding birch rods. Of the seven professors in the college, four were gentlemen-scholars rather than professional teachers: Charles W. Hanson, a state judge, was professor of philosophy; George Ralph, an Episcopal rector, was professor of English and rhetoric; Samuel Brown, a physician, was professor of Latin and Greek; and John E. Hall, an author and magazine editor, was professor of history. The latter position was particularly interesting for it was probably the first separate chair of history in any American institution. The other three professors—John Allen of mathematics, John D. Craig of Latin and Greek, and Archibald Walker of science —were professional teachers or principals in local academies.[40]

With no one else taking the initiative, the mathematics professor John Allen, in 1814, quietly assumed it for himself, announcing that his academy would offer an entire college education and a degree from the University of Maryland. To his colleagues, this was going too far, and the ambitious principal was forced to apologize for his presumption. Three years later, undaunted though perhaps still interested in advertising his academy, Allen announced a four-month series of public lectures, presented on Tuesday and Saturday evenings, on mathematics, astronomy, navigation and surveying. The first few lectures were free, and the entire series cost $10. This was the procedure the medical professors wanted, and newspapers, growing interested in the experiment, expressed warm approval. Yet Allen's colleagues found themselves too busy to join him. During the next few years at irregular intervals, Craig and Hanson offered public lecture series, and Dr. Elisha DeButts from the medical school tried to encourage the program with a course in chemistry which featured spectacular "magical demonstrations," but their efforts met with an indifferent response.[41]

[40]Ibid., 6 January 1813; City Director of Baltimore . . . 1813 (Baltimore, 1813).
[41]Federal Gazette, 24 November 1814; 5 April 1821; 11 April 1821; 20 September

With the disorganized public lecture approach an obvious failure, Allen again tried to provide leadership by enlisting the faculty, or at least persuading them to lend their names, for a more ambitious scheme. Large newspaper advertisements appeared in 1824 giving detailed plans for a four-year residence college featuring an eleven-month term. Admission standards were high, and the broad curriculum offered all the traditional courses in Latin and Greek, mathematics, science and "Christianity." But there was also a vagueness in the advertisements. No one knew exactly where the campus was to be located, and while the only other educational institutions in the city actually were academies, the advertisements promised no more than an education "as good as any in Baltimore." Even as the professors advertised they were, in fact, waiting for students to materialize before they established a college. In the following months, with students failing to appear, most of the arts and science faculty managed to forget the scheme, and the proposed opening date for the college passed unnoticed. For the time being the college had failed.[42]

The School of Divinity, if it ever had been intended to go into operation, met with a similar fate. Many prospective clergymen still apprenticed themselves to established ministers, and conceivably they could have systematized such training into formal lectures as the physicians had done. Actually, however, this nondenominational approach hardly was feasible for theological training, and perhaps the real purpose of the school was to temper the public impression of godless medical students by lending to the University the names and support of prominent clergymen. Joining the faculty were Episcopalians James Kemp and Frederick Beasley, Presbyterians James Inglis and William E. Wyatt, Methodist George Roberts and Lutheran Daniel Kurtz. Their ecumenical outlook appeared in their ready approval of a Roman Catholic archbishop as the University provost.

The clergymen took their appointments seriously, regularly filling the vacancies which occurred in their numbers and keeping minutes

1821; 19 October 1821; 24 March 1824; *Baltimore American,* 29 October 1818; 1 November 1819; 25 October 1820; Faculty Minutes, 26 March 1819; John D. Craig, *Introductory Lectures to a Course of Experimental Philosophy* . . . (Baltimore, 1819) ; *Journal of the House of Delegates* . . . *1825,* 309.

[42]*Federal Gazette,* 20 September 1821; 24 March 1824; *Journal of the House of Delegates* . . . *1825,* 309.

of their meetings for almost 50 years. Once or twice yearly they gathered to talk of the importance of religion in educational institutions. Occasionally one of them descended upon the medical students to deliver a sermon. At least twice, in 1820 and 1828, "Professor" Wyatt provided weekly required-attendance lectures on "such subjects as may appear most likely to promote correct principles and pious habits among the young Gentlemen of the Institution." Wyatt's colleagues authorized him to charge $10 for attendance upon his lectures, but either he was too generous or else he lacked the courage to do so.[43]

David Hoffman's Law School

By far the most significant of the new schools in the University was David Hoffman's one-man school of law which inspired a system of legal study that dominated the United States for half a century. Although his was the first university law school in the nation, the important influence was Hoffman rather than the school. The august professor cared little about degrees. His classes ceased after nine years, and in fact his school hardly differed from the independent chairs of law that existed in other institutions or in the apprentice schools prevalent outside of colleges. By publishing his lecture notes, however, Hoffman gave students a syllabus which almost replaced the classroom. As Blackstone in the previous century had organized the law itself, David Hoffman organized the study of law to the point that law schools were almost unnecessary.

Too self-righteous to obtain fame through politics, Hoffman was generally recognized as the greatest lawyers' lawyer of the Maryland bar. His distinguished colleagues on the law school faculty—William Pinkney, Robert Goodloe Harper, Robert Smith, John Purviance, Nicholas Brice and Nathaniel Williams—immediately acknowledged him as their dean and never ventured to interfere with his unusual educational experiment. Born in Baltimore, educated at St. John's, a novelist and historian in his spare time, he was a scholarly common sense lawyer whose proper place was in a law

[43]Minutes of the Divinity School, 24 March 1819; 22 March 1821 and *passim.* This small book of minutes is preserved in the archives of the medical school, Baltimore. Also, *Journal of the House of Delegates . . . 1825,* 309.

school. Active from the start in the creation of the University, he had been insistent upon the sovereignty of the faculty. He was one professor—indeed he was an entire school—who could benefit from the absence of administration.[44]

Law was one of the oldest subjects in the college curriculum. Taught in the colonial era as a one-semester introduction to legal training, the course was general and philosophical, a composite of modern courses in history, government and philosophy. Beyond this, to obtain practical knowledge of the law and of courtroom technique, students clerked for practicing attorneys, read haphazardly in Blackstone and in court reports and, after a few years, passed a perfunctory oral examination before a state judge which qualified them to argue cases. This was Hoffman's own training. However imprecise their education, lawyers held an exalted position, and the French traveler Tocqueville noted that they were the closest group to an American social aristocracy.[45]

After the Revolution occasional attorneys, following the example set by physicians, offered special lectures to small groups of students. Most prominent of these apprentice schools was that of Judge Tapping Reeve at Litchfield, Connecticut, which lasted from 1784 to 1833. Hoffman's classes at the University of Maryland followed the established pattern. Although the University charter was one of the first in America to authorize degrees for law students, Hoffman preferred the older tradition, ignoring formal requirements in the pious hope that only the legal knowledge mattered.

He began planning his law school in 1813 while the University still was being organized. For the systematic course which he envisaged, no syllabus or textbook existed in England or the United States and no guide whatever to content or organization. Instead of proceeding with a few apprentices and no plan of study, Hoffman went to the libraries to reduce the mass of laws and precedents into a discipline suitable for students and to produce the textbooks and lectures from which to begin a worthwhile course.

Five years later, in 1817, Hoffman's great work, *A Course of Legal Study, Respectfully Dedicated to the Students of Law in the United*

[44]See, Francis S. Philbrick, "David Hoffman," *Dictionary of American Biography,* Allen Johnson and Dumas Malone, eds., 22 vols. (New York, 1928-1944), IX, 111-112.
[45]Richard Hofstadter and C. DeWitt Hardy, *Development and Scope of Higher Education in the United States* (New York, 1952), 71-81; Johns S. Brubacher and Willis Rudy, *Higher Education in Transition; an American History: 1636-1956* (New York, 1958), 197-207.

States, appeared in print. It was not a textbook, but a syllabus which organized the subject and presented a list of readings for each topic. His thirteen categories were close to the course divisions today: political theory, the English constitution, property rights, personal rights, equity, business law, criminal law, international law, maritime law, Roman civil law, the United States Constitution, state constitutions and politics and economics. The readings consisted of two annotated bibliographies estimated to require six years if read entire, or four years if the student chose the abbreviated list. In the selection of topics, in the readings and in the commentaries which ranged from methods of note taking to professional ethics, Hoffman displayed a strikingly modern combination of history and jurisprudence with practical courtroom applicability.[46]

The greatest jurists of the day acclaimed the work, recognizing its significance as the basis for a virtual revolution in legal study. Chief Justice John Marshall and Chancellor James Kent wrote to Hoffman praising his book; Dewitt Clinton called it "invaluable" for all future students; Joseph Story pronounced it "by far the most perfect system for the study of law which has ever been offered to the publick." Praise encouraged Hoffman, and some years later he expanded his work into two volumes with longer commentaries and topic summaries. The author acquired a pedagogue's egotism too, for the second edition included a student's prayer and detailed instructions on how to awaken early, dress properly, take daily exercises and control the "youthful emotions."[47]

Hoffman continued work on his syllabus and lectures, and in 1823 after ten years of preparation, he announced that the University law school, called the Law Institute, was ready for operation. Three four-month terms constituted the course, with two-hour lectures five evenings a week.[48] Hoffman took pains to emphasize that the lectures were not a substitute for four years of reading, but were designed to stimulate students by placing each topic in the broad perspective of history, by pointing out the contradictions and rele-

[46]David Hoffman, *Course of Legal Study, Respectfully Dedicated to the Students of Law in the United States* (Baltimore, 1817).

[47]*North American Review, VI* (November, 1917), 76. For a digest of reviews and letters see David Hoffman, *Course of Legal Study . . .,* 2 vols.; second edition (Baltimore, 1836), I, i-vi.

[48]David Hoffman, *Syllabus of a Course of Lectures on Law, Proposed to be Delivered in the University of Maryland* (Baltimore, 1821). For a history and plan of the Institute, David Hoffman, *Address to the Students of Law in the United States* (Baltimore, 1824).

vance of various readings and by providing insight into matters which "students have neither time nor books to investigate." Lectures were only a diversion from reading, adding a freshness and realism to the law which was unobtainable in private study.[49]

On Saturday afternoons the professor stood aside to advise as the students held moot courts. Assigned to play the roles of judges, plaintiffs or defendants in specific cases, the students imitated county, district and circuit courts, chancery courts, courts of appeal and even the United States Supreme Court.[50]

Anticipating that many students would come from other states to attend his institute, Hoffman was the first at the University to be concerned with dormitories. Breaking with the centuries-old tradition of student poverty, he declared that "too little regard has been paid in all countries to the comforts and convenience of those engaged in the toils of a long and arduous course of study." Details of this first University of Maryland dormitory are vague, but Hoffman apparently arranged at his own expense for "a spacious and commodious building" on Market (now Baltimore) Street, "the apartments of which have been handsomely fitted up, and arranged in every respect for the accommodation of students." Strict rules governed the hours of study and the most minute details of daily life. Dormitory expenses were never published, but they must have been high by the standards of the day if other costs provided a measure. For lectures, attendance at the moot courts, examinations, consultation and use of Hoffman's library facilities, the fees totaled approximately $120 a term.[51]

But the vision was greater than the reality for the institute. No record exists of how many students attended in its nine years of operation but expressions of disappointment abound. At best there were about 30 students attending lectures at any one time, and Hoffman declared that he lost $20,000 in the school.[52] The trouble was that a student could study on his own, using Hoffman's published guides and saving both the time and the tuition of formal lectures. In addition to his syllabus Hoffman, in 1829, began publishing his lectures—two large volumes of model addresses, each

[49]Hoffman, *Address to Students of Law*, 9.

[50]David Hoffman, *A Lecture Being the Third of a Series of Lectures Now Delivering in the University of Maryland* (Baltimore, 1826), 50-59; *Federal Gazette*, 4 June 1827.

[51]Hoffman, *Address to Students of Law*, 10-15.

[52]Charles Varle, *Complete View of Baltimore* . . . (Baltimore, 1833), 27; *Journal of the House of Delegates* . . . *1825*, 311.

complete with outline and bibliography.[53] With the books available for a few dollars, students were not anxious to pay much more to hear them read aloud.

While various universities continued to offer introductory courses and occasionally provided a poorly attended chair of law, not until after the Civil War, with the emergence of a new type of law and a new method of case study, was legal training again institutionalized. Following Hoffman's example, many other famous jurists, notably James Kent and Joseph Story, published textbooks so that the man who initiated the movement was deprived of large royalties as well as of students. When the State of Maryland gained control of the University and established trustees over the proud Hoffman he could take no more. He resigned in 1833 and went to Europe to write novels.

The University and the College of Medicine

While the undergraduate college and the school of divinity foundered and the law school in a grand manner devoured itself, the medical school made the most of the University of Maryland name. From the establishment of the University structure in 1812 until the coming of troubles about 1826, the Medical College enjoyed a golden era. Its classrooms were full; its mood was progressive. In the second and third decades of the century only the University of Pennsylvania School of Medicine regularly graduated larger classes, but the Marylanders acknowledged no one as their superior in quality.

The strength of the Medical College came in part from its stable faculty. Davidge, Potter, DeButts, Baker and Hall remained from the founding of the school, dedicated not only to the institution, but also, except possibly for Hall, to outstanding education and scholarship. The brilliant William Gibson, joining the faculty in 1812, appeared to be an academic vagabond when he left after seven years, and even Maxwell McDowell, a well-known Pennsylvania doctor who arrived in 1814, remained a comparative newcomer after twenty years in the institution. Gibson was particularly noteworthy

[53]David Hoffman, *Legal Outlines, Being the Substance of a Course of Lectures Now Delivering in the University of Maryland,* 2 vols. (Baltimore, 1829-1836).

as the first American surgeon to tie the common illiac artery, the first to ligate the subclavian artery and the first to perform successfully a Caesarean section twice on the same patient.[54] But two other professors raised the faculty from the noteworthy to something approaching greatness.

John Crawford was the first of these remarkable men. He taught only two courses at the University, in 1811-1812 and in 1812-1813, and he may not have completed both of them. In his first set of lectures, however, he closely approached the germ theory of disease 50 years before Pasteur, and his second course concerned evolution 45 years before Darwin. Although far from the first to champion either theory, his linkage of the two involved genius as well as luck. Born in Ireland, educated at Leyden, he came to Baltimore soon after the Revolution and became a leader in the medical and civic life of the city. In the summer of 1800, together with Benjamin Waterhouse of Boston, he first introduced vaccine into the United States as a means of halting the dread smallpox scourge. Learned, opinionated and zealous, he had labored for the creation of the Medical Society of Maryland and of the College of Medicine. Never popular because of his unusual and strongly held theories, he probably had to ask for the privilege of delivering the University lectures which were the culmination of his life's work.[55]

Disease, Crawford maintained in his first lectures, was caused "by the introduction into the human body of some form of animacular life so minute as to escape observation," and he insisted that "each of these minute organisms produces its own peculiar disease." The destruction of these germs should presumably be the aim of all therapy.[56] To his friend, Benjamin Rush, Crawford confessed that his lectures were poorly received, but the following year he spoke out even more boldly.[57] Lecturing on natural history off college property, he noted "the chain of life" developing from the lowest to the highest forms. "I have been deemed an innovator," he confessed with some bitterness. "I am accused of having descended

[54]Cordell, *University,* I, 143-149, 194.

[55]Raymond N. Deutsch, John Crawford and His Contribution to the Doctrine of *Contagium Vivum," Bacteriological Reviews,* XXVIII (March, 1964), 87-96; also Julia E. Wilson, "An Early Baltimore Physician and His Medical Library," *Annals of Medical History,* IV (January, 1942), 63-80.

[56]John Crawford, *Lecture Introductory to a Course of Lectures on the Cause, Seat and Cure of Diseases* (Baltimore, 1811); *Federal Gazette,* 21 September 1802.

[57]Crawford to Rush, January 1806, Rush Papers, Library Company of Philadelphia, cited in Deutsch, "John Crawford."

from the dignity of my species, and placing myself on a level with the most ignoble of the creation. What others may consider as a degradation, I esteem of high value."[58]

Crawford does not deserve the credit that belongs to more famous names. While he used some of the same arguments as Darwin and Pasteur, he relied on theory rather than experimentation and consequently failed to convince others. His colleagues, who would have been astonished to hear of his being selected as one of their greatest, were pleased when he resigned. It was a day when scientific theories flourished, but it remained for others to prove his theories right and those of his colleagues wrong. If Crawford deserves limited acclaim for prescience, however, his colleagues must not be accorded undue ridicule when their equally imaginative theories proved wrong.

So far as the University was concerned Crawford's wife did them a greater service than he. After he died in 1813, she sold to the University his private medical library, one of the best collections in the country, for the remarkably charitable price of $500. For the University library, the purchase was an auspicious beginning, and it spoke well for the faculty members that they could appropriate that amount of money for books instead of for salaries or buildings. They fitted up a large room at the front of the medical building to house the collection. Called the "Green Room" because of its handsome carpeting and draperies of that color, the atmosphere was that of a lounge, provided with stationery and the popular magazines of the day at no charge. The University received numerous other gifts of books. By 1830 the faculty had spent $2,600 on the library and were providing it with an annual appropriation of at least $50.[59]

To most students and Baltimoreans, however, there was no doubt that the greatest professor at Maryland was the eloquent Scottish lecturer, Granville Sharp Pattison. He made no lasting medical discoveries, and his vanity destroyed his promise before he was forty. But his energy, his reputation and his incredible charisma invigorated the Medical College. He radiated greatness whether he

[58]John Crawford, "Doctor Crawford's Theory," *Observer and Repository of Original and Selected Essays*, II (November, 1807), 311.
[59]*Baltimore American*, 23 September 1815; 20 July 1816; *Memorial of the Trustees of the University of Maryland and the Trustees of Baltimore College to the Legislature of Maryland* (Baltimore, 1830), 19; Ruth Lee Briscoe, "A History of the Library of the University of Maryland," *Bulletin of the School of Medicine, University of Maryland*, XXIII (October, 1938), 44-57; Wilson, "Early Baltimore Physician," 70-75; Cordell, *University*, I, 138.

possessed it or not, and more importantly he gave his associates a sense of greatness. For himself and for the institution he provided the example that self-confidence is half the assurance of success.

Wherever he went Pattison attracted admirers. Students regularly applauded his lectures, and most of them assumed, as did he, that they had heard the world's greatest authority on whatever subject he had discussed. His colleagues caught his enthusiasm, electing him dean of the medical faculty within a year of his arrival and willingly giving him credit for the institution's progress. Extraordinarily handsome, he especially impressed women. Wives and debutantes of Baltimore pursued him with notorious success, and 50 years after he left Maryland his amours were legendary. It was said that he had "taken so much mercury [for veneral disease] that he was afraid to take hold of a door bell for fear of electric shock."[60]

Pattison arrived in Baltimore in 1820 with the usual storm of controversy in his wake. He had left Glasgow two years before because of an adultery charge concerning the wife of a fellow professor. Landing in Philadelphia, he advertised his presence in the newspapers, and informed the University of Pennsylvania Medical School that he was willing to assume its chair of surgery. Infuriated by its refusal, he helped to organize a rival group of physicians, hoping to drive the older school out of business. Tiring of that, he offered his services and his student following to the University of Maryland.[61]

Apparently as a part of the conditions on which he came, Pattison sold to the University a magnificent collection of anatomical specimens to which he had somehow acquired title before leaving Glasgow. Containing over a thousand beautifully pickled examples of normal and diseased organs, the collection was invaluable for teaching and probably was the best in America. Pattison received a staggering $7,800 for the collection, and evidently the University considered it a bargain. In addition, Professor Davidge obligingly took the chair of anatomy so that Pattison could have the chair of surgery that he demanded.[62]

[60]*Federal Gazette,* 15 November 1821; 10 February 1824; 11 April 1824; William Snow Miller, "Granville Sharp Pattison," *Johns Hopkins Hospital Bulletin,* XXX (October, 1919), 98-104; Cordell, *University,* I, 149, 169.

[61]*Federal Gazette,* 31 October 1821; *Daily Advertiser,* 25 October 1820; *Federal Gazette,* 15 May 1821; *Niles Register,* IX (September 16, 1815), 34.

[62]*Report of the Joint Committee,* 1839, 7; *Annual Circular of the Medical Department . . . 1839-1840* (Baltimore, 1840), 6.

Throwing himself into University affairs, Pattison was fully as dedicated to its financial well-being as to his own. Immediately he assumed the direction of another lottery which the faculty had obtained permission to conduct and money flowed into the treasury. The professors thought of paying their debts, but the more ambitious Pattison persuaded them to pour the money into improvements and to borrow more besides. DeButts, the chemistry professor, pushed his perennial request for additional laboratory apparatus, and with the effervescent Pattison at the meeting an expenditure of approximately $5,000 was quickly authorized. This particular appropriation led to difficulties, for the agent who was to buy the equipment in Paris absconded with the money. Eventually recovering the funds, DeButts went to Europe for the apparatus. As a result of such improvements the University was able to advertise its laboratories, along with its anatomy museum, as the finest in the country.[63]

To house the new facilities and the swelling enrollment, Pattison next persuaded the faculty that their eight-year-old building required an addition. Completed in 1821, the new, two-story, $8,000 structure was just northeast of the older building. The first floor contained chemical laboratories and classrooms, and the second was devoted to Pattison's anatomical museum. The building was known as the Museum, although after a third story was added later it came to be known as Practice Hall.[64]

Undoubtedly Pattison's greatest University project was the establishment of a teaching hospital adjacent to the school and administered solely by the professors for the instruction of their students. Most American medical schools, in reaction against empirical apprentice instruction, placed such emphasis on classroom lectures that clinical training was badly neglected. Cocke and Davidge had tried to remedy this by giving their students regular tours through Baltimore hospitals, but Pattison rejected halfway measures. Failing to persuade the Baltimore city council to build the hospital for the University and failing also to influence the banks to extend further credit to the University corporation, Pattison prevailed upon the

[63]*Federal Gazette*, 16 April 1821; 15 May 1821; 10 February 1824; 14 September 1824; *Report of the Joint Committee*, 5-6; *Baltimore American*, 23 April 1821; Faculty Minutes, 6 February 1817; 29 March 1822; *Baltimore American*, 20 July 1816; 30 September 1819; 25 October 1820; *Annual Circular . . . 1839-1840*, 6.

[64]*Baltimore American*, 24 August 1820; 25 October 1820; Cordell, *University*, I, 149-151; Varle, *Complete View of Baltimore*, 25.

professors to extend their personal credit. At any rate, there was no doubt that the hospital would belong to the professors.[65]

The infirmary, as it usually was called, was the third University building. Situated across Lombard Street from the medical school and about a half block west of Greene, the 60-bed hospital was ready for patients and classes by the fall term in 1823. A handsome 4-story building in the Federalist style, it cost the faculty $14,109 for construction plus $2,520 for beds and furnishings. Two curved stairways led to a porch and entrance on the second floor where offices and quarters for nurses and residence students were located. The rest of the building was divided into four wards, one specially designed for ophthalmic cases. At the rear of the hospital was a semicircular operating theater with seats for student observation. Behind the building were wooden shacks which served for laundries and "necessaries." Resident students could obtain room and board in the hospital for $300 annually; for patients the fee for board, nurses and doctors was $3 per week.[66]

Nurses rather than doctors transform a house of death into one of hope, and Pattison's magnificent solution to the problem of securing them guaranteed the hospital's success. Because of the absence of trained nurses most early nineteenth century hospitals were little better than pesthouses where the indigent came to die, and because of the grimness of nursing modest women who willingly plowed in the fields never dreamed of following the profession. Pattison turned to the Roman Catholic nuns who had served so heroically in the European hospitals and were beginning to work as nurses in America. To his invitation to serve in the University infirmary, the Sisters of Charity from nearby Emmitsburg, Maryland, responded with eagerness. "I can hardly express the joy they felt," wrote a priest after the final arrangements were made. The Sisters, he said, were "ready and willing to fulfill the most menial or disgusting offices."[67] Sister Superior Joanna Smith soon arrived as the first

[65]Davidge, *Physical Sketches*, III, 9-10; *Baltimore Medical and Physical Recorder*, I (1809), 53-54; *Baltimore American*, 20 July 1816; *Federal Gazette*, 30 March 1822; *Report of the Joint Committee*, 5-6; Arthur J. Lomas, "As It Was in the Beginning: A History of the University Hospital," *Bulletin of the School of Medicine of the University of Maryland*, XXIII (April, 1939), 182-209.

[66]Lomas, "University Hospital," 188-190; John H. B. Latrobe, *Picture of Baltimore* . . . (Baltimore, 1832), 169-170. There is a modified etching of the building on most of the University catalogues from 1838 to 1855. Also *Federal Gazette*, 18 October 1823; 24 October 1823; 30 October 1823; 10 February 1824; Cordell, *University*, I, 157.

[67]Father John DuBois to Pattison, 16 May 1822, St. Joseph College Archives, Emmitsburg.

manager of the hospital and under her were Sisters Ann, Adelle, Rebecca and Barbary.

Hard bargaining between Pattison and the Sisters established a detailed system of rules which set model standards for a nursing order and for a teaching hospital. To the attending physicians the nurses promised "implicit obedience," and to the faculty who owned the institution they promised detailed monthly reports. Otherwise they obtained absolute control over daily operations, finances, patients and resident students. Most difficult was the regulation of the residents, for the nurses had strict notions of discipline and irrevocably locked the hospital doors at ten o'clock each night. The nuns provided daily Bible reading to the patients, but attempted no evangelism, and they promised "to interrupt their religious exercises . . . or even omit them altogether if necessary." The University supplied them with "simple" quarters and meals in the hospital, free medical care, annual transportation to and from the convent at Emmitsburg, and $42 apiece each year for clothing. The University allowed them to hire orderlies to carry fire wood, move patients and render those "services repugnant to female delicacies or propriety." The Sisters agreed to wash patients' clothes at no cost, but required the University to provide free pajamas because "many of the sick brought to the Infirmary, particularly the blacks, may have ragged, dirty clothes, even with vermin." Under the efficient management of the nuns the hospital broke even financially and provided incalculable dividends in the education of students and in service to the suffering humanity of the state. During the fifty-six years the Sisters served the University of Maryland, almost every decade saw the expansion of the hospital. The quixotic Pattison rightly could claim credit for bringing Maryland's medical education to the forefront. In claiming credit he was never hesitant.[68]

From seven medical students hiding from the hostile populace of Baltimore in 1807, there had emerged at Lombard and Greene Streets by 1826 one of the finest American medical colleges, a school of which the state was justly proud. The faculty, medical buildings, library, laboratories, museum, hospital and nursing system were

---

[68]Agreement between the Faculty and the Sisters of Charity, 1823, MS. in St. Joseph College Archives, Emmitsburg; Lomas, "University Hospital," 190-209; Faculty Minutes, *passim.*

among the best in the country. Over 300 students from almost every state in the nation were attending classes each year.[69]

The annual commencement in April had become a city-wide holiday, and each seemed to mark a new triumph or distinction. Awarding an honorary degree to Lafayette in 1824 focused nation-wide attention on the campus. The main lecture hall of the medical building was fitted with green carpets and red cushions as more than a thousand state and national dignitaries listened to the Revolutionary hero praise the University as one of the illustrious flowers of American independence.[70] The following year the University displayed a more scholarly insight, awarding an honorary degree to the backwoods ovariatomist Ephriam McDowell, first recognizing the man now considered one of America's greatest physicians.[71] In 1826 the University awarded 89 medical degrees, the largest graduating class of the next half-century.[72]

Such spectacular accomplishments set many people to marveling at how well Maryland's unique proprietary University had worked, at least for medicine, and how far the medical school had come in

[69]See, *Daily Advertiser,* 25 October 1820; *Federal Gazette,* 28 November 1821; 22 October 1824; *Baltimore American,* 9 October 1826; Potter, *Some Account,* 12; Faculty Minutes, 1813-1826, *passim.* The following medical school balance sheet, exclusive of fees, gifts and salaries, is from *Journal of the House of Delegates . . . 1825,* 309-310:

Income:

Lottery of 1812	$18,000
Lottery of 1813	20,000
Lottery of 1816-1824	31,404
Loans guaranteed by professors	30,000
Losses assumed by professors	6,425
	105,829

Expenses:

Lot for University, 1807	$ 9,000
University Building, 1813	45,000
Wall around Building, 1813	1,500
Heat for Building, 1817	1,000
Anatomical Collection, 1820	7,800
Museum Building, 1821	8,000
Lot for Infirmary, 1822	8,000
Infirmary Building, 1823	14,109
Infirmary beds, etc., 1823	2,520
Library, 1815-1825	1,000
Laboratory, etc., 1807-1825	8,900
	105,829

[70]Faculty Minutes, 23 September 1824; *Niles Register,* XXVII (October 16, 1824), 109-110; (October 23, 1824), 118-119; *Federal Gazette,* 11 October 1824.

[71]Faculty Minutes, 31 March 1825.

[72]Faculty Minutes, 17 March 1826. For a complete list of University graduates to 1905 see Cordell, *University,* II.

only twenty years. But the marveling only signified difficulties ahead. To the faculty success pointed toward a growing concern for the profits that should accrue to them for their sacrifices. To other physicians the Medical College's success suggested the possibility of establishing rival schools in which, perhaps, enrollments could be encouraged by slightly lowering standards. To the people of Maryland, the medical school's success pointed toward the failure of the other University schools, and suggested the wisdom of some outside guidance. William Smith and David Hoffman had been crushed by their success; so often the University's problems seemed to come from its triumphs.

3

The State Takes Control

Jacksonian democracy offered great opportunities but also met with sweeping rebuffs on American campuses. In an age of reform enthusiasm, of crusades for human rights and of ideas fermenting, Americans seemed almost obsessed with the desire for moral and intellectual improvement. Free public schools spread—the first state school board was established in Maryland in 1826—adults flocked to self-improvement lyceum meetings and new colleges sprang up by the score. At Thomas Jefferson's University of Virginia exciting experiments began with a greatly broadened curriculum and student electives. On the other hand, more than almost any other institutions and perhaps with less reason, colleges resisted internal reform. The multiplication of such schools did little to democratize their aristocratic aims; Jefferson's innovations failed; and the moral urgency of the Jacksonian era only confirmed the ancient academic emphasis on morality rather than on useful knowledge. Often the creation of new colleges only weakened the established ones.

In Maryland, despite the success of professional education and the existence of a number of struggling denominational colleges, the absence of a firmly crystalized academic tradition offered unusual opportunities to create new educational patterns. The general assembly, reflecting the reform sentiment of the day, seized the University of Maryland in an effort to transform it into a true state university combining the English system of classical undergraduate education with the Scottish-Continental system of professional education. The time was not ripe for academic reform, however, and the state's experiment, from 1826 to 1839, reflected the shortcomings rather than the advantages of both systems.

Proprietary Problems

When the University emerged out of a medical school in 1812, no one realized that its unique system of faculty self-government had so many implications for higher education. Although other private schools in America, including the famed academies, had long depended solely upon tuition for support, the University of Maryland was the first institution of higher learning to grant degrees on a proprietary basis. Put most bluntly, the University was able to sell degrees and the precedent had far-reaching results. Theoretically, faculty control provided great dignity to the professors, since it placed academic policies in the hands of those most capable of determining them. Theoretically, the laws of the market place guaranteed good teaching, since ineffective professors soon found themselves without students. And, again theoretically, the pay-as-you-go policy insured outstanding education, since students set their own pace and realized in an immediate financial way the value of study. The very success of the College of Medicine advertised the virtues and camouflaged the difficulties of the system. The problems, however, became increasingly evident.

The most obvious failure of the proprietary system was the inability of the University to establish an undergraduate college. Medical and law students were willing to advance their professional competence by paying for the best type of professional training available, but almost no one wished to pay for undergraduate lectures when subsidized colleges were available. There were other reasons for the failure apart from financial ones. The European colleges—oriented in aims, teaching methods and curriculum around the delight in knowledge—succeeded by appealing to students willing to sacrifice for this delight. The English and American colleges—oriented in aims, methods and curriculum around character building—succeeded by appealing to parents to improve their children. But the University of Maryland combined the aims, methods and curriculum of the English and American colleges with the nonresident, proprietary structure of the Scottish-Continental institutions, so that it appealed to neither students nor parents. Its tuition-supported lectures were at best a system of adult education, with little prospect of growing into a successful college.

For most Marylanders the reasons for failure were less important than the fact that the state was lagging in education. With well-established denominational colleges and new state universities flourishing North and South, even men little concerned with education felt the rivalry which the American federal system promoted. Far from appreciating the efforts of the medical college to launch a university, many felt that somehow the failure to establish an undergraduate college was a violation of the state's trust in awarding a charter.[1]

The state found it difficult to aid a private institution based on faculty profits and even more difficult to control the favors it did provide. Although the dominant medical faculty spoke enthusiastically about the values of a college, it was quick to use the lottery profits for itself. Faculty self-government, in other words, caused the large departments to grow larger and the small ones to languish. When the assembly investigated the institution in 1826, it could not find a single University appropriation to nonmedical subjects. The School of Law had been financed by Hoffman personally. Profits from the lotteries, the second of which had been intended primarily for the college, had been spent solely "for the benefit, and under the direction, of the Faculty of Physic."[2]

As the desire for a college grew complaints about the medical school mounted. Never far from the surface was the feeling of ignorant men that the medical professors were godless grave robbers, and that medical education was a method of creating monopoly, raising fees and eliminating cheap miracle healers. Just as the grave-robbing charge of 1807 contained an element of truth, so

[1]*Federal Gazette*, 24 October 1826; 21 December 1830; 3 January 1831; 20 August 1831; 12 August 1834; *Baltimore Sun*, 22 August 1840; *Baltimore American*, 23 July 1836.
[2]*Journal of the House of Delegates of Maryland . . . 1825* (Annapolis, 1826), Report of a Committee, 25 February 1826, 310.

the monopoly charge was coming to have a respectable basis by the mid-1820's. The medical society, always in close collaboration with the College of Medicine, was accused of making it difficult for non-Maryland graduates to obtain licenses. Able physicians, the charge ran, refused to migrate into the state because they were unable to practice until they paid for expensive "refresher" courses at the University. Approximately ten percent of the young men at the University already possessed the M.D. degree from other reputable institutions.[3]

The ever-controversial Pattison became a particular focus of hostility. Conservative physicians throughout the state were skeptical, and possibly jealous, of the "foreigner" who dominated the University with his newfangled clinical teaching methods. To many Maryland physicians it seemed that they, or at any rate other native Americans, should be hired for all posts in the University. If this argument was unworthy of the jealous physicians, they could always depend upon Pattison to provide them with better grounds for attack. Following Pattison's attempt to destroy the school of medicine at the University of Pennsylvania, Dr. Nathaniel Chapman, a leading professor at that school, launched a scurrilous diatribe on his medical attainments, his marital life and his character. Published just after Pattison arrived in Baltimore, the hot-blooded Scotsman demanded satisfaction on the dueling ground. Chapman pleaded that he was too old to fight, and for three years insults flew back and forth between the two men and their rival institutions. Finally, in 1823, Chapman's brother-in-law, General Thomas Cadwalader, a hero of the American wars against the British, took up the challenge. With Davidge attending as "Surgeon," the two met in Delaware. Neither was seriously hurt in the exchange of shots, but the general received an arm wound. Patriots and moralists alike were shocked, and besides blaming Pattison and foreigners generally, they also blamed the University for harboring such a man.[4]

Less obvious to the public than the failure of the college or the supposed faults of the College of Medicine, but a more basic prob-

[3]*Federal Gazette*, 22 August 1831; 26 November 1833; 27 November 1833; 28 October 1836.

[4]*Ibid.*, 20 July 1830; 26 July 1830; 29 July 1834; *Baltimore American*, 23 July 1836; Nathaniel Chapman, *Official Transcript of Proceedings in the Case of Divorce of Andrew Ure, M.D. v. Catherine Ure, for Adultery with Granville Sharpe Pattison* (Philadelphia, 1821); Frank H. J. Figge, "Granville Sharp Pattison, the Dueling Anatonist," *Bulletin of the School of Medicine of the University of Maryland*, XXIII (October, 1938), 81-92; *Federal Gazette*, 9 May 1821; 10 May 1821; 17 May 1821.

lem for a proprietary school, was the lack of leadership inherent in the system. With no one to define university-wide goals or to act as spokesman, the professors tended to place loyalty to subject matter above loyalty to the institution or to the cause of higher education. With no center of authority, self-government produced indifference rather than responsibility for the university cause. During the first fourteen years of the University's existence, the faculty assembled a quorum for only twelve meetings.[5] The medical professors had no desire to consult about their affairs with the nonmedical faculty, and the nonmedical faculty had few affairs to discuss. Even within the College of Medicine, a potentially dangerous power vacuum existed as professors settled matters informally, generally on the basis of who took the initiative rather than who happened to be the elected dean. Although the process was democratic, danger existed when there was no one to decide disputes.

The inevitable internal controversies, along with the state's desire for a true state university, finally led to confiscation by the government. Quarrels among equals were more bitter and devouring than rebellion against a remote board of trustees or against a dean or a president who was an undisputed superior. Disputes over educational policy became disputes within a business partnership, flared into the open and became power struggles. There was no finality in the censure of colleagues. Some of the University's disagreements would have occurred under any system of administration, for by 1826 a number of the professors were growing old and crotchety. According to the trustees who took control for the state, the faculty "was a scene of perpetual disputes and cabals . . . of total chaos."[6]

The first serious quarrel alienated Davidge and DeButts and prompted them to attack the University in ways they came to regret. Both professors always had worked closely with the students, advising and assisting them when they had difficulties with their studies. By 1822 the two doctors had organized their advisory sessions into a series of coaching classes held in a nearby schoolhouse each Wednesday and Saturday evening. At first the sessions were free, but by 1824 the doctors were renting off-campus coaching rooms on a regular basis and were charging students $10 a term for these extra

[5] Faculty Minutes of the University of Maryland, 1813-1837. Bound MS. volume in archives of the College of Medicine, Baltimore.
[6] *Annual Report of the Trustees of the University of Maryland to the General* XIV (June, 1943), 14-29.

"Medical and Chymical Conversations." Soon the extra classes became a school within a school, as students found the coaching sessions to be unlisted requirements. Pattison and other faculty members felt that Davidge and DeButts were enriching themselves at the
students' expense. When remonstrance failed, Pattison took the unprecedented step of forcing the matter to a vote before the entire
University faculty, and by a tally of 12 to 6 (with 10 absentions) the
private lectures were forbidden. Two founders of the institution
were censured, and the censure burned more deeply than anyone
knew. They bided their time until a second dispute gave them a
chance to strike back at their colleagues.[7]

The second quarrel, a much more portentous one, arose when the
faculty refused to appoint Horatio Gates Jameson, a particularly
ambitious physician, to the staff thus making him so angry that he
tried to establish a rival school. Jameson was one of the most
brilliant students ever to attend the University, and apparently some
of the professors promised him a faculty position even before he
graduated. Other professors were angered by the fact that they had
not been consulted, and with Pattison particularly disliking the
brash young man, they managed to block the appointment. Perhaps
Jameson and Pattison were too much alike, for the entire episode
resembled the latter's experience in Philadelphia. Jameson's disappointment turned to bitterness blended with ambition. Rallying
whatever University enemies he could find, he offered them the
prospect of a rival institution, and in January, 1826, he appealed to
the general assembly for a charter. The assembly referred the
matter to a committee, inviting testimony from whomever was
interested.[8]

Rivalry was the ultimate threat overhanging the University, and
upon receipt of Jameson's application the legislature suddenly realized the hopeless problem it had created for itself with proprietary
education. If the state granted rival charters, it assured a cutthroat
war for obtaining high enrollments by lowering standards; if it
refused rival charters, it assured a profitable monopoly to a single

---

[7]*Federal Gazette,* 20 October 1825; Faculty Minutes, 12 November 1824; 16 November
1824; Nathaniel Potter, *Some Account of the Rise and Progress of the University of
Maryland* (Baltimore, 1838), 14-15.

[8]Horatio Gates Jameson, "Synopsis of the Hintze Trial," *American Medical Recorder,*
XVI (January, 1829), 71; *Baltimore American,* 30 September 1826; *Journal of the
House . . . 1825,* 17 January 1826, 81; Genevieve Miller, "Nineteenth Century Medical
School: Washington University of Baltimore," *Bulletin of the History of Medicine,*
XIV (June, 1943), 14-29.

group of professors. With the finest of intentions the State of Maryland and the College of Medicine had fathered a monster for American education, and medicine suffered more than other fields. By 1826 at least six medical colleges had been established outside of the state on the Maryland model, and already the Maryland catalogue had become unprofessionally flamboyant in its appeal for students. By 1910 almost 200 proprietary medical schools competed for enrollment. The most disreputable ones made their degrees easier to obtain than they had been a century before.[9]

The University dispatched Potter and DeButts to Annapolis to argue against Jameson's charter and in favor of maintaining the University's monopoly. Each went his own way buttonholing legislators. For DeButts, remembering the censure of his colleagues, here was his long-awaited opportunity. Discreetly, careful to avoid Potter, he opposed Jameson's charter yet he also talked about the University, its internal quarrels and its tendency, already evident, to lower standards to attract enrollment. He wondered aloud whether the state should take over all medical education in Maryland as well as the entire University. Perhaps DeButts, as his colleagues believed, wanted to punish them by urging confiscation of their property; or, perhaps, he better than they saw state control as a brake to the chaos ahead. At any rate the legislative committee broadened its investigation.[10]

Late in February, 1826, the committee reported, curtly recommending rejection of Jameson's charter and roundly condemning the University's charter as "radically defective." Unanimously the committee scored the University for its failure to establish a college, its lack of leadership and its internal quarrels. Noting the failure of the faculty to cooperate with the investigation, the committee significantly observed that "many" professors, speaking privately, had expressed sympathy for state control. Finally, the committee concluded that the state should assume control by establishing a board of 21 trustees, appointed by the governor, "none of whom shall be professors, or have any personal interest to be affected." The report was strong medicine for the physicians. University bills had previ-

[9]Richard Wilmot Hall to Franklin J. Smith, 22 September 1832, Hall Papers, Maryland Historical Society, Baltimore. See *Annual Catalogues* of the medical school; Nathan Smith Davis, *Contributions to the History of Medical Education and Medical Institutions in the United States of America* (Washington, 1877), 43; Abraham Flexner, *Medical Education in the United States and Canada, A Report to the Carnegie Foundation for the Advancement of Teaching* (Boston, 1910), 5-9.

[10]Potter, *Some Account*, 15-17.

ously passed quietly in the general assembly, but now debate raged openly and furiously.[11]

As the academic year ended, on March 6, 1826, the lower house approved the committee bill, confiscating the University by a vote of 36 to 17, and the upper house concurred by a voice vote. The University of Maryland became a state university in fact. In language that seemed almost vindictive, the new charter made plain that the professors were hired employees of the trustees, without tenure, replaceable at will and possessing no voice in the institution's management. As to a financial settlement, the law was vague, appropriating about $41,000 for the trustees to spend largely at their discretion, but presumably to reimburse the professors for their investments and to launch the institution on its new course with broadened objectives.[12]

As individuals the trustees commanded respect.[13] Six of them had served, or were to serve, in Congress, four in a presidential cabinet and two as state governors. To replace Bishop Kemp as provost, the trustees elected Roger B. Taney, a future Chief Justice of the Supreme Court. Again, however, as in the earlier appointments of provosts and some of the professors, prominent personages were not necessarily effective leaders. Not a single professional educator was in the group, nor a single man ready to devote his career to the institution. Taney viewed his position as had his predecessors, offering advice and awarding degrees at commencements; but he refused a salary and took no part in daily administrative affairs. Most active of the trustees was Nathaniel Williams, a United States district attorney and a long-time state senator from Baltimore. As vice-provost and head of the trustees' executive committee, he became the center of the new University government.

The trustees took over as diplomatically as possible, but even DeButts and Davidge, who had instigated the assumption of power, felt a loss of status and a resentment toward their new superiors. The trustees announced that all teaching professors would be retained, but that the inactive professors of arts and sciences, law, and divinity

[11]*Journal of the House* . . . *1825*, 307-312.

[12]*Journal of the House* . . . *1825*, 371-373; *Laws of Maryland* . . . *1825* (Annapolis, 1826) , Chap. 188, 190.

[13]They were Stephenson Archer, Theodrick Bland, E. F. Chambers, Dennis Claude, Thomas B. Dorsey, William Frick, Robert Gilmore, J. P. K. Henshaw, John C. Herbert, John Eager Howard, Reverdy Johnson, Isaac McKim, John Nelson, George Roberts, B. J. Semmes, Robert Smith, James Steuart, Roger B. Taney, Henry Wilkins, Nathaniel Williams. *Laws of Maryland* . . . *1825*, Chap. 190.

would be relieved of their honorary positions. For the time being the faculty might continue to collect student fees instead of receiving salaries; only the $5 matriculation fee and the $20 graduation fee would be collected by the trustees for a general maintenance fund. The faculty awaited future developments apprehensively.[14]

The College

Marylanders wanted an undergraduate college, and the trustees like good public servants tried to build exactly what the people wanted as inexpensively as possible. Most colleges are built by educators who try to persuade the public to accept their program and fight to obtain every penny they can get for it. In this case, however, the trustees were responding to a call, not making one. Never once did the general assembly question the modest sums the trustees requested. The college that resulted was an odd combination of traditional educational principles and fiscal innovation that reflected only too well the popular will.

The trustees launched an undergraduate program for the University of Maryland by acquiring a full-blown college. Little Baltimore College had grown out of a successful private academy established in 1798 by James Priestly, one of the great teachers of his day, and subsequently founder of the present George Peabody College in Tennessee. In 1803 Priestly obtained permission from the Maryland legislature to change the name of his academy to Baltimore College, although he continued to offer only secondary school instruction. When Priestly left for Tennessee a few years later, Samuel Knox, the ambitious proponent of a national university, took over the institution. Knox hired three additional teachers, attracted an impressive group of trustees and began offering a four-year college course in addition to the regular high school program. He also obtained lottery rights from the state, won certain favors from the Baltimore city council and obtained a few gifts from the trustees. In 1810 he erected a large $80,000 building on Mulberry Street, and for the

[14]Minutes of the Executive Committee of the Trustees, bound MS. volume in archives of the medical school, Baltimore, 6 June 1826; 24 July 1826; 9 December 1826. Minutes of entire body of trustees exist only through published newspaper accounts. See *Baltimore American*, 15 July 1826; 9 October 1826. Also, Potter, *Some Account*, 24, 29; *Journal of the House . . . 1825*, 7 March 1826, 380-381.

next ten years the liberal arts institution prospered. Each year there were about a score of graduates from its secondary school, and about a half dozen from the college. In 1820 Knox resigned, and thereafter the institution struggled along under various principals, the number of its graduates dropping by about half.[15]

With the trustees of both Baltimore College and the University of Maryland supporting the plan, in February, 1830, the general assembly unanimously approved a merger of the two institutions. There was no question of sale or purchase; the University simply took over the Baltimore College building, its three faculty members and its $7,000 in debts. The college, said the trustees, would be "the principal feature in the design of a State University."[16]

The trustees, however, were distressingly unambitious for the college, and content to allow it to prosper on its own. Instead of utilizing the reform fever in the air, they promised to "cooperate with the spirit of the times"; instead of appealing to state pride to lead the nation, they expressed the hope that Maryland could "keep up" with her neighbors; instead of promising greatness, they begged for the "indulgence of the community." For all the firmness of the general assembly in seizing the University from its owners, the trustees viewed themselves as guardians of the public purse, eager to compromise with the proprietary system if it offered a chance to save money. Instead of hiring an able faculty, the trustees renovated the brick building on Mulberry Street.[17]

The old faculty of Baltimore College continued as if little had happened. They were not scholars nor concerned with scholarship; they were disciplinarians more suited for an academy or a pulpit than for a university. The same could be said for most American professors of the 1830's, and the chief indictment of the trustees lay in their acceptance of the condition. Most able of the faculty was

[15]MS. Journal of John Pendleton Kennedy, 30 January 1831, Peabody Library, Baltimore; Memorial of the Trustees of the University of Maryland and the Trustees of Baltimore College, To the Legislature of Maryland (Baltimore, 1830); Bernard Christian Steiner, History of Education in Maryland (Washington, 1894), 245-247; J. Thomas Scharf, History of Baltimore City and County . . . (Philadelphia, 1881), 225; A. L. Crabb, "James Priestley," Allen Johnson and Dumas Malone, eds., Dictionary of American Biography, 22 vols. (New York, 1946), XV, 222-223.

[16]Laws of Maryland . . . 1829 (Annapolis, 1830), Chap. 50; Memorial of the Trustees of the University and Baltimore College, 4.

[17]Address of the Trustees of the University of Maryland to the Public (n.p., n.d. [1830]), 3-4, 8; also William Frick, Address Preparatory to Opening the Department of Arts and Sciences in the University of Maryland (Baltimore, 1831); John Pendleton Kennedy, Address Delivered on Behalf of the Faculty of Arts and Sciences on the Occasion of the Opening of the Collegiate Department in the University of Maryland, On the 3rd of January, 1831 (Baltimore, 1831).

Charles Williams who served as dean of the college and as professor of ancient languages and philosophy. A former Episcopal minister in Baltimore, he had been director of Baltimore College before its merger with the University. Other members were Reverend John Ulhorn as professor of Greek, John Carr as tutor in Latin and Richard Cotter as tutor in mathematics. Except for Williams, who had graduated from Cambridge University in England, none possessed a college degree, and none remained in Baltimore over two years. Replacing them were other mediocre, transient teachers who came and went every few years, often remaining only until they could obtain a pastorate or a well-paying position as a family tutor. Williams resigned in 1833, and John Prentiss took over as dean for four years; William Hamilton lasted two years; and Horace Morrison headed the college from 1839 to 1854.

Perhaps Maryland's trustees recognized the problems of a mediocre faculty better than those of other institutions, for they tried to strengthen the staff as the medical faculty had done, by naming prominent local citizens to deliver occasional guest lectures until student demand required their full-time employment. These honorary faculty members included John Pendleton Kennedy, Charles Hanson, John G. Morris, Joshua Cohen and George H. Calvert, all able gentlemen-scholars. Their occasional lectures, however, never became a significant part of the educational program.[18]

The trustees also continued the proprietary experiment of doing without dormitories, but for them it was a matter of economy rather than educational theory. Instead of stimulating freedom and maturity by encouraging students to live on their own in the European manner, the trustees intended to guarantee even stricter discipline than residential colleges by maintaining them under "rigid and wholesome parental control." Although promising to find quarters for enrollees from outside Baltimore, the college never attracted such students. If real scholarship had pervaded the institution, or if the subject matter had been sufficiently attractive, then a nonresidential college might have succeeded. With mediocre teachers and a traditional curriculum, however, dormitory life provided the greatest vitality to the early American college, and at Maryland this internal vigor was lacking.[19]

The trustees further weakened the academic spirit of the campus

[18]*Address of the Trustees to the Public*, 8-11; *Federal Gazette*, 2 September 1833; *Baltimore Clipper*, 1 June 1841; Cordell, *University of Maryland*, I, 470.
[19]Kennedy, *Address Delivered on Behalf of the Faculty*, 18; *Address of the Trustees to the Public*, 7.

by continuing both the secondary school program of Baltimore College, and the adult education program of the proprietary experiment. They claimed that the secondary school was necessary to assure the highest college admission standards, and that the admission of adults was a community service to "bring to every man's door the wares of intellect." Businessmen, gentlemen of leisure and "even the fairer sex" were invited to attend classes as "a pleasant diversion." In fact, however, the presence of children and of part-time adult students only further weakened the college atmosphere. By striving to keep the four professors fully occupied and by trying to serve everyone, the trustees obscured their ultimate aims.[20]

Still the college seemed to prosper, at least in a modest way, for the desire for higher education was greater than the leadership provided. Over 500 people attended the elaborate ceremonies in January, 1831, when the college first opened as part of the University of Maryland.[21] There is no complete record of the number of students in attendance or even of the number of graduates, for most of the school archives have been lost. Indeed, there is no certain evidence that the college produced any graduates before 1859, although the number in attendance indicate that at least a few must have graduated. In 1833 there were "about a hundred" students in the secondary school and the college combined, and in the next year there were 130. By 1841 there were 14 in the secondary school and 39 in the college.[22]

Although the trustees' parsimony prevented the success expected of a state university, the finances of the little college were much like those of scores of other struggling institutions throughout the country. The trustees paid the $7,000 debt hanging over the college building, and each year appropriated up to $500 for supplies and building repairs. Occasionally they appropriated as much as $300 to pay one of the medical professors for a series of scientific lectures which were opened to the public and intended for advertisement as much as for instruction.[23] In 1836 the trustees approved an expendi-

[20]Kennedy, *Address Delivered on Behalf of the Faculty*, 14-17; Frick, *Address Preparatory to Opening*, 11; *Address of the Trustees to the Public*, 18-19.

[21]Journal of John Pendleton Kennedy, 28 December 1830; 3 January 1831; *Federal Gazette*, 3 January 1831; 20 August 1831; *Baltimore American*, 4 January 1831.

[22]Charles Varle, *Complete View of Baltimore* (Baltimore, 1833), 27; *Federal Gazette*, 9 August 1834; *Matchett's Baltimore Directory* (Baltimore, 1837), Appendix; *Baltimore American*, 25 July 1836; *Annual Circular of the Collegiate Department of the University of Maryland, 1842* (Baltimore, 1842), 7-8.

[23]Minutes of Executive Committee Trustees, 7 April 1830; Complete annual budgets also appear in *Annual Report of the Trustees of the University of Maryland to the General Assembly* (Annapolis, 1831 and 1833).

ture of $331 for "work on the gymnasium," a particularly significant item of which there is unfortunately no further record, for this is one of the earliest references to physical education in an American college.[24] Student tuition was about $50 a year in the academy and about $75 a year in the college. These fees provided approximately $5,000 annually which the three or four professors divided as their salaries.[25]

The unimaginative attitude of the trustees and the mediocrity of the college gave it special significance in reflecting the "typical" education of the day. Although student life was curtailed by the absence of dormitories, the educational aims and teaching methods reflected well what the public expected from higher education and what it usually received in the half century before the Civil War. The good old days would appall a modern student.

Eager to expound on the purpose of higher education, the early nineteenth century professor had developed a close-knit argument for colleges as a means of expanding the mental capacities and the moral sentiments of its charges. More simply, it was the aim of the college to build character. Generally unconcerned with the value of knowledge itself, much less with expanding the boundaries of knowledge, higher education was a force of conservatism rather than of change, an attempt to maintain existing values rather than to seek new ones. The colleges, like the churches, were designed to strengthen the moral fiber of the student and thus, as the University charter declared, "to raise the tone of society." By rigid discipline, by expanding the mental "faculties" of judgment and conscience, by buttressing the values in which society believed, a college education would shape a more perfect man. In grandiose language, without a word about imparting knowledge, the Maryland trustees explained how the college would "mold the character" and "fix the principles" of adolescents:

> It will be the care and study of professors and teachers throughout all the collegiate courses . . . to impress notions of order, decency and good manners; to form the habits of industry and attention, by which youth are secured from idleness and consequent depravity; to inculcate an enlightened and well-principled moral sentiment, and inspire that purity and refinement of taste, which is so important to

[24]Minutes of Executive Committee Trustees, 2 December 1836.
[25]*Address of the Trustees to the Public*, 18-19; *Federal Gazette*, 30 December 1830; 3 January 1831; 20 August 1831; 2 September 1833; 9 August 1834; 29 August 1837; 23 August 1839; Varle, *Complete View of Baltimore*, 27-29; *Address of the Trustees to the Public*, 11-17.

form and adorn the moral character. It will be the primary object, to elevate the student . . . by inspiring the principles of virtue at an early age, and exciting a sense of character and manly deportment; to check the follies and extravagances of youth . . . and to check the denunciations of religion against dissipation and immorality. Moral and intellectual elevation of character, is the great object sought to be obtained.[26]

Individual trustees tirelessly reiterated the concept. According to John Pendleton Kennedy, speaking at the college opening, "improvement of the moral deportment" of students promised to "lift this whole society into a higher scale of being." Said Francis Scott Key on another occasion, "Parents cannot guide [their son's] morals, direct his judgment, restrain his passions, and guide his pursuits with the same advantages as a well-conducted college." And to trustee William Frick the purpose of the college was to "refine the taste . . . elevate the moral sentiment . . . and enkindle lofty feelings in the heart."[27]

Educators were ready to translate this rhetoric into everyday applicability by illustrating and justifying the moral, social and political ideals of the day. To the early nineteenth century educator, it was not falsifying the facts to select only those which proved, for example, the past triumph of morality over immorality, for the triumph of morality was certain while the exact facts of history and observation were not. The facts which demonstrated this triumph, therefore, were the relevant facts, the ones worth using in a textbook or a lecture, while those which did not illustrate an accepted truth were falsely understood, irrelevant and in all probability simply untrue. By fortifying in all men the ideals which society accepted, all society would be strengthened and elevated. The system worked so long as men agreed, in general, about what was right and good.[28]

Of the specific certainties which education tried to buttress, the

---

[26]*Address of the Trustees to the Public,* 3-6.

[27]Kennedy, *Address Delivered on Behalf of the Faculty,* 21, 26; Francis Scott Key, *Discourse on Education* (Annapolis, 1827), 10; Frick, *Address Preparatory to Opening,* 13.

[28]See, for example, the following textbooks in use at the time: Alexander Fraser Tytler, *Elements of General History* (Concord, N. H., 1825), 11; Salma Hale, *History of the United States* (New York, 1837), iv; Samuel G. Goodrich, *Pictorial History of the United States* (Philadelphia, 1845), iv; Samuel Whelpley, *Compend of History* (Burlington, Vt., 1808), 160; also, Carl Becker, *Heavenly City of the Eighteenth-Century Philosophers* (New Haven, 1932), 16-19 and *passim*; Richard Hofstadter and

most important was personal virtue—a Protestant ethic emphasizing individual integrity, industry, piety, duty, earnestness, courage, work, character and dependability.[29] By examining classical literature and history the student discovered the "noble examples" and "striking incidents" which set forth these principles, and "the youthful heart shall kindle into desires of imitation." If the desire to emulate were not enough, the competent teacher pointed out threats and rewards as clearly as any preacher. "In the faithful delineations of history," said one textbook writer, "vice always appears odious, and virtue desirous and productive of human happiness." Education invariably "presents us with pictures of the vicious overtaken with misery and shame," said another.[30]

Besides personal ethics the existence of God was another specific certainty for education to illustrate. Although the trustees made a great point of being nondenominational by retaining Catholics, Protestants and Jews on the faculty, each of the deans was a clergyman, and "Evidences of Religion" was the course that seniors considered the capstone of the entire curriculum. Since God was a certainty, the facts which revealed His presence were the true and important ones. "To show that one supreme, eternal God . . . controls all events is the great design of this work," said a textbook. "With a steady eye to the special designs of God . . . I have . . . prosecuted my work with an unbiased inquiry after truth." The author saw no conflict between his steady eye and his unbiased inquiry.[31]

Finally, patriotism was another fundamental principle for education to instill. In an age of nationalism and manifest destiny Americans liked to view their government as the pinnacle of historical development, and patriotism meant veneration for the United

---

C. DeWitt Hardy, *Development and Scope of Higher Education in the United States* (New York, 1952), 13-15; Eva Channing, trans. and ed., *Pestalozzi's "Leonard and Gertrude"* (Boston, 1885), 125-131; Johann Friedrich Herbart, *Outlines of Educational Doctrine*, A. F. Land, trans. (New York, 1901), 7, 24, 97, 223-240.

[29]See *Federal Gazette*, 9 August 1834; William C. Taylor, *Manual of Ancient History* (New York, 1855), 5; Emma Willard, *Ancient Geography* (Hartford, Conn., 1827), v.

[30]Emma Williard, *History of the United States* (New York, 1845), v; Joseph Emerson Worcester, *Elements of History* (Boston, 1840), 3; Charles A. Goodrich, *History of the United States* (Hartford, Conn., 1841), 5; Francis Weyland, *Elements of Political Economy* (Boston, 1837), 32.

[31]*Address of the Trustees to the Public*, 17; Frederick Butler, *Complete History of the United States* (Hartford, Conn., 1821), iii.

States, for democracy, for American liberty and even for progress itself. Instead of training for citizenship, as later generations would require, instead of providing specific knowledge for training statesmen and voters, education provided the character and wisdom from which students could make use of knowledge gained in the world. Like ethical behavior, and like belief in God, patriotism reflected character, and with that everything else would fall into place.[32]

The aims of the little Maryland college, so well-understood and so unhesitatingly accepted, dictated a traditional, conservative academic curriculum with an overwhelming emphasis on classical languages. Latin and Greek were the fountainheads of culture, the common languages of learned men, the ideal subjects for training the mind; but above all they offered a "pure" literature, uncontaminated by modern prejudices, in which professors could find endless illustrations for moral principles. Professors pointed to the virtues of the Greeks and Romans which had led to their glory, and to their vices which seemed to have led to their decline.[33]

Most students at Maryland, both in the academy and the college, spent about two-thirds of their time studying Latin and Greek. Although the precollege program offered a special terminal course emphasizing English and arithmetic, college-bound students studied Latin, Greek, mathematics and philosophy. After about five years in the academy, the student was about fifteen years old and had about nine years of education. To enter the college he passed a written and oral examination proving his ability to read Caesar, Ovid, Virgil and Xenophon and to write grammatical Latin prose from English dictation. There are no records of what proportion of the applicants met the entrance requirements, and probably the faculty looked favorably on most students who had the price of admission. On paper, however, these entrance requirements were among the highest in the country. Freshmen at the University studied Cicero, Virgil, Horace, Homer and Herodotus; sophomores added Livy, Catullus, Terence, Demosthenes and Euripides; the junior class studied Lucan, Juvenal, Tacitus, Xenophon, Thucydides and Sophocles; and seniors finished up with Pliny, Aeschylus, Longinus and a host of lesser writers. All the while the students labored over classical

[32]Frick, *Address Preparatory to Opening*, 36-37; Butler, *Complete History of the United States*, vi-viii; Hale, *History of the United States*, 5; Whelpley, *Compend of History*, viii; Tytler, *Elements of General History*, 11; Worcester, *Elements of History*, 3.
[33]Frick, *Address Preparatory to Opening*, 33-34; Kennedy, *Address Delivered on Behalf of the Faculty*, 19; *Baltimore American*, 5 March 1860.

grammar and composition by translating passages into English or from English into the two ancient languages.[34]

Students were left about a third of their time for other studies. Mathematics was taught through all four years of college, progressing from geometry to algebra, trigonometry, surveying, navigation and calculus. There were scattered courses in history, religion, rhetoric, belles lettres—which meant English literature, especially Milton— and philosophy which meant ethics. Finally there was "natural philosophy," which included chemistry, physics, astronomy, geology and biology. This general science course, usually the most popular, most often was taught by a professor from the medical school or by one of the honorary lecturers only technically on the faculty. The lectures, seldom subject to examinations, were frequently attended by numerous townspeople who were unqualified for admission to the college.

The teaching methods at Maryland, rooted in the peculiar theory of "faculty psychology," combined with the curriculum to reinforce the institution's aim of expanding the mental and moral capacities of its students. According to this theory the human mind was compartmentalized into separate "faculties," such as sensibility, will, reason, judgment, imagination, conscience, memory and attention. The well-formulated theory dated from Aristotle, was modified by Descartes and Rousseau and was accepted educational dogma in America until after the Civil War. Education would exercise specific faculties just as an athlete trained specific muscles. This was "the method of science, and the law by which the mind is governed in the acquisition of knowledge."[35] According to one Maryland professor, "colleges [were] not so much places for acquiring general information, as intellectual gymnasia, where the mental and moral faculties were trained and strengthened, and the student instructed how to use his powers to best advantage." Students could not expect the exercise to be pleasant.[36]

Forced learning, rigid control and severe discipline marked every step in the college program. At first, by doing without dormitories and shifting much of the disciplinary burden to parents, Maryland

[34]For curriculum of the college, *Address of the Trustees to the Public*, 15-19, and *Annual Catalogues* which appear after 1841.

[35]Jay Wharton Fay, *American Psychology Before William James* (New Brunswick, N. J., 1939), 52-128; Royal Robbins, *Outlines of Ancient and Modern History* (Hartford, 1839), 3.

[36]Memorial of William Reynolds, a graduate of the college in 1860, to E. A. Dalrymple, cited in Cordell, *University of Maryland*, I, 490.

hoped to avoid corporal punishment, relying instead on an oath of obedience from students and weekly deportment grades to the parents. From the standpoint of conduct the policy seemed to work, for generally Maryland avoided the riots and violent pranks which characterized other colleges. From the standpoint of education, however, the professors were dissatisfied, for punishment seemed essential to enforce regular study. Maryland soon relapsed to the more traditional pattern, and even the best college students long remembered Dean Morrison and Dean Dalrymple for their severe whippings.[37]

The daily classroom procedure at Maryland would seem impossibly grim to a modern student. From half past eight until half past ten o'clock in the morning a class sat through the first lesson, often with the youngest academy students and the college seniors suffering together. After a thirty-minute break, from eleven until one o'clock the class of twelve or fifteen students went to a second professor. During the two-hour dinner recess most students went home for the main meal of the day and a nap. The final session, under a third professor, met from three until five in the afternoon. On Saturdays the week officially ended after the first morning session, but students who had been unruly or remiss in their lessons were compelled to remain for additional sessions. The academic year of three terms lasted for eleven months, from early September until late July.[38]

Classrooms in the old college building were large and bare. At the front of the room probably was a low platform on which the professor sat at his desk. Behind him was a blackboard, a new installation of the trustees which in 1837 made the college feel progressive.[39] The students sat in upright chairs, balancing their textbooks and writing pads on their knees. Pupils in some academies still carried slates, but all college students were expected to have paper.

Except for the rare treat of an outside lecturer, instruction rarely varied either with the professor or the subject. Usually the professor "heard" the lessons, by citing the day's assignment and listening to the students recite. He called a name at random, and the frightened student translated the passage from his book, "parsed" the verb, related the fact, or worked at the blackboard on the selected

[37]*Prospectus of the Collegiate Department of the University of Maryland For the Academical Year 1841-1842* (Baltimore, 1841), 8-9; *Address of the Trustees to the Public,* 12-13, *Baltimore American,* 1 August 1836; Cordell, *University of Maryland,* I, 473.

[38]*Address of the Trustees to the Public,* 13-14, and subsequent *Annual Catalogues.*

[39]Minutes of Executive Committee of Trustees, 15 March 1837.

problem. Questions from students still were considered a bit impertinent. Toward the end of the two-hour session the professor might read the next day's assignment, demonstrate a series of problems or read from a book not available to students. By the 1830's the end-of-the-class citation, or moralizing, was beginning to evolve into the lecture method of instruction, but most professors still stuck close to the textbook.[40]

Students received daily grades on their recitations and weekly grades went to their parents. The academic year ended with oral examinations open as public exhibitions which insured impartiality in grading, served to advertise the college and provided a popular amusement of the day. One Maryland student recalled the grueling premium on memorization:

> I remember that my entire class was able to repeat the whole *Ars Poetica* of Horace containing 476 lines, from beginning to end in the original Latin, and it was part of our final examination exercises for each one of us, after being started . . . at any place in the poem, to repeat what followed in the original until we were told to stop, then to go back and construe into English what we had repeated, and finally to parse and scan as many lines as requested, giving all the rules of syntax and prosody which might be applicable, and all this without once opening a book.[41]

Following the examinations each student was ranked in order, with failure requiring him to repeat a term or an entire year. Like God, the professors balanced punishment with reward. The best students in recitations, in attendance and in deportment received gold medals; the second best received silver ones. Other students whom the faculty felt particularly deserving for some reason were rewarded with medals of bronze.

Perhaps the most serious weakness of the University of Maryland's undergraduate program was the fact that the trustees were so pleased with it. In the annual reports which they submitted to the general assembly, they congratulated themselves on the "flourishing condition" of the college, and also on the fact that the funds appropriated for its use "have been fostered and increased."[42] As a going institution, however, the college was at least established, its very creation

[40]See, John S. Brubacher and Willis Rudy, *Higher Education in Transition: An American History, 1636-1956* (New York, 1958), 82-85.

[41]Memorial of William Reynolds, cited in Cordell, *University of Maryland*, I, 491; see also, *Baltimore American*, 1 August 1836; 29 July 1837; 26 July 1839.

[42]*Annual Report of the Trustees . . . 1833*, 2.

reflecting the deeply felt and growing needs of the people of Maryland. It was the heart of a state university. Its fate now depended on the ability of the trustees to hold the fine old professional schools around it.

Professors versus Administrators

In the prospering medical school prideful professors and impatient trustees were destined from the start for conflict. Even though some of the professors had spitefully urged state control and even though they were torn with personal quarrels, they were justly proud of their role as founders of the institution and of their unique independence and authority in guiding its fortunes. The trustees, on the other hand, though entirely well-intentioned, were important men of affairs, impatient, as they said, to get the professors "straightened out." They offered the medical professors $3,800 for their personal investment in the institution, while announcing that the faculty was responsible for the $30,000 debt contracted in building it. They stated that the professors held no tenure and must re-apply for their jobs. Curtly they refused to allow the faculty to send representatives to meetings of the trustees. They took control of the hospital from the doctors, who always had directed it and contributed their services to it without pay, and set up as its supervisor the son of one of the trustees at a salary of $800 annually.[43]

The first forewarning of serious trouble came to the trustees when the great Granville Sharp Pattison walked out. For the past six years he had practically run the University, and he did not take a back seat easily. One of the most active figures in American medicine, and certainly the strongest magnet for attracting students to Maryland, he sailed to England in the spring of 1826, confiding his plans to no one. A few weeks later he wrote the trustees that he had accepted a position at the University of London because he believed they were destroying the University of Maryland. In vain they begged him to return.[44]

[43]Potter, *Some Account*, 21, 32; *Laws of Maryland . . . 1825*, Chap. 188, 190; Minutes of Executive Committee of Trustees, 9 December 1826; 21 February 1831; "Memorial to Legislature against the Faculty Bill to Include them as Trustees," MS. scrap dated 7 March 1837, in Minutes of Executive Committee Trustees, 52-63.

[44]Minutes of Executive Committee Trustees, 24 July 1826; 7 March 1837; *Federal Gazette*, 27 June 1827; William Snow Miller, "Granville Sharp Pattison," *Johns Hopkins Hospital Bulletin*, XXX (October, 1919), 98-104.

Three other popular professors died within a few years after the trustees took control. In January, 1829, Dr. Davidge contracted a sinus cancer, suffering a painful death a few months later. In 1831 Dr. DeButts died of pneumonia, and three years later Dr. Samuel Baker succumbed to heart failure. If not great physicians, all of them were great teachers whose careers dated back to the original College of Medicine. Probably a majority of the physicians then practicing in the state had sat in their classes, and with their deaths a glorious age of medical education in Maryland had passed.[45]

For a time the trustees were able to capitalize on the school's reputation to attract some extraordinarily able replacements. Nathan Ryno Smith, M.D. from Yale and son of the founder of the Dartmouth Medical College, was procured from the faculty at Jefferson Medical College. Robley Dunglison, M.D. from Erlangen, Germany, the most prolific medical writer of his day, was employed from the faculty at the University of Virginia. Eli Geddings, M.D. from the Medical College of South Carolina, was acquired from that institution. Rounding out the new acquisitions were Robert Griffith, former professor of pharmacy at Philadelphia, and Jules Ducatel, professor of chemistry from the Mechanics' Institute of Baltimore. As the newcomers joined the University during the 1830's, each was entangled, on one side or the other, in the unhappy dispute between the older professors and the trustees. With other universities eager for their services, every one of these outstanding men left Maryland within a decade.[46]

The trustees also managed to inherit a petty janitorial problem which turned out to be more disrupting than some of the disputes with the distinguished professors. The janitor, known simply as Vickers, was a disagreeable fellow who had served Dr. Davidge devotedly since the school opened. Living on the campus of the medical school he assumed a lordly air, ordering about both students and professors. Possibly he turned especially bad tempered after Davidge died, for at about that time the minutes of the trustees began to fill with accounts of the dissension he created.

The trouble began about 1827 when he was accused of beating a student who attempted to take a friend into the school. The trustees yielded to his abject apology: "I ought to have reflected that I am a poor man with a wife and family," he pled, "and I have nothing to look forward to for their support but the place I hold under Your

[45]For biographical sketches see Cordell, *University of Maryland*, I, 175, 186, 193.
[46]*Ibid.*, I, 249, 197, 198, 201.

Honors."[47] A few months later Professor Potter caught the janitor gambling and selling liquor to some students. The puritanical professor was horrified and insisted that either he or Vickers would have to go. The trustees again listened to the janitor's pleas of long service and again dropped the matter with a resolution: "That hereafter the janitor not be permitted to sell liquors of any kind, nor fruit, nuts, cigars or tobacco—nor shall he permit the Students to play cards or any other game in his house for money or any other thing." Potter decided to keep his job, but for the rest of the year he carried a pistol to class in order to protect himself from "further outrage." A few months later Professor Smith complained of insubordination on the part of Vickers, but the matter was passed over. Not until 1832 did the trustees finally discharge the janitor, yielding to a petition signed by most of the students and every member of the faculty. Trivial as it was the entire commotion further strained relations between the faculty and trustees, strengthening the professors all the more in their conviction that trustees had no business running their school.[48]

The most severe blow the trustees suffered came with the loss of David Hoffman and his law school. Again, it was a matter of failure of good intentions, for a majority of the trustees were lawyers who admired Hoffman and wanted to encourage his work. The law school was the only one in which they did not attempt to save money. Generously they offered Hoffman $5,000 for his library, which the students were using anyway, and $400 annually for rent which he had previously paid.[49] Hoffman, however, had been deeply devoted to Pattison and Davidge, and he had committed himself to fight the trustees on the legal grounds that confiscation of the University was an impairment of contract which was granted to the University under the charter of 1812. By the 1830's Hoffman may have been discouraged that the wide use of his textbooks was contributing to the decline of his classes, or perhaps he simply tired of the law school experiment. In any case, he accepted the $5,000 for his library, but kept that portion of it which he believed worth more than that amount and departed. Angrily the trustees attempted to sue him for the remainder of the library, but the courts seemed to ignore their protests and after five years they dismissed the case. Hoffman's name remained in the

[47]Minutes of Executive Committee Trustees, 7 January 1827.
[48]Potter, *Some Account*, 38-39; Minutes of Executive Committee Trustees, 4 December 1828; 6 December 1828; 15 December 1828; 27 March 1829; 28 March 1829.
[49]Minutes of Executive Committee, 24 January 1832.

University catalogues as professor of law until 1837 when Judge R. B. Magruder was named to the post, but no more law was taught at the University until after the Civil War.[50]

As if internal disputes were not enough, the trustees and the medical faculty finally were confronted by the long-threatened rivalry of a second medical school in Baltimore. Horatio Gates Jameson did not accept the rebuff given him by the general assembly of Maryland, and the dissension within the University made him all the more confident of success in opening a rival institution. Off he went to Washington College, a tiny liberal arts school chartered by the State of Pennsylvania and located just south of Pittsburgh, where he convinced the trustees that they had nothing to lose by permitting him to establish a medical branch of their institution in Baltimore. Washington College never so much as mentioned a medical department in its catalogues, but in 1827 Jameson announced that the Washington Medical College of Baltimore was ready for students.[51]

The quality of Jameson's institution was as flimsy as its legal status. He advertised lower fees than the University of Maryland, and quietly assured students that a medical degree could be obtained more easily. Ironically, the state was attempting to avoid this decline of standards just when competition emerged, but now it was too late. In an effort to retain its own students the University immediately abolished the $20 graduation fee which previously had gone for supplies and new equipment. Still Jameson's institution flourished, and in 1833 the general assembly gave him a charter similar to the University charter of 1812, with the same right, though it was never exercised, to establish schools of law and liberal arts.[52]

With internal warfare, with the best professors leaving, and with competition from Jameson's degree mill the medical school enrollment began to drop ominously, and the professors' incomes began to shrink. From 89 graduates in 1826, the number was down to 55 by

[50]*Journal of the House* . . . *1825*, 310; *Memorial of the Trustees of the University and Baltimore College*, 4; *Report of the Trustees to the General Assembly* . . . *1831*, 6; Minutes of Executive Committee Trustees, 16 April 1833; 6 May 1833; *Federal Gazette*, 26 June 1837.

[51]Miller, "Washington University of Baltimore," 15-16; Varle, *Complete View of Baltimore*, 27.

[52]*Annual Report to the General Assembly* . . . *of the Washington College of Baltimore* (Annapolis, 1839); *Annual Circular of the Washington Medical College of Baltimore* . . . *1841* (Baltimore, 1841); Miller, "Washington University of Baltimore," 16-20; *Memorial of the Medical Faculty of the University of Maryland to the Public and the General Assembly of Maryland* (n.p., 1833), 7; Benjamin Lincoln, *Hints on the Present State of Medical Education* (Burlington, Vt., 1833), 23.

1829. The trend continued until there were only 20 graduates in 1839.[53]

The trustees could have remedied the situation by placing the faculty on a direct salary basis, but they were frightened by the enormous sum they would have to pay, since each of the medical professors in 1826 was earning about $4,000 annually. This amount equalled the salary of the state governor and was triple that of a liberal arts professor. Timidly the trustees put off the matter, and continued to allow the professors to collect their lecture fees. Due to the decline in enrollment, however, the professors' incomes dropped to one-fifth of what they had been and they blamed the trustees for their loss.

The trustees tried sincerely to understand the chaotic financial records of the University, but they never came close to a figure which coincided with the professors' demands for their personal investment in the institution. The records were a hodgepodge of careless notations and reminders of verbal agreements. No one could estimate what portion of the University property came from lotteries, what resulted from student fees paid into the common fund or what came from bank loans. To top off the confusion were incredibly informal records of loans which professors had made to the University or to colleagues, and of loans which the banks had made with a given professor's home as security. The wonder is that such delightful mutual trust had not produced more quarrels. When the trustees attempted to untangle the records, the professors could be certain only that they were losing. The general assembly concluded that $3,800 was a fair settlement for the confiscation of the institution; the trustees were persuaded that $9,000 might be a closer figure; the professors insisted that the proper sum was nearly $30,000. The disagreement never was settled, and on this point the trustees must have felt sheer relief when they abandoned the University.[54]

The final cause of a showdown was the appointment of Dr. Henry Willis Baxley as professor of anatomy. A graduate of the medical school, Baxley was a laboratory assistant, or "demonstrator," who attended the morning lectures of the anatomy professor with the students, and in the afternoon laboratory sessions directed their dissections. The demonstrator was furthering his own education as a sort of graduate student, but as a junior staff member, he received

[53]Cordell, *University of Maryland*, II, Appendix.
[54]*Journal of the House . . . 1825*, 7 March 1826, 380-381; *Report of the Trustees to the General Assembly . . . 1831*, 5; *Memorial of the Medical Faculty* (1833), 5.

a fee of $5.00 from each student who attended the laboratory. The students traditionally disliked any demonstrator and Baxley was particularly officious.[55]

Somehow Baxley managed to ingratiate himself with the trustees, so that the professors also came to dislike the pompous young man, and even imagined that he was a spy at their lectures and faculty meetings. When the trustees raised Baxley's fee to $10 at a time when they were trying to reduce the professors' fees, rebellion resulted. Many students refused to pay the fee and began attending a private laboratory conducted by Dr. Samuel G. Baker just outside the college walls. Tacitly the faculty encouraged the students, for Baker was the son of their long-time colleague, Professor Samuel Baker, who recently had died. Baxley's pomposity grew with his increase in salary, however, and those students not in his dissecting session began to tease him. They made a game of usurping his favorite seat during the anatomy lecture periods, and even Professor Eli Geddings joined the students in laughing at his fury.[56]

When Baxley complained to the trustees of Geddings' "ridicule," they took the unprecedented step of censuring the eminent professor.[57] At the end of the 1837 academic year Geddings left for a better position and his post was vacant. Previously the trustees always had insisted upon their right to appoint new staff members, but they had made a point of asking the faculty for nominations and invariably had chosen one of its nominees. Now the faculty unanimously supported young Baker for the position, and quietly announced their unanimous resignation should a certain other "individual" be chosen.[58]

The trustees tried honestly to avoid the impending clash. They could not accept Baker, for despite his popularity as the son of a former professor his college record was poor, his practice undistinguished and his research nonexistent; and at stake was the whole principle of who ran the University. On the other hand, they respected Baxley as a brilliant student who already had published more

---

[55]Charles Russell Bardeen, "Henry Willis Baxley," *Dictionary of American Biography*, II, 60-61; William Frederick Norwood, *Medical Education in the United States Before the Civil War* (Philadelphia, 1944), 393; MS. scrap in Minutes of Executive Committee Trustees, 55-58.

[56]MS. scrap in Minutes of Executive Committee Trustees, 58; *Circular of the Regents Medical Faculty of the University of Maryland* (n.d., n.p. [1837]), 7; Samuel George Baker, *Introductory Lecture Delivered Before the Medical Class of the University, November 1837* (Baltimore, 1837), 27; Cordell, *University of Maryland*, I, 77-78.

[57]Potter, *Some Account*, 11; *Federal Gazette*, 18 March 1837.

[58]Faculty Minutes, 2 May 1837.

articles than many of his professors. To appease the faculty the trustees looked eagerly for a compromise candidate, even going so far as to advertise in the newspapers for applicants, but no respectable physician was willing to accept a position where his colleagues would despise him. Late in June, 1837, the trustees announced that Dr. Baxley was the University's new professor of anatomy. The faculty immediately replied that Dr. Baxley was the University's only professor.[59]

The medical faculty called a meeting of all those who had been professors of divinity, law and arts and sciences prior to state confiscation. To test the constitutionality of the confiscation act of 1826, they named an imposing battery of lawyers headed by Daniel Webster. Defiantly they elected Baker to the medical faculty, and announced that classes would continue as they had before the trustees took over in 1826. With that the minutes of the meeting officially were closed and everyone was sworn to secrecy.[60] Then, displaying the instincts of revolutionists, the faculty began plotting ways of re-acquiring the University buildings.

Late in the afternoon of September 21, 1837, the professors launched their quixotic attack on the properties which officially were state owned. Baker tricked the janitor away, another professor lured the janitor's wife into the street and a third carried out the couple's squalling baby. Soon the high-walled medical buildings were crowded with doctors and trusted students who guarded the gates and posted lookouts. The fortress was theirs.[61]

The trustees were not amused when they met in emergency session the following day. Viewing the matter as seriously as the faculty, they appointed their own battery of distinguished lawyers, headed by Reverdy Johnson and Roger B. Taney. On the morning of the 23rd lawyers from each side began to negotiate, and late in the afternoon, when the rebelling professors must have been getting hungry in their stronghold, they were persuaded to evacuate the property pending a court decision. The keys to the building were deposited at a neutral spot and the antagonists themselves never met. Later, when the trustees went through the buildings, they found

[59]Minutes of Executive Committee Trustees, 29 March 1837; *Federal Gazette,* 23 June 1837; 24 June 1837; 26 June 1837; *Baltimore American,* 24 June 1837.

[60]Faculty Minutes, 18 September 1837.

[61]The trustees collected detailed testimony from the janitor and all concerned. See, "Documents on the Faculty Seizure of the University," in Minutes of Executive Committee Trustees, 65-68.

all in order except for three empty liquor bottles and a broken sword which the professors and their students apparently had left behind.[62]

While the dispute made its way slowly through the courts, medical education in Maryland reached its lowest ebb. Theoretically, there were three medical schools in Baltimore—that of Jameson, that of the trustees and that of the old University faculty. In fact, all were weak and the better students found their way to one of the rapidly growing out-of-state institutions. Almost every week the newspapers of Maryland and the surrounding states carried advertisements for physicians to fill vacancies in one of the three Baltimore colleges.[63]

With Baxley as their key man, the trustees determinedly recruited a group of second-rate Baltimore physicians to continue at the University of Maryland. Aided by the financial backing of the state, they kept the hospital in operation and held regular classes in the University buildings. Because of its superior facilities it may have remained the best of the three schools in the city.[64]

The seceding faculty rented rooms in the old Indian Queen Hotel and for some of their lectures they used the Presbyterian Church on Hanover Street. Here they met their small classes for two years. Of the professors who had rebelled only the more stubborn remained embroiled in such a situation. Already Pattison and Geddings had been driven away, and within a year Smith, Dunglison and Griffith departed; but Professors Potter, Hall and Baker doggedly continued instruction, aided occasionally by transient part-time lecturers who happened to be available.[65]

When the state took control of the University in 1826, lawyers realized at once that a far-reaching legal question was involved. The state acted on the principle that it could destroy what it could create, and it had created the College of Medicine in 1807 and the University in 1812. The University charter, and the lottery privileges which helped to build the institution had stipulated carefully that the University existed solely for the public good. Presumably the state could determine what was the public good and control the institution according to its concept of that good. The state argued

[62]Minutes Executive Committee Trustees, 22 September 1837; 23 September 1837; Cordell, *University of Maryland*, I, 80-81.

[63]*Federal Gazette*, 6 July 1837; 7 July 1837; 25 July 1837; 3 August 1837; *Baltimore American*, 4 July 1837; *National Gazette* (Philadelphia), 23 July 1837.

[64]*Federal Gazette*, 29 August 1837; *Annual Circular of the Medical Department of the University of Maryland* (Baltimore, 1838).

[65]*Federal Gazette*, 27 October 1837; *Baltimore American*, 26 October 1838; *Circular of the Regents Medical Faculty* (1837).

further that faculty acquiescence to trustee administration for eleven years constituted recognition which could not now be repealed.[66]

The medical professors also had a strong case. According to their argument, the charters of 1807 and 1812 constituted private contracts which granted them incorporation, and thus the right to invest their money in hopes of future profit, as in any business corporation. Contrary to the state's argument, they maintained that they never had received a penny in appropriations for the public good. They had been given the right to conduct a lottery just as any huckster at a fair conducted a gambling device, and they had, in fact, paid the state a share of their profits in the form of a license or tax.[67]

To prepare for any eventuality, the medical professors had obtained legal counsel as soon as the trustees took over, winning assurances that they were protected by the famous Supreme Court case of *Dartmouth College vs. Woodward.* Just seven years earlier, yielding to the dramatic pleas of Dartmouth alumnus Daniel Webster, Chief Justice John Marshall had held that New Hampshire could not transform Dartmouth from a private institution to a state university. One of the famous decisions of American history, it seemed to place private corporations outside the control of the state which had created them, foreshadowing enormous power and eventual abuses by future corporations. William Wirt, Attorney General of the United States, assured the faculty that the confiscation act of 1826 could be declared unconstitutional at any time that it was in their interest to have it done. As if this were not enough, the great Webster went on record: "I concur entirely with the Attorney General." The action of the trustees, he added, "is *void* by the constitution of the United States."[68]

As the case dragged on, as the lawyers' fees mounted and as both sides approached exhaustion, the general assembly gave up the fight. In 1837, soon after the faculty seceded, the Baltimore court ruled for the trustees, but in 1839 the court of appeals ruled for the faculty. The lawyers on both sides already had collected $10,000,

[66]*Report of the Trustees to the General Assembly* (1838); *Baltimore Gazette,* 14 October 1837.

[67]*Circular of the Regents Medical Faculty of the University of Maryland* (1837), 3; Potter, *Some Account,* 17-25; *Baltimore American,* 27 March 1839.

[68]The reports of Wirt and Webster are in MS., bound with the Minutes of the Faculty. There is also a MS. copy of a report sent by the faculty to the Governor of Maryland, dated 22 May 1826, in which these opinions are quoted. Also Potter to Webster, 14 May 1826, Webster Papers, Library of Congress; Benjamin Chew Howard to Potter, 28 March 1838, and Potter to Howard, 10 April 1838, Howard Papers, Maryland Historical Society, Baltimore.

and they had just begun.[69] On April 3, 1839, by a vote of 40 to 29, the assembly repealed the act of 1826 and ordered the trustees to return the disputed property, including the undergraduate college, to the old University faculty. A few weeks later the legislators considered a bill which would start afresh in building a state university, and in 1850 there was talk of providing for a state university in the new state constitution adopted a year later; but such halfhearted discussion came to nothing, and the legislature scarcely mentioned the University again until after the Civil War. The state was fed up. The private University of Maryland could get along as best it could.[70]

On April 10, 1839, the lawyers for both sides met for the last time. The faculty members, or what was left of them, received full title to the medical college buildings on Greene Street, then valued at $150,000, and to the arts and science building on Mulberry Street, appraised at $87,000. They also received about $18,000 in bonds and cash held by the trustees.[71]

When the trustees abandoned the University of Maryland few realized what a severe blow the state had suffered. For decades to come no true center of ideas and leadership was to exist in Maryland. In Massachusetts, on the other hand, a thousand future Union officers were bound together at Harvard by a common education. Such men as Emerson, Thoreau, Bancroft, Longfellow, Lowell, Holmes and Channing studied as classmates, jointly forging a culture and a series of concepts which helped to shape a nation. Similarly, at the University of South Carolina almost a thousand future Confederate officers studied together and such men as Hampton, Harper, Brooks, Pinckney and Legaré became the fire-eating spokesmen for a different set of values. Almost every state boasted a coterie welded by friendships and common learning and serving as the focal point for

[69]"Regents of the University of Maryland vs. Joseph B. Williams," Richard W. Gill and John Johnson, eds., *Reports of Cases Argued and Determined in the Court of Appeals of Maryland*, 12 vols. (Baltimore, 1830-1845), IX, 1837-1838, 365-425; Eugene Fauntleroy Cordell, *Historical Sketch of the University of Maryland School of Medicine* . . . (Baltimore, 1891), 59; *Report of a Joint Committee* [of the General Assembly] *on the Memorial of the Regents of the University of Maryland* (Annapolis, 1839).

[70]*Journal of the House* . . . *1838* (Annapolis, 1839), 29 March 1839, 582-583; *Journal of the Senate* . . . *1838* (Annapolis, 1839), 22 March 1839, 222-223; *Proceedings of the Maryland State Convention to Form a New Constitution* (Annapolis, 1850), 122; *Journal of the House* . . . *1838*, 1 April 1839, 614; *Baltimore American*, 26 March 1839; Ashton Alexander to Samuel McCulloh, 18 March 1839, Alexander Papers, Maryland Historical Society, Baltimore.

[71]Letters and receipts of transfer appended to Minutes of Executive Committee Trustees, 1-10 April, 1839.

a dynamic society. In Maryland, of course, there were also great leaders—Taney, Kennedy, Johnson, Wirt, Key and Latrobe. Many, indeed most of them seemed to hover around the fringes of the University of Maryland as if they should have been graduates. But none of them were classmates, and none shared the bond which other antebellum colleges provided. If, during the first half of the nineteenth century, the University of Maryland could have flourished under the Unionist Josiah Quincy from Harvard, or under the secessionist Thomas Cooper from South Carolina, if it had employed any one of a score of powerful university leaders at the then going rate of $3,000 annually, a lot of history might have been different.

The nineteenth century failure to establish a state university in Maryland stemmed from historical conditions, from bad luck and from mistakes. Conditions contributed to the premature failure of William Smith's university, and to the consequent premature success of professional education before a proper base was built for it. Bad luck contributed accidents of history like an ill-tempered janitor and a conspiratorial graduate student. Mistakes included the trustees' costly parsimony and their decisions to do without an executive, without direct salaries and without dormitories. By a patchwork approach to the building of a university, the state which so sorely wanted higher education was rapidly falling behind other states which were two centuries younger.

Many Marylanders felt a sense of relief in 1839 when the professors again took over their private institution. People were aware that the trustees had presided over the collapse of fine schools of medicine and law without building the strong undergraduate college they had promised. People were correct in believing the professors could do better on their own. If everything seemed to go wrong for the trustees, everything seemed to fall into the lap of the professors. During the next several decades, the breaks continued to fall their way.

4

Professional Pre-eminence

During the 1840's and 1850's Americans turned increasingly to professional schools to meet the practical needs of the expanding nation. While traditional undergraduate colleges rejected academic reform and piously continued building character with their old-fashioned curriculum and birch-rod discipline, people demanded new institutions which they hesitated to dignify as colleges. Congress created academies at West Point and Annapolis to provide practical military knowledge; industrialists encouraged polytechnic institutes to train technicians and engineers; reformers established normal schools for teachers; and various ancient trades made themselves into professions by transforming the apprentice system into one of formal education.

The University of Maryland, again a proprietary institution, was ideally suited to meet the demands for such professional training. The school of medicine regained a high position in the medical profession. Entirely new schools of dentistry and pharmacy appeared and helped to found new professions, and in addition to possessing a fund of practical knowledge, the graduates of these schools also appeared to have reasonably good character. The traditional colleges had much to learn from the professional institutions they pretended to despise, and the University's responsiveness to public demand made it a leader in the movement for a more utilitarian type of learning.

The College of Medicine

The old medical faculty took over the University in 1839 with enthusiasm, boasting about its victory over the state and promising great things for the future. As if striving to prove to themselves that they could make faculty administration work, the professors organized new committees, drew up elaborate bylaws and began preparing detailed agendas for their monthly faculty meetings. The substantial sum of money left by the departing trustees promptly was appropriated for clearing up old debts and restoring the buildings and equipment to top condition. Baltimore newspaper editors, invited to tour the renovated campus, quickly caught the enthusiasm and began to speak of the rising phoenix.[1]

Minor problems arose at first, for enrollment did not increase as quickly as expected, and the faculty spent its surplus money too fast. The janitor had to be dismissed to save his $250 annual salary, and each professor became responsible for cleaning a portion of the buildings. In addition, the hospital showed a deficit of about $1,000 a year. Such circumstances forced the University to curtail services and mortgage some land, but these were temporary problems. By 1845 enrollment was up to about 200 students with about 65 graduating each year, a level maintained until the Civil War. The figure was approximately a third below the enrollment of 1826, for the College of Medicine did not regain its earlier eminence. It remained, however, one of the eight or ten largest and strongest medical schools in the nation.[2]

The medical faculty once again took the initiative in keeping alive the over-all University structure by calling together what

[1]Bound MS. volume entitled "Regents Minutes, 1839-1900' in the archives of the medical school, Baltimore, 4 April 1839; 16 April 1839; 6 May 1839; 19 January 1840; 27 March 1840; *Baltimore Clipper*, 30 October 1839; *Baltimore American*, 31 October 1839; *Baltimore Sun*, 26 May 1840; *Baltimore Patriot*, 27 May 1840.

[2]Regents Minutes, 15 April 1840; 29 December 1841; 14 November 1842; 3 January 1843.

remained of the faculties of divinity, law and arts and sciences to elect another provost. To replace Roger B. Taney the faculty elected a locally prominent physician, Ashton Alexander, repeating the mistake of selecting a provost with no interest in leading the University. Even by the standards of his predecessors the venerable old doctor neglected the position. When he resigned in 1850 the faculty elected the prominent John Pendleton Kennedy who served, unfortunately, for twenty years.[3]

Kennedy was a brilliant and wealthy dilettante who could have done much for the University. As a novelist and man-of-letters he numbered Poe, Irving, Thackeray and Macaulay among his literary friends; as a polite dabbler in Whig politics, he served occasionally in the general assembly, in Congress and briefly in Fillmore's cabinet as secretary of the navy. He included four United States presidents among his political friends. In another environment he might have been a great leader of men, but in the easy life of Baltimore he frittered away his talents as a dandy and a conversationalist. Instead of feeling called upon to lead the University, his attitude was one of amused indifference. In a letter to a friend following his election, his mild delightful cynicism reflected the attitude of too many people in the state:

I found myself one morning, by some process of which I was certainly ignorant, Provost of the University of Maryland. I learned afterwards that old Doctor Alexander . . . had resigned his post, and that, the Regents coming together to make a new selection, first debated the point whether they would give it to Bishop Wittingham and decided thereupon unanimously in the negative; holding that one layman was worth a dozen priests. . . . The election preceded the Commencement which was to be held in a few days and this threw me into a vortex of business among the learned clerks of the College, where I had to sign some diplomas and do sundry other professional things most strangely incongruous with all my habits, even to the breaking up of my billiards for two or three evenings. Think of a Provost with his coat off at billiards! Then I had to meet the *young gentlemen* the evening before Commencement, to give them the light of my provostial or prefectial countenance at a social entertainment; then the next day, Tuesday last, a grand glorious churchful of beautiful girls, with the Germania band and a great array of Regents and Faculties, and seventy-two diplomas to distribute with

[3]*Ibid.*, 4 April 1839; 6 March 1850; 18 March 1850; John Pendleton Kennedy Journal (bound MS. volume in Kennedy Papers, Peabody Library, Baltimore), 11 March 1850.

suitable words of encouragement and sage advice delivered provost-wise—all of which I went through to the minutest point of customary observance, without flinching. . . . And so ended that morning—after which I took my dinner and went to billiards with an increased earnestness, by way of disabusing my mind of the humbug I had been practicing before the world.

I don't know whether I have done right in accepting this post, which, in many respects is incompatible with my character. There is a make-believe in all these masquerades which require a better actor than I am to play off before the world. . . . I have a Theological Faculty to look after as well as the Medical, and a Law Faculty and the Arts and Sciences which, again, are connected with a college,—all of which puts upon me the necessity of a certain sobriety both of walk and opinion which nature has utterly denied me, and which I shall not condescend to counterfeit. So, that if you ever hear that I have brought scandal on the learned bodies, say that I made a protest early to you against the responsibility of it. I shall see how it works and then determine how long to hold it.[4]

If the school of medicine failed to find leadership to awaken the central University government, it was extraordinarily successful and fortunate in recruiting new professors. Within six years after the trustees departed, every chair in the medical school had been given to new men. The younger generation of professors brought a different approach to medicine and a new atmosphere to the institution. Before 1837 Davidge, Potter, DeButts, Baker and Hall had constituted a stable core, attracting for short periods some of the most brilliant professors in the world. This early faculty had combined basic sciences with daring medical theory, producing students who were confident that they knew most of what could be learned in medicine, and who made many mistakes in their confidence. Actually the new faculty members, from about 1840 to 1865, were more able than their predecessors, but were unable or unwilling to attract the truly great names in the profession. By combining the basic sciences with experimentation rather than theory the new faculty produced students who made fewer mistakes simply because they were less sure of themselves. In a paradoxical way the new faculty was less great but more able.

Of the new professors the central figure was Nathan Ryno Smith. He had taught briefly in the University when the trustees were in control but had left Baltimore as the dispute threatened to ruin the institution. Returning in 1840, he became the most powerful

[4]Kennedy to R. C. Williams, 24 March 1850, Kennedy Papers.

and respected surgeon in the state. He carried a teaching stick which he snapped against his trousers like a field marshal's baton. Students and even colleagues cringed before him in awe and called him "the Emperor."[5] Scarcely less distinguished, at least in appearance, was William E. A. Aiken, remembered later for his flowing white beard and white wig, but also widely known as an able teacher and scholar who served the University for fifty years.[6] From Harvard came Joseph Roby, a man too shy to practice medicine or publish the results of his research, but one who inspired a devotion akin to reverence among his students. One of his closest friends, Oliver Wendell Holmes, believed that Roby's letters—which have never been found—would someday be recognized as masterpieces of American literature.[7] Finally, from Maryland came Samuel Chew and George Miltenberger, both of whom attained modest national reputations as teachers and scholars.

During the years in which the young faculty took over from the old, relations between the two generations often were strained. Potter and Hall particularly were reluctant to yield power, while the newcomers and most of the students considered the old men impossibly out-of-date. Resentment reached a peak in 1843 when the young professors, led by Smith and Aiken, bluntly asked Hall for his resignation. When Hall refused Smith called together the entire faculty, including the inactive professors of the inactive schools within the University, to bring formal impeachment charges. As a case of tradition versus progress, the trial reached the newspapers, causing old graduates, editorial writers and the general public to take sides. To the young men's charge that Hall refused to assume his share of University expenses, he replied that he was bankrupt because he had put over $28,000 into the institution. To their complaint that he neglected students, failed to record attendance or give regular quizzes, and that his views of medicine, particularly of obstetrics, were hopelessly antiquated, the older physician answered that he had taught more students and delivered more healthy babies than the lot of them. The lawyers for Hall presented sentimental testimony from 104 of his former students, and took every advantage of legal loopholes and parliamentary maneuvers.

[5]*Baltimore Sun*, 4 July 1877; Samuel Clagget Chew, "Address Commemorative of Professor Nathan Ryno Smith . . .," *Maryland Medical Journal*, III (September, 1878), 407-430.

[6]"William E. A. Aiken," *Maryland Medical Journal*, XIII (August, 1888), 388-398.

[7]*Daily Advertiser* (Boston), 7 June 1860; Eugene Fauntleroy Cordell, *University of Maryland, 1807-1907 . . .*, 2 vols. (New York, 1907), I, 229-233.

With 10 abstentions the subsequent faculty vote was 13 to 3 against the old man—short of the two-thirds required by the charter for dismissal.[8]

Certainly Hall had become a handicap to the University—perhaps he always had been—but the whole affair was unfortunate. Some weeks later when he and Smith met in the hospital, the old man whacked at his antagonist with his cane. Smith easily wrenched it away, drew forth the sword which it contained and contemptuously threw it on the ground. Within three years both Hall and Potter died, and their mourners were sadly few.[9]

By the end of the 1840's the new faculty was firmly in control, relative harmony prevailed, enrollment was steady and the school was on its feet financially and scholastically. Although the faculty remained limited to seven, new courses appeared in auscultation (listening to body sounds), pediatrics, pathology, histology and microscopy.[10] In every field Maryland was in company with the best schools in the country. Probably it was the first to introduce microscopy as a distinct course. The faculty-edited *Maryland Medical and Surgical Journal* became the official organ of the medical departments of the United States Army and Navy, and in 1848 the University played host to the first annual meeting of the American Medical Association.[11] Unable to meet such competition the Washington Medical College closed in 1851, leaving the University again with a monopoly of medical education in the state.[12] So pleased were the medical professors with their affairs that in 1852, with the aid of a $5,000 legacy, they expanded their 90-bed hospital with a 60-bed addition. The new three-story building on the southwest corner of Lombard and Greene Streets was an ugly square structure in an eclectic warehouse style.[13] It stood in ostentatious contrast to the chaste neo-classic and Federalist buildings on the campus, as the expansive 1850's stood in contrast to the modesty and dignity of the 1810's and 1820's.

[8]Regents Minutes, 11 July 1843 through 31 October 1843 and appended testimony; Cordell, *University*, I, 97-99.

[9]Cordell, *University*, I, 99.

[10]See annual *Catalogues of the Medical College* [titles vary slightly], 1841, 1845, 1848, 1854, 1856.

[11]*Baltimore Sun*, 3 May 1848; 5 May 1848.

[12]Genevieve Miller, "A Nineteenth Century Medical School . . .," *Bulletin of the History of Medicine*, XIV (June, 1943), 19-20.

[13]Arthur J. Lomas, "As It Was in the Beginning, A History of the University Hospital . . .," *Bulletin of the School of Medicine, University of Maryland*, XXIII (April, 1939), 203.

In all of the expansion the continuing absence of leadership again seemed to leave the school just short of greatness. Following the few years in which Pattison had given the professors vision, they seemed content with success. They never appealed for state aid to expand medical services or build the University. They took little part in the creation of public health boards and public hospitals, or in drafting the sanitation and quarantine laws which citizens pushed so actively. Schools of dentistry and pharmacy gravitated around the University because of the needs of those professions, not because of the foresight of the medical faculty. Typical of the lack of vision was the outright refusal of a $10,000 gift. In 1851, a Philadelphia chemical manufacturer and philanthropist, Campbell Morfit, offered the money to establish an institute of applied chemistry to be administered by the faculty as it saw fit, either as a research institute or as a teaching department in arts and sciences. He provided complete plans and cash for a new building and implied that more was to come. Although apparently no strings were attached to the offer the faculty rejected it as "outside their scope." They thanked the philanthropist, gave him an honorary degree and for fifty years were bothered by no more benefactors.[14] In the Baltimore of the 1840's and 1850's three of the greatest philanthropists in the city's history—George Peabody, Enoch Pratt and Johns Hopkins—considered means of aiding education, especially in the field of medicine. There is no evidence that they were approached by the University.

The Origin of Modern Dentistry

Even if the proprietary system lacked the leadership for greatness, its responsiveness to the needs of society sometimes thrust it to the forefront of American education. The first such incident occurred within the shadow of the University, when two ambitious men—Horace H. Hayden and Chapin A. Harris—forged a new profession. Together they launched the first American dental textbooks of significance, the first dental journal, the first dental association and, above all, the first dental school. As the earliest such school in

[14]Lyman C. Newell, "Campbell Morfit," *Dictionary of American Biography*, eds. Allen Johnson and Dumas Malone, 22 vols. (New York, 1946), XIII, 162; Cordell, *University*, I, 222.

the world, the Baltimore College of Dental Surgery was, in large measure, the fountainhead of dentistry as a profession. For many years its graduates dominated the field in both America and Europe. Historians have debated heatedly the extent to which the University encouraged the development of the dental school. The debate is relatively unimportant, however, for certainly the two institutions maintained a close contact, and eventually the Baltimore College of Dental Surgery became a part of the University of Maryland.

At the beginning of the nineteenth century professional dentists were virtually unknown. Various people worked on teeth—doctors, barbers, blacksmiths who made forceps, and craftsmen such as Paul Revere who made artificial dentures. George Washington was one of the first Americans to wear a complete set of false teeth and, aside from the pain they are known to have given him—which may have affected the course of American history—they lent him a grandmotherly look that has made it difficult for Americans to think of him as the forceful general his contemporaries knew him to be. One set of his false teeth, made of ivory and gold, is in the University of Maryland dental museum. During the 1830's, however, ivory artificial dentures became widely fashionable, and many ignorant "tooth drawers" toured the country supplying this profitable item. Occasionally they traveled with a brass band, and sometimes their newspaper advertisements were as artful as their dentistry:

> He also cures effectively the most stinking Breaths, by drawing out and eradicating all decayed Teeth and Stumps . . . and putting in their stead, an entire Set of right Africa Ivory . . . so nicely fitted to the Jaws, that People of the first Fashion may eat, drink, swear, talk, Scandal, quarrel and shew their Teeth without the least Indecency, Inconvenience, or Hestitation whatever.[15]

Despite the flamboyance of most practitioners a handful of devoted men were eager to make dentistry a reputable science. Washington's dentist, John Greenwood, was one of these as were Solyman Brown and Eleaser Parmley of New York. Denouncing the florid advertising of charlatans and the popular notion that democracy implied the right of any man to practice dentistry, they emphasized the need for the organization and licensing of dentists, for professional literature and especially for professional education. Of all such advocates, however, the most prominent were Hayden and Harris

---

[15]Cited in M. D. K. Bremner, *Story of Dentistry* . . . (Boston, 1946), 97.

of Baltimore. Horace Hayden was old, patient and intellectual; Chapin Harris was young, brash and a practical man of action. The closest of associates, they never would have admitted to being friends, even though contemporaries spoke of "Hayden and Harris" in the same breath. Probably neither would have accomplished much without the other.

Hayden, the older man, had been a seaman, a schoolteacher and an architect until, one day in New York, he had a tooth pulled by John Greenwood and immediately thereafter became an apprentice of that pioneer dentist. In 1800 Hayden settled in Baltimore where he quietly practiced dentistry for the next forty-five years. He studied medicine on his own and became a surgeon in the War of 1812. Accepted into the Maryland medical society, he associated chiefly with physicians. In his spare time he wrote an outstanding work on geology and was a noted member and critic of the best literary clubs of Baltimore. But for all his interests, Hayden believed that dentistry was the noblest profession, and dentists the nation over properly looked to him as the foremost of their profession.[16]

Chapin Harris, the man in a hurry, had no time for literary or other idle cultural pursuits. He purchased college degrees from a diploma mill in Illinois, studied medicine for a year under his brother and then simply assumed an M.D. degree. Sensing profit in dentistry, off he went to study under the most famous practitioner in the business, the great Hayden of Baltimore. Making his headquarters in the city he traveled over the South for a decade, advertising disgracefully, but serving his patients magnificently.[17]

Always eager for fame Harris turned to publication. He recorded all he had learned from his old teacher, added what he could from foreign authors and his own practice, and in 1838 published *The Dental Art,* a work which was not only the first significant dental textbook in America, but probably the most widely used dental work of the nineteenth century.[18] The following year he organized

---

[16]J. Ben Robinson, "Foundations of Professional Dentistry," *Proceedings Dental Centenary Commission . . .*, ed. George M. Anderson (Baltimore, 1940), 1016-1017; L. Parmley Brown, "Horace H. Hayden," *Dictionary of American Biography*, VIII, 442-443.

[17]Robinson, "Foundations," 1019-1021; L. Parmley Brown, "Chapin A. Harris," *Dictionary of American Biography*, VIII, 305-306.

[18]Subsequently entitled *Principles and Practice of Dental Surgery,* it went through 12 English editions by 1900 and was translated into several languages. Robert W. McCluggage, *History of the American Dental Association* (Chicago, 1959), 30.

the pioneering *American Journal of Dental Surgery,* dedicated to publicizing the trade secrets which most practitioners guarded jealously. Hayden, possessor of the profession's most valuable secrets, objected to having his techniques made public and never fully forgave his pupil. Yet Harris' textbook, and especially his *Journal,* guaranteed that dental information—like any other truly scientific knowledge—would be available for the benefit of all humanity. His ambition for fame, and indeed for service, was greater than his ambition for riches, for he edited the *Journal* as a public service for twenty years, pouring his entire fortune into it and dying as a pauper. Publication was the first great step in creating the profession.[19]

Hayden's ancient professional dream, meanwhile, had been the creation of a national dental society, modeled after the successful Maryland Medical and Chirurgical Society and empowered to license reputable practitioners. To accomplish his goal, Hayden used Harris just as Harris had used him as the chief source of data for publication. Once in 1817 and again in 1838 Hayden had talked casually of his ambition, but nothing came of it. Finally, in 1840, when the two happened to be in New York City, things began to happen. Hayden used his influence and prestige to call together the outstanding dentists of the area, and Harris used his energy to dash off a constitution for the group, thus creating in August, 1840, the American Society of Dental Surgeons, the model organization for all subsequent dental societies. Its purpose was "to give character and respectability to the profession, by establishing a line between the truly meritorious and skillfull, and such as riot in the ill-gotten fruit of unblushing impudence and empiricism." The society established high dues, rigid standards of admission, and offered the title of "Doctor of Dental Surgery" to all elected to membership. Organization was the second step in creating the profession.[20]

The founding of an independent dental college also stemmed from the disagreements and grudging cooperation of the two men. To the young Harris dentistry was primarily a mechanical art to

[19]Solyman Brown, "Early History of Dental Surgery," *Dental Science and Art Journal,* III (February, 1875), 5.

[20]Solyman Brown, "Extracts from the Minutes of a Convention of Dentists," *American Journal of Dental Science,* I (August, 1840), 159-164; "Editorial," *American Journal of Dental Science,* I (January, 1841), 246; McCluggage, *History of the American Dental Association,* 35-102. There was an unsuccessful attempt to create a local society in New York in 1834.

be learned by practice. Basically he approved the apprentice system and continued to teach apprentices even after the dental school had opened. To Hayden, on the other hand, dentistry was primarily a science to be studied like any other specialized branch of medicine. Gradually they both discovered, as they had in the fields of publication and organization, that neither could progress alone. Harris became increasingly disturbed at the poor background and slow pace of his apprentices, and Hayden learned even more forcibly that medical students were uninterested and often incompetent in dentistry. Invited to lecture at the University of Maryland in 1819 and again from 1823 to 1825, Hayden only bored the students.[21] One of them wrote:

> I was one of his class and found the lectures very speculative and unsatisfactory. Certain it is, that those engaged in tooth pulling, filling and filing, which then seemed to be the sole business of the craft, took no interest in Dr. Hayden's attempt to enlighten them. Nevertheless, he is entitled to credit for an effort, however unsuccessful to give dentistry better claims to public confidence.[22]

From the increasingly apparent failure of dental education through apprenticeship or medical school, a separate college emerged to guarantee the establishment of dentistry as a distinct profession. In that independent college a compromise was worked out between Harris' apprentice instruction and Hayden's medical instruction, and a proper balance established between mechanical art and medical science. Following publication and organization, professional education was the third and greatest step of Harris and Hayden toward creating a new profession.[23]

Ambitious for their new college and aware that the initial expense for a building and equipment would be staggering, in 1839 the two men apparently petitioned for support and inclusion within the University of Maryland as a distinct dental school. The medical faculty, just emerging from their exhausting fight with the state, and perhaps too self-centered to envision a real university, seems to have rejected the dental school as being "of too little conse-

[21]Photostat of MS. note signed by Hayden in dental school archives, Baltimore; J. Ben Robinson, "Testing Certain Evidence Relating to Horace H. Hayden's Influence on Dental Education," *Dental Cosmos*, LXXV (September, 1933), 857-859; Chapin Harris, *Dictionary of Dental Science* (Philadelphia, 1849), 360.

[22]H. Willis Baxley to unidentified person in Baltimore, 29 September 1874, dental school archives, cited in Cordell, *University*, I, 282-283.

[23]Charles W. Ballard, "Dental Education," *American Journal of Dental Science*, II N.S. (October, 1851), 67.

quence." This remark has rankled the dental profession ever since, and some of its historians have denied that Hayden and Harris ever appealed to the University.[24] Recalling the incident ten years later, Harris claimed that the University requested unification only to be turned down by the dentists.[25]

Whatever the exact association of the new school with the University, the two institutions remained friendly. In 1840 the University awarded Hayden an honorary degree, and at the first dental commencement in 1841 one of the dental professors thanked the physicians for their support: "To the medical profession, too, we are happy to acknowledge ourselves under great obligation. From the first they have been our warm and zealous friends." Dentistry emerged in cooperation with medicine, not in opposition to it.[26]

Harris and Hayden designed their college with the single aim of improving the standards of dentistry. On the most elevated plane this meant genuine service to the public by improving people's health and lessening pain; and on the most immediate level it meant driving out competition from untrained dentists and providing dignity to the profession. The only serious opposition stemmed from those practitioners who resented the "clear line of discrimination" which a degree would provide for the well-trained dentist. "Against this resentment," said Harris, "we have been prepared to contend . . . though we have found it more extensive and powerful than we would have anticipated."[27]

[24]The original copy of this much-disputed letter of the University to Harris no longer exists but it is frequently quoted. See James Taylor, "Life and Character of Chapin A. Harris," *Dental Register of the West,* XV (January, 1861), 84; B. J. Cigrand, *Rise and Fall and Revival of Dental Prosthesis* (Chicago, 1893), 205; R. B. Winder [Dean of Dental College, 1882-1894], "Baltimore College of Dental Surgery," *Medical and Dental Register of the City of Baltimore . . .,* ed. William H. Wilson (Baltimore, 1884), 137-139; William Simon, "History of the Baltimore College of Dental Surgery," *Transactions of the Fourth International Dental Congress* (St. Louis, 1904), 11; Frederick C. Waite, "Background of Modern American Dentistry," *Journal of Dental Education,* I (February, 1937), 102-103; Carl P. Lewis, "The Birth of Professional Dentistry, 1839-1840" (M.A. thesis, University of Maryland, 1961), 55-57. J. Ben Robinson has written several articles to argue the letter never existed. See especially his article, "Foundations," 1032-1033.

[25]Chapin A. Harris, "Editorial," *American Journal of Dental Science,* I N.S. (April, 1851), 399.

[26]Thomas E. Bond, "Valedictory Address to the Graduates of the Baltimore College of Dental Surgery," *American Journal of Dental Science,* I (August, 1841), 242; also, W. E. A. Aiken to Horace H. Hayden, 7 April 1840, dental school archives, Baltimore; Chapin A. Harris, "Introductory Lecture . . .," *American Journal of Dental Science,* I (January, 1841), 210.

[27]*Catalogue of the Baltimore College of Dental Surgery . . . 1844* (Baltimore, 1844), 4; *Catalogue . . . 1840,* 3-5. [Annual titles of catalogues vary slightly.]

The General Assembly of Maryland on January 30, 1840, passed the bill establishing the Baltimore College of Dental Surgery. Trying to avoid the pitfalls of faculty autonomy, the legislature created a board of trustees, consisting of nine physicians, four ministers and two dentists, which possessed absolute control in establishing salaries and standards. Although in close contact with Hayden, Harris and the dental faculty, none of the trustees held a financial interest in the college, but served only to guarantee the general welfare of dentistry and the public. Hayden was president and professor of dental pathology and physiology; Harris was dean and professor of practical dentistry; Thomas E. Bond, son of one of the medical college founders, was professor of special dental pathology and therapeutics; and H. Willis Baxley, source of the University's troubles in 1837, was professor of special dental anatomy.[28]

Five students entered the little college on November 3, 1840, and after a week of introductory lectures, classes formally began. The faculty had borrowed heavily to launch the school, but it did not compromise with standards to save money or attract students. Acquiring a beautiful little three-room building on Hopkins Place, its members furnished one room as a lecture hall, another as a dental workshop and the third as a museum for dental specimens. Although the college was widely discussed and advertised, the faculty never begged for students—as many medical schools were doing by now—and never intimated that the course was cheap or easy. No formal entrance requirements were necessary, but a degree could be earned only after two years—the same time as in medicine. One year of work could be transferred from an "approved" medical college. Fees were $30 annually for each of the four courses, plus charges of $5 for entrance and $30 for graduation—a total of about $135 a year exclusive of board, almost exactly the cost of a medical education. In addition to completing specified courses, students were required to undergo a comprehensive examination on theory, to demonstrate their skill in dental operations and in setting false teeth, and to write a thesis.[29]

On March 9, 1841, Robert Authur and Richard Covington Mackall were awarded the first two dental degrees in history. Hayden and

[28]*Laws . . . of Maryland . . . 1839-1840* (Annapolis, 1840), Chap. 155; Robinson, "Foundations," 1035-1040.

[29]*Catalogue . . . 1840*, 3-7; Eleazer Parmley, "Dental Education in Baltimore," *Boston Medical and Surgical Journal*, XXXVI (March, 1847), 235-236; *Baltimore American*, 20 May 1840; *Baltimore Clipper*, 3 November 1840.

Harris even invented the name of the degree—Doctor of Dental Surgery, abbreviated as D.D.S. "For the first time in the history of the world," proclaimed Professor Bond at the valedictory, "the practice of dentistry is legally recognized as a profession."[30]

People were impressed and formal dental education developed rapidly. Within the next six years Harris encouraged one of his friends in the establishment of a similar institution in Ohio, and Robert Authur, one of the first two Baltimore graduates, founded a third institution in Philadelphia. By 1850 the Baltimore school was producing fifteen graduates annually and by 1860 about forty. In an effort to publicize the D.D.S. degree, the college awarded it on an honorary basis to many of the better practitioners during its first years of existence, but once recognized, the degree was limited almost entirely to those earning it in the classroom.[31] The prestige of institution was far more than local—7 percent of its students before the Civil War were from abroad, 14 percent from Maryland, 30 percent from northern states and 49 percent were from the South. In London, Paris and Rome the "Baltimore Dentist" was famous, and at least one French printer apparently made a sizable sum by selling counterfeit diplomas from the Baltimore college.[32]

The faculty kept abreast of its reputation, improving the college faster than the enrollment grew. When Hayden died in 1844 Harris became president. In the same year students began required anatomical dissections and a clinic was established. Two years later the college moved to new quarters on Lexington Street and added an infirmary. In 1856 it moved again to larger quarters on Lombard Street; and by 1861 it was offering new courses in surgery, metallurgy, chemistry and microscopy, and had a faculty of eight regular professors.[33]

Dental students generally spent their mornings working under the careful supervision of their professors in the infirmary where they gave the people of Baltimore free dental care. In one typical

---

[30]Bond, "Valedictory," 247; also, Robinson, "Foundations," 1040-1041.

[31]From 1841 to 1853 the college awarded 136 honorary degrees; from 1853 to 1897 it awarded 16. *Catalogue . . . 1870*, 4; Cordell, *University*, II, Appendix.

[32]*Triennial Catalogue of the Baltimore College of Dental Surgery* (Baltimore, 1867), 5-6; Harry Bryan McCarthy, "History of Dental Education in Maryland" (M.A. thesis, University of Maryland, 1948), 138-139; Simon, "Baltimore College of Dental Surgery," 26-34; Lewis, "The Birth of Professional Dentistry, 1839-1840," 68.

[33]*Catalogue . . . 1844*, 4-7; *Catalogue . . . 1846*, 3-5; *Baltimore Sun*, 20 November 1857; Simon, "Baltimore College of Dental Surgery," 17-21.

year, 1855, they extracted 2,430 teeth, filled 982 and replaced 736, in addition to cleaning, filing, straightening and treating various mouth diseases. During their afternoons, from November to late March, they attended lectures and worked in the laboratories, and in their evenings many of them worked on dissection or read in the private libraries of the professors.[34]

By the Civil War, however, the Baltimore College of Dental Surgery was losing its overwhelming pre-eminence because of its very success in launching a movement. The great Chapin Harris, by far its most noted professor, died on the eve of the conflict. As a tribute to him and his predecessor, Hayden, the college never elected a successor to the presidency, thus making the deanship its highest office. Since almost half the students were from the South, enrollment dropped sharply after Fort Sumter, and two of the regular professors resigned to join the Confederacy.[35] In addition five other dental colleges were flourishing in various areas, and although they were competitors the faculty of the Baltimore College of Dental Surgery observed them with pride, declaring that professional education in dentistry was "no longer an experiment; it has become, with the majority of the profession, an acknowledged necessity."[36]

The School of Pharmacy

Pharmacy was another occupation which, much like dentistry, developed in the shadow of medicine, evolved its own system of higher education and grew into a true profession. An ancient trade, long related both to science and magic, pharmacy took its biggest step toward professionalism in 1821 when the first college of pharmacy was established in Philadelphia. Other colleges emerged in Boston and New York, and in 1841 the Maryland College of Pharmacy became the fourth. More than its predecessors, the Maryland college emerged under the aegis of a university and established its program in an academic framework.

Almost everyone loved the nineteenth century apothecary shop with its dark, musky atmosphere, its walls lined with myriad bottles

[34]Simon, "Baltimore College of Dental Surgery," 20-26; *Catalogue . . . 1855*, 3-6; also see Lewis, "The Birth of Professional Dentistry, 1839-1840," 70-75.
[35]Simon, "Baltimore College of Dental Surgery," 20-26; *Triennial Catalogue*, 5-6.
[36]*Catalogue . . . 1860*, 3.

and urns of exotic odors. Often the proprietor was a taxidermist, and from the ceiling hung an alligator, symbol of pharmacy, along with other stuffed animals and birds. Mysterious potions bubbled in the fireplace. Scattered here and there were scales, grinders, filters, sieves, mortars and pestles of every size, equipment for distilling and pressing and, perhaps, a human skull beside a crucifix. Paints and dyes were usually mixed or manufactured on the premises, for the apothecary shop was the town laboratory. About the middle of the century some enterprising druggists began distilling mineral water and manufacturing medicated candies, paving the way for the soda fountain which eventually destroyed the old apothecary shop.

Everyone liked druggists except the doctors. Between the two groups the utmost in cooperation might have been expected, but often they were bitter rivals. Druggists disliked the competition of doctors who dispensed their own drugs, debased the apothecary trade by maintaining poorly equipped shops in their offices and left those shops to their apprentices while they concentrated on patient care. Doctors, on the other hand, had little use for druggists who were too willing to offer on-the-spot diagnoses, were more interested in peddling patent nostrums than in filling prescriptions and too often left the shops to untrained apprentices while they concentrated on the manufacture of drugs and candies.

The hostility served to bring the druggists closer together. In the cities where the better physicians did not need or wish to engage in retailing, they were able to exert pressure on the druggists to specialize in dispensing and to educate themselves to do so efficiently. In the smaller towns where druggists most keenly felt the competition of physicians, druggists demanded some form of organization to improve their profession and drive out the competition. In Philadelphia, New York and Boston an identical sequence of events followed. First the city physicians tried to license a small number of druggists whom they considered reputable. Then, indignantly, the druggists rejected the licenses in order to establish their own standards. They organized informally and immediately recognized that effective licensing, high standards and legal protection depended upon professional education.[37]

[37]Edward Kremers and George Urdang, *History of Pharmacy, A Guide and a Survey* (Philadelphia, 1940), 140-146, 173-180; William S. Thompson, "History of the Maryland College of Pharmacy," MS. dated 1871 in archives of the School of Pharmacy, Baltimore.

In Maryland the hostility between the druggists and the doctors never was quite so open. Instead of antagonizing and attempting to dominate the druggists, the medical faculty at the University of Maryland quietly led them, willingly providing aid and acknowledging their independence as the pharmacists desired. In 1820 the University's professor of chemistry, Elisha DeButts, had been one of the six scholars invited to draw up the original *United States Dispensatory*, the index of drugs which has been the basic handbook for pharmacists ever since. During the 1830's several members of the University faculty wrote of the need for special pharmaceutical training. DeButts' successor, Professor W. E. A. Aiken, made a point of inviting pharmacists and their apprentices to his lectures which he opened to them as a public service. In 1839 another University chemistry professor, William R. Fisher, took the initiative which led directly to the founding of the Maryland College of Pharmacy. A practicing pharmacist as well as a professor and physician, Fisher petitioned the Medical and Chirurgical Society to call together the pharmacists of the state. When they met in June, 1840, Fisher was ill, but another University professor, Samuel G. Baker, was there to preside.[38]

Throughout the following summer the pharmacists met regularly, drafting a constitution for their organization and planning for the founding of a college. On July 30, 1840, seventeen of the leading druggists in Maryland formally signed the constitution and elected Thomas G. Mackenzie as their president. They promised not to sell adulterated medicines, to admit new members upon proof of their competence and to require their own apprentices to attend their projected school. When the general assembly met in 1841 the druggists' association was officially chartered as the Maryland College of Pharmacy. The pharmacists established committees to obtain quarters, design a seal and arrange for lectures.[39]

The college started slowly. Even though the lectures were free and there were no requirements for admission, only six students

[38]Minutes of the Maryland College of Pharmacy, 1840-1872 (MS. Minutes in archives of the School of Pharmacy), 8 June 1840; Kremers and Urdang, *History of Pharmacy*, 240; William R. Fisher, "Brief Sketch of the Progress and Present State of Pharmacy in the United States," *American Journal of Pharmacy*, II N.S. (January, 1837), 271-279; Charles Schmidt, "Short History of the Maryland College of Pharmacy," MS. dated 1894 edited by B. Olive Cole (1946) in archives of the School of Pharmacy; *Maryland Medical and Surgical Journal*, I (July, 1840), 397-399.

[39]Minutes of the College of Pharmacy, 22 June 1840; 30 July 1840 ff.; *Laws of Maryland . . . 1841 . . .* (Annapolis, 1841), Chap. 32; *Baltimore Sun*, 9 July 1840; 22 December 1840.

began the first course in November, 1841, in a rented room at Baltimore and Gay Streets. A graduate of the University, David Stewart, agreed to deliver a series of chemistry lectures without pay, and seven Baltimore druggists agreed to take turns lecturing on *materia medica,* but the instructors had little concept of educational methods. Each of the lecturers agreed:

> in order of his name to take the chair and read 30 minutes from the English edition of Pereisa's Materia Medica continuously, omitting, however, unimportant sections and parts, and being at liberty to refer to . . . other authors . . . or give his own views in the form of a lecture or essay.[40]

Although only one course, lasting from November to February, was required for a degree, only three of the original six students were able to endure. Yet the first, Frederick A. Cochrane, became one of the most successful druggists of Maryland; the second, William S. Thompson, obtained national renown as a pharmaceutical writer and professor; and the third, Alphonso P. Sharp, became founder of the Sharp and Dohme chemical corporation. In its second year the college offered no lectures, and in the third year only one graduate completed the course.[41]

With the college obviously foundering, the University of Maryland again took a hand, offering to provide quarters for the pharmacy school and to allow its students to attend the medical school lectures on chemistry free of charge. The offer was hard on the pharmacists' pride, but they readily accepted with the proviso that, in exchange, medical students should be allowed to attend the pharmacy lectures.[42] To augment the chemistry lectures, the pharmacists named W. S. Reese as their professor of *materia medica,* and David Stewart as professor of the theory and practice of pharmacy. Stewart's course, begun in 1844, often is cited as the first separate course in pharmacy as distinct from chemistry or *materia medica* ever offered in the United States. It was a practical course dealing with pharmaceutical weights and measures and with "pharmaceutical manipulations," such as filtering, distillation and crystallization. Students paid $10 for the three-lecture courses, and Reese and Stewart received a total of $100 each. In 1844-1845 only

[40]Minutes of the College of Pharmacy, 3 July 1841; also, 12 October 1843; 22 April 1844.

[41]*Ibid.,* 25 January 1842; 31 May 1842; Schmidt, "Maryland College of Pharmacy," 3-4; *Baltimore Sun,* 23 June 1842.

[42]Minutes of the College of Pharmacy, 24 April 1844; *Baltimore Sun,* 2 November 1844.

fifteen students enrolled, and the druggists had to make up the amount owed to the professors.[43]

With membership in the pharmacy association at $10 annually, the majority of Maryland druggists did not join, and despite the support of the University the school did not prosper. There were no graduates in 1845, none in 1846, only three in 1847, and for the next nine years the lectures ceased altogether. The passage of time only increased the need for organization, however, and in 1856, under the vigorous new leadership of a Baltimore druggist, Israel Graham, the pharmacy association and the college got onto their feet again.[44]

Under Graham's leadership over fifty druggists joined the association, and that fall the school reopened with band music, enthusiastic speeches and twenty regular students. Graham was professor of pharmacy; Dr. Charles Frick, graduate and sometime professor at the University, was professor of *materia medica;* and Dr. Lewis H. Steiner, later first librarian of the Enoch Pratt Library, was professor of chemistry. Following the example of the medical school, the druggists accepted the proprietary system and transferred the costs and responsibilities of education to the students. Fees were set at $8 for each course to be paid directly to the professors. In 1858, with the school finally prospering, standards were revised sharply upward. The college required graduates to be 21 years old, to have served a four-year apprenticeship, attended two annual terms, written a thesis, passed a written examination given by the professors and an oral examination given by the pharmacy association.[45]

Except for fewer courses each term and lower fees, the training of pharmacists had become equal to that of dentists or physicians. Established on a professional basis and sure of themselves, the druggists were ready to declare their independence from the physicians. Although two professors in the pharmacy school were doctors, physicians were prohibited from joining the pharmacy association.[46]

[43]Minutes of the College of Pharmacy, 24 April 1844; Schmidt, "Maryland College of Pharmacy," 5-6; Kremers and Urdang, *History of Pharmacy,* 208; "Lectures in the Maryland College of Pharmacy," *Journal and Transactions of the Maryland College of Pharmacy,* I (June, 1858), 23-24.

[44]Minutes of the College of Pharmacy, 24 April 1844; 29 April 1844; 26 May 1846; Schmidt, "Maryland College of Pharmacy," 5-8.

[45]Minutes of the College of Pharmacy, 7 February 1856; 13 March 1856; 17 May 1856; 5 June 1856; 28 February 1857; "Lectures in the Maryland College of Pharmacy," Lewis H. Steiner, *Valedictory Address Delivered at the Maryland College of Pharmacy . . . 1859* (Baltimore, 1859).

[46]Minutes of the College of Pharmacy, 13 March 1856.

William S. Thompson, graduate of the first class in 1842, began publication of the quarterly *Journal and Transactions of the Maryland College of Pharmacy*. By 1860 thirty-five men, about half of them from outside the state, had received degrees in pharmacy from the college. As yet no legal sanctions existed to prohibit an untrained druggist from opening a shop, but increasingly both physicians and patients could assume that a pharmacist, especially in Baltimore, was qualified and proud of his profession.

Nor was progress halted by the Civil War. Each year about ten men received degrees, and each year the pharmacy association appropriated substantial sums for new college equipment. In 1864 the association placed the faculty on a direct salary of $300 a year.[47] Thereafter student fees went to the association so that the faculty could not be tempted to sacrifice standards for popularity and high enrollment. Although the Maryland College of Pharmacy was not formally a part of the University of Maryland, it would come back into the arms of the institution which had helped it to become established.

The College

The undergraduate college always seemed to be starting, petering out and beginning again. The state desperately needed colleges, and students flocked to the University's undergraduate branch when it offered promise, but always it seemed to be waiting for a dynamic leader who never came. In the 1820's William Allen had lacked the force to bring it to life; in the 1830's the state trustees failed; and twice again, first in the 1840's and then in the 1850's, the college struggled back to life.

In 1840, the year after the faculty assumed control from the trustees, the University turned over the college to a secondary school principal named Horace Morrison. He received generous grants from the University for new equipment, published a pretentious catalogue and began his tenure with accolades from the press. Maintaining the preparatory school and the college program outlined by the trustees, he added a third distinct program which offered special "practical" training "adopted to the needs of the mercantile community." To the existing staff he added six part-time instructors in such subjects as engineering, German, French, Spanish, Italian and music. According to the catalogue, the undergraduate school matched the finest course offerings in the country, and during the first year 53 new students entered at various levels.[48]

But personally Morrison was unpopular; grandly he promised too much, and by his third year the college could not afford to publish a catalogue. In 1843 the City of Baltimore offered to buy the college building for use as a high school and the University refused the offer only because it had pledged the state to keep it. For ten more years Morrison and one or two assistants continued to occupy the building, earning whatever they could from college preparatory classes. In 1852, a faculty investigating committee from the other schools of the University reported that Morrison was using the property for personal gain, that he had allowed the building to depreciate from a value of $80,000 to $25,000 for lack of repairs and that until he was forced to resign the University would not be "properly discharging its trust to the public."[49]

In 1854 the University again thoroughly reorganized the college, this time placing in charge an able Episcopal clergyman, Edwin Dalrymple. Old-fashioned and believing in no nonsense, he held that "Latin and Greek and Mathematics" were about all that a college needed to provide since these subjects were the "foundation of all sound learning." If students thought otherwise, he stood ready to convince them with a birch rod. He mortgaged the building for $5,000 which he spent for repairs and equipment, and talked the University into giving him $5,000 more to acquire a competent faculty. Although he maintained the prep school, he abolished the program for the "mercantile community," and renamed the college the School of Letters of the University of Maryland. Dalrymple acquired five college-educated instructors, and within three years his enrollment was up to 127 students. Once again the college seemed to be on its way.[50]

Late in June, 1859, in a quiet ceremony at the college building, Isaac Brooks received a Bachelor of Arts degree. Although there

[48]Regents Minutes, 8 October 1839; 29 December 1841; 3 January 1843; *Prospectus of the Collegiate Department of the University of Maryland . . . 1841-1842* (Baltimore, 1841); *Annual Circular of the Collegiate Department . . . 1842-1843* (Baltimore, 1842); *Baltimore American,* 26 July 1839; 23 August 1839; *Baltimore Clipper,* 1 June 1841.

[49]Regents Minutes, 3 March 1843; 5 April 1852.

[50]*Ibid.,* 13 August 1854; 18 October 1854; *Register of the Faculty, Officers and Students of the Academic Department . . . of the University of Maryland . . . 1855-1856,* also Register . . . *1856-1857, 1857-1858, 1858-1859* (Baltimore, 1855-1859); *Baltimore Sun,* 19 June 1857; 26 June 1858.

may have been graduates from the college during the 1830's, Brooks is the first student known to have received an undergraduate degree from the University of Maryland. In the following year the faculty of all the University schools attended the commencement, and John Pendleton Kennedy awarded degrees to four graduating seniors; in 1861 there were three graduates. The ceremonies were held apart from those of the medical school, almost as if the doctors were unwilling to recognize the undergraduate college as a part of the same institution.[51]

One of the healthiest signs for the young college was the organization in 1860 of the Literary Society of the University of Maryland. Through this group, for the first time, undergraduate college life had some momentum of its own. As the focus of college intellectual life and of school loyalty, the nineteenth century literary society was often an accurate measure of the vitality of a college. The Maryland society, composed of elected students and alumni, met weekly to debate the political and literary issues of the day. Membership was coveted, expulsion was a disgrace and the campus hero was the man who devastated his opponent with a particularly sparkling oration. Although the University still lacked dormitories and its college classes often met with classes from the preparatory school, the literary society gave the college a clear delineation of its own.[52] The students, perhaps even more than the faculty, were building toward academic respectability. The needs of the state and of the students were pushing the University forward so that, sometimes at least, it seemed to be succeeding in spite of itself.

With the coming of the Civil War, however, Dalrymple's institution began to crumble. College enrollment dropped sharply. There were no graduates in 1862, only one in 1863 and a final one in 1866. Following the example of his predecessors, Dalrymple shifted his emphasis to preparatory work for children, half-heartedly continuing such instruction as a means of livelihood until his retirement in 1874.[53]

[51]*Baltimore Sun,* 24 June 1859; 26 June 1861; John Pendleton Kennedy Journal, 20 June 1859; 27 June 1860.

[52]*Constitution and By-Laws of the Literary Society of the University of Maryland* (Baltimore, 1860) ; Cordell, *University,* I, 475.

[53]*Register of the Faculty, Officers and Students of the Academic Department . . . of the University of Maryland . . . 1863-1864,* also *Register . . . for 1864-1865, 1865-1866* (Baltimore, 1864-1866) ; Regents Minutes, 2 February 1872; 10 June 1878; 24 June 1878; MS. scrap entitled "Financial Report of Arts and Sciences," appended to Regents Minutes, no date.

Even if the Civil War had not come there was no guarantee that the college would have succeeded. Fundamentally burdened by its proprietary system, it lacked sufficient outside support, dormitories and salaried professors. Most of all it lacked imaginative leadership. Many American colleges faced this problem in the mid-nineteenth century as popular needs seemed to push colleges faster than they wanted to move. Few professional scholars were available to step into a college presidency, and often the professional secondary school teachers or clergymen who usually took over were of mediocre quality. Had the Civil War not occurred, Dalrymple might have provided the impetus necessary to establish a college or, perhaps, another leader might have assumed control. The people in Maryland were hoping almost desperately for a college. The City of Baltimore and the State of Maryland were ready to provide money for almost any institution that offered a chance of success. Ideally located and associated with the flourishing professional schools, the college of the University of Maryland appeared almost ready, when the war came, to take its place as the center of a true state university.

More than the University professors realized, the professional and intellectual life of the state was beginning to gravitate around the institution by 1860. Despite its deficiencies the college was growing in popularity, the medical school flourished, and training for the new professions of dentistry and pharmacy blossomed in the shadow of the University. Most important of all, far out in the country—in the area now known as College Park—the farmers of Maryland were beginning to build a school which was to be the focus of their profession, and which also was to become a vital part of the University of Maryland.

5

Life and Learning in the Medical School

When the College of Medicine of Maryland opened in 1807, physicians still practiced medicine much as they had a thousand years earlier. Most people assumed that disease was punishment for sin and were angered when such men as Wiesenthal and Davidge undertook to probe further. Only a handful of Americans had attended a medical college, and they had no body thermometers, no stethoscopes, no hypodermic needles, no antiseptic and no understanding of germs and infection. Operations were frequently performed with kitchen knives, and anethesia was unknown. Infant mortality in 1807 was 30 percent; life expectancy was 34 years.

Early in the nineteenth century, however, important signs of progress were appearing. Gradually, hospitals and dispensaries multiplied, public health boards promoted sanitation and quarantine laws, the first American medical journals were printed and vaccination came into use. Above all, medical societies and medical licensing boards began to distinguish effectively between the physician and the charlatan, while new medical colleges established basic standards for the would-be physician. The life of the medical student began to fit a pattern which did not change substantially until after the Civil War. The story of medical school life at Maryland, available through remarkably abundant records, is the story in miniature of the nation's developing scientific tradition.[1]

The Students Who Came to Maryland

Entrance requirements and high tuition meant that the early nineteenth century medical student usually came from a prosperous home. The father of a prospective student may have been a physician, lawyer or shopkeeper; perhaps he was a clergyman since ministers to the soul and body had long maintained a friendly association. Or he may have been a planter or farmer successful enough to help with his son's education.

Geographically, about a third of the students were from Baltimore, a somewhat surprising figure since the city comprised less than a fourth of the state's population in 1860, and less than a tenth in 1810. Urban centers breed professionalism, however, and Baltimore long had been a medical center. The young boys of the town must have been impressed by the mysterious building behind the high walls, by the imposing professors who moved in the highest social circles and by the people who came to the University from far away. Medical students in Baltimore went to the University as a matter of course, while many back-country students continued to study on their own to pass the licensing examination without the benefit of formal courses.[2]

Another third of the students came from the rural districts of Maryland, especially from the Eastern Shore and the southern counties of the Western Shore. Far from reflecting the traditional suspicion of Baltimore, these slaveholding counties tended to place greater emphasis on medical training than the German and English residents of the western counties. This support also appeared in the

[1]Richard Harrison Shryock, *Development of Modern Medicine* (New York, 1947), 102, 133 and *passim;* Lester S. King, *Medical World of the Eighteenth Century* (Chicago, 1958); John Allen Krout and Dixon Ryan Fox, *Completion of Independence, 1790-1830* (New York, 1944), 293-312.

[2]*Catalogue of the Alumni of the School of Medicine* (Baltimore, 1850). Most nineteenth century catalogues of the medical school list the names, preceptors, thesis topic, and home town of the graduates.

general assembly, for the medical college often found its staunchest supporters across the Bay.

A final third of the students who came to the school were from outside the state. At first they came because of the absence of medical colleges in their home states, but by the 1820's their continued migration to Baltimore was testimony to the school's outstanding reputation. Of the out-of-state students, about 60 percent were from Virginia and the District of Columbia, about 25 percent from other southern states, about 10 percent from Pennsylvania and the North and about 5 percent from abroad. The University faculty often addressed itself "To the Friends of Southern Institutions" and made conscious appeal to the slave states. The faculty placed advertisements in such southern journals as *DeBow's Review, Southern Literary Messenger* and *Niles' Register,* and these journals in turn made flattering editorial comment about the University.[3]

Wherever he came from, the future student probably had graduated from a local academy where he had been drilled in Greek and Latin and excited by a taste of "natural philosophy." Possibly he had shocked his parents with the statement that he wanted to become a doctor, for with the exception of a few eminent professors, the profession promised neither glamor nor prestige nor high income. Most men thought of medicine in terms of filth and pain and of the charlatanism still widely practiced. One Maryland professor lamented that parents sent their more intelligent sons into law, the ministry or farming, and believed that a medical education was worthy only of those young men "the strength of whose intellectual powers they have some doubt."[4] One student recalled the displeasure with which his father learned of his ambition:

> He said to me: 'My son, I confess I am disappointed in you. . . . I suppose that I can not control you; but it is a profession for which I have the utmost contempt. . . . There is no honor to be achieved in it; no reputation to be made, and to think that *my* son should be going around from house to house in this country with a box of pills in one hand and a squirt in the other . . . is a thought I never supposed I should have to contemplate.'[5]

[3]*Catalogue,* 1841-1842, 60; *Catalogue,* 1870-1871, 5-6. These annual publications are variously called catalogues, announcements, prospectuses and circulars. They are here referred to simply as *Catalogue,* along with the academic year which they cover. All were published in Baltimore and may be found in the medical school archives.

[4]Robley Dunglison, *The Medical Student, Aids to the Study of Medicine* (Philadelphia, 1836). 8.

[5]J. Marion Sims, *Story of My Life* (New York, 1888), 23. Sims graduated from Jefferson Medical College in 1835.

Beyond the academy, the next step before entering medical school was apprenticeship with an established physician, perhaps a distant relative or a close neighbor. Life was still intimate in the nineteenth century, personal ties were close and seldom did a boy proceed blindly in search of a master. The same ties generally insured the apprenticeship agreement would be an informal one which either party could end at any time. Sometimes the boy moved in to live with the physician and paid a nominal board. More often he remained at home, working for his master during the day for his instruction so that no money changed hands.

The apprentice arrived at the doctor's house early in the morning. He swept the floor, made the fires and probably milked the cows. During the day he pounded out powders, washed bottles and made up pills in his master's laboratory; he accompanied the doctor on his rounds, watching him practice, handing him instruments and running errands. Often he had breakfast or lunch with the doctor, asking questions and discussing cases. In his spare time the student repeatedly pored over the ten or fifteen medical books which the doctor owned. Late in the afternoon he returned home to attend the chores there. If the physician were particularly conscientious, on Saturday mornings he quizzed his pupil on the reading which he had done during the week, but often such formalities were sloughed over in the close personal association between student and physician. As the boy's knowledge grew, he increasingly took a hand in the practice, extracting teeth, bleeding a patient or making a distant call on a case that did not seem serious.[6]

If the young man were exceptionally bright, and if his master were influential in medical circles, he probably was able to pass the oral licensing examination of the Maryland Medical and Chirurgical Society after two or three years of apprenticeship without attending medical school. Increasingly, however, formal training became essential to top off apprenticeship. The intelligent boy was eager for the schooling and the dullard scarcely could pass without it. Often the examining board was closely associated with the University, and frequently its professors made up the board's majority. By 1830 about 60 percent of the Maryland licenses granted went to

[6]William Frederick Norwood, *Medical Education in the United States before the Civil War* (Philadelphia, 1944), 380-386; Henry Burnell Shafer, *American Medical Profession, 1783 to 1850* (New York, 1936); Dunglison, *The Medical Student*, 3-45.

medical college graduates, and by 1860 the rate was about 80 per-cent.[7]

For all the practicality of the apprentice system, it was high time that Americans attended formal medical classes. European travelers in America were shocked at the backwardness of its medicine and the inadequate training of its physicians. Almost certainly the appren-tice had never dissected a cadaver; his books of symptoms and remedies were usually old; he had little, if any, knowledge of chem-istry and practically no system to his study. Most students welcomed the coming of medical colleges, looking upon them not as obstacles to their licensing, but as places which provided exciting opportu-nities to study subjects they longed to understand.

As medical schools grew in importance the apprentice system underwent changes. Students began turning to their professors to guide their apprenticeship until, by the late 1850's, three-fourths of the Maryland medical students were apprenticed to a member of the faculty.[8] Instead of following the physician in his day-to-day prac-tice, the student paid his preceptor up to $100 a year for which he received access to the physician's library, to regular clinical demon-strations and to guided tours through Baltimore hospitals. Early in the century students had completed most of their apprenticeship before entering medical school, but by the 1850's many waited until they had begun classes and then served between terms under their preceptors. Often they continued their association for a year after they had received their degrees. Too much responsibility still re-mained with the students, and many of them cut corners; but the apprentice system was evolving into the modern post-graduate in-ternship.

At the University professors were concerned that it was almost impossible to spell out specific rules for admission, and that almost anyone who could afford the tuition could attend the lectures. In theory, the faculty required students to have graduated from an academy and to have completed "most" of their two-year apprentice-ship. In an individualistic age, however, there was no agreement as to what constituted an academy or a complete apprenticeship. In fact, the Medical College could only establish standards for the de-gree and not those for admission, so that by 1850 its catalogues

[7]Eugene Fauntleroy Cordell, *Medical Annals of Maryland, 1799-1899* (Baltimore, 1903) , 241, 297-637; William Travis Howard, *Public Health Administration and the Natural History of Disease in Baltimore, Maryland* (Washington, 1924) , 11-17.
[8]*Catalogue*, 1849-1850, 15; *Catalogue*, 1858-1859, 18-19.

admitted frankly that the University "does not dictate the quantity or quality, of preliminary education."[9] Yet the unqualified student soon found life in the college so uncomfortable that he returned home to complete his preparation or find another profession. It stood to the credit of the University standards that only about half of the entering students remained through the two years to receive the degree. While the minimum standards for admission probably were higher in 1810 than in 1860, the average student's preparation in 1860 was considerably better. During the 1810's and 1820's about 10 percent of the students had attended college before entering the medical school, but by 1860 about 35 percent were college men.[10]

Throughout the period the average age of entering students remained about 19.9 years. The figure indicated that they possessed at least two years of experience beyond the academy and were somewhat older than college freshmen. The youngest students were sixteen, but some were in their thirties.[11]

Fired with excitement and anticipation, the future medical student arrived at the University early in October. For many students the occasion was their first visit to a city, and for almost all it was their first admission to the strange sights and smells behind the University walls. Many of them saw a skeleton for the first time and first heard the screams of patients undergoing operations without anesthesia. Whether the student had served a complete apprenticeship or was getting by with no previous training, he usually remembered those first days of medical school for the rest of his life. "How wonderful," wrote a Maryland student in his fresh notebook while he waited for Dr. Davidge, "I am not now bending over the pescle [sic] and morter [sic] in the Country but am travercing [sic] over the fare [sic] field of Science."[12] Another student drew a determinedly striding skeleton with horns and a tail and captioned it "I'm off."[13] A student at Harvard Medical School summed up what many at Maryland must have felt:

[9]*Catalogue*, 1851-1852, 7.

[10]John B. Davidge, *Nosologia Methodica: Classicum et Generum et Specierum et Varietatum Series Morbedum Exibens* (Baltimore, 1813), v-vi; Samuel Chew, *Lectures on Medical Education, or The Proper Method of Studying Medicine* (Philadelphia, 1864), 113-141; *Baltimore Sun,* 6 November 1846; Cordell, *Medical Annals,* 297-637.

[11]Cordell, *Medical Annals,* 297-637.

[12]The Health Sciences Library in Baltimore has collected about 40 notebooks belonging to students who attended the University from 1807 to 1862. Many are fragmentary, lacking names and dates. These notebooks provide the primary source for this chapter. Notebook, anon., "Notes on Potter and Davidge," no date, 1.

[13]Notebook, Thomas J. McGill, "Notes on Lectures," 1833-1834.

There is something very solemn and depressing about the first entrance upon the study of medicine. The white faces of the sick that fill the long row of beds in the hospital wards saddened me, and produced a feeling of awe-stricken sympathy. The dreadful scenes in the operating theatre—for this was before the days of ether— were a shock to my sensibilities, though I did not faint as students occasionally do. When I first entered the room where the medical students were seated at a table with a skeleton hanging over it, and bones lying about, I was deeply impressed, and more disposed to moralize upon mortality than to take up the task in osteology which lay before me.[14]

The student usually arrived on a Thursday or Friday and, after finding a room, went to the college on Saturday morning to sign up for classes. First he found the dean to pay the $5 matriculation fee. In those days the dean was merely one of the professors, elected to the post annually, and besides collecting this fee, he had no more duties or prestige than the other professors. A few faculty members who wanted offices usually found a closet, corner or classroom which was more or less their own; but probably the dean simply brought the huge, old matriculation book from home that day and carried it with him as he went his rounds through the hospital.

In a brief interview the student presented his academy diploma and a letter from his preceptor; perhaps the dean then talked lightly about local lodging places or about mutual acquaintances. Possibly he doubted that the student's background was adequate and offered frowning advice. At any rate the student's name, home county and preceptor's name were entered in the matriculation book and marked paid.[15]

The student's major expense, however, was his lecture tickets. Beginning with the dean, he hunted up his seven professors to pay each one $20 for a ticket which would admit him to his lectures or laboratory sessions. Slightly larger than a playing card, the handsomely printed ticket included the name of the course, and spaces for the professor's and the student's signatures. During the student's second year at the University he omitted the matriculation fee, but paid the dean $20 for the right to take the final examination and

---

[14]John T. Morse, *Life and Letters of Oliver Wendell Holmes,* 2 vols. (London, 1896), I, 81-82.

[15]The matriculation book is in the archives of the medical school, Baltimore.

receive his diploma. Although the fees varied slightly from year to
year, until the Civil War they remained close to $140 annually,
making the course one of the most expensive in the United States.
Western medical colleges advertised costs less than half those of
Maryland, and Washington College in Baltimore provided training
for less than $100. Those who attended the University were willing
to pay for what they believed was the best medical education available.[16]

Ceremony and introduction marked the opening week of school.
Each morning, and again on Saturday afternoon, the students assembled to hear a two-hour oration by one of the professors. Each
speech was full of rhetorical flower and classical allusion, apotheosiz-
ing the medical profession and exhorting the young men to study
diligently. In each talk the professor outlined his theory of disease,
praised the University as the beacon light of civilization, warned the
students of discouragements that lay ahead and offered advice for
study and success. Seemingly the platitudes did not bore the students. Always they applauded, sometimes they took up voluntary
collections to have the lectures published and occasionally they may
have been inspired. The general public and visitors from other
medical schools frequently attended these speeches and spoke highly
of Maryland's custom of introductory orations. During the 1850's,
however, even the professors tired of the clichés, and reduced the
introductory orations to a single one which they took turns delivering on the first Monday morning of the term.[17]

What Students Learned

Students and faculty were happy, though, when actual study began, for consistent in notebooks and orations was the students' certainty that they had something marvelous to learn, and the professors'

[16]See annual catalogues. Also, Eugene Fauntleroy Cordell, *Historical Sketch of the
University of Maryland School of Medicine, 1807-1890* (Baltimore, 1891), 126; Norwood,
Medical Education in the United States, 387-395; *Annual Circular of the Washington
University Medical College of Baltimore, 1841-1842* (Baltimore, 1841), 3-6; Dunglison,
The Medical Student, 307.

[17]Notebook, "Lectures of John S. C. Monkur," 1845-1852; Notebook, Johannis Bowie,
"Introductory Lectures," no date; Dunglison, *The Medical Student*, 139-145; *Baltimore
American*, 28 October 1813; 5 June 1860.

certainty that they had something important to teach. The school of medicine was infused with a sense of intellectual mission and message. The students may have gained less practical knowledge than they imagined from their dissections, but they felt they were becoming wiser; and the professors' theories were more mistaken than they imagined, but they seemed to provide understanding for phenomena which had not been understood before. In the process modern medical science was slowly emerging.

The modern scientific method was born during the Renaissance when men first recognized the necessity for testing theories empirically. During the seventeenth and eighteenth centuries the new empirical approach yielded practical results for such physicians as William Harvey who discovered the circulation of the blood, and Thomas Sydenham who began compiling statistical case histories. By the first decades of the nineteenth century, however, a reaction had set in. Men of that romantic era, impatient for results, began to feel that empiricism was unproductive. They wanted to do for medicine what Sir Isaac Newton had done for physics, to discover grand universal laws which would explain all disease and all therapy. Searching for a unifying system, physicians turned to speculative theories to organize their knowledge and provide a basis for their therapy. When the University of Maryland was established, "empiricism" had come to mean the methods of the uneducated quack who relied only upon his experience with drugs he did not understand. The medical colleges, on the other hand, abounded with theories. The more learned the professor, the more daring and dangerous were apt to be his nosologies. The philosophically oriented German universities took the theories furthest with such systems as Brunonism, Mesmerism, vitalism and homeopathy.[18]

British and American universities were not far behind, and the University of Maryland offered some theories as daring as the rest. "The philosophy of . . . disease," said Dr. Davidge, was to be understood only "on the grounds of deductive reasoning."[19] The faculty argued heatedly whether diseases were "natural" or "artificial," whether they could be traced to Europe, the Flood or the Garden of

[18]Shryock, *Development of Modern Medicine*, 57-78, 109-119 and *passim*.
[19]MS. dedication of Davidge to John Glendy in a copy of Davidge, *Nosologia Methodica* located in Peabody Library, Baltimore; also, Notebook, anon., "Dr. Davidge's Lectures on the Institutes," no date, 10-11; Richard Wilmot Hall, *Oration Delivered by Appointment before the Medical and Surgical Faculty of Maryland . . . 1815* (Baltimore, 1815), 8.

Eden, and whether a change in climate or diet could change a disease from, say, mumps to measles.[20]

The Maryland faculty, however, generally agreed on a set of basic assumptions similiar to those prevailing in medical circles throughout the country, but recognized in certain of its implications as the "Maryland theory." Actually an ancient hypothesis and Aristotelian in its roots, it had filtered into Baltimore through William Cullen and his colleagues at Edinburgh who had taught Davidge, Gibson, DeButts, Shaw and Baker, and also through Cullen's most famous pupil, Benjamin Rush, who had taught Potter and Hall at Philadelphia. The theory dominated medical thinking at Maryland until well into the 1830's. According to this hypothesis, health was a natural balance of basic elements within the body, and disease was an imbalance to be corrected. Some of the professors—Gibson, DeButts and Baker—viewed the balance in chemical terms; others—Potter and Hall—saw health as a balance of stimulants, such as food, heat, exercise and emotion. Too much of any chemical or stimulant, they argued, caused a debility or excitement which was transmitted through the blood to produce a "spasm" in the vessels and which erupted as a specific irritation or disease. Davidge spoke of the "plurality of disease," suggesting that chemicals, stimulants and "yet unidentified principles of animation" might all be equally basic body elements which could become unbalanced. But in general he agreed: "That every disease is an irritation, or morbid excitement, is a position, so plain and true that it neither admits of refutation or illustration."[21]

Proceeding from the basic assumption of balance and imbalance, all of the professors agreed that medical therapy was essential. Nature, left to itself, did not correct the imbalance, but tended to increase it. "If nature comes in at the door," said Professor Potter, "she must be thrown out of the window."[22] In any case, the cures were simple and traditional—emetics and purges to clean the stomach of excess chemicals or stimulants and massive bloodletting to restore the "natural" balance of the blood. Davidge emphasized counterstimulants which would build up the weaker elements in the body

[20]Notebook, Johannis Bowie, "Introductory Lectures," no date, 4; Notebook, Samuel Mainster, "Notes on Lectures Delivered by Nathaniel Potter," 1827-1828, 1; Davidge, Nosologia Methodica, xii-xxv.

[21]Davidge, Nosologia Methodica, xi.

[22]Francis Donaldson [a student of Potter], "A Physician's Note-Book," Weekly Gazette [Baltimore], 22 November 1873.

rather than reduce the offending element. Instead of using purges for diarrhea and bleeding for fevers, as most doctors did, to clean out the offending digestive system or to lower the temperature, Davidge bled for diarrhea and purged for fever. "No two general actions can take place at the same time," he wrote. Purging and sweating a fever patient "establishes action in the system opposite to the fever . . . which ceases."[23]

But the Maryland theory was never a rigid dogma, and while the theoretical approach made the professors feel superior to the uneducated "empirics," their remedies were remarkably similar. The theory was merely an attempt to comprehend a mass of unrelated data in an era before modern theories of germs and infection. The theories of cures always seemed to fit the observable results, and the remedies themselves were really only two: bleeding and calomel. Every good doctor, said Potter, carries "the lancet in one hand and calomel in the other."[24] Differences in theories came down to which one of these was used first and most freely.

Calomel is a compound of mercury, white and tasteless in powder form, which acts as an heroic purgative, tends to lower temperature and if taken in sufficient quantities dries out the body through sweating, urination and salivation. It is mildly antiseptic and possesses some therapeutic value for certain venereal diseases. But as used in the nineteenth century it served, like bleeding, primarily to weaken the patient. Professor Baker called it the only fully "proven" therapeutic drug; and Professor Davidge believed that few "patients have ever died after the full treatment."[25] By 1830 some physicians were coming to question the reliance on calomel, and one patient, in full revolt, wrote a verse that gained considerable contemporary renown:

> And when I must resign my breath,
> Pray let me die a natural death,
> And bid you all a long farewell,
> Without one dose of Calomel.[26]

[23]John B. Davidge, *Treatise on the Autumnal Endemial Epidemic of Tropical Climates . . . Together with a Few Reflections of the Proximate Cause of Disease* (Baltimore, 1798), 3 and *passim;* also, Cordell, *Historical Sketch,* 70.

[24]Donaldson, "Physician's Note-Book," *Weekly Gazette,* 22 November 1873; Notebook, Thomas Munroe, "Notes on Potter," no date, 20.

[25]Notebook, Thomas Duval, 1842-1843, 9; Davidge, *Treatise on the Autumnal Endemial Epidemic,* 4.

[26]Cited in Shryock, *Development of Modern Medicine,* 253.

Bleeding patients to release the poisons in the body, or to restore the "balance" of nature, was the other favorite remedy during the first three decades of the nineteenth century. It fitted many of the seemingly logical theories, and appealed equally to the uneducated empirics. A pint or two of blood taken from the arm or neck usually reduced fever and tension and frequently lessened pain, allowing the patient to relax into quiet sleep. For sharper more local pains, such as arthritis, gout or appendicitis, the approved method of bloodletting was cupping. The physician scarified a few inches of skin near the pain with his lancet and applied a suction cup to draw out the blood. The effect was superficial pain, more severe but less frightening than the internal one, and if the internal pain happened to disappear in the meantime then obviously it had been "cured." Leeching was a third method of bleeding. For local inflammation around a wound or for hemorrhoids, the repulsive little animals were applied. After sucking about an ounce of blood they would drop off, and when dipped in vinegar would disgorge the blood so that they could be applied again. With no hypodermic needle for taking blood, doctors used the animals to make an inflamed area white. Akin to bleeding was the rarer remedy of blistering. Professor Hall prescribed blistering for a kidney ailment, and his therapy must have caused many of his patients to forget their previous complaints. Apply a coating of gunpowder to the back, he advised; then apply a match.[27] Again, such treatment drew out the poison and substituted a superficial pain for an internal one.

In one subtle way, however, the Maryland theory differed from other medical theories in America, and the difference made it possible for the University to keep the door open to experimentation more easily, probably, than any other American institution. The difference was that everyone at Maryland strongly opposed the theory of Benjamin Rush which held that all diseases were identical, and that an identical "universal cure" was appropriate for all. Davidge at Maryland and Rush at Pennsylvania both agreed on the basic balance-of-nature theory, which came from Cullen, but Davidge believed that Rush had perverted the master with his corollary that diphtheria in one man or one climate might be hydrophobia in another man or climate. Rush was the greatest figure in American medicine, and his views came to dominate Amer-

[27]Richard Wilmot Hall to Franklin J. Smith, 24 November 1837, Hall Papers, Maryland Historical Society, Baltimore.

ican medical opinion almost everywhere except at Maryland. Davidge convinced his colleagues, however, that each disease must be studied, catalogued and treated separately, and the Medical College of Maryland was established with this basic difference in mind. The rivalry between Davidge and Rush reached the point of personal animosity, and the rivalry between Maryland and Pennsylvania, generally the two most prominent medical schools in the country, amounted to a fundamentally different approach to science.[28]

Specifically, the Maryland theory involved an emphasis on diagnosis and a consequent emphasis on the basic science of physiology and pathology, such as existed nowhere else in the United States. Wrote Dr. Potter:

> We soon came to the conclusion that the science could not be successfully taught, under the usual organization of medical schools. We either did see, or thought we saw, that without the aids of physiology and pathology, either associated with anatomy, or as a separate chair of Institutes, the philosophy of the body, in sickness and in health, could not be understood.[29]

This emphasis on physiology and pathology still allowed for abundant theorizing—Potter, for example, still spoke of "the philosophy of the body." But the emphasis meant that medicine was being approached, to a unique degree, through the basic sciences.[30] When Professor Crawford presented his startling germ theory in 1811, he expressed a scientific approach which was even more modern. "We must not forget," he said, "that these are only conjectures, and that our hypothesis must not claim the credit of proofs, until they are supported by incontrovertible evidence."[31]

By the 1840's, as the older generation of Davidge, Potter, Hall, Baker and DeButts was replaced, untestable hypotheses gave way even further to experimentation. Thoroughly conscious of the distinction between theory and observation, the younger generation made experimentation their rallying cry. Medicine "is emphatically an experimental science," said the newly installed Professor

[28]Rush to Maxwell McDowell, 11 June 1812, L. H. Butterfied (ed.), *Letters of Benjamin Rush*, 2 vols. (Princeton, 1951), II, 1140-1141.

[29]Nathaniel Potter, *Some Account of the Rise and Progress of the University of Maryland* (Baltimore, 1838), 5.

[30]Dunglison, *The Medical Student*, 161 and *passim*.

[31]John Crawford, *Lecture Introductory to a Course of Lectures on the Cause, Seat and Cure of Diseases* (Baltimore, 1811), 27.

Aiken in 1837, "all its deductions are based on experiment."[32] When Potter died in 1844 his chair of theory and practice was changed to principles and practice, and his successor, Elisha Bartlett, declared that, "Hypothetical speculations, which . . . have generally occupied . . . so large a space in this department of instruction, wasting the time and perverting the minds of the pupils, will be wholly discarded."[33] Inspired to prepare a book-length attack on the Rush-Davidge-Potter approach to medicine, Bartlett published *The Philosophy of Medical Science* which has sometimes been cited as a milestone in the development of the modern scientific method.[34] By the 1850's the Maryland catalogues proclaimed almost belligerently: "The faculty bestow no time or attention upon fanciful theories, speculations, and conjectures."[35] Even the ancient therapy of calomel and bleeding came under attack:

> *Modern medicine differs* from that which preceded it mainly in this: that while it esteems at their full value the powers of Art, it also regards the powers of Nature, teaching the true wisdom of watching patiently, observing patiently, acting cautiously.[36]

While the philosophical approach to medicine may have been evident to the brightest students from the introductory orations, it assumed a concrete shape for everyone in the daily classes. Five days a week, sometimes six, the students spent at least an hour in classes under each of the seven professors.

The most popular course was anatomy. The University had emerged from Davidge's anatomy classes; unusual emphasis on anatomy revealed the institution's devotion to basic science; and through anatomy classes it had introduced microscopy to American medicine. Such famous professors as Davidge, Cocke, Pattison, Geddings, Roby and Miltenberger had held the chair. The aim of the course, said the catalogue, "is not to coax the memory into retention of the barbarous nomenclature of the brain, bones, and muscles," but to demonstrate the function of organs and fluids, and to provide a bridge to physiology and pathology.[37] One professor entitled the

[32]William E. A. Aiken, *Introductory Lecture, Delivered before the Medical Class of the University, November, 1837* (Baltimore, 1837), 16.

[33]*Catalogue*, 1845-1846, 9.

[34]Elisha Bartlett, *The Philosophy of Medical Science* (Philadelphia, 1844), see especially 224-225; Shryock, *Development of Modern Medicine*, 4.

[35]*Catalogue*, 1858-1859, 5.

[36]*Catalogue*, 1851-1852, 19.

[37]*Catalogue*, 1846-1847, 9.

course "anatomy and pathology," and another called it "anatomy and physiology." Regardless of the name, anatomy, with all of its laboratory work, required at least twice as much of the student's time as any other course. In 1817 the University employed a laboratory demonstrator to aid the professor, and until the Civil War it remained the only two-man department in the school. Students particularly liked the laboratory where, at any time of the day, they could dissect for themselves.[38]

The striking success of the anatomy department, and indeed of the medical school, stemmed in part from the ready availability of cadavers. Despite the riots in 1788 and 1807, the college catalogues referred to Baltimore as "the Paris of America, . . . where the abundance of subjects is greater than any other city in the United States."[39] As early as 1815 one student claimed to have dissected six subjects.[40] In deference to parents who might object, dissection was not officially compulsory until 1848 (second to Pennsylvania), but almost every student since the school's opening imagined himself the discoverer of some new fold or tissue.[41] Indeed, the University actually supplied cadavers to colleges as far away as Maine. In a highly confidential letter to a professor at Bowdoin, Nathan Ryno Smith described Maryland's method of procurement and shipment:

> It will give me pleasure to render you any assistance in regard to subjects. I think you may rely upon having them. I shall immediately *invoke* Frank, our body-snatcher (a better man never lifted a spade), and confer with him on the matter. We can get them here without any difficulty at present but I would not [tell] the world that any but ourselves should know that I have winked at their being sent out of the state.
>
> I will cause about three to be put up in barrels of whiskey. I suppose they will require about half a barrel each, of whiskey. This at 35 cents a gallon will be $16.80. The barrels a dollar each; the subjects, the putting up, etc. $10. each, making in all $50.00.[42]

[38]Thomas Sewall, *An Eulogy on Dr. Godman* . . . (Washington, 1830), 15; *Baltimore American*, 24 August 1820; Cordell, *Historical Sketch*, 34-36.

[39]*Catalogue*, 1838-1839, 4; *Catalogue*, 1846-1847, 5.

[40]Alexander Clendinen, "Surgery of the Dislocated Shoulder Joint" (Thesis, University of Maryland, 1815), 3.

[41]*Catalogue*, 1848-1849, 4; Dunglison, *The Medical Student*, 147-166.

[42]Smith to———[probably Parker Cleveland], 25 September 1830, archives, Bowdoin College. I am indebted to Dr. Oliver S. Haywood, of the National Institutes of Health, Washington, D. C., for calling this to my attention.

Students dreaded the course in the "medical institutes" as much as they liked the one in anatomy. Taught for twenty years by Maxwell McDowell—who apparently never quite understood what his colleagues intended when they created the position—the course was a conglomeration of physiology and diagnosis, including lectures on muscles, fibers, blood, urine, milk, acids, absorption, air, temperature, nerves, hearing, smell, sleep and decay. Other departments, especially anatomy, took over the exciting experimental work in physiology and pathology, and in the 1850's the "Institutes," as such, was abolished.[43]

The course called "theory and practice," or "principles and practice," was the most practical one in the University. All kinds of diseases were listed with descriptions of their symptoms and suggested treatments. Old Dr. Potter delivered the lectures for almost forty years from the same crumbling yellow notes: "Miasmic feavers, dysentery, pneumonia, mumps, brain diseases, gout, . . . gastritis, enteritis, measles, smallpox, hemorrhoids,"—they all fit a system— ". . . whooping cough, epilepsy, apoplexy, paralysis . . . dropsy, nymphomania and hydrophobia."[44] Sheep dung was good for measles, and calomel would do for almost anything.[45] "Emptying the bowels is especially good for diseases of the Head."[46] The old bachelor had a particular interest in lovesickness which he believed was a major cause of fevers, hysteria and "mania." This type of malady, he observed, was most common to women and to "men of delicate minds," but "sometimes it occurs and may be produced by indolence, and hence it is that monks are more subject to this disease than other people. . . . It is also frequent among New England men."[47] Potter cited many examples. "I once saw [this mania] in an *athletic* young man who was constantly laughing and crying because he was obliged to be seperated [sic] from his *sweet-heart* for 3 weeks." The prescribed cure was a diet of bread and water, cold baths, a hard bed and a "massive dose" of calomel. The permanent cure, he admitted, was "matrimony."[48] At least two hours a week Potter led his students to the infirmary to match the lecture

---

[43]Notebook, Charles McGill, 1827, no pagination; Dunglison, *The Medical Student*, 154-166. These courses are also described in the annual catalogues.

[44]Notebook, Thomas J. McGill, "Notes on Lectures," 1833-1834, no pagination.

[45]Notebook, Samuel Mainster, "Notes on the Lectures of Dr. Potter," 1827-1828, 27.

[46]Notebook, anon., "Notes on Potter," no date, 113.

[47]*Ibid.*, 109, 123-125; Notebook, Johannis Bowie, "Notes," no date, 139.

[48]Notebook, Samuel Mainster, "Notes on the Lectures of Dr. Potter," 1827-1828, 90-91.

material with diagnosis, therapy and observable results. When he died in 1844, William Power and Samuel Chew assumed the course, eliminating much of Potter's theory, expanding the clinical assignments and bringing into use the stethoscope which Potter had ridiculed as a "conjuring horn."[49]

Chemistry was a routine course in general science, a sort of introduction to more important fields. Students seldom worked in the laboratories themselves, but watched the demonstrations of the popular professors, Elisha DeButts and W. E. A. Aiken. The University claimed to have chemical apparatus which was "the most complete and splendid in the United States."[50]

The course in *materia medica* literally meant the materials of medicine, but it also included general therapeutics, chemical properties, the manufacture of drugs and the use of surgical instruments. During the first twenty years Samuel Baker taught the course, covering narcotics, tonics, aromatics, astringents, emetics, cathartics and diuretics, and proceeding to methods of bleeding, treatment of hemorrhage and methods of surgery.[51] In the 1830's Robley Dunglison occupied the chair, placing such emphasis on hygiene that the University claimed to be the first American school to teach the subject.[52] Samuel G. Baker, George Miltenberger, William E. A. Aiken, Samuel Chew and Edward Warren subsequently taught the course, each adding his own emphasis and interest. The Maryland professors generally maintained a well-balanced interest in chemistry, refusing to embrace the extreme herbalism which hampered American pharmacy in other schools.

The obstetrics course, taught for so many years by Professor Hall, was never popular. Actually it was considered daring to teach the subject at all in the early part of the century, for the professor was still called a "male midwife," and midwives obtained most of the cases until after the Civil War. At first the course was taught by lectures, illustrations and manikins, but in 1838 the University was among the earliest institutions to allow students to attend and participate in deliveries at the infirmary. Hall's real love was

[49]Donaldson, "A Physician's Note-Book," *Weekly Gazette*, 22 November 1873; *Catalogue*, 1845-1846, 10.

[50]*Baltimore American*, 1 November 1819; *Catalogue*, 1839-1840, 6; *Federal Gazette*, 24 March, 1824; *Baltimore American*, 31 August 1840; *Baltimore Clipper*, 28 June 1841.

[51]Notebook, Thomas Duval, 1842-1843, no pagination; Notebook, Thomas Munroe, 1827-1828, no pagination.

[52]*Federal Gazette*, 30 May 1833; *Catalogue*, 1846-1847, 8.

medical jurisprudence and at least half of his lectures concerned the laws of marriage, abortion, poisons, quarantine, sanitation and the detection of violence. In the 1850's Professor R. H. Thomas brought the course more up to date with an emphasis on gynecology and pediatrics.[53]

Finally came the glamorous, horrifying course in surgery. Davidge, Gibson and Pattison first taught the subject at Maryland, but after 1830 it was dominated by imperious Nathan Ryno Smith. The course dealt with the care of wounds, inflammations, burns and ulcers which were beyond the theories and remedies of medicine. Increasingly, though still as a last resort, surgeons attempted to cure internal ailments such as tumors and kidney stones. At least once a week, in addition to lectures, the students attended the operating theater to watch the master perform, and during the week they followed him on his rounds through the infirmary to hear him explain the results. Surgery was probably not as progressive at Maryland as many believed, but Smith's personality, his dexterity and his speed —essential for a surgeon before anesthesia—his willingness to adopt new procedures and his spectacular successes made it seem the most dramatic course of all. Smith insisted that pathology was the basis of surgery; in the 1830's he adopted the new procedure of tying instead of cauterizing blood vessels, and in the 1850's he was quick to adopt the newly discovered anesthesia. Always his students were amused by his fetish for cleanliness.[54]

Student Life

The main building, Davidge Hall, dominated the University neighborhood before the Civil War, and the green lawn and tall oak trees were almost enough to make a campus. The professors regretted the necessity of putting a fence around the building, but remembering the earlier mob actions, they yielded to prudence,

[53]*Catalogue,* 1838-1839, 6; *Catalogue,* 1846-1847, 6.
[54]Notebook, Lewis W. Knight, "Notes on Professor N. R. Smith's Lectures on Surgery," 1866-1867; Thomas J. McGill, "Notes on Lectures," 1833-1834; Samuel Mainster, "Notes on Lectures of N. R. Smith," 1827-1828; *Federal Gazette,* 22 October 1817; Samuel Clagget Chew, "Address Commemorative of Professor Nathan Ryno Smith . . .," *Maryland Medical Journal,* III (September, 1878), 407-431.

first erecting a high iron railing and later a 10-foot brick wall. Still, from the portico of the building one could see over the wall, and as late as 1840 the vista was clear to the harbor. The unfinished blank space above the portico was intended to be filled by a relief frieze with a medical motif. In the trees behind the main building was the museum, plain and unpretentious. Diagonally across Lombard and Greene Streets was the handsome hospital building, with small trees lining its sidewalk.[55]

The southwest was always a neglected area of Baltimore, and as the neighborhood grew it became second-rate, occupied with boarding houses, livery stables, factories and railroad repair shops. The nuns in the hospital became fearful of walking into town alone.[56] Ever since—at least until the urban renewal projects of the 1960's—the University has been blighted by its surroundings and apparently unaware of the importance of environment in establishing an academic atmosphere.

Since there were no dormitories, students found rooms in the nearby boarding houses. A few stayed with relatives, and six or eight lived in the infirmary; but from October until March the neighborhood was overrun with student boarders. Frequently the school catalogues listed "approved" boarding houses, with those of Mrs. Norman, Mrs. Buckley and Mrs. Pollett among the ten or twenty usually on the list. Extremely expensive by the standards of other cities, room and meals cost from three to four dollars a week, with three students in a room and firewood available at extra cost. Privies were behind the houses.[57]

Costly board plus high tuition often drove students to frantic financial calculations which they sometimes compiled to the last quarter of a cent. "My supply of money from home being limited," wrote one student, "I boarded my self, while in college, living very cheaply on roast potatoes, pudding and milk."[58] The account of Thomas McGill in 1833 was typical and revealed much about the kind of life he led:[59]

[55]*Baltimore American*, 25 October 1820; Charles Varle, *Complete View of Baltimore* . . . (Baltimore, 1833), 24-28; *Baltimore Clipper*, 30 October 1839; *Baltimore Sun*, 5 January 1849.

[56]Father John DuBois to Granville Sharp Pattison, 10 May 1822, archives of St. Joseph's College, Emmitsburg, Maryland.

[57]*Catalogue*, 1846-1847, 16; *Catalogue*, 1848-1849, 13.

[58]Cited in Isaac Newton Donfork, *Life of Nathan Smith Davis, 1817-1904* (Chicago, 1907), 33.

[59]Notebook, Thomas J. McGill, "Notes on Lectures," 1833-1834, no pagination.

Rail Road	2.50
Lecture tickets, Infirmary, Anatomy	135.00
Books. Medical. Owned 6; bought 6 new	19.65
Books. Shakespeare, Thompson's Poems, Spectator, Novel, Cooper's Poems, Album of Poems, Cooper's Poems, Novel, Misc. books	9.85
Board [listed in part in four places]	55.00
Cane Couch	.43
Chair	1.50
Plates	.75
Wood and candles [listed four places]	4.15
Candy [listed three places]	.25
Tobacco [listed seven places]	1.37½
Postage [listed four places]	.82½
Clothes, Umbrella, Gloves, Thimble, etc.	16.00
Quills and Pencil [listed three places]	.67¼
Theatre	1.00
Museum	.25
Lost at Whist	3.31¼
Steel Pins	.37½
Knife	1.25
Sundries	6.60
Other [illegible]	8.50
Total for Year	271.23

Able to lose at whist and to buy novels, McGill was apparently better off than most students. Thomas Duval's budget in 1842 totaled $261.50 and was similar to McGill's except that regularly every two weeks he underlined a mysterious item *"Comfort .12½"* and at the end of the term he wrote "COMFORT .37½."[60]

The medical students were a remarkably mature group of men. In contrast to most college undergraduates of the nineteenth century, the ante-bellum Maryland students were characterized by a high seriousness that sometimes bordered on the dull. Except for a casual remark that "good manners" were requisite for success, the school catalogues never mentioned deportment, and in more than fifty years the faculty dealt with specific disciplinary problems only six times.[61] The nuns regularly complained that the resident students stayed out too late, but after investigation, the faculty scolded the boys only for working too late in the laboratory. "The fact

[60]Notebook, Thomas W. Duval, 1842-1843, no pagination.
[61]*Catalogue*, 1848-1849, 5; Minutes of the Faculty, 13 May 1813; 4 February 1828; 9 October 1843; 2 October 1860; Minutes of the Executive Committee of the Trustees, 7 January 1827; 6 December 1828.

of being a student at the University," said a Baltimore newspaper, "is considered by our best society, as a sufficient passport to their homes and hospitality."[62] When the legislature's investigating committee made its highly critical report on the University in 1826, it added a special encomium to the students:

> We cannot permit this occasion to pass without expressing . . . gratification at the uncommonly respectable appearance of the students, their devoted attention to the lectures, their orderly and respectable behaviour to the professors, and their decorous and gentlemanly deportment towards each other.[63]

Each university breeds its distinct traditions and atmosphere, and somehow Maryland's spirit was one of serious dedication which may have stemmed in part from the commanding personalities of several remarkable professors, and in part from the students' keen awareness of standing at the frontiers of knowledge. In addition medical students were generally older and more career-minded than undergraduates. Perhaps the relatively isolated neighborhood was a contributing factor, while the high standards and fees undoubtedly kept the frivolous away.

The young gentlemen seemed to remain serious even when their fancies turned to love. The age was prudish and sentimental, and love was a strange and wonderful thing of pining and swooning, of blushes and stammers, of lady fair and dashing swain. Students—like Thomas McGill—seemed to buy books of romantic poetry instead of books of naughty jokes. As they listened to their professors drone on about leeches and dysentery, their minds soared outward, and they wrote in the margins of their lecture notes thoughts about the "tender sweetness" of their true love's heart or the "impassioned rapture" of their own. When Professor Potter spoke of the maladies of lovesickness they took copious notes.[64]

One story of love at Maryland is especially famous. Samuel Carr from South Carolina and William Martin from the Eastern Shore

[62]Minutes of the Executive Committee of the Trustees, 15 December 1828; *Federal Gazette*, 25 April 1823; also, Edward Warren, *A Doctor's Experiences in Three Continents* (Baltimore, 1885), 129.

[63]"Report of a Committee," *Journal of the House of Delegates of Maryland . . . 1825* (Annapolis, 1826), 309.

[64]Notebook, anon., "Dr. Davidge's Lectures," no date, on cover; Notebook, Thomas J. Davis, "Notes from the Lectures of Dr. Nathaniel Potter," 1825-1826, on cover; Notebook, Alexander Stewart, "Notes," 1829-1830, *passim;* Notebook, Samuel Mainster, "Notes on Lectures of N. R. Smith," 1827-1828, no pagination.

of Maryland were best friends and roommates at the medical school until they both fell in love with Dr. Davidge's 14-year-old daughter Mary. During Christmas vacation, when Carr was in South Carolina, Martin learned that absence had affected Mary's heart; she was in love with his rival. Distraught, Martin wrote to his roommate suggesting foul play, and demanding that he be quick to pay what he owed on the bill they had just received for wood. Carr replied with insulting condescension, as only a victor can. The injury and insult were too much to bear and Martin demanded a duel with pistols. Early in the morning on February 2, 1828, the roommates met on the dueling grounds at Bladensburg. The South Carolinian was an experienced duelist and offered to pay for the wood on the spot, but his lovesick opponent insisted that the duel go on and was killed. Great crowds gathered when the body was returned to Baltimore and on to his home in Cambridge. Death did not end the story, for while most people sympathized with Carr, the University felt compelled to expel him, and this was more than Mary could stand. She eloped with the young man and they fled to Louisiana. Five years later they returned to Baltimore and Carr finished his degree at the University only to die a few years later. Mary, still young and beautiful, married David Dudley Field, a famous American jurist. The tale was in the grandest romantic tradition.[65]

As in European schools, student maturity appeared—and was doubtless produced by the wide degree of independence which the faculty allowed its charges. The catalogues said "it is urged" instead of "it is required," and the professors promised to "help the student to learn for himself" instead of promising to serve up knowledge on a platter. The faculty seldom recorded attendance, but classes were always full; all drills and all examinations except the final one were optional, and the students begged for more. Frequently the professors offered extra lectures at night which were "entirely optional," or they promised that, if invited, they would meet the members of the class "in small clubs" to give them additional attention.[66] From the first, one of the finest rooms in the college building, located to

[65]*Federal Gazette,* 4 February 1828; Eugene Fauntleroy Cordell, *University of Maryland, 1807-1907* . . ., 2 vols. (New York, 1907), I, 173-175.
[66]*Catalogue, 1845-1846,* 10; *Catalogue, 1846-1847,* 12; *Catalogue, 1848-1849,* 13; *Catalogue, 1850-1851,* 11; *Catalogue, 1855-1856,* 6; *Catalogue, 1858-1859,* 6; *Catalogue, 1862-1863,* 8.

the right of the entrance, was fitted as a student lounge with free stationery, up-to-date European and American medical journals and a library of about 600 books for students to use as they wished. During the 1840's free newspapers were added, current books were placed on sale and a yearly charge of $5 was made for use of the lounge.[67] On their own the students organized study groups, with election into the Rush Medical Club being especially coveted.[68] Professor Dunglison, after he left Maryland, cited the University's voluntary quiz clubs as an ideal to be copied elsewhere:

> By mutual interrogation, the topics, that have been discussed by the different professors, are constantly reviewed, and re-impressed upon the minds of the members,—not, simply, a short time before the examination for the degree, but throughout the whole of the session.[69]

Even the length of the term and the daily schedule were student responsibilities to a degree seldom known in American education. According to the charter, attendance upon the lectures of any three professors constituted the minimum requirements for a year's work, but the announcements "urged" students to attend all classes and by the 1830's no one dreamed it possible to do less. Most of the time there were seven courses, counting the laboratory, and students registered for the same course for the first two years. Professors sometimes varied their lectures in alternate years—emphasizing, for example, febrile diseases one year and nervous diseases the next— but essentially each year the course was complete and students were expected to repeat it in full. Professor Chew urged students to spend the first year merely listening to the lectures and concentrating on the laboratory work; the second year they should take verbatim notes on lectures and spend as much time as possible in the clinic.[70]

Usually two years of classes were necessary to receive the degree. At first classes began late in October and continued simply "until the course is finished." By 1812 the term was set at four months, but during the 1840's the faculty allowed students to attend for four or six months, as they wished, for the same cost and the same credits:

[67]*Baltimore American*, 25 October 1820; *Catalogue*, 1844-1845, 16.

[68]Notebook, Joseph James O'Donnell, "Notes," 1853-1854, no pagination; Cordell, *Historical Sketch*, 154.

[69]Dunglison, *The Medical Student*, 181; also, *Federal Gazette*, 18 September 1826.

[70]Chew, *Lectures on Medical Education*, 80.

In extending their term of Lectures to *six months,* the Faculty have been governed by a desire to increase the opportunities for their Students in acquiring a knowledge of their Profession—while for the few who cannot conveniently spend six months in the city, they will consider an attendance during the last four months as equivalent to a full course.[71]

Subsequently fixed at four and a half months, from mid-October until early March, the term was one of the longest of any medical college. About 10 percent of the students accepted the "recommendation" of the faculty to return for a third year of courses after they had received their degrees.[72]

As an example of a student's daily routine, Thomas McGill's schedule in 1833 was typical. He awoke late—apparently a custom then in the medical school. At nine o'clock on Monday and Wednesday he followed Potter through the infirmary to observe the medical cases, and on Tuesday and Thursday he followed Smith to inspect the surgical cases. At ten o'clock, Monday through Friday, he attended the surgery lectures; at eleven he went to *materia medica;* at twelve to theory and practice; and at one o'clock he went to anatomy. Since the dinner break lasted two hours, from two to four, he could spend at least an hour reading. At four o'clock McGill attended obstetrics; at five he went to chemistry; and after six he spent at least an hour in the dissecting laboratory. The building was heated after 1817, but until gas lighting came in 1848 night work had to be done by lamps. Students also had parallel reading to do—one professor recommended spending two hours of reading for each hour of lecture. On Saturdays, somewhat irregularly, the professors held oral examinations, designed, they said, "to inspire emulation and expose ignorance." Almost everyone went to church on Sunday. Except for a week at Christmas, there was no holiday; classes continued on New Year's day as usual.[73]

Two tests were required for a degree—a thesis and a final examination. In Europe, where the M.D. was a graduate degree, the thesis had merit, for while medicine was in an infant stage of cataloguing

[71]*Federal Gazette,* 21 October 1807; *Baltimore American,* 26 July 1811; *Catalogue,* 1840-1841, 6.

[72]Norwood, *Medical Education in the United States,* 402; Dunglison, *The Medical Student,* 307-308; *Catalogue,* 1849-1850, 3-5; *Catalogue,* 1853-1854, 17.

[73]Notebook, Thomas J. McGill, "Notes on Lectures," 1833-1834, no pagination; also, Notebook, Joseph James O'Donnell, 1853-1854, no pagination; Dunglison, *The Medical Student,* 139-145; *Federal Gazette,* 22 October 1817; *Catalogue,* 1848-1849, 4; Notebook, John S. C. Monkur, 1848-1849, 39; *Catalogue,* 1848-1849, 12; *Catalogue,* 1858-1859, 6.

and reporting, student observations provided original contributions to science. The early Maryland theses were formidable—hundred-page essays on some disease, symptom or anatomical phenomenon, often beautifully illustrated with hand drawn sketches. They were written in Latin since this was also a test of the student's general education. The author of the best one received a gold medal. As medical knowledge increased, and as school time became more valuable, the thesis became more of an obstacle than a test or contribution. In 1817 the publication requirement was dropped, after 1824 the thesis could be written in English, and after 1850 students could substitute a clinical case study.[74]

As the importance of the thesis declined, that of the examination grew. Since the University of Maryland was the only institution in the country where the degree automatically carried a license to practice without further questions from the state board, the faculty took its examining responsibility seriously. Students were never allowed to forget the ordeal which lay ahead, and physicians seldom forgot the trauma which lay behind. Describing the experience, Professor Dunglison wrote that "the students frequently lost their composure, and sometimes their dinner as well."[75]

It cost $20 for permission to take the examination. At the end of the second year of study a week was set apart during which from early morning until late at night the candidates, one at a time, were examined. The nervous young man was invited to sit at the head of a large table around which the entire faculty was assembled. Slowly at first, and then faster, the professors fired questions. After stammering answers for an hour, the lad was invited to leave the room while the professors discussed his performance and decided his fate by secret ballot. A majority vote was necessary to pass; a tie qualified the student for a second exam. Each year three or four students failed, and their names were published along with those of the graduates. Some were allowed to return for a third year of study, while others were advised to find another profession.[76]

Commencement, which was as festive as the examinations were grim, finally came early in April. The night before the event the

[74]*Baltimore American*, 26 August 1812; Cordell, *Historical Sketch*, 47; *Catalogue*, 1850-1851, 14; see theses in Health Sciences Library, Baltimore.

[75]Dunglison, *The Medical Student*, 12, 311.

[76]*Catalogue*, 1846-1847, 13; *Baltimore American*, 5 March 1860; Notebook, Samuel Mainster, "Notes on Lectures," 1827-1828, inside cover; Notebook, Joseph James O'Donnell, 1853-1854, no pagination; Norwood, *Medical Education in the United States*, 406.

faculty gave a banquet for the graduates. John Pendleton Kennedy attended only one of these affairs while he was president of the University. "I had ordered the carriage to come for me at 10 o'clock," he wrote, but "at that hour . . . supper was not yet announced."[77] On the next morning crowds gathered to watch the young men parade. It was a gala social occasion, attracting not only relatives and friends, but the fashionable elite of the city as well. During the first decades the commencements were attended by "hundreds" of people crowded into the University's largest lecture hall which was decorated with banners and white muslin. By the 1850's "thousands" were attending the affairs, held in one of the nearby churches or in the great hall of the Mechanics' Institute. According to the newspapers the assemblage was "mostly ladies" who threw kisses and "showers of bouquets" to the graduates.[78]

A band led the procession, "playing delicious music," followed by the faculty of all the colleges in the University, and then the graduates. During the 1820's there was a special round of applause when Professor Davidge, "father of the University," came down the aisle, and a roar of approbation when Professor Pattison appeared. After prayers and speeches, one or two honorary degrees were awarded, not to potential benefactors, but to worthy physicians the world over whom the faculty desired to recognize. Finally came "the moment of hushed excitement" as the candidates came forward for their degrees. The president of the University addressed them:

> Gentlemen, in the public bestowal and acceptance of this diploma, the authorities of the University recognize an obligation on your part to uphold the honor of your profession, indulging in the employment of no secret remedies nor unprofessional practice, but devoting all your capacities and discoveries to the good of your fellow man in the advancement of medical science. I ask you, gentlemen, in the presence of these witnesses here assembled, do you admit this obligation?[79]

They answered the question affirmatively and received their Latin-inscribed diplomas. After more music and prayers, cheers and a recessional, there were more kisses and bouquets.

[77] John Pendleton Kennedy, Journal, 16 March 1850, Kennedy Papers, Peabody Library, Baltimore.
[78] Local newspapers regularly carried full accounts of these affairs. See, for example, *Baltimore American*, 25 April 1823; *Baltimore Sun*, 12 March 1841; *Baltimore American*, 5 March 1860.
[79] John Pendleton Kennedy, Journal, 19 March 1850; 9 March 1852.

A hard path lay ahead for the fledgling physician, for medicine was an unappreciated and underpaid profession in the nineteenth century. His status hardly equalled that of a graduate from a classical college, and for many years he would be fortunate to earn $600 annually from his practice.[80] Approximately 3,150 students received the M.D. degree from the University before the Civil War.[81] While most of them lived respectable lives, a few were outstanding. The *Dictionary of American Biography*, the most comprehensive list of America's greatest men, includes some 15,000 Americans; 340 of these are Marylanders of whom 160 reached college age between 1810 and 1865, and 19 were graduates of the University of Maryland College of Medicine. One Marylander in two thousand attended the University; but of the greatest Marylanders, one in ten was a graduate.[82]

Many graduates, probably a third, became planters, merchants, politicians, writers or clergymen instead of practicing physicians. The ante-bellum M.D. degree was in large measure the equivalent of the modern bachelor of science degree and was taken by men who wanted a scientific education which was unavailable in the classically-oriented colleges. Of Maryland's nineteen most outstanding graduates, nine made their mark in nonmedical fields. Bartholomew Fussell was an abolitionist; R. H. Graves was a missionary in China; Francis Chatard and Charles Krauth were clergymen; William Hand Browne and C. S. Davis became historians; John W. Palmer was a poet; Lunsford P. Yandell was a geologist; and John Wesley Davis became Speaker of the United States House of Representatives.

Most graduates, however, did practice medicine either full time or as a sideline to another occupation. By 1860 Maryland had one doctor for every 628 people, one of the highest ratios in the country, and clearly above the present ratio of physicians to population.[83] Of the graduates most distinguished as physicians, each was a medical professor, a position that was unquestionably the top of the medical profession. Thomas Buckler was a pioneer in the treatment of tuberculosis; Aaron Friedenwald was a pioneer in ophthalmology;

[80]Shryock, *Development of Modern Medicine*, 265-266.
[81]Cordell, *University of Maryland*, II, Appendix.
[82]Allen Johnson and Dumas Malone eds., *Dictionary of American Biography*, 22 vols. (New York, 1946). In addition, before 1865 there was one graduate of the law school, Brantz Mayer. Since 1865, all schools combined, including those at College Park, have produced 15 entries.
[83]*Population of the United States in 1860; Compiled from the Original Returns of the Eighth Census . . .* (Washington, 1864), 217.

Theodatus Garlick worked in plastic surgery; Henry Wilson in gynecology; James C. Palmer was Surgeon General of the Navy; and Horatio Gates Jameson was one of the first surgeons to use animal ligatures. Roberts Bartholow, James Cabell, H. W. Baxley and John D. Godman were authors of technical articles and medical textbooks.

The graduates left with a feeling of fondness for the University. The excitement of scientific research and the subsequent difficulties of practice seemed to make of the medical school a particularly glowing ivory tower. College loyalty was not yet organized by school songs and colors, by professional alumni directors and reunions or by publicized football teams; but graduates cherished the old alma mater with the sentimentality they bestowed upon the ladies they loved. Old classmates wrote of weeping when they met together to recall bygone college days.[84] One graduate wrote in 1837 as if the University were already mellowed by the centuries:

> For the old University, I inherited an ardent and devoted attachment which has increased with every hour of my life. . . . This venerable temple of science is regarded by [the graduate] with the same affection, and cherished with the same endearment as the place of their birth or the scenes of their early attachment. Under the beautiful dome they have spent many hours of happiness.[85]

The Professor's Life

The professors at the University tended to outshine their students. Thirteen of the thirty ante-bellum professors are listed in the *Dictionary of American Biography,* almost as many as from all the alumni. Never since in American education, and in almost no other field of scholarship, has a group of professors been so genuinely the elite of their profession. Because of the prestige, high income and generally happy faculty relationships at Maryland, the University could attract to its staff almost any physician in the United States. Of the thirty regular professors before 1860, twenty came from

[84]Notebook, "Lectures of John S. C. Monkur," 1844-1845, no pagination; also, *Federal Gazette,* 23 March 1833; Warren, *A Doctor's Experiences,* 356 and *passim.*

[85]Samuel George Baker, *Introductory Lecture, Delivered before the Medical Class of the University, November, 1837* (Baltimore, 1837), 4-5; also, Richard Wilmot Hall to Franklin J. Smith, 22 September 1832, Hall Papers, Maryland Historical Society, Baltimore.

outside Maryland and three from abroad. While there was pressure to choose local men to fill the chairs, and while friendships sometimes resulted in mediocre men obtaining posts, in general the faculty filled vacancies with deliberation and wisdom. As part of the faculty's recruiting program, it customarily dispatched one of its members to attend several lectures of an able professor elsewhere. If the report were favorable, the faculty presented the prospect with an offer.[86]

Although a professor lectured only an hour a day, the University consumed most of his time, at least during the five-month term. The lectures themselves were serious matters, far different from the holding-a-book type of instruction which most teachers provided in undergraduate colleges. Each professor assumed that a lecture should combine up-to-date research with literary polish, that it should be written out, memorized and delivered with oratorical flourish. At least twice weekly throughout the school year, the professor toured the infirmary. Each took his turn, more or less, to serve as general administrator of the infirmary or as dean of the college. Most professors spent at least an hour a week, and some an hour or more each day, conducting quiz sessions and providing individual instruction. "The amount of midnight oil consumed in preparing for my daily duties can hardly be estimated," wrote one new professor who could find time for nothing else.[87]

In addition to formal teaching duties, the professors felt the ever-present academic expectation to do research and publish their findings. Most of them found research to be an opportunity rather than a pressure, for promotions were not involved and the frontiers of knowledge were painfully evident. Still, research was a major criterion in the selection of a professor, and was one of his unspecified duties. Maryland's publication record was remarkable. In addition to pioneering in operations and therapies, the 30 faculty members published 46 monographs, 14 textbooks, at least 390 scholarly articles and edited 14 medical journals. The figures averaged two books and thirteen articles for each man. Seldom, if ever, did this kind of writing produce royalties for the author.[88]

After his teaching and administrative and research duties, the

[86]Minutes of the Faculty, 14 November 1842 and *passim;* also, Cordell, *Historical Sketch,* 107.

[87]Warren, *A Doctor's Experiences,* 245-246.

[88]John R. Quinan, *Medical Annals of Baltimore from 1608 to 1880* . . . (Baltimore, 1884), 55-185.

professor was free to practice. Most of the professors devoted about half their time to private practice, and most were able to double their academic incomes. The public recognized them as outstanding physicians, and much of their practice took the form of consultation in difficult cases with their former students.

With an average of 200 students paying $20 for each course, professors averaged about $4,000 annually from their academic duties. Actually the incomes showed considerable variation, ranging to almost twice the average for men like Davidge, Pattison and Smith. Some students took obstetrics, institutes or chemistry only once, but many returned to take anatomy, surgery or practice for a second or third time. Also, the $5 entrance fee and the $20 examination fee, generally used for repairs and equipment, sometimes were divided by the faculty as a bonus to its most valuable members. Occasionally the professors charged fees for special coaching sessions, and by the 1850's many of them accepted students as apprentices during the summer months, charging each one up to $100. Professor Chew, during one year, had forty such apprentices.[89] In at least one case a professor was appointed with the provision that he return $500 annually from his lecture fees to the general University fund; and in another case a professor was considered a liability and was paid $10,000 to resign.[90]

Even more than the students, the professors appreciated the University of Maryland as an ivory tower. One noted "the incredible joy" of continuing his own education, and another glorified in being "the idol of an enthusiastic class, the pet of an admiring community."[91] Still another professor, just before he died, wrote touchingly of his association with the University and the appeal of academic life:

My connection with the University formed the realization of professional hopes and plans long cherished. To feel secure in a position where I could pursue the profession as an ennobling science, not as a necessary trade, where there was a constant stimulus given to self-culture and improvement, to constant fresh study and daily progress in the search after truth, to be entrusted with the responsible and noble mission of interpreting and disseminating this truth; finally, to have the conviction from the friendly and cheering

[89]Catalogue, 1849-1850, 13; also, Catalogue, 1858-1859, 14.

[90]Minutes of the Faculty, 13 March 1858; 16 April 1839; also, 14 November 1842; 16 June 1859; 20 January 1860.

[91]Notebook, Louis W. Knight, "Notes on Professor N. R. Smith's Lectures," 1866-1867, 176; Warren, A Doctor's Experiences, 356.

intercourse of colleagues and the respectful demeanour of the classes that I had the approbation and confidence of both, and that my efforts to be useful and give satisfaction were not in vain, all this made my situation dear to me. My chair was the ruling interest of my professional life, that in which all my pleasures, hopes and ambition centered, and my determination to resign it involves the virtual and formal adieu to all lingering hope of future usefulness.[92]

The University of Maryland prospered through its own morale, and through the sense of usefulness it gave its associates. That was the proof of its worth.

[92]William Power to the Medical Faculty, 5 January 1852, medical school archives, Baltimore; also, Cordell, *Historical Sketch,* 117.

6

The Maryland Agricultural College

While professional men created special professional schools to outflank the old-time colleges, American farmers also began to catch a vision of the benefits which a practical education might offer them. Indeed, in the changing world of the new telegraph, railroad and reaper, farmers faced the problem of keeping abreast of the times. In Europe intensive farming had long before forced farmers to learn scientific procedures and to build agricultural training schools. In America, as the once plentiful new farm land began to dwindle during the early nineteenth century, such farm leaders as Simeon DeWitt of New York, Jonathan B. Turner in Illinois, and Charles Benedict Calvert of Maryland, talked of the need for agricultural experimentation and agricultural schools. Pennsylvania chartered the first such institution in 1854, the Farmer's High School which later became Pennsylvania State University; in the following year Michigan chartered the institution that became Michigan State University; and in 1856 Maryland chartered the Maryland Agricultural College. These three institutions foreshadowed the Morrill Land-Grant Act of 1862 which eventually led to the establishment of sixty-five other agricultural and mechanical colleges. Today, of course, these institutions are far more than agricultural and mechanical. Most of them are among the nation's strongest educational establishments.

In Maryland, particularly, the founders of the college struggled over questions that long plagued the land-grant movement: Should the institution specialize in agricultural experimentation, or should it provide a scientific education for the aristocratic planter? Should it provide a genteel education inexpensively for the common man, or should it provide practical information about plowing and milking for the ordinary farmers throughout the state?

The Farmers' Plight

Just as Maryland was one of the first states to experience urban prosperity and create professional schools, so it was one of the first to experience "worn out" soil and agricultural depression. Tobacco had been the gold of Maryland, making eighteenth century Annapolis one of the richest cities on the Atlantic but also it depleted the soil of potash and nitrogen, and without plentiful livestock to replenish the soil with manure, tobacco prosperity slowly succumbed during the early nineteenth century to the virgin lands of the West. Tobacco prices declined from 20 cents a pound in 1810 to 5 cents in 1850, and land values dropped by half. One third of Maryland's young men were leaving the state by 1850, the slave population had declined by a third, and six rural counties possessed smaller populations than a half century before. "Ask those who have gone, or are going West, why they left or intend to leave their native hills," said one farmer, "and they will tell you 'the soil is wore out.'"[1]

The Maryland farmer was concerned especially to see his profession outstripped by rapid urban expansion. Businessmen were more prosperous than planters, skilled workers lived better than small farmers and factory workers earned more than farm hands.

[1]Avery O. Craven, *Soil Exhaustion as a Factor in the Agricultural History of Virginia and Maryland, 1606-1860* (Urbana, Ill., 1926), 120-160; Leland Griffith Worthington, "Forces Leading to the Establishment of the Maryland Agricultural College" (M. A. thesis, History, University of Maryland, 1933), 1-17; *American Farmer*, II (September 1822), 106-107.

The Maryland farmer was falling behind his city cousin and could not afford the luxuries of the budding industrial revolution. His influence, too, was declining, for while the state government had appropriated $15,000,000 from 1820 to 1855 for internal improvements, the farmer had wrested less than one-hundredth that amount from the government for agricultural improvements. The farmers' plight mystified the optimistic Americans of the mid-century.[2]

In their frustration many planters in the south Atlantic states blamed the central government and its tariff laws for their problems and demanded secession, but wiser men looked to scientific farming for the solution. This meant evolution from soil exploitation to intensive farming; it meant experimentation with new crops and fertilizers and the dissemination of knowledge; and it meant—even as in medicine and dentistry—the organization and professional education of the farmer. In the long run scientific farming only increased production so that, ironically, the cities benefited most with cheaper food. In the end, and contrary to the aims of their founders, agricultural colleges may have helped the farmer most by providing him with training for urban occupations.

Hard-pressed by the tobacco depression, Marylanders assumed the leadership in the movement for societies, fairs and publications to aid the farmer. The first agricultural society was organized by a Marylander in 1785 in Philadelphia; by 1850 there were 250 such societies scattered over the country, and by 1860 nearly 1,000. Rapidly they became focal points for the social and political life of isolated rural people, reflecting the farmers' changing struggles and aims. After the Civil War the societies concentrated on pricing, marketing and political problems; but the ante-bellum societies were primarily concerned with the technical problems of production, attempting to promote better farming methods by awarding prizes, sponsoring contests, conducting experiments and fostering lectures and publications about farm efficiency. Maryland societies took an active part in organizing the first agricultural fair in the District of Columbia in 1807. By the Civil War state, county and community fairs had become an American institution where farmers came to display their wares, to learn about the most successful techniques of their neighbors and to admire displays of new farm machinery. Probably the most important boost to scientific farming

[2]Percy Wells Bidwell and John I. Falconer, *History of Agriculture in the Northern United States, 1620-1860* (New York, 1941), 259-452; *American Farmer*, XI (February, 1856), 253.

came from the agricultural press which began in Georgetown in 1807, and reached its apogee in John S. Skinner's *American Farmer*. Growing up on a worn-out Calvert County tobacco plantation, Skinner moved to Baltimore in 1819 to found the journal which dominated its field for seventy years and was to become a major influence in the establishment of the Maryland Agricultural College.[3]

During the 1820's and 1830's the societies and journals crusaded for public schools rather than agricultural colleges. Since most farmers could scarcely read, they wanted free elementary education with lessons on farming introduced into the public schools. In Maryland a Somerset County planter, Littleton Dennis Teackle, served as the farmers' spokesman in the general assembly, where, in 1822, he introduced a resolution asking congress for federal lands to endow public schools. Two years later he sought state legislation to provide agricultural teachers in private academies.

Supported by petitions from a score of agricultural societies and by the agricultural press, Teackle, in 1826, demanded state-supported high schools combined with an experimental farm for every county of the state. As if to quiet him, the assembly passed the bill without appropriation, and appointed him the first state superintendent of education in the United States. Serving without salary and publishing reports at his personal expense, Teackle pled the cause of education generally and of agricultural education in particular. Vainly he begged for funds, but the legislature was too busy financing canals and railroads, most of which were destined for bankruptcy. Public schools and agricultural education were closely related in Maryland, and Teackle may have been the father of both.[4]

During the 1830's, with the public school movement seemingly a failure, the farm societies and journals concentrated upon other demands, almost pitiful in their modesty. For a time they were

---

[3]Vivian Doris Wiser, "The Movement for Agricultural Improvement in Maryland, 1785-1865" (Ph.D. thesis, History, University of Maryland, 1963); also, Wayne Caldwell Neely, *The Agricultural Fair* (New York, 1935); Albert Lowether Demaree, *The American Agricultural Press, 1819-1860* (New York, 1951), 23-28.

[4]Worthington, "Forces," 72-86; Wiser, "Agricultural Improvement," 220-223; *Journal of Proceedings of the House of Delegates of Maryland . . . 1822* (Annapolis, 1822), 11, 92-94; *Proceedings . . . 1824*, 61, 142; *Proceedings . . . 1835*, 125; *Proceedings . . . 1836*, 242, 290, 399, 410, 454; *Proceedings . . . 1837*, 29, 108; *Laws of Maryland . . . 1825*, Chap. 162; *House and Senate Documents of Maryland, 1828-1836*, especially *Report of the Select Committee Appointed to Enquire into the Expediency of Establishing an Agriculutral School and Pattern Farm in Each of the Counties of This State* (Annapolis, 1835).

interested in the creation of a state geological office, headed by a man who would map the state with particular attention to analyzing its soils. Farmers imagined the discovery of some magical kind of soil or fertilizer which would improve their crops, and businessmen backed the appropriation of $2,000 annually because they wanted maps to assist in the laying out of new railroad routes. The railroad men got their maps, and when the state geologist discovered deposits of marl a fad developed to use it as fertilizer; but the chief ones to profit were the railroads which hauled it.[5]

During the 1840's a state chemist was appointed, with instructions to spend a month in each county analyzing soil for local farmers and educating them in the crops and fertilizers best suited to their particular fields. Dr. James Higgins, a hard-working graduate of the University's College of Medicine, could not talk to every farmer in the state, and he did not revolutionze agriculture. He used his office largely to convince the farmers that what they needed was an agricultural college. So far, talk was outrunning action, but meanwhile some of the wealthy planters were beginning to become interested from a slightly different point of view.[6]

The Planters' Solution

As usual in a declining and frustrated economy, Maryland's richer planters became more powerful while the poorer farmers either slid into marginal existence or migrated to the West. Planters bought up the latters' lands and slaves to assume an increasingly dominant leadership over the farm community. They read the new farm journals, experimented with rotating crops and invested in the new farm machinery. While the planter could not keep pace with the businessman, his ascendency over the small farmer, plus a moderate improvement in farm prices during the 1850's, gave him renewed confidence in his ability to solve the farmers' plight.

In Baltimore a small group of gentlemen planters created a new

[5]Worthington, "Forces," 92-98; Wiser, "Agricultural Improvement," 212-253.
[6]Worthington, "Forces," 88-132; *Fifth Agricultural Report of the State Chemist to the House of Delegates . . .* (Annapolis, 1856), 11; *American Farmer*, IV (November, 1837), 227; XI (February, 1856), 241-243; XIII (May, 1858), 362. For similar movements in other states, Alfred Charles True, *History of Agricultural Education in the United States, 1789-1925* (Washington, 1929), 23-94.

kind of agricultural society designed, somewhat condescendingly, to educate their rustic neighbors. The Farmers' Club, located on Baltimore Street, boasted liveried lackeys in its dining room, a fine library and a lounge where members might "partake of the intellectual and physical conveniences of the Club." With membership limited "to *intelligent* farmers," no one with overalls or muddy shoes was welcome.[7] By 1848 the club regulars seemed to be in substantial agreement that an agricultural college and experiment station were necessary. To emphasize their new purposefulness, the club changed its name to the Maryland State Agricultural Society and sent invitations to selected other planters who might become interested:

> This is the time, gentlemen of talents, influence and wealth, for you to act—let me entreat you to come to the rescue; alleviate the misfortunes of the laboring farmer—save your State from poverty and disgrace, and immortalize your own names as benefactors of Maryland.[8]

The best-remembered of the group—and certainly the most justly so—was Charles Benedict Calvert who not only gave the old planters' club its cause and led the crusade for public support, but also supervised the building of the college which eventually emerged and became its acting president. Descended from the Lords Baltimore, the son of a wealthy planter and an aristocratic Belgian mother, handsome, debonaire and charismatic, Calvert was a patrician in the finest Jeffersonian tradition. Graduating from the University of Virginia at 19, he returned to Riverdale in Prince George's County to take over his father's estate. The plantation mansion, which still stands about a mile from the institution he founded, then looked out upon marble terraces, fountains, arbors, lakes, pagodas and immense greenhouses. His 2,200-acre hay and dairy farm became nationally famous for its use of machinery, fertilizers, irrigation and experimental crops, but his agrarian interests took the direction of philanthropy as well as of scientific experimentation. Typically, within a year he might donate a score of prize bulls to neighboring farmers who agreed to breed and care for them according to his instructions.

From time to time Calvert sat in the state legislature, and in

[7]*American Farmer,* I (September, 1845), 82; III (February, 1848), 246-247.

[8]*Ibid.,* IV (August, 1848), 44. A similar announcement appeared four years later, "Letter Sent Out to the Public by Chas. B. Calvert," handbill dated 30 January 1852, Calvert Papers, McKeldin Library, College Park.

1861 he went to Congress, but love of the farm remained his only political loyalty. His instincts were with the planter South before the Civil War and he particularly opposed abolitionist activity; but he also loved the Union and, after the South's secession, he believed it was in the best interest of Maryland farmers to remain loyal. For many years the president of the Maryland State Agricultural Society, he was also a leader of the powerful United States Agricultural Society and active in the creation of the United States Department of Agriculture.[9]

Other founders of the Maryland Agricultural College were of the same type. Many of them dabbled in politics, most were wealthy and almost all boasted proud old Maryland names. From the Eastern Shore came James T. Earle, William T. Goldsborough, John C. Groome and Samuel Hambleton; from the southern counties were John S. Skinner, Nicholas B. Worthington, Robert Bowie, John H. Sothoron, Allen Bowie Davis and William N. Mercer; from near Baltimore came Ramsay McHenry, Charles Carroll, John Merryman and Thomas Swann; and from the western counties came John O. Wharton, Thomas Perry, J. Dixon Roman and George R. Dennis. After Calvert, these men, remarkably evenly distributed over the state, were almost equally prominent as planners, early trustees and large stockholders in the new institution.[10]

Conflicting ideals and motivations buffeted the planters who set out to ennoble agriculture by the creation of a college, but their conscious, and probably their paramount motivation was philanthropic—to elevate the ordinary farmer to prosperity and cultural refinement. The upper class planters were convinced that the rural masses were composed of "the indolent, the apathetic and the ignorant"; that except for a fortunate few, the once "noble farmer has become a 'clodhopper.' " What the people needed, therefore, was special scientific training which would help them to earn a living, plus ample moral and religious training to develop their character and manners.[11]

In the planters' attitude were notes of democracy and of arro-

[9]Curtis W. Garrison, "Charles Benedict Calvert," *Dictionary of American Biography*, eds. Allen Johnson and Dumas Malone, 22 vols. (New York, 1946), III, 427-428; *Country Gentleman*, X (3 September 1857), 161-162; X (10 June 1858), 361-362; Wiser, "Agricultural Improvement," 212-493 *passim*.

[10]*Report of the Register of the Maryland Agricultural College, to the Board of Trustees* . . . (Baltimore, 1858); *First Circular of the Maryland Agricultural College* (Baltimore, 1859); *American Farmer*, (1848-1860), *passim*.

[11]*American Farmer*, X (October, 1854), 97-101.

gance. While they planned, the founders never imagined that their sons would attend the institution. They assumed that the college would be patterned after the "manual labor" agricultural schools of Europe where the underprivileged paid their way by working on the experimental farm, and after the Mechanics' Institute of Baltimore, designed by businessmen to convert the city poor into skilled workers.[12] Occasionally a farmer expressed doubts about the proposed institution, suggesting that the poor wanted public schools instead of technical "colleges" which would set them apart, but the founders seemed to think they knew better what was good for their neighbors.[13] "It remains to be seen how far the mass of the farmers of Maryland will second [our] arduous efforts and sacrifices," said one report on the college. "Will the farmers of Maryland for whose benefit it is especially designed, take hold of the work and carry it to completion, or will they leave it to the charities of those, who without any personal interest, look only to the noble ends it is to accomplish."[14] The planters did sacrifice much and selflessly. The Agricultural College was not the result of a movement of the small farmers, but of a movement for them and one which the founders considered democratic.

A few planters expressed less democratic attitudes, desiring to perpetuate their own positions rather than to elevate the poor. A college would make the masses "obedient to those placed over them, and . . . likewise cheerful and happy under a sense of their peculiar advantages." Moreover, the writer declared, it would develop competent overseers for plantations. "It is our deliberate expectation that such of the graduates of our proposed institution as are not landowners themselves will [become] managers for, or employees of extensive proprietors."[15] Few spoke so frankly, but the idea appealed to some. One man argued that the masses would be easier to govern "if the present tillers of the soil have the benefits of instruction." The first College catalogue noted that instruction "would acknowledge no difference of class," and the founders apparently felt that the comment was necessary.[16]

Finally, belief in scientific experimental farming motivated some

[12]*Ibid.*, VIII (January, 1853), 233; XI (March, 1856), 259; XI (April, 1856), 289-291; XII (February, 1857), 246.
[13]*Ibid.*, VIII (January, 1853), 227-228; VIII (February, 1853), 268; II (April, 1847), 297-299; V (February, 1850), 271.
[14]*Ibid.*, XIII (May, 1858), 363-364; also XII (December, 1856), 176.
[15]*Ibid.*, X (October, 1854), 97-100.
[16]*Ibid.*, III (February, 1848), 247; *First Circular*, 6.

of the early planners. Initially some of them, including Calvert, were more interested in the agricultural experiments which a college would conduct than they were in education. The limitless possibilities of applied science fascinated the practical American who never fully understood why schoolmen were so reluctant to accept it into the curriculum. It seemed logical to expect that a curriculum emphasizing science, plus an experimental farm, could settle once and for all—and for the benefit of all—the endless arguments over superior seeds or breeds of animals, whether horses or mules were better for plowing, and what types of feed would produce the fattest hogs and the best milk. Above all, the College could test the many brands of commercial fertilizers and the new types of farm machinery coming into the market. Although no one really opposed such experimental work, the small farmer with two old cows and forty acres of corn remained indifferent. Actually the planter-philanthropist stood to benefit most from his gifts, and in the end he became so fascinated with the prospects of scientific education that he began to think of sending his own sons to the College.[17]

The College emerged through a maze of resolutions, committees, hearings, alternate plans and votes. On the day the Maryland State Agricultural Society was created in 1848, the founders considered three separate resolutions introduced by Skinner, Earle and Wharton, all favoring agricultural schools.[18] In 1851 Calvert headed a committee which offered a solution to the problem of financing by suggesting the sale of $50,000 in stock certificates. The committee petitioned the legislature for permission to issue stock, but farm support was unorganized. Some farm representatives still supported Teackle's concept of experimental farms combined with state high schools, and others suggested that a state-supported chair of agriculture at St. John's College might prove more effective than a separate college.[19]

Committees of the state agricultural society continued debating and modifying plans, while advocates of the College rallied support.

[17]*American Farmer*, VII (November, 1851), 171, 182; X (October, 1854), 97-101; XI (January, 1856), 193-195,

[18]*Ibid.*, IV (October, 1848), 107-112; IV (December, 1848), 171-172, 182. For details of action by the committees and passage through the Assembly, Worthington, "Forces," 139-188, 212-217; Vivian Wiser, "Maryland in the Early Land-Grant College Movement," *Agricultural History*, XXXVI (October, 1962), 194-199.

[19]*American Farmer*, VII (November, 1851), 182; VII (May, 1852), 388; VIII (December, 1852), 193; IX December, 1853), 174-179; *Proceedings . . . 1851*, 275, 469; *Journal of the Proceedings of the Senate of Maryland . . . 1852* (Annapolis, 1852), 274.

Governor T. Watkins Ligon endorsed the College, and Calvert shocked the legislature into reality by suggesting casually that it should appropriate $150,000 to the new institution. In January, 1856, a large deputation from the society appeared before the assembly's agricultural committee which was headed by a society member, Colonel John H. Sothoron. Their request was modest: permission to sell stock for a college and experimental farm, and a promise of $6,000 annually from the legislature provided the founders demonstrated their good faith by purchasing $50,000 in shares within two years.

Halfhearted opposition appeared, not from the industrial interests of Baltimore, but from some small farmers, particularly on the Eastern Shore, who objected to the aristocratic origin of the institution and feared they had nothing to gain but increased taxation. Nevertheless, Allan Bowie Davis led the bill through the House of Delegates by a vote of 40 to 24, and Colonel Sothoron pushed it through the Senate by a vote of 20 to 2. On March 6, 1856, the bill became law.[20]

Although some planners had boasted they could raise $500,000 if necessary, acquiring the $50,000 set by the legislature proved to be difficult. Robert Bowie served as agent to raise the required sum by selling 2,000 shares at $25 each. Although he encouraged the notion that dividends might result from student fees and the profits of the experimental farm, most planters knew their investment was gratuitous. Almost every member of the state agricultural society bought shares. William N. Mercer, a once-bankrupt Maryland tobacco planter who had moved to Louisiana to make a fortune in sugar cane, became the largest stockholder with 300 shares; Calvert was next with 176. Thomas G. Clemson, a friend of Calvert and later founder of the agricultural college in South Carolina, persuaded his friends in the South to buy. W. W. Corcoran, the Washington banker who founded the Corcoran Art Gallery, bought 40

[20]*American Farmer,* IX (March, 1854), 288; X (October, 1854), 97-101; XI (February, 1856), 243-244, 254-255; XI (March, 1856), 273; XI (April, 1856), 292-295; T. Watkins Ligon, "Message of the Executive of Maryland to the General Assembly," *House and Senate Documents* (Annapolis, 1856), 4; *Proceedings [House]* . . . *1856,* 358, 509, 512; *Proceedings [Senate]* . . . *1856,* 22-23, 55-84, 109, 144-146, 262; *Laws of Maryland* . . . *1856,* Chap. 97; *Baltimore Sun,* 3 March 1856; *Baltimore Republican,* 1 March 1856; *Baltimore American,* 1 March 1856. What is now Michigan State was chartered in 1855 and opened in 1857; Pennsylvania State was chartered as a high school in 1855, opened in February, 1859, and became a college in 1862.

shares; and Johns Hopkins in Baltimore bought 20. Yet two months before the deadline, supporters of the College were still $8,000 short of the required sum, and members of the agricultural society agreed to subscribe the remaining amount. All told there were about 300 stockholders of whom 20 had a majority holding.[21]

The shareholders met in January, 1958, to elect a board of trustees who would purchase land, erect buildings, select a faculty and establish the academic policies of the institution. They elected Calvert president of the board, and Nicholas B. Worthington, editor of the *American Farmer,* secretary. Dr. John C. Wharton, one of the small stockholders, became the first employee, a kind of executive officer of the board with the title of registrar, at a salary of $1,000 annually.[22]

During the next few months Calvert worked the trustees furiously. Committees met in Baltimore several times weekly, investigating every facet of education. One group surveyed farms that might be turned into a campus. Allen Bowie Davis offered 100 acres in Montgomery County as an outright gift, and others tendered farms at discount rates. After combing various possibilities and visiting a number of sites, the committee voted to accept the northern plot of Calvert's Riverdale plantation—420 acres at $50 an acre, a total of $21,400. This was relatively inexpensive for land so near a railroad, but the real inducement was Calvert's offer of $10,000 toward payment in the form of an indefinite loan without interest.[23]

Other committees consulted architects and let contracts for renovating the old Rossborough house and the barns around it, and for building faculty homes and a five-story college building. Calvert, on horseback, was at the site almost every day to supervise the construction. Deciding that commercially sold bricks were too expensive,

[21]Stock Subscription Ledger, 1856-1906, bound MS. in Maryland Room, McKeldin Library, College Park. Also, *Baltimore Sun,* 2 June 1856; *American Farmer,* XI (April, 1856), 319; XIII (September, 1856), 63; XIII (October, 1857), 134-135; XIII (December, 1859), 194; Alester G. Holmes and George R. Sherrill, *Thomas Green Clemson . . .* (Richmond, 1937), 123-131; *Report of the Register . . . 1858,* 13-20.

[22]Most College records were destroyed when the main building burned in 1912, but until 1865 the *American Farmer* and the *Rural Register,* both edited by stockholders, carried reasonably full accounts of the trustees meetings. See *American Farmer,* XIII (May, 1858), 363-364.

[23]*American Farmer,* XIII (October, 1857), 130; XIII (May, 1858), 363-364; *Baltimore Weekly Sun,* 23 January 1858; *Report of the Register . . . 1858,* 4-8; Plat of the "Rossborough Estate," 1857 or 1858, Rossborough Inn, College Park; *Maryland Farmer* XV (April, 1878), 107-110; XV (May, 1878), 150-151.

he set up a kiln to produce them. On August 24, 1858, Calvert's birthday, he laid the cornerstone for the main building and delivered an address to the assembled trustees.[24]

Soon, of course, the trustees were out of money but that did not deter them. A committee recommended a 5-to-1 stock split and sold about 1,000 additional shares to small farmers at $5 a share. The trustees' Louisiana admirer, William N. Mercer, contributed another $2,500. Meanwhile, other committees were outlining a course of study, interviewing potential faculty members and preparing for the College opening. Calvert was bursting with happiness. "We will have," he said excitedly, "the best Institution *in the world!*"[25]

The College Opens

Early Monday morning, October 6, 1859, the 9:15 Baltimore-Washington train, after an hour and a half journey, stopped in what seemed to be the middle of a field, and about 250 well-dressed, cheerful people got off. From the railroad they could see a cloud of dust rising from the hill three-quarters of a mile away where approximately another 250 persons were arriving by carriage from the surrounding countryside. Most of the Baltimore crowd walked toward the hill, but wagons from Calvert's plantation transported the ladies and the aged. A half hour later a train arrived from Washington and another 250 people disembarked.

Since it was the opening day of the College as well the day of formal dedication, a number of students struggled with trunks, but most conspicuous were the dignitaries in their black frock coats and stove pipe hats. Most of the trustees were present as well as many members of the legislature. From Washington came Justice James M. Wayne of the United States Supreme Court, and Jacob Thompson, Secretary of the Interior. W. W. Corcoran's presence caused excitement since some said that he was the richest man in America. The orator of the day, emphasizing the scientific character of the institution, was the country's foremost scientist, Joseph Henry, head of the new Smithsonian Institute.

For at least an hour the crowd wandered about inspecting the

[24]*Country Gentleman*, XI (3 June 1858), 353; *American Farmer*, I (December, 1859), 176; XIV (September, 1858), 65-66; *Rural Register*, I (15 July 1859), 26.
[25]*American Farmer*, XIII (May, 1858), 363; I (December, 1859), 176.

College. The prominent walked with Calvert, congratulating him abundantly. Since the land, about half woods and half field, was once part of his estate it had been beautifully kept. The terrain reminded one observant reporter of a great saucer, rising to a series of small hills in the center. Farmers thought much of the soil was poor, but that made it all the better for practical teaching, and they were impressed to see experimental work already far along. Just south of the main building Calvert had planted an orchard with a wide variety of fruit trees; and near the road were fifty-seven plots, carefully marked off by cords, where he was testing nineteen different varieties of manure.[26]

Farmers were particularly pleased by the institution's location. It was reasonably near the center of the state, close to a railroad, and above all it was sufficiently far from any city where the boys might be tempted to dissipate on week ends. Never would cheap urbanization corrupt the neighborhood, and the very thought of this isolated beauty brought tears of joy to one farmer. Here, he said, the young men of Maryland

> may begin to live, growing up like young plants in their simple dependence, rivalling the flowers in their innocent beauty, and the birds in their careless joy; and away from the unhealthful atmosphere and the impure, corrupting associations of the city, the nation's children may be nursed into vigorous bodily health, and simple-minded virtue, and pure and undefiled religion.[27]

The main College building was an ivory-painted brick structure, five stories high and almost gothic in style, located on the highest hill beside the present main dining hall. Originally planned as one wing of a far larger building which was never built, it looked complete as it stood. Calvert's landscaping had done much to set it off handsomely with "proper walks and an ornamental arrangement of borders and shrubbery." On the ground floor was an auditorium which doubled as a dining room, plus kitchen facilities and a bathroom "furnished with iron tubs and every comfort for the bather." On the second or main floor were eight carpeted lecture rooms of various sizes and a few offices. On each of the upper three floors were 18 rooms, 12 by 23 feet, and furnished with two iron beds and two wardrobes. All told, quarters were available for 104 students

[26]*Baltimore Sun,* 4 October 1859; 6 October 1859; *Baltimore Republican,* 6 October 1859; *Washington Star,* 6 October 1859; *Rural Register,* I (15 October 1859), 121-122.
[27]*American Farmer,* I (November, 1859), 144.

and at least two faculty members. Especially were the trustees proud of the modern steam heat in the building—although it never worked very well—and the lighting which a Baltimore gas company had donated. An elaborate machine behind the building manufactured the gas from coal and pumped it to a fixture in every room. A delighted newspaper reporter wrote that the glow in each room was "as brilliant as a city street-light."[28]

Crossing the farm far down the hill was a narrow dirt road that was the once busy Washington-Baltimore Turnpike, now much quieter since the advent of the railroad. Beside the road stood the sturdy old Rossborough house, built in 1798 and much too old-fashioned and stodgy to the trustees to serve as the president's house, but satisfactory enough for the registrar and for overnight guests of the College. A contemporary dismissed it as "the old tavern which travellers, before the days of railroads, may remember as the first stage station after leaving Washington." Behind the house was a large barn and across the road were three sheds. For the College president and for the most distinguished professor, the trustees had built identical frame houses with fashionable gingerbread decoration. The president's home was located close to the present infirmary, and the other stood behind the present College Park shopping center. The other professors were expected to live in the main building or to erect their own homes.[29]

At about half past eleven in the morning, after everyone had made various observations about the College grounds, the crowd pushed into the auditorium to hear the dignitaries. A neat eight-page catalogue was distributed, setting forth the aims of the institution and listing the trustees, the faculty and the courses to be offered. As the people rustled through its pages, Calvert introduced himself as the presiding officer of the day and asked everyone to buy more stock. An Episcopal minister from Washington prayed, and blessed the College. Joseph Henry orated at length on science, education and character. Secretary of the Interior Jacob Thompson, from Mississippi, congratulated the trustees, reminding them that "southern planters who undertake to control the labor of others" must set a good example for their inferiors. Calvert closed

[28]*Baltimore Sun,* 6 October 1859; *Baltimore Republican,* 6 October 1859; *Report of the Register . . . 1858,* 8-9.

[29]*Country Gentleman,* XI (3 June 1858), 353; William F. Kellerman, "Rossburg Inn, Landmark of a National Route," *Maryland Historical Magazine,* XXXIII (September, 1938), 273-280; *Historic Rossborough Inn, 1798-1940* (n.p., 1940); Plat, Rossborough Inn, College Park.

the ceremonies by again requesting people to buy stock, and every-one flocked outside for a picnic lunch.[30]

Many of the audience must have commented during the cere-monies at the absence of the College president, listed in the cata-logue as Benjamin Hallowell, and also at the inconspicuous part played by the three members of the faculty who were present. If the crowd had known why the president was absent, or why the professors had been shunted aside, they might been even more disturbed. In fact, Hallowell had no idea that he had been elected, and the trustees were not altogether satisfied with their faculty.

Hallowell came from a well-known Montgomery County Quaker family. A huge, kindly man who followed the Friend custom of using "thee" and "thou," he had distinguished himself in Alex-andria as principal of an academy where Robert E. Lee had been his most famous pupil. A short time before the College opened he had retired to write scientific articles and perform agricultural experiments on his farm near Sandy Spring. Recognizing him as a noted teacher, scientist and practical farmer, the trustees had sought his advice from the beginning, and he had devoted much attention to his careful replies. Although the board would have preferred someone with more of a national reputation, belatedly they asked Hallowell to serve as president and, in addition, as professor of philosophy, English and history at an annual salary of $2,500. While the trustees had deliberated, Hallowell was in New York, totally unaware of the offer; but the board decided to rush the catalogue into print, assuming that the public announcement would guarantee his acceptance. In November, three weeks after classes began, he arrived to assume the duties which had been so gracelessly thrust upon him. He accepted the position with the provision that no slaves would be used on the College farm, and with the agreeable stipulation that he serve without salary.[31]

Little was known about the other three members of the faculty. George C. Schaeffer, a physician from somewhere in the West and a part-time instructor at Georgetown Medical College, was named professor of agriculture, which meant chemistry, geology and min-eralogy. Hugh Dorsey Gough, a farmer from Harford County, was

[30]*Baltimore Republican*, 6 October 1859.

[31]Benjamin Hallowell, *Autobiography of Benjamin Hallowell* . . ., second edition (Philadelphia, 1884), 163-166; *American Farmer*, I (December, 1859), 176; *Rural Register*, I (1 December 1859), 169; I (15 December 1859), 184; Harris Elwood Starr, "Benjamin Hallowell," *Dictionary of American Biography*, VII, 159-160.

named professor of mathematics, astronomy and engineering. Bapista Lorino, an academy professor from Mississippi who claimed he could speak in a dozen tongues, became professor of languages. Probably none of the faculty, including Hallowell, had graduated from a college. According to the catalogue two additional professorships, one of veterinary medicine and the other of botany and entomology, would be filled shortly. The trustees preferred to pass over the faculty matter on the day of opening ceremonies, and to point instead to the fine physical plant.[32]

Behind the faculty problem lay the far more serious question of the actual aims of the new institution. During the years of planning, the founders of the College had been so busy with the practical problems of raising money and acquiring land that they had managed to neglect their conflicting concepts of its aims as well as the bothersome questions of the types of students they would attract and the curriculum and faculty they desired. As the opening approached, however, these problems became more pressing to the trustees and they could not agree on a course of study or the selection of professors. Increasingly, they came to realize that a European-style manual labor institution was not practical in America, that the great mass of ordinary farmers in Maryland were uninterested in their philanthropy, contemptuous of their ideals of refinement and unprepared for college work. Moreover, in the process of building the College, the trustees had grown immensely fond of it, and when Calvert proclaimed it the best *"in the world,"* he and many of the trustees had persuaded themselves that it must be dedicated to educating their own sons.

In a series of tumultuous meetings held before the opening ceremonies, the manual labor, charity-school advocates were decisively defeated. The decision centered upon tuition charges, for recognizing that neither the philanthropic endowment nor the tiny state appropriation was sufficient to run the institution, the trustees turned in the opposite direction and set board and fees at a stiff $260 a year. This amount was double the cost of most state universities and placed the little College among the half dozen most expensive in the country.[33] At one stroke the founders had rejected

[32]*American Farmer,* I (August, 1859), 52; *First Circular,* 4; Thomas L. Bissell, "The Maryland Agricultural College, The First Teachers and the Opening in 1859" (MS. in possession of Thomas L. Bissell, Department of Entomology, University of Maryland).

[33]*American Farmer,* I (November, 1859), 145; Frederick Rudolph, *The American College and University* . . . (New York, 1962), 177-200.

their earlier democratic ideals and turned the College into an institution for those who could afford the best. Of the 34 students who enrolled the first day, at least 13 were related to the founders—Calverts, Carrolls, Bowies, Pacas, Goldsboroughs, Whartons, Sothorons, Sands, Skinners and the rest. W. W. Corcoran sent his son; the Governor of Delaware, William H. Ross, sent his; and Johns Hopkins sent a relative.[34] No doubt many mediocre boys attended, but not many had mediocre fathers. "The object of the Institution," said the catalogue, "is not so much designed to teach the pupils to be farmers, as to make liberally educated gentlemen."[35]

The Maryland Agricultural College opened not as a democratic farmers' school, but as a planters' College designed to train students for leadership: first, by refining their intellects and tastes, as the traditional colleges did; second, by adding a new kind of professional education in science; and third, by insuring an aristocratic *corpora sana* through spartan discipline and outdoor exercise. The officials liked to compare their College with West Point and the Naval Academy, institutions which turned out officers in their profession.[36] By developing "the whole man in all departments of his being" and by the "symmetrical development and instruction of the religious, the intellectual, and the physical qualities," the College would produce a more powerful and enlightened agrarian leadership. It was, in short, designed to develop superior men, "if not rulers, at least fit to rule."[37]

Originally the trustees meant to flatter their institution by calling it an "Agricultural College," but with their transformed aims the title embarrassed them. It seemed to carry a hayseed connotation which confused the public and produced the opposite of the image they wished to project. The first catalogue devoted three of its eight pages to explaining away the term: "It is not to be supposed then, that what we designate an Agricultural College, aims merely at professional education in agriculture." For many years they

[34]Register of Students, 1856-1906, bound MS., Maryland Room, McKeldin Library, College Park; *Second Circular of the Maryland Agricultural College* (Baltimore, 1860), 11-12; *Rural Register,* I (15 October 1859), 121-122.

[35]*Third Circular of the Maryland Agricultural College* . . . (Baltimore, 1861), 9; also *First Circular,* 5-7; *Baltimore Sun,* 6 October 1859; *American Farmer,* I (November, 1859), 145.

[36]*American Farmer,* XI (March, 1856), 257-258; *First Circular,* 7; *Rural Register,* I (1 November 1859), 139-140; *Third Circular,* 7.

[37]*American Farmer,* XIV (July, 1858), 18-19; I (October, 1859), 86-87, 105; I (December, 1859), 183; *Country Gentleman,* XVIII (14 November 1861), 320; *Rural Register,* I (1 December 1859), 169.

fought bitterly the "notion generally entertained that the educational studies of the pupils are subordinated to agriculture." The
College provided unique specialized training, not in farming, but
in science and leadership; it was designed to be "pre-eminent among
the Colleges of the country."[38]

An important influence in the shift from farm education to
scientific education was the absence of teachers for a purely agricultural school and of anything to teach boys who had already
grown up on a farm. These deficiencies plagued the country's
agricultural schools for decades, and the Maryland trustees were
foresighted in accepting the fact and proceeding to scientific training
instead. Hallowell warned the trustees that there were no textbooks
on agriculture, insufficient formal agricultural knowledge and, that
indeed, there was little for a purely agricultural institution to do.
He urged them to provide botany, entomology, chemistry and
geology, believing that someday these subjects would grow into an
agricultural science; but meanwhile the trustees had better content
themselves with offering a moderate liberalization of the traditional
academic curriculum which had been tested by the centuries.[39]

Agricultural colleges in Pennsylvania and Michigan were unwilling to accept the absence of academic agricultural knowledge,
and for years they foundered while attempting to teach what did
not exist. Because of its weakness after the Civil War, the Maryland
Agricultural College was not strong enough to influence greatly
the curriculum of later agricultural colleges. It remained for Andrew
D. White, at Cornell University in the 1870's, to provide the scientific basis for agricultural education which Maryland was attempting to introduce two decades earlier.[40]

The Maryland founders established five departments within the
College, and students took all courses offered by any four:[41]

1. *Ancient Languages*—Latin and Greek.

2. *Modern Languages*—French and either German, Spanish
or Italian.

---

[38]*Rural Register,* I (15 October 1859), 121.

[39]*American Farmer,* XIV (June, 1859), 380-381.

[40]Allan Nevins, *The State University and Democracy* (Urbana, Ill., 1962), 23-68;
Rudolph, *American College and University,* 265-267.

[41]*American Farmer,* XIV (July, 1858), 18-19; *First Circular,* 4-7; *Second Circular,*
18-21; [Fifth] *Circular of the Maryland Agricultural College* . . . (Baltimore, 1863),
Appendix.

3. *Natural Sciences*—Botany, Entomology, Chemistry, Physics, Geology, Practical Farming.

4. *English*—Rhetoric, Composition, World History, United States History, Bookkeeping, Philosophy, Ethics, Evidences of Christianity.

5. *Mathematics*—Alegbra, Geometry, Trigonometry, Calculus, Surveying, Civil Engineering, Astronomy.

This curriculum, developed by Hallowell, Wharton and Calvert, resembled the earlier suggestions of Benjamin Franklin and William Smith, and those which Thomas Jefferson had drawn up for the University of Virginia. Actually, only the natural science courses made the curriculum different from those of a hundred other struggling colleges. During the first two years, however, every student selected the science course, while many omitted ancient languages. By doing so they were helping to shape an educational revolution.

Teaching procedures in most classes were traditional, with students spending at least six hours each day in classroom recitations. Also traditional was a stern discipline that was all any father could have wanted to make a man of his son. The usual academic rules prevailed against tobacco, profanity, alcohol and "morals calculated to destroy the established order." Students were prohibited from "loud talking, scuffling, boisterous behavior, or unnecessary noise of any kind," and also from "attempts to injure any member of the Faculty, in his person." Special rules appeared to be directed at aristocratic scions: no gambling, no guns, no duels—even attendance at duels was specifically forbidden. All students were required to deposit their pocket money with the registrar and to ask his permission before they spent a nickel. On every fifth week-end, if a student's behavior were "perfect" and his studies in order, he might apply for permission to leave the campus at noon on Saturday and return by sunup Monday. Other absences from the campus were forbidden. One officer reported that the College was fortunate in its students, totally lacking "that venial kind that so often characterizes College life."[42]

Religion, like discipline, was "rigidly nurtured." Every morning the students listened to the president lead prayers and read scriptures; during the day a professor led the blessing at each meal; and

[42]*Second Circular*, 24-25, 17; *Report of the Trustees of the Maryland Agricultural College to the Legislature . . . 1864* (Baltimore, 1864), 10.

every Sunday a visiting preacher from a different denomination conducted long services. Although religion was carefully designed "to rise above denominational differences and discussions," no one questioned its usefulness. With about a third of the students Roman Catholic, this consensus probably would not have been reached in other states.[43]

Eager to provide for physical training and fearful that their sons might grow up with "contempt for physical labor," the trustees accepted Hallowell's recommendation that instead of requiring the boys to take gymnastics, they be put to work on the College farm. For at least an hour each day under the supervision of the registrar and farm manager, Dr. Wharton, they underwent a stiff round of hoeing or plowing. Such work provided exercise, profited the farm, sapped the students' energy for delinquency, and "refreshed the mind for renewed intellectual endeavour."[44]

Other outdoor work was more educational and imaginative. To beautify the campus each student had to plant a group of trees, shrubs or flowers, placed wherever he chose and cared for by him throughout his college career. During the first year one team of boys was told that the supply of ice for their drinks would depend upon their success in building a pond—located at the present site of McKeldin Library—and an ice house. The mealtime desserts for another team depended upon their success in cultivating a strawberry bed. "The well informed mind and the cunning right hand will learn to work together," said the catalogue, thus "dignifying labor by its connection with intellectual and moral culture."[45]

Since most nineteenth century professors considered contemporary ideas beyond the scope of formal education, intellectual stimulation was often the most neglected aspect of student life, and students made up the deficiency through their major extracurricular activity, the literary societies. All students belonged to either the Calvert Fraternity or the Mercer Literary Society, and rivalry between the two was keen. Each society had a better library than the College itself. Their members met weekly to hear invited speakers discuss, or to debate among themselves, the burning questions of the day—slavery, secession, Sir Walter Scott's poetry, the rights of women,

[43]Second Circular, 22; American Farmer, XIV (July, 1858), 18-19.

[44]Report of the Trustees . . . 1864, 6; Rural Register, II (15 November 1860), 145; Hallowell, Autobiography, 165-166; American Farmer, XIV (June, 1859), 380-381.

[45]Hallowell, Autobiography, 165-166; First Circular, 6; American Farmer, XI (March, 1856), 257-258.

the future of railroads. When distinguished guests appeared on campus, each society put forth its best orators to entertain the visitors or to instruct them as to the society's views.[46]

As with the other agricultural colleges in Pennsylvania and Michigan which were "weakly struggling into existence," the first years were hard for the Maryland school with aims which were new and sometimes vague. To begin with, the trustees were disappointed at the enrollment. They had worried that the quarters for 104 students might be insufficient, but on the first day only 35 appeared. Then, after all the confusion over Hallowell's arrival and after he had endeared himself to the students, illness forced him to resign after only a month on the job. Considering the manner in which he had been employed, perhaps he was justified in allowing the trustees to read about his resignation in the newspapers.

Hallowell's departure was a loss but not a disaster because Charles Benedict Calvert, president of the trustees, agreed to take over as acting president. Although no educator, he was a powerful administrator, and it seemed that whatever he undertook proved successful. His presence impressed other planters so that by the end of the year a total of 68 students had dribbled in. Calvert had rigid standards, and students who could not meet academic requirements were tossed into a stiff, no-credit preparatory program under a specially hired tutor. To the empty chair of botany and entomology, he attracted a prominent Washington scientist, Townsend Glover, who proved especially able. Schooling his students in field work and research methodology, Glover's course was probably the first entomology course offered in America. On the other hand, when Schaeffer and Gough did not measure up to Calvert's standards, he persuaded them to resign.[47]

As the second year began under the shadow of impending war, the trustees repeated their blunder of advertising a president who had not accepted the position. James Work Scott, a former president of Washington College in Pennsylvania, proved to be unavailable after the second annual catalogue had gone to the printer, and in desperation the trustees turned to a local academy principal, John

---

[46]*Rural Register*, I (1 February 1860), 232; II (1 March 1861), 264; *Washington Star*, 22 January 1860; *American Farmer*, II (January, 1861), 211.

[47]Register of Students, 1856-1906, 1-6; *Rural Register*, I (1 July 1859), 16; I (1 October 1859), 105; I (15 October 1859), 121-122; II (15 December 1859), 184; *Country Gentleman*, XVI (2 August 1860), 80; *American Farmer*, I (January, 1860), 208; I (April, 1860), 306; I (May, 1860), 336; *Baltimore American*, 14 April 1860; *Second Circular*, 10.

M. Colby, to head the institution. In addition to Lorino and Glover, three new men, all reasonably able, appeared on the faculty —Montgomery Johns, Benjamin Shoemaker, and his son, Benjamin Shoemaker, Jr. Enrollment during the second year reached 78, a respectable number for a college in the mid-nineteenth century, but before the session's end the figure fell sharply with the approach of war.[48]

In 1861, after two years of operation, no one quite knew whether or not the Maryland Agricultural College was a success. The oldest students were rising juniors who had still not quite developed loyalty to the institution. The campus was handsome and the finances, faculty and enrollment were adequate.[49] The real questions lay in the curriculum and the aims. Born in the democratic impulses of the planter gentry and transformed into a school for planter leadership, it was at once related to, and different from, the nation-wide movement for land-grant colleges. Its pedagogical direction, modifying the traditional curriculum with a particular emphasis on science, pointed the way for the most important movement in American higher education. Its social orientation, however, pointed to difficulties, for the day of the planter was almost over.

[48]*Rural Register,* II (15 December 1860), 186; III (15 July 1861), 17; III (15 September 1861), 82; *American Farmer,* II (September, 1860), 86; *Washington Star,* 14 July 1862; *Report of the Trustees . . . 1864,* 10; Bissell, "Maryland Agricultural College."

[49]Judging primarily from the *Report of the Trustees . . . 1864,* 13-15, finances during the first two years of operation were approximately as follows:

Expenses:

428 acres @ $50.00	21,400
Main Building	46,902
Two faculty homes	7,352
Repair of barns	900
Furniture for college	6,000
Farm implements	1,000
Farm stock	2,000
Garden and orchard	3,000
Labor, manure, etc. for farm	9,000
Faculty salaries	12,000
Student board, books, apparatus, labor, taxes, etc.	28,000
	$137,554

Income:

Sale of stock	44,000
State appropriation	12,000
Student board and fees	28,000
Sales from farm	11,000
Loan of C. B. Calvert	10,000
Outstanding bills	32,554
	$137,554

7

The Civil War

When the guns of the Civil War began to rumble, the colleges which eventually made up the present University of Maryland resembled the state itself. They possessed vitality but lacked unity; they were advanced in the professions but lagged in classical culture; they strangely combined a practical democracy with a social aristocracy. Both the state and the colleges were reasonably successful by the standards which other states and institutions might set, but neither seemed to have quite come to terms with itself.

Like the state, too, the colleges began the war with strong southern sympathy, and ended it attempting to adjust to the forces which made the North victorious. The state legislature in 1861, even with nineteen members in jail for treason, still defiantly resolved its sympathy "for the South in the Struggle for their rights." Slaveholding planters who controlled the Agricultural College and fashionable Baltimoreans who influenced the professional schools retained their southern allegiance longer than most Marylanders, almost until the end of the conflict. From Washington, however, came the Morrill Land Grant Act, evidence of the rise of the yeoman in the midst of war, a promise of practical education for the small farmers and city workers. From Annapolis came a similar self-assertion of the middle class, demanding public schools and public colleges. The war served as a catalyst for Maryland and for education, weakening classical aristocratic ideals, and strengthening the forces of unity, practicality and democracy. The colleges which make up the present University of Maryland hovered between defeat as proponents of the old, and victorious renaissance as proponents of the new.

Legends of the South

Of the four schools in Baltimore vaguely related as the University of Maryland—medicine, dentistry, pharmacy and undergraduate—southern sympathy was most prominent in the school of medicine. To many outsiders Baltimore has seemed to be a Yankee city, but most well-bred Baltimoreans have pretended they were southerners, and the medical students considered themselves very well-bred. The better residential wards of the city cast a larger majority for Breckinridge, the extreme southern candidate in 1860, than the large slave-owning southern counties of the state. With the socially prominent environment of most of the professors, and the southern origin of many students, the medical school seemed to set a pattern for the entire University.

The southern legend rather than southerners themselves dominated the faculty. The most powerful personality in the school was Nathan Ryno Smith, born in New Hampshire, educated at Yale, but enchanted with moonlight and magnolias. Anonymously he published a fanciful volume, *Legends of the South, By Somebody Who Desires to Be Considered Nobody.*[1] Romantic essays about plantation life of which he knew little, the stories typified the attitude of many Maryland professional men. Students knew who was the author and what were the political views that pleased him. Similar romance must have influenced Professor Aiken who had grown up in New York and was accused of helping Union army deserters escape into the Confederacy.[2] In 1862 when most of the southern-born students had fled from Maryland, the medical students elected

[1] (Baltimore, 1869).
[2] *Baltimore American*, 22 July 1864.

as president of their graduating class the one "gallant Virginia gentleman" who remained. To his birthplace, apparently, more than to him, they dedicated a poem:

> But hark! the tramp of Southern braves,
>   Maryland, dear Maryland,
> For you they come, your honor to save,
>   Maryland, dear Maryland.
> Hark the shouts of victory!
> See them in their majesty!
> Thy shackles fall, and thou art free!
>   Maryland, dear Maryland![3]

The medical faculty delighted in flaunting their sympathy one step short of treason. Each year the professors ostentatiously refused to fly the United States flag at commencement, and each year the Union troops in Baltimore ordered them to do so. John Pendleton Kennedy observed that graduates known to be southern sympathizers received great applause and many bouquets at commencement, but that Unionists were roundly hissed. When the rumor spread that Unionists always seemed to fail their examinations, the faculty announced proudly that the 1862 class included two known Union sympathizers.[4] So blatant was faculty disloyalty that one newspaper demanded that the general assembly require "the officers of the institution to take an oath of allegiance." The newspaper particularly accused the faculty of keeping open vacancies in the staff "to be filled after the war by some Southern men."[5] Actually the vacancies probably had nothing to do with politics since the declining enrollment required economy.

While enrollment fell from about 150 in 1860 to about 100 in 1863, the country needed doctors, and the school of medicine remained relatively prosperous. Advertising that "the present unhappy condition of public affairs . . . will not interfere with their duties," the faculty created a new, up-to-date course in military surgery.[6] Buoyed by wartime morale, the students endured class-

---

[3] *These Lines Are Respectfully Dedicated to William P. Morgan, of Virginia, President of the Graduating Class of the University of Maryland, by His Fellow Students* (n.p., 1862). This was the same sentiment and meter as the state song, "My Maryland," by James R. Randall.

[4] *Baltimore American*, 10 March 1863; 13 March 1863; 24 February 1864; Charles H. Bohner, *John Pendleton Kennedy* (Baltimore, 1961), 229.

[5] *Baltimore American*, 24 February 1864.

[6] *Baltimore Sun*, 10 October 1861; 21 October 1861; *Baltimore American*, 17 August 1861; 12 September 1863.

room routine much as before. Even the graduation balls and gay commencements continued undiminished. Faculty jealousies and policy struggles were put aside so that often the war years seemed more harmonious for the medical school than ever before.[7]

The hospital made handsome profits from the war. Offering its facilities to the United States government for wounded soldiers, it charged $5 per soldier per week, while private patients paid only $3. The Roman Catholic nuns who worked as nurses complained that the Protestant troops were "over-zealous" in trying to convert them, but the United States surgeon general quickly issued orders "prohibiting such conduct in the future." For all their southern sympathies, the medical professors served their patients heroically, winning commendations from the federal authorities.[8]

Little information remains about the other Baltimore schools, for it was not a time of innovation and the quarrels and the beauties of academic life seemed less worthy of recording than before. The College of Pharmacy suffered least, maintaining its ante-bellum enrollment of about 20 or 30 students annually. The College of Dental Surgery, drawing most of its students from outside the state, saw enrollment fall from over 100 to less than 30 students. One of its graduates, Adalbert J. Volck, became the South's finest caricaturist, especially famous for his satanic pictures of Lincoln.[9]

The undergraduate college of the University in Baltimore suffered the fate of many backward looking classical schools, barely struggling through the war and finally expiring. It produced four graduates in 1860, three in 1861, one in 1863, and one in 1866. A sad demise after a half century of struggle, its end was perhaps inevitable for a small, proprietary, classical college without adequate support or leadership in an age that had passed it by. Its principal, Edwin A. Dalrymple, continued to offer precollege instruction for a number of years. Almost no one noticed that the little college had closed,

[7]*Baltimore Sun*, 5 March 1860; 9 March 1863; 6 March 1864; *Baltimore American*, 13 March 1863.

[8]Minutes of the Medical Faculty, 9 May 1861; 15 July 1861; 24 May 1864. These minutes are in manuscript in the archives of the medical school, Baltimore. Also, Arthur J. Lomas, "As It Was in the Beginning: A History of the University Hospital," *Bulletin of the School of Medicine of the University of Maryland*, XXIII (April, 1939), 203.

[9]Annual catalogues of the Maryland College of Dental Surgery and the Maryland College of Pharmacy, 1860-1866.

and no one suggested again that the professional schools try to sponsor an undergraduate college.[10]

Statistics on alumni participation in the war are difficult to obtain, but a sampling indicates that hundreds must have served on both sides. From the class of 1860, at least 30 percent fought for the Confederacy and about 10 percent for the Union:

College	Total Graduates 1860	Confederate Service	Union Service
Medicine	52	17	5
Dentistry	35	11	3
Pharmacy	6	1	0
College	4	2	1
Total	97	30	9

Drama lies in the cold figures, for it was not easy to make the decision to fight against one's friends and classmates. No doubt it was more difficult in Maryland to go to war for one's convictions than in the deep South or in most of the northern states. From the medical school faculty of 1860, Edward Warren became a general in the Confederate army, and William A. Hammond a general in the Union army; from the dental school, two professors fought for the Confederacy; from the pharmacy school, two professors fought for the Union; from the college, one professor fought for the Confederacy. The alumni were about evenly divided between the medical and nonmedical units and between officers and enlisted men.[11]

[10]Eugene Fauntleroy Cordell, *University of Maryland, 1807-1907* . . ., 2 vols. (New York, 1907), I, 475-480; *First Annual Report of the State Superintendent of Public Instruction . . . 1866* [Document "K," House Documents, 1867] (Annapolis, 1867), 51.

[11]Service records, National Archives, Washington, D. C. The list is not entirely accurate for the records are sometimes incomplete, illegible, or duplicated.

In Confederate service, from the medical school: Surgeon Alexander Bear, Lt. Samuel Beck, Surgeon Powhatan Bledsoe, Pvt. John S. Daniel, Surgeon Frank Gale, Surgeon Charles L. Gwynn, Pvt. Hiram W. Harding, Surgeon Horace M. Heath, Surgeon John W. Hebb, Surgeon William R. Hodges, Surgeon James F. Hughes, Surgeon Henry M. Jones, Surgeon Alexius L. Middleton, Pvt. William H. Pue, Surgeon Samuel A. Raborg, Pvt. William H. Robbins, Lt. Col. Hiram H. Walker; from the dental school: Surgeon Thomas E. Besseliew, Capt. John Bland, Surgeon Hugh Phillips Bone, Surgeon Memory Bonner, Pvt. Conrad S. Boyd, Capt. William N. Cunningham, Pvt. John H. Dickson, Pvt. John W. Doniphan, Pvt. John S. Moore, Sgt. George Patterson, Sgt. Bryant S. Traywick; from the pharmacy school: Pvt. John H. Bolton; from the college: Pvt. William S. Pinkney, Pvt. William Reynolds.

In Union service (ranks not always available), from the medical school: Pvt. Charles Benson, Capt. W. M. Hilleary, James Earle Mathews, Surgeon Harry W. Owings, Surgeon B. M. Patterson; from the dental school: William Brown Dennis, Adam A. May, William H. Waters; from the college: Pvt. Henry McElderry.

The Old South Ball

At the Maryland Agricultural College practically all of the trustees sympathized with the South if not with secession. At least five of the trustees were arrested or fled the state to escape arrest during the war, and most of them lost substantially when slaves were emancipated. Calvert, for example, owned more than forty slaves, and Earle, McHenry, Merryman and Carroll each owned more than a hundred.[12] Until Hallowell arrived with his Quaker conscience, slaves were used in constructing the College buildings and for work on the farm. Most students came from slave-owning families, and Prince George's County where the College was located was dominated by a southern-oriented community.

Despite the near-unanimous feeling on the part of the officials, they took pains to freeze the sectional conflict out of College affairs. The state agricultural society and the agricultural journals maintained rigid rules against any mention of the slave question, and the College catalogues prohibited secret political clubs or the expression of political opinions on the campus. Although students inevitably resorted to innuendo in literary society debates about "Liberty" or "The Heroes of the World," the president of the College could boast that, "In the lecture room, and literary societies, as also in social intercourse, mere political issues and questions are practically ignored." The trustees obeyed their nonpolitical dictum in the appointment of the first presidents—Hallowell who was a Quaker pacifist, Calvert who was a pro-slave Unionist, and Scott and Colby who were moderate Unionists.[13]

The Agricultural College was only in its second year when the long sectional conflict erupted into war. There was no telegraph or direct mail to the campus, but each morning President Colby or a deputy went down to the railroad tracks where the trains had begun to stop regularly at "College Station." By dinner

[12]Slave Schedules of the Eighth Census of the United States, National Archives, Washington, D. C.

[13]*First Circular of the Maryland Agricultural College* (Baltimore, 1859), 6; *Washington Star*, 14 July 1862; Charles M. McGee and Ernest M. Lander (eds.), *A Rebel Came Home, The Diary of Floride Clemson* . . . (Columbia, S. C., 1961), 54; *Second Circular of the Maryland Agricultural College* (Baltimore, 1860), 25; *Report of Samuel Register, Esq., President, in Regard to the Condition of the Maryland Agricultural College* [House Document "H," 1872] (Annapolis, 1872), 5.

time, which was two o'clock, the professors had picked up their newspapers and mail from the president's office, and the day's news percolated among the students. At supper the president quietly and impartially explained events to the assembled student body.

How momentous was the news that second year! In the fall, soon after classes began, came word of Lincoln's election, even though he had obtained only 2,000 votes in Maryland out of 92,000 cast. In December came news of South Carolina's secession, and during January, 1861, six other states left the Union. A month later, as rumors of assassination spread, Lincoln passed through Baltimore in a sealed coach, and there were riots in the city. Then, on the cold spring morning of April 12, came the most dramatic news of all—Fort Sumter had been fired upon. Within a week, Lincoln called for volunteers, and Virginia, only ten miles from the little College, formally severed ties with the United States. Maryland was in turmoil, with troops everywhere and the governor resolutely refusing to allow the general assembly to meet in special session.

We can only guess what went through the minds of the students that year. Twelve were from the seceded states, and most of them left about Christmas of 1860. Of the rest, some must have been afraid and others thrilled at the excitement; some must have been pleased that examinations would probably not be very severe that year, and all must have wondered when they said good-by to their friends and professors whom they would soon be trying to kill. The fall term had begun with 78 students and 6 professors; only 17 students and 3 professors remained until commencement day in July. The others had more important things to do: President Colby became an officer in the Union army; the Shoemakers, father and son, joined the Confederacy; of the 78 students at the start of the year, at least 20 fought for the Confederacy and 9 for the Union.[14]

In the fall of 1861, as classes opened for the third year, Colby was gone, Calvert was in congress and the other trustees were too

[14]Service records, National Archives, Washington, D. C.

In Confederate service: Pvt. William N. Bean, Capt. C. L. Beaty, Pvt. William Berry, Lt. C. F. Brickhouse, Pvt. E. S. Calvert, Pvt. James W. Corcoran, Lt. John Crudup, Pvt. Josiah Crudup, Capt. A. D'Antignac, Lt. William Groom, Capt. William Henderson, Pvt. J. C. Lawton, Lt. John Maynard, Sgt. James J. McCalop, Pvt. E. T. Paca, Pvt. Robert W. Smith, Pvt. M. L. Sothorn, Pvt. Richard Tilghman, Pvt. William W. Waring, Pvt. William F. Wharton.

In Union service: Pvt. Charles H. Brown, Lt. Thomas Fassitt, Pvt. Thomas E. Franklin, Thomas Gale, Pvt. W. B. M. Hardesty, Col. George W. Houck, Sgt. George W. Maynard, Lt. William Lee Scott, Lt. Col. Benjamin F. Taylor.

scattered by war to be much concerned with the College; but with rare fortune they acquired the able Henry Onderdonk to take over as president. A southern sympathizing Quaker schoolmaster from Washington County, Onderdonk guided the struggling young institution during the next three years with tact, economy and inspiration. His ultimate ambition was to reshape the College to the original plan of its founders, away from its aristocratic bent and back to a manual-labor, charity, technical school for poor farmers. He argued particularly for a tuition cut to swell enrollment and hopefully to increase income. For the time being, however, he and the trustees avoided controversy.[15]

At the Agricultural College, as in the schools in Baltimore, many hours and even months dragged on with little thought of the fighting. Small military units moved regularly along the road in front of the College, and occasionally food was in short supply. There were frequent rumors that the College would be taken over as a Union training camp or hospital. But still the Latin recitations, the algebra, the field trips to search for insects went on as usual. For an hour or more each day the students worked under the farm director, getting their exercise and learning about the dignity of work. Working along with the students were five or six hired hands, and after Hallowell left, probably a few hired slaves labored on the farm. Actually the officers of the institution had almost stopped calling it an "experimental" farm and ignored the provision in the charter requiring annual reports on the experiments which were conducted. Instead, they called it a "model" farm, and as such it was a success, at least with wartime prices, for it not only fed the students but also made a moderate profit.[16]

The little College awarded its first two degrees in June, 1862, with the festivities only slightly diminished by war. William B. Sands who had chosen the classical curriculum received the A.B. degree, and Thomas Franklin who preferred the new science courses received the new B.S. degree which was awarded by only a handful of other institutions in the country. Sands orated to the crowd on "Labor," and Franklin spoke on "Education," after which there

[15]Thomas J. C. Williams, *History of Washington County, Maryland*, 2 vols. (n.p., 1906), II, 1286-1289; Henry Onderdonk, *Circular Letter to the Trustees* [dated 15 April 1863] (n.p., n.d.); *Report of the Trustees of the Maryland Agricultural College to the Legislature of Maryland . . . 1864* (Baltimore, 1864).

[16]Thomas L. Lockorman [student] to Joseph Burchinal, 11 May 1861, MS. scrap, Washington College Library, Chestertown, Maryland; *American Farmer*, I (May, 1867), 349; *Report of the Trustees . . . 1864*, 3-15.

were parties and dances for the graduates. The following year there were two more graduates, and in 1864 came a third commencement with four receiving degrees. Reconstruction was to be harder for the College than war, for during the next eight years only one more student graduated from the Agricultural College.[17]

At nearby Riverdale in Congressman Calvert's home, lovely Floride Clemson, daughter of Thomas G. Clemson and grand-daughter of John C. Calhoun, waited out the war, confiding to her diary her impressions of the "beautiful boys" from the College. Apparently she had no difficulty obtaining Confederate sympathizing escorts from the students, even if they could get out only once every five weeks. She came often with her girl friends to the literary society debates, recording that the boys spoke "wonderfully well," but that the professors' speeches "on Literary Culture or something of the sort, [were] awfully dull, & long." Her favorite of the College boys was the president's son, Henry Onderdonk, Jr. Her favorite time of the year, by far, was the College graduation ceremonies in June or July, and carefully she recorded the most important facts:

I went to the Commencement ball, & to the commencement in the morning. I was dressed in a white spotted muslin, & danced every set. We got to bed at 5 o'clock in broad day-light! There were more than a hundred, at least . . . We stayed at the Wharton's [Ross-borough House].

Floride found the following commencement to be even more rapturous. "It was a lovely moon light cool night," she wrote, "and the band serenaded *me*." "Mr. Onderdonk," she reported, was in attendance "*constantly*."[18]

As the war entered its final year, the troops passing along the turn-pike sometimes swelled to great armies, not always friendly. In April, 1864, General Ambrose E. Burnside moved his Ninth Army Corps from Annapolis, where it had been regrouping, to join Grant in Virginia. On April 24, the entire corps, some 6,000 men, camped on the College grounds before moving on to Washington the next morning. All of this was delightful for the cloistered students, and uneventful enough, except that two years later Professor Worthington remembered that the Union troops "burned a stone barn" and some 300 feet of fencing. Stone barns do not burn easily, but the

[17]*Washington Star*, 14 July 1862; McGee and Lander, *Diary of Floride Clemson*, 35, 53-55.
[18]McGee and Lander, *Diary of Floride Clemson*, 35, 44, 53-55.

College would not forego an opportunity to press claims against the Union.[19]

Far more costly was the Confederate raid two months later, for it left a scar on the institution that took many years to erase. General Jubal A. Early's Confederate expedition in July, 1864, was almost the last glorious moment for the dying Confederacy. Sweeping through Harper's Ferry and imposing a $25,000 ransom on Hagerstown and a $100,000 ransom on Frederick, Early routed the army of General Lew Wallace at Monocacy Junction. With Baltimore and Washington open to him, Early chose to drive on the national capital. Washington was in panic as army clerks and partially recovered wounded soldiers manned the fortifications on the northern outskirts of the city until Grant's men could arrive from Virginia to rescue them. On July 11, Early camped in Rockville while one of his cavalry officers, General Bradley T. Johnson, a Marylander, swept through the countryside with about 400 men to cut communications between Washington and Baltimore. About noon on the 11th Johnson and his men blew up the railroad near Beltsville, swung through Bladensburg, and arrived at the Agricultural College late in the afternoon.[20]

The College officials seemed to be waiting for Johnson. President Onderdonk met the raiders a half mile from the campus, and the kitchen appeared ready for guests. Johnson set up headquarters in the Rossborough House and chatted pleasantly with the faculty about the local roads. Although the Negro servants "had all decamped," the housemother and kitchen manager, "Miss Bettie," provided a fine meal for the men and even found a few jugs of whiskey, all of which Johnson paid for punctiliously in Confederate script. No one knows what happened later that night, except that passers-by along the road reported they saw carriages of ladies moving toward the hill and imagined they heard music. Floride would have been the first to know, but her diary is silent for that night.[21]

The Old South ball has remained only a legend, but for many

[19]Benjamin Perley Poore, *Life and Public Service of Ambrose E. Burnside* . . . (Providence, R. I., 1882), 230; *American Farmer*, I (April, 1867), 315-316.

[20]Millard Kessler Bushog, *Old Jube, A Biography of Jubal A. Early* (Boyce, Virginia, 1955), 192-208.

[21]"Baker-Turner Records," File 4091, R. G. 94, Adj. Gen. Off., National Archives, Washington, D. C.; also, *War of the Rebellion: A Compilation of the Official Records of the Union and Confederate Armies*, 130 vols. (Washington, 1880-1901), Series I, XXXVII, Pt. II, 171, 180, 185-187, 248, 256, 283, 299, 307-308; *National Republican* (Washington), 21 July 1864; *Baltimore American*, 22 July 1864; 27 July 1864; 28 July 1864.

years the College officials cared for little mounds of earth around the main building where lookouts were said to have stood guard during the dance. Next morning the troops were gone to rejoin Early before Fort Stevens on what is now Georgia Avenue. That same morning Grant's men landed at the Potomac River docks at the foot of 4th Street, and in the afternoon Early began his retreat back to Virginia.

For the College, the real storm was political. Angry newspaper editorialists and swarms of United States army investigators wanted to know how the Negroes all seemed to have advance warning of the raid, and why the College officials did not flee; they wanted to know why the kitchen, on the spur of the moment, when classes were out, happened to be ready to feed several hundred men; and especially they wanted to know about the party that the officials and the surrounding community were said to have given for the invaders.[22] President Onderdonk swore that the charges were a *"pretty romance . . . the offspring of malignity and cowardice,"* and perhaps they were.[23] As romantic as the legend was in retrospect, the abuse was almost more than the faltering young institution could bear. As the United States moved closer to victory and as the morale of the College officials faded, the hardships became increasingly oppressive.

The institution was approaching bankruptcy. Calvert had loaned it $10,000 which the trustees never expected him to collect, but when he died in 1864 his brother pressed for immediate payment. A three-year $10,000 bond issue of 1862 was coming due. The trustees had counted on a promise of $2,500 from their Louisiana philanthropist, William N. Mercer, but the war had bankrupted him. Two of the professors—Wharton and Johns—had each loaned the institution about $8,000, and there was still another $10,000 of miscellaneous debts and unpaid bills. On top of all this, members of the general assembly were impatient with the institution because of its activities during the war. Some darkly suggested that its officials were guilty of mismanagement or even misappropriation of funds.[24]

The long suffering Onderdonk had taken all he could bear; in

[22]"Baker-Turner Records," File 4091; File 2669; Margaret Leech, *Reveille in Washington, 1860-1867* (New York, 1941), 243; *National Republican*, 21 July 1864; *Baltimore American*, 22 July 1864; *Official Records*, Ser. I, XXXVII, Pt. II, 307-308; *Debates of the Constitutional Convention of the State of Maryland . . . 1864 . . .*, 3 vols., (Baltimore, 1864), II, 846, 974-975.

[23]*Baltimore American*, 28 July 1864.

[24]*Report of the Trustees . . . 1864; First Report of the State Superintendent of Public Instruction to the Governor of Maryland . . .* [Document "E," House Documents, 1866] (Annapolis, 1866), 18-20.

November, 1864, he resigned and went to Baltimore to open a private academy. Nicholas B. Worthington, trustee, former editor of the *American Farmer* and part-time professor, agreed reluctantly to take over as acting president. To meet the most pressing bills he sold 205 acres of the original 428-acre tract, including the present business section of College Park. To attract students he advertised the institution as a prep school open to any boy over 12 years old who could read and write. Although there were no graduates, the College struggled through 1864-1865 and 1865-1866 as a school for youngsters. The following fall, however, September, 1866, the institution failed to open. It appeared that the planters' College had died with the planter ideal.[25]

Reconstruction from Washington

And yet, even as the Agricultural College seemed to die, and during the year which it lay dormant, the Morrill Land Grant Act from Washington offered the means for beginning a new era. The Civil War had been a democratic revolution, overwhelming aristocracy in the South and transforming many American institutions elsewhere. In American higher education, the people were reshaping aristocratic colleges with emphasis on morality into technical schools and universities with a practical emphasis on knowledge. The transformation was not always easy. The founders of the Maryland Agricultural College fought the change and never learned to appreciate what the land grant movement had done. But eventually that movement helped the Maryland Agricultural College struggle to its feet and eventually to leadership.

The Morrill Land Grant Act was the culmination of the same agrarian reform movement which had created the agricultural societies, fairs, journals and the first agricultural colleges. Since the passage of the Northwest Ordinance in 1787, Congress had been generous in appropriating unsettled western lands to endow educational institutions, and with the agricultural distress of the 1850's farm demands for federally endowed technical education increased. Marylanders, such as Calvert, Skinner and Earle, had been among

[25]*Baltimore American*, 9 August 1865; 17 August 1865; *Maryland Farmer*, I (September, 1866), 87; I (January, 1867), 215; I (February, 1867), 248; I (April, 1867), 315-316.

the most vigorous in calling for federal aid for agricultural education.[26]

Justin S. Morrill, a Republican congressman and subsequently senator from Vermont, first introduced his bill in 1857 when it encountered bitter opposition from the southern cotton states. The planters were still prosperous, and they feared the precedent of federal aid to education; the well-established southern universities feared possible competition and despised the democratic aims of agrarian colleges; and if these reasons were not enough, there was the fact that the bill was introduced by a Vermont Republican. Morrill won a hairbreadth victory for his bill in congress, but President Buchanan, fearful of further aggravating sectional hostility, quietly vetoed the measure.[27]

President Lincoln, however, supported the scheme, and soon after the election Morrill introduced his bill again. With the South out of the Union, the bill passed with ease, and in July, 1862, was signed into law. The act offered to each state 30,000 acres of federal land for each of its senators and representatives in congress. Each state was to use the proceeds from the sale of this land to endow a college for "agriculture and the mechanical arts" and for military tactics. The military provision was added to the second Morrill bill as an afterthought during the war. The federally endowed college could teach anything else it wished, but these three subjects were required. To encourage the states to bear part of the cost of the new institutions, no money from the land could be used for the physical plant of the colleges.

Otherwise the act was wisely vague, leaving details to be worked out independently by the states and to be modified by the needs of succeeding generations. Morrill explained that he himself was the son of "a hard-handed blacksmith," and that he intended to provide technical schools for farmers and blacksmiths who could not obtain an education elsewhere. He did not want the land-grant institutions to compete with established colleges, but to meet the immediate, unphilosophical needs of a different class, to raise the poor farmer to a skilled agriculturalist and to lift the blacksmith and stonemason to

[26]*Baltimore Sun*, 8 May 1840; James T. Earle to Charles B. Calvert, 5 February 1848, letter in possession of H. C. Byrd, College Park, Maryland. *American Farmer*, IV (October 1848), 107-112; IV (January, 1849), 219; IV (June, 1849), 400; X (August, 1854), 42-45.

[27]Earle D. Ross, *Democracy's College: The Land Grant Movement in the Formative Stage* (Ames, Iowa, 1942); Alfred Charles True, *History of Agricultural Education in the United States, 1789-1925* (Washington, 1929).

engineers. Here was the original European, manual-labor school concept of the founders of the Maryland Agricultural College, a concept far from the school for gentlemen planters that they finally created. Eventually, as the public schools assumed many of Congressman Morrill's aims, the land-grant colleges raised their sights to become, not technical schools, but true universities.[28]

The democratic ideals implied by the Morill Act were precisely what Onderdonk always had wanted for the Agricultural College. As soon as the act passed congress he called the trustees into special session to remind them that Maryland, with two senators and five representatives, stood to receive 210,000 acres, and that the Agricultural College would receive the proceeds. Onderdonk urged that the faculty be increased immediately from 5 to 9, that tuition be lowered to $50 annually and that free tuition be provided for 75 scholarship students. He urged that students be put to work seriously, not merely for exercise, on the farm to pay for their board. He calculated that if all students were required to work four hours each day there would be no boarding expense whatever. Despite the glowing prospects of receiving money for the institution, however, this was not what the trustees wanted for the College. They quieted Onderdonk, made no recommendation to the general assembly to accept the Morrill Act and awaited developments.[29]

The farming and industrial interests in the assembly, however, proved more interested than the trustees in the land grant promise. In February, 1864, the legislature voted to accept the Morrill grant, and the following year voted 61 to 5 to give the proceeds to the Agricultural College which had not requested it. The legislators made plain that they would withdraw the money if it were not used in precisely the approved manner, and they understood among themselves that this was only a first step in placing the College under state supervision.[30]

Since there was little available federal land in Maryland, the state received land script, or land title, to federal property scattered through Michigan, Wisconsin, Nebraska and Kansas. Dismayed at the prospect of negotiating individual sales, defending titles and pay-

[28]True, *Agricultural Education,* 98-111.
[29]Onderdonk, *Circular Letter; Report of the Trustees . . . 1864.*
[30]*Laws of the State of Maryland . . . 1864* (Annapolis, 1864), Chap. 90; *Journal of Proceedings of the House of Delegates of Maryland . . . 1865* (Annapolis, 1865), 335, 511, 620; *Journal of Proceedings of the Senate of Maryland . . . 1865* (Annapolis, 1865), 311-312.

ing taxes on the land, Maryland impatiently sold its entire tract to an Ohio speculator for 53½ cents an acre, receiving a total return of $112,504. It was one of the least profitable dispositions of land made by any state. The money was invested in bonds yielding about $5,000 annually. Although the sum was disappointingly small and was received too late to prevent the closing in 1866, the Morrill Act funds insured the eventual success of the little Agricultural College. It tied the institution to a national system of land-grant colleges, and eventually it provided supplementary federal appropriations of almost $1,000,000 annually. Even more important, the act linked the Agricultural College to the state which was henceforth pledged to guarantee its continued existence or, presumably, to return the 210,000 acres of land to the federal government.[31]

The ultimate significance of the Morrill Act lay, not in new institutions, but in new directions for higher education. In the shadow of battle for the American democracy and in the storm of reconstructing the nation, the American congress and the Maryland legislature affirmed their belief that a bridge existed between higher education and the needs of the masses. The act pointed to the new subjects and the new attitudes which would build that bridge. Yet even its most optimistic supporters could not have foreseen the role that sixty-eight land-grant colleges and universities would play in later times. After a hundred years, some historians have suggested that the act written by the otherwise obscure Vermont congressman changed the face of America more than all the laws offered by the great Calhoun and Clay and Webster combined.[32]

Reconstruction from Annapolis

Ever since the eighteenth century, Marylanders seemed fascinated with ambitious plans to develop a public school system with a state university as its capstone. During the 1780's and 1790's William Smith and Samuel Knox had tried to develop elementary and col-

[31]"Agricultural College Script (Maryland) ," R. G. 49, National Archives, Washington, D. C.; Arthur J. Klein, *Survey of Land Grant Colleges and Universities* (Washington, 1930) , 9-14; *Annual Report of the Comptroller of the Treasury . . . 1864* [Document "E," House Documents, 1865] (Annapolis, 1865) , x; *Annual Report of the Comptroller of the Treasury . . . 1867* [Document "C," House Documents, 1868] (Annapolis, 1868) , xii-xiii.

[32]Allen Nevins, *The State Universities and Democracy* (Urbana, Ill., 1962) , 16-47.

legiate institutions simultaneously; during the 1820's the general assembly appointed Teackle to build a school system at the same time it tried to take over the University of Maryland; and during the 1850's the perceptive governor, T. Watkins Ligon, worked to build schools and higher education in harmony. Despite all these efforts, however, the state had failed to create public schools or colleges because the upper classes resolutely opposed taxation to educate the masses in elementary schools, and equally resolutely the lower classes opposed taxation to educate the few in colleges. Again with reconstruction came a new opportunity as far-reaching as the term implied. With the planter aristocracy discredited, a new generation of leadership arose with ability and vision. One of the new leaders, Libertus Van Bokkelen, almost singlehandedly created the Maryland public school system, and while he failed to complete a unified university superstructure he laid the basis for its eventual triumph. Just as the Morrill Act showed the way for higher education to reach the people, so Van Bokkelen helped the people and the state to reach the colleges.

The son of Dutch emigrants to New York, Van Bokkelen spent most of his life in Baltimore as an Episcopal minister and advocate of education. He turned down the presidency of the Maryland Agricultural College and of St. John's College to work for an entire educational system, and that opportunity came with the Maryland Constitutional Convention of 1864.[33] Although not a delegate to the convention—which was called to abolish slavery and disfranchise Confederates—Van Bokkelen attended as a lobbyist to capitalize on the prevailing democratic sentiment and to crusade for his long cherished public school system. Adopting his words almost intact, the convention wrote provisions into the new constitution requiring the governor to appoint a superintendent of schools and compelling the general assembly to levy taxes to support his program. Another provision, and a most unusual one, required the superintendent to present a plan for a school and university system, and in the event that the legislature did not act on it, his plan would become law.[34]

As expected, Governor Augustus Bradford appointed Van Bok-

[33]*Biographical Cyclopedia of Representative Men of Maryland and the District of Columbia* (Baltimore, 1879), 408-409.
[34]L. E. Blauch, "Education and the Maryland Constitutional Convention, 1864," *Maryland Historical Magazine*, XXV (September, 1930), 225-251; James Petrie Rouleau, "Governors of Maryland and Education" (M. A. thesis, Education, University of Maryland, 1951), 8-21 61-76; *Debates of the Constitutional Convention . . . 1864, passim.*

kelen superintendent, and early in 1865 the vigorous Dutchman presented his plan to the assembly. With only slight hesitation, the legislature approved his sweeping plan for elementary and secondary schools and gave the superintendent one-third of the entire income of the state government to operate the system. The centralized system of public schools, supported by teacher's colleges, emerged as one of the strongest in the nation.[35]

The most interesting and controversial part of the superintendent's plan was the university structure designed as the apex of the educational program. Van Bokkelen recommended that the state university be composed of four undergraduate institutions—St. John's, Washington, the Maryland Agricultural College and the undergraduate college of the University of Maryland. This included all of the colleges in the state except the Baltimore Female College and those controlled by the Roman Catholic Church. The first two years of work in each of the four colleges would be identical. In the last two years students who wished to major in medicine, dentistry or pharmacy would attend the University in Baltimore; those who majored in the liberal arts would attend Washington College; students majoring in law would attend St. John's; and those who majored in agriculture, engineering, commerce or military science would attend the Maryland Agricultural College. The colleges would be combined under a single board of trustees composed of the presidents of the four institutions, four state officials and four appointees of the governor. Remarkably resembling the university system which emerged in most states a century later, Van Bokkelen foresaw the unified University of Maryland as providing a national model for efficient centralization and diversified centers for wide-reaching public service. Since the trustees were to establish policies for the entire system down to the elementary grades, higher education possessed a unique influence over the public schools.[36]

The general assembly was not fundamentally opposed to the ambitious university system, but with many advocates of higher education disfranchised, it hesitated. In principle it approved the plan, declaring the four colleges united as the University of Maryland. Thus for the third time—in 1784, in 1826, and in 1865—the legis-

---

[35] L. E. Blauch, "First Uniform School System of Maryland, 1865-1868," *Maryland Historical Magazine*, XXVI (September, 1931), 205-227.

[36] *Report of the State Superintendent of Public Instruction to the General Assembly of Maryland* . . . [Document "P," House Documents, 1865] (Annapolis, 1865), 102-127 and *passim*; Bernard C. Steiner, *Education in Maryland* (Washington, 1894), 143-145.

lature created a state university. Actually, however, it put off its zealous superintendent by delaying an appropriation to acquire the colleges from their owners.[37]

When the legislature reconvened in 1866, Van Bokkelen was on hand virtually demanding purchase of the Maryland Agricultural College. As his favorite of the four colleges, it would, he thought, serve to launch the rest of the university system. His maneuvers were masterful. To the stockholders who balked at state control, he argued that state aid was the only hope for reopening the bankrupt institution, and he promised to block state aid that did not include controls. He mobilized the College's democratically inclined former president, Henry Onderdonk, and its acting president, Nicholas B. Worthington, to use their influence with the stockholders. To the legislators who balked at appropriations for the Agricultural College, Van Bokkelen argued that state support guaranteed them control over the land grant institution. Finally, to cement both sides to his scheme, he arranged a compromise: the state agreed to appropriate $45,000 for half ownership of the College, and the stockholders retained seven of the eleven seats on the board of trustees. In February, 1866, the Maryland Agricultural College became, at least in part, a state institution.[38]

Except for the state's brief experiment with a university in the 1780's and again in the 1820's, this was Maryland's first actual ownership of an institution of higher learning. The Morrill Act tied the College to the federal government, and Van Bokkelen linked it to the state. Long to be torn between the state and the remaining stockholders its future would be difficult, but the eventual emergence of College Park as the center of the university system was fixed.

During his own tenure as superintendent, Van Bokkelen failed to persuade the legislature to move further. Washington and St. John's Colleges were so debt-ridden that the assembly paled at the cost of bailing them out, while the regents of the University of Maryland in Baltimore, enjoying postwar prosperity and remembering the problems of state control thirty years earlier, bitterly opposed government

[37]*Laws . . . of Maryland . . . 1865*, Chap. 160, Title II, 288-290; Blauch, "First Uniform School System," 220-221.
[38]*Journal . . . of the House . . . 1866*, 63, 349; *Baltimore Sun*, 9 February 1866; *First Report of the State Superintendent of Public Instruction* [House Document "E," 1866], *First Annual Report of the State Superintendent* [House Document "K," 1867], 47-51; *Report of the Committee on Education . . .* [Document "K," House Documents, 1868] (Annapolis, 1868), 35-38; *Laws . . . of Maryland . . . 1866*, Chap. 53, 103-105; *American Farmer*, I (April, 1867), 315-316.

ownership. Van Bokkelen's annual reports on the public school system continued to include accounts of the various colleges of Maryland as if they were part of the system, but in fact they were not. When the people of Maryland again rewrote their constitution in 1867, undoing the idealism of reconstruction, the provisions for a university system were eliminated, and the ardent superintendent was replaced by a less ambitious one. Most people expressed greater concern for making money than for cultural frills such as universities.

Strangely, perhaps, even the setbacks of the Civil War and reconstruction had served higher education well. For the Maryland Agricultural College—despite declining enrollment and bankruptcy—failure of planter ideals paved the way for federal and state support, and opened new curriculums and new goals. For the professional schools in Baltimore, the taint of disloyalty served to attract large postwar enrollments from the deep South where schools had been destroyed. Despite the failure of Van Bokkelen's ambitious university system, he built a public school system which, more than most college planners realized, was a basic requirement for higher education. Revolutions occur slowly, but the transformation from the old classical college to the modern university had begun.

8

An Agricultural College in an Industrial Age

During the next twenty-five years, from 1865 to about 1890, only a few leaders caught the vision of what higher education might really offer. Andrew D. White at Cornell, James B. Angell at Michigan, Charles W. Eliot at Harvard, and Daniel Coit Gilman at the new Johns Hopkins University began to transform the English model institution with its emphasis on morality into the German university with emphasis on scholarship. Rote memorization slowly gave way, electives came into use, the concept of academic freedom emerged and philanthropists like Ezra Cornell and Johns Hopkins became interested in the promise of education. For the great majority of people, however, college education was still aristocratic and impractical. The land-grant colleges particularly seemed to have failed. Farmers especially were skeptical of formal education, scholars to develop the new technical subjects were lacking, and the institutions languished from the mistaken popular belief that the Morrill Act had left them well provided for. At first the farmers ignored the land-grant colleges. Then, increasingly frustrated by the industrial world during the 1870's and 1880's, they turned on the colleges with unreasoning fury for seeming to have betrayed their promise.

The Maryland Agricultural College suffered more indifference and far more hostility than most. For twenty-five years it stood proud and drab on the hill, a little military school bristling with guns like a fortress, while the politics of Maryland swirled around it. The old planters, the angry farmers and the booming towns and cities of the state were developing a new social order on which a modern university could be based.

Looking Backward

It was an inhospitable age for an agricultural institution of any kind, especially one tainted with discredited planter leadership. The farmer had represented over half the wealth of Maryland in 1860, but only one-fifth by 1900. It was an age of industry, of the business-man, of the city. Baltimore surged ahead, adding 50 percent to its population each decade, until by 1900 almost half the people of Maryland lived within the city limits. The city possessed influence beyond its numbers, for urban politics, urban economic interests and urban ideals radiated out to dominate and intimidate the rural countryside.[1]

While the influence of the farmer declined, the dominance of the planter aristocracy collapsed completely. The average size of a Maryland farm declined from 200 acres in 1860 to barely more than 100 acres in 1900. Some of the old planters who founded the Agricultural College—the Davises, McHenrys and Sothorons, for example—rented their lands to tenants and remained poor and proud on the old homestead. Others among the founders—such as the Calverts, Mercers, Earles, Sands and Goldsboroughs—accepted the new era for what it was, sold their lands for what they could get and moved to the city to begin new careers in business. Symbolic of the times, the old fraternal Maryland State Agricultural Society gave up its rural interests, purchased a race track and became a club for sportsmen. Symbolic for the College, the trustees' meetings and even

[1]U.S., *Eighth Census, Agriculture in the United States* (Washington, 1864), 72-73; *Twelfth Census, Statistical Atlas* (Washington, 1903), Plates 136, 184.

the inaugurations of its presidents were no longer held on the campus, but in Baltimore.[2]

Educational leadership, like so much else, had shifted to Baltimore. There, growing slowly and greater than most people realized, was the towering Johns Hopkins University. Chartered in 1867, it officially opened in 1876 with an operating budget forty times that of the Maryland Agricultural College. Two old Baltimore institutions, Loyola College and the Mechanics' Institute, revived vigorously; and three entirely new institutions appeared—the State Normal School, the Woman's College and Baltimore City College. Within a decade of the Civil War, each of the new schools boasted an enrollment at least double that of the little farmers' College. However loyal to the Agricultural College he might be, no longer could a man like Calvert think of its soon becoming "the best Institution *in the world.*"[3]

While Johns Hopkins represented the finest scholarship of the age, the new colleges reflected its ruthless practicality and materialism. Many so-called colleges were really technical high schools where students learned accounting and mechanics. "The 'humanities' as certain studies used to be called, are less and less considered to be an essential part of education," declared a Baltimore newspaper editor approvingly.[4] Students "must be kept free from the musty classic rubbish of the old collegiate course . . . the student must enter college as young men do the accounting room or machine shop—to *learn a trade.*"[5]

For the agricultural colleges, despite the intentions of the Morrill Act, it was not easy to teach even a trade. There were no textbooks on agriculture and no available body of agricultural information that did not appear in every farmer's almanac. Farming had not yet become an academic discipline. Scientists shared the disdain of the age toward things agricultural and were not easily attracted to the struggling rural schools. All of the agricultural colleges faced the dilemma, and the annual meetings of the American land-grant col-

[2]*Maryland Farmer,* VI (October, 1869) , 307; X (October, 1873) , 308; XVII (September, 1880) , 289. See also, Comer Vann Woodward, *Origins of the New South, 1877-1913* (Baton Rouge, 1951) .

[3]*Annual Report of the State Board of Education, 1867,* ff.; Bernard C. Steiner, *History of Education in Maryland* (Washington, 1894) ; *Baltimore American,* 9 October 1876; 27 March 1877; 13 October 1882; *American Farmer,* V (January, 1876) , 34.

[4]*Baltimore American,* 14 May 1882; also, 18 October 1867; 28 January 1868; 9 October 1876; *Baltimore Sun,* 27 May 1877.

[5]*Maryland Farmer,* X (September, 1873) , 276; also, XXVII (30 July 1890) , 514; *American Farmer,* VI (April, 1877) , 147-149.

lege representatives became exercises in hand wringing despair. By 1875 the trustees of the Maryland Agricultural College were ready to admit privately that "agricultural education is a failure."[6] Except for Cornell, California, Wisconsin and Minnesota—each privately endowed—the next largest land-grant college had a faculty of nine. After a tour of the agricultural colleges in 1886, one observer reported that they were things of the past: "In this country they have pretty generally gone out . . . they are useless concerns, doomed to early extinction."[7]

All that the colleges needed, of course, was time and research. Calvert, realizing in 1859 that agriculture was not an academic discipline, developed a curriculum combining traditional subjects with science. A few institutions, Cornell for example, had the money for the basic research which eventually brought about the revival of agricultural education.[8] The trustees and presidents of the Maryland Agricultural College pleaded for the opportunity to develop botany into horticulture and biology into scientific livestock breeding. One after another of the presidents begged for "*time* to develop a scientific institute," promising that eventually Maryland would gain "a reputation as a school of science." But neither time nor money was available, and the College struggled to stay alive.[9]

Overwhelmed by the urban world and unable to develop agriculture as a science, the trustees of the Maryland Agricultural College held on tenaciously. With finances and enrollment at pitiful levels, they gradually and almost entirely gave up scientific research and retreated to the ancient program in which two or three low-paid professors dutifully went through the lessons in Latin, Greek, mathematics and philosophy. The trustees knew the College was out-of-date, but they were trapped. Still they were devoted to the little school and convinced that it was better to maintain a proud old academic curriculum for their own sons than to turn it over to the state to become a high school teaching plowing and horseshoeing. Oliver Wendell Holmes had commented on such institutions:

[6] *American Farmer,* IV (April, 1875), 153-154; also, III (March, 1869), 268.

[7] *New York Sun* cited in *Maryland Farmer,* XXIII (August, 1886), 237; also, *Baltimore American,* 7 March 1880; 13 October 1882; *Maryland Farmer,* IV (December, 1868), 369; XXIII (January, 1886), 26-27; Allan Nevins, *The State Universities and Democracy* (Urbana, Ill., 1962), 50.

[8] Earle Dudley Ross, *Democracy's College, the Land-Grant Movement in the Formative Stage* (Ames, Iowa, 1942), 113-151; Alfred Charles True, *History of Agricultural Education in the United States, 1785-1925* (Washington, 1929), 126-127, 192-195, 210-219.

[9] *American Farmer,* I (April, 1867), 315-316; IV (April, 1875), 155; *Maryland Farmer,* XXI (February, 1884), 66-68; *Baltimore American,* 11 June 1887.

> And who was in the catalogue, when college was begun?
> Two nephews of the president, and one professor's son.

Defiantly the trustees stuck to their old-fashioned ideals. Determinedly looking backward they elected eight successive Confederate veterans to head the College. Students dressed in military uniforms closely resembling those worn by Confederate soldiers, and until the 1890's most of them still came from once-aristocratic families. These "snobbish literary students," said one critic, "look upon the agricultural students and laugh." They "heap [on] those unfortunate sons of our farmers—'clod-hoppers' as they call them—all the sneers, insults and outrages they can—they *haze* them unmercifully."[10]

The trustees stepped into trouble almost as soon as the war was over when they appointed a new president, George Washington Custis Lee. It was one thing to appoint a Confederate sympathizer or even a Confederate veteran, but Lee was the son of Robert E. Lee and had been a major general on Jefferson Davis' personal staff. Wiser than the trustees, Lee insisted that public opinion be tested by the announcement of his election before he accepted the position. Unionist newspapers were horrified, a storm of abuse broke over the College and Lee understood. Graciously he turned down the position, and a few years later in more friendly surroundings he succeeded his father as president of Washington and Lee University.[11] The storm even caused the general assembly to consider a resolution, although it did not pass, which would have censured the trustees and withdrawn support from the College "forever":

> *Whereas*, the Trustees of said College have recently appointed to the Presidency and chief Professorship a notorious Rebel and traitor, a certain Gen. Custis Lee, late of the Rebel army, the influence of whose public character, as well as his professional labors, would have a dangerous tendency to corrupt the minds of pupils with treason and disloyalty to the Government; therefore,
> *Resolved by the General Assembly of Maryland*, that the State Agricultural College would be an unsafe place for the education of our young men, and wholly unworthy of either State or Federal patronage, with a man of that cast at its head. . . .[12]

---

[10]*American Farmer*, VII (March, 1878), 110-111; VI (July, 1877), 250; *Maryland Farmer*, XXVII (17 September 1890), 629-630; XXVIII (August, 1891), 19-20.

[11]*Baltimore American*, 12 December 1866; 1 February 1867; 3 March 1867; *Maryland Farmer*, IV (January, 1867), 20.

[12]*Journal of Proceedings of the House of Delegates of Maryland . . . 1867* (Annapolis, 1867), 658-659.

The trustees next turned to Charles L. C. Minor, a graduate of the University of Virginia, once a successful planter and formerly a captain in the Confederate army. Minor's well-developed educational philosophy resembled that of Calvert's and, in fact, the program of most ambitious land-grant college presidents. He would develop a classical-scientific college for the sons of farmers. It was to be a college of the highest standards, designed to train farmers' sons for leadership in the modern world. It was not to be a charity school for the poor, not a playground for young gentlemen waiting to inherit estates, not a mere technological training institute. But like other able land-grant college presidents, Minor found it hard to comprehend the farmer's supreme indifference.[13]

The College reopened in October, 1867, with the president, four other professors, and eleven students. Bravely, Minor abolished the preparatory school and insisted that entering students prove their knowledge of Caesar and Ovid, Greek grammar, algebra and world history. A special arrangement with State Superintendent of Schools Van Bokkelen allowed Minor to offer a number of $100 scholarships, but the tuition was a forbidding $300 annually. Although all students took the same basic course, Minor continued Calvert's highly progressive program of allowing students to major under the professors of natural science for the B.S. degree, or under the professors of languages and mathematics for the A.B. degree. In the future, he promised, "the College is to be rather a school of science rather than a school of classical learning," but he warned that change would come gradually. To critics who suggested that farmers' sons could not meet the requirements, could not pay the tuition and even might not want this kind of education, Minor replied that it was more democratic for the farmers to be exposed to the best than to be segregated by an inferior education. To critics who complained that the curriculum might drive students from, rather than to, the farm, he replied calmly that such a development might be the farmers' eventual salvation.[14]

Minor's administration, unlike those following him, was defeated by indifference rather than hostility. In a day when personal contacts

[13]*Maryland Farmer,* IV (June, 1867) , 178; *Baltimore Sun,* 27 August 1867; *Baltimore American,* 5 October 1867; *American Farmer,* I (April, 1867) , 315-316; II (July, 1867) , 19-20; V (September, 1867) , 274-275.

[14]*American Farmer,* II (July, 1867) , 19-20; II (September, 1867) , 84-85; *Catalogue of the Maryland Agricultural College . . . for the Years 1868-1869* (Baltimore, 1868) . Hereafter cited *Catalogue, 1868-1869.*

were important, few Marylanders had ever heard of the young Virginian or his professors. Few students could meet the entrance requirements, and in the immediate postwar years many young men found it more important to get a crop started than to take time for an education. Finally, the heavy Confederate shadow hanging over the College frightened many away, former Confederates and Unionists alike. In any case, because of the small enrollment, Minor was compelled to release both of his scientific professors at midyear, thus ending the B.S. program and any pretense of agricultural study. His program a failure, the ambitious president resigned. Like Custis Lee before him, he returned to Virginia, where as president of Virginia Polytechnic Institute during the 1870's, he pushed that college far ahead of Maryland.[15]

The trustees looked again for a prominent leader, and this time picked the highest ranking admiral in the former Confederate navy, Franklin Buchanan. Born in Baltimore, the first superintendent of the United States Naval Academy, lionized hero of the *Merrimack*, Buchanan was suave, popular and eager to please. Without much conception of educational philosophy, Buchanan re-instituted the prep school, reduced tuition, re-hired a professor of science and in general continued the program of his predecessor. It offered something for everyone, and enrollment soared to almost one hundred students.

Buchanan, however, viewed himself as an honored hero in retirement and took College affairs lightly. He did not get around to completing the annual report required by the legislature, and when the trustees asked how he was financing his expanding program he replied casually that he had committed the institution to some $6,000 in debts. The trustees were anxious not to antagonize their popular president, but relations after that disclosure were strained. Some weeks later when two professors—half of the faculty—insisted that he expand the work in science, he dismissed them on the spot. Before they could complain to the trustees Buchanan himself resigned. College administration was apparently more than he had bargained for. He departed for Alabama to serve as the figurehead president of an insurance company at double his Maryland salary.[16]

[15] *Second Annual Report of the State Superintendent of Public Instruction* . . . (Annapolis, 1868) , 22-24.
[16] *American Farmer*, III (September, 1868) , 82; *Maryland Farmer*, VI (August, 1869) , 247; VII (January, 1870) , 4-5; Charles Lee Lewis, "Franklin Buchanan," *Dictionary of*

Still trying to hit upon the right combination for an effective leader, the trustees called in another Marylander and former Confederate, a huge and overpowering Methodist preacher, Samuel Register. A graduate of St. John's, Register was more inflexible than his predecessors in demanding "a *thorough* collegiate education" with old-fashioned discipline and no frills. He promised to continue the College farm as an "example" for students, and to establish blacksmith and carpentry shops for students "who may have a taste for these mechanic arts," but this was to be no newfangled technical school. Register abandoned the B. S. degree and for two years neglected to employ a professor of agriculture. He regularly omitted the derogatory word "agriculture" when he referred to "the Maryland *College*."[17]

The preacher-president's real interest was "to instill Christian *morality*," and so much did this endear him to country people that they almost accepted his abandonment of agriculture. He believed the College was isolated providentially seven miles from Washington and consequently "seven miles from sin." Register made himself "Professor of Revealed Religion," employed a special instructor of religious music and promised that even "the incorrigible . . . whether in lessons or behavior" could be taught the Christian way by "severe punishments." He required the professors to eat with the students in order "to exercise supervision over their manners and morals." They attended chapel morning and evening. To the general assembly the president announced proudly, "Our care for their intellectual, spiritual and moral welfare is largely requited."[18]

From 1869 to 1873 Register maintained enrollment at nearly one hundred students and paid off most of the College debt; but his administration was, perhaps, less requited than he imagined. Each year four or five students were expelled, and six or eight more have beside their names in the College register the cryptic remark, "Ran Away." Some trustees disliked the religiosity surrounding the institution, and others expressed concern because the institution was not

---

American Biography, eds. Allen Johnson and Dumas Malone, 22 vols. (New York, 1946), III, 206-207.

[17]James Edward Armstrong, *History of the Old Baltimore Conference* . . . (Baltimore, 1907), 440-441; *Maryland Farmer,* X (February, 1873), 53; *American Farmer,* IV (September, 1869), 82; *Catalogue, 1870-1871,* 8, 12; *Catalogue, 1871-1872,* 5-12.

[18]*Catalogue, 1871-1872,* 5-10, 22-24; *Report of the Board of Trustees of the Maryland Agricultural College to the General Assembly of Maryland* (Annapolis, 1870), [Document "K," House and Senate Documents, 1870], 5.

growing. Farmers became increasingly outspoken about the lack of technical farm training. Just before classes began in the fall of 1873 the trustees announced the complete "reorganization" of the College and asked for Register's resignation.[19]

In the eight years following the war, the trustees had turned to five different presidents with similar disappointing results. Worthington, Lee, Minor, Buchanan and Register each was strong in his own way, but each had failed to establish the Maryland Agricultural College as part of the modern world, and each had failed to fulfill the promise of the Morrill Act. The eight years and five presidents had produced exactly six graduates—one in 1871 and five in 1873. The Confederate ties, the emphasis on classics and religion, even the dedication to high standards and service to the farmer seemed strangely backward. Desperately seeking a way forward, the trustees never guessed that it lay with their enemies.

Guns and Butter

During the 1870's and 1880's, as the great mass of Maryland farmers began to find their voice in farmers' associations and Grange meetings, they turned on the Maryland Agricultural College with astonishing fury. To them it was the one farmers' institution in the state supported by the government, and yet it was doing nothing for agriculture. The small farmers had always feared and hated the planter-Bourbons who controlled the institution. Now these "so-called aristocrats" were robbing them of the Morrill Act funds and were deliberately denying them the practical, technical education that was making the cities rich.

Leading the attack were two of the finest farm journals in the United States, William B. Sands' Maryland Farmer and Ezra Whitman's American Farmer, both published in Baltimore. Both editors held enough College stock to attend shareholder meetings and enjoy an inside view of all disputes; Sands, ironically, had been one of the first two graduates of the school in 1862. Both editors usually courted their subscribers by lambasting the institution, but when one occasionally supported a particular administration, the bitter-

[19]"Register of Students, 1856-1906," bound MS., Maryland Room, McKeldin Library, College Park; Report of Samuel Register, Esquire, President, in Regard to the Condition of the Maryland Agricultural College (Annapolis, 1877), [Document "H," House and Senate Documents, 1872]; Baltimore American, 13 April 1871; Maryland Farmer, X (July, 1873), 215-216.

ness of his rival only increased. Roused by the two journals, the various farmers' organizations began passing resolutions to condemn the College. In a single month the resolutions of censure provided a cross section of the agrarian organizations of Maryland: the State Grange, the Patapsco Grange, the Olney Grange, the Garrison Forest Grange, the Montgomery Farmers' Club, the Montgomery Enterprize Club, the Baltimore Gunpowder Club and the Harford County Deer Creek Club. Each year the general assembly received dozens of petitions demanding investigations, reorganization or withdrawal of state support.[20]

As criticism mounted it seemed to feed on itself until the College became a kind of a scapegoat for the farmers' woes. Much of the criticism was ignorant and vindictive. Pretending to demand technical training for the masses, many critics simply assailed the institution for failing to aid the farmer. Bitterly they attacked the stockholders as a class, "still lamenting the loss of their slaves and talking of the crops they used to raise 'before the wah'."[21] Furiously they raved against the traditional academic curriculum which induced students to leave the farm instead of attracting them to it. The humanities were "effiminate," "absurd studies for a farmer's son," "useless luxuries for the idle rich." Studying Latin, or even English, in an agricultural college seemed "the very height of imbecility."[22]

Far from encouraging research, the enemies of the College hated science almost as much as they scorned the classical course. "We have very little faith in an Agricultural Experiment which can be carried on in a room twenty feet square, by a couple of professors who know nothing beyond their retorts and chemicals." Another critic claimed that research automatically turned an institution into "a pleasant home for incompetents." The ordinary farmer stood squarely behind the advice of his almanac: "Scientific farming stands today with phrenology and biology and magnetism. No farmer ever yet received any benefit from any analysis of the soil and it is doubtful if any one ever will."[23]

[20]*American Farmer*, I (15 March 1882) , 89.

[21]*Ibid.*, VI (15 August 1887) , 232; also, II (May, 1873) , 164; V (February, 1876) , 69; VI (July, 1877) , 250; *Baltimore American*, 18 October 1867; 29 January 1868; 9 October 1876; William B. Sands to James T. Earle, 10 May 1877, Earle Papers, McKeldin Library, College Park.

[22]*American Farmer*, IV (April, 1875) , 158-159; V (March, 1876) , 105; *Maryland Farmer*, XXVIII (October, 1891) , 23-25; also, XIX (September, 1887) , 278; XXVII (30 July 1890) , 514; XXVIII (August, 1891) , 19-20.

[23]*Maryland Farmer*, XXIV (September, 1887) , 280; XXIX (February, 1892) , 29; Almanac cited in Samuel Eliot Morison and Henry Steele Commager, *Growth of the*

The most extreme enemies of the College were determined to sow its fields with salt. "Destroy! destroy!" cried one farmer, "blot out entirely and forever this superfluous and worse than superfluous institution." Not content with recommending the withdrawal of government appropriations, the *American Farmer* in 1887 considered the College the greatest political issue of the day: "No candidate for the legislature this fall should receive a vote from the farmers who is not pledged to uproot . . . this so-called Agricultural College [which is] the most stupendous fraud in the state."[24]

Bewildered at the excitement but always eager to economize, the general assembly began to give in. In 1876 it withdrew its $6,000 annual appropriation to the institution. The trustees obtained a ruling from the attorney general that this was a violation of the state's acceptance of the Morrill Act, but in 1882 he was persuaded to change his ruling. For the next six years the College subsisted entirely on tuition plus the pittance from the Morrill Act. Meanwhile, in 1880, the legislature reorganized the board of trustees, reducing the stockholders' representatives to five and increasing the state-appointed representatives to seven, thus giving the state majority control of College affairs for the first time. In 1888 the legislature increased the state-appointed trustees to thirteen. Yet all such actions seemed to make little difference. The new trustees generally understood the dilemma of the College and willingly continued the old policies, so that the critics remained unappeased.[25]

Violent criticism first came into the open about 1873 when the trustees appoined to top positions two military-minded officers, Samuel Jones and William H. Parker. Perhaps the main reason why the trustees asked for Register's resignation was their discovery of these two men who promised to infuse new life into the College with an emphasis on engineering and military tactics. Together they formed a continuous administration which lasted from 1873 to 1882. When Jones arrived as president, Parker came as professor of engineering; and when Jones was driven off by criticism in 1875, his associate stepped in to continue his program.

American Republic, 2 vols. (New York, 1942), II, 195; also, *American Farmer,* VII (January, 1878), 4.

[24] *American Farmer,* V (January, 1876), 35; I (15 February 1882), 57; VI (1 July 1887), 199.

[25] *Journal . . . of the House . . . 1876,* 123; *American Farmer,* V (September, 1876), 300; VII (January, 1878), 35; I (15 February 1882), 57; *Laws of the State of Maryland . . . 1880* (Annapolis, 1880), Chap. 231; *Laws . . . of Maryland . . . 1882,* Chap. 432; *Laws . . . of Maryland . . . 1888,* Chap. 326.

John Beale Davidge

John Crawford

Granville Sharp Pattison

Horace H. Hayden

Chapin A. Harris

David Hoffman

Nathaniel Potter

Louisa Parsons

Nathan Ryno Smith

The University Hospital on the eve of the Civil War

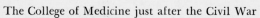

The College of Medicine just after the Civil War

An anatomy laboratory about 1900

An operation before a class about 1900

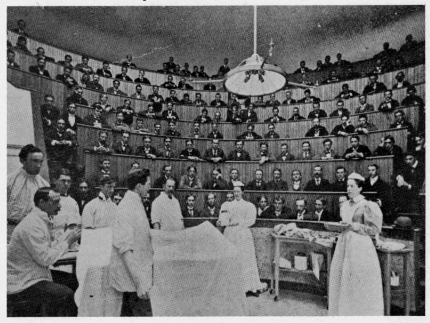

An operation before a class about 1900

The Baltimore College of Dental
Surgery in the 1840's

The Dental Clinic about 1910

Charles Benedict Calvert, founder of The Maryland Agricultural College

The Barracks, main building of the College from 1859 to 1912

The Rossborough Inn about 1885

The cadets in 1898

An engineering laboratory in 1898

The first President's House

Agricultural Extension in 1900

The College on the hill in 1905

The two were alike in background and personality. Samuel Jones was a Virginian, a graduate of West Point and another former Confederate major general. William H. Parker, one of the ablest of all Maryland's presidents, was a New Yorker who had graduated first in his class from the Naval Academy, become a captain in the Confederate navy and founder of the Confederate Naval Academy in Richmond. During the hardest years of reconstruction he went west as commander of a Pacific steamer. In his spare time he wrote at least three notable books on naval tactics and one of the most charming books of memoirs that came out of the Civil War.[26]

Jones and Parker obtained their interests in engineering from West Point and Annapolis, probably the best engineering schools in the country. By bringing the new subject to Maryland they made the institution one of the first agricultural and mechanical colleges to develop the mechanical studies as something more than blacksmithing and carpentry. They established seven distinct one-man departments in the College: three traditional ones in languages, mathematics and English; three new departments in physics, chemistry and civil engineering; and one department in agriculture which they hoped would appease agrarian critics. Students could choose six of the seven departments in which to work. Although a sound basic education remained, emphasis had shifted still further from classics to science. The educated farmer's son, who was probably going to the city anyway, would be led in that direction through engineering rather than through the ministry, medicine or law.[27]

Aware that farmers demanded courses in practical agriculture, Jones and Parker also knew that no agricultural knowledge existed on a college level, and that students did not want it if it did exist. Nevertheless, they offered a "certificate" to any student completing a year's study of agriculture. The course was a pretense, for the handful of such students did manual labor on the farm, and they were the "clod-hoppers" laughed at by the others. While Jones and Parker declared publicly that the agricultural department was the "most important" one in the College, the classes met once a week while the others met daily. Still trying to appease farmer

[26]"Samuel Jones," *National Cyclopedia of American Biography*, 42 vols. ff. (New York, 1897 ff.), IV, 466; Allan Westcott, "William Harwar Parker," *Dictionary of American Biography*, XIV, 243-244; William H. Parker, *Recollections of a Naval Officer, 1841-1865* (New York, 1883); *Maryland Farmer*, X (October, 1873), 308; XII (August, 1875), 243.

[27]*Catalogues*, 1873-1882, *passim*.

critics, Parker arranged for the agricultural students to take trips to county fairs, receive gold medals for essays on farming and hear lectures at the College "by some of the most famous agriculturalists of the State." Finally, with much fanfare, Parker employed a certain Professor Grabowski, the first Ph.D. on the College faculty, from the Wiesbaden Academy of Agriculture in Germany. Parker called him "Professor of Agriculture," but actually he taught engineering and physics.[28]

While Jones and Parker pointed to the future with their engineering emphasis, and while they appeased the farmer with their agricultural masquerade, they invited criticism with an emphasis on spit-and-polish military training. Eager to expand the institution, they hit upon the unfortunate notion of advertising the Maryland Agricultural College as a preparatory institution for West Point and the Naval Academy. This would expand the College prep school, and they hoped that some of the students would remain for the College course. Without consulting the trustees, Jones and Parker published a pamphlet intended for select distribution among their many personal contacts. The pamphlet promised long daily drills, daily inspections and instruction in military tactics. Officers wore white gloves and swords. Students were "cadets" who ate their meals in perfect silence, marched to classes and recited their lessons at attention.

As the prep school prospered, Jones and Parker widened their appeal to "Captains and Mates in the Merchant Marine Service wishing to improve themselves." Parker somehow managed to obtain use of a vessel in Baltimore harbor for summer training missions and promised "navigational exercises" on the College "lake." Actually the lake was an ice pond three feet deep, and Parker's enemies were able to make many jokes about his campus fleet. The new program attracted about twenty out-of-state students each year during most of the 1870's and for a while the College almost subsisted on their tuitions. In the long run, however, militarism only drove students away.[29]

Military training was a peculiarity in the Morrill Act which

[28]*Catalogue, 1873-1874*, 20; *Catalogue, 1878-1879*, 5, 14; William H. Parker, *Letter of Acceptance of the President of the Maryland Agricultural College* ("Published by Order of the Trustees," 1875) ; *Report of the Board of Trustees of the Maryland Agricultural College to the General Assembly of Maryland*, 1876, also 1878, 1880, 1882 (Annapolis, 1876, 1878, 1880, 1882) .

[29]*Maryland Farmer*, XII (May, 1875) , 164-165; XIII (January, 1876) , 22; *American*

even today remains the subject of emotional debate. The act contains only four words on the subject, providing that land-grant colleges might offer any course they wished so long as they taught agricultural and mechanical training "and including military tactics." Added as an afterthought to the act and inspired by the feeling that southern military schools had given the South an initial advantage in the war, the phrase did not require uniforms nor did it make military training compulsory. In the first months after the war, however, with military fervor still strong, with surplus uniforms the cheapest clothing available and with retired officers heading many of the new colleges, no one particularly objected when most of the land-grant colleges adopted certain military characteristics. This development occurred at Maryland, and students had worn uniforms and drilled casually for about an hour a week since 1867 when the College reopened. Now Jones and Parker were carrying militarism much further than their predecessors and much further than other land-grant colleges.[30]

The new military emphasis invited criticism because by the 1870's the typical postwar wave of antimilitarism had set in. As usual, this feeling was particularly strong among rural people. In Maryland, moreover, it was particularly strong because it reopened hatreds that neighbors were trying to forget. Southern sympathizing parents were horrified to see their sons wearing uniforms with a United States insignia, and northern sympathizing parents were shocked to see their sons drilled by former Confederates. Jones and Parker argued that military training inculcated the virtues of strength, obedience, neatness and courtesy. Farmers suspected that it inculcated arrogance, pettiness, pretense and that "it dulls the boys." Many parents who visited the campus were not honored by the roar of cannon which greeted them. They were repelled by the chapel walls which "bristled with muskets" and by the chapel platform "ornamented with crossed swords, shot guns and evergreens."[31]

Farmer, IV (February, 1875), 77; V (September, 1876), 300-301; VI (July, 1877), 246-249; *Baltimore American,* 13 July 1872; 10 June 1875; 30 December 1875; *Baltimore Sun,* 25 August 1877; 25 February 1882.

[30]Ross, *Democracy's College,* 122-128, 196-197.

[31]*Catalogue, 1885-1886,* 24-25; *American Farmer,* VI (September, 1877), 311; VI (November, 1877), 388; also, *Baltimore American,* 18 October 1867; 12 September 1877; 7 March 1880; *Washington Republican,* 15 January 1887; *American Farmer,* IV (April, 1875), 153-154; V (September, 1876), 300-301; VI (July, 1877), 246-249; VII (March, 1878), 110-111; VI (1 July 1887), 199 and *passim; Maryland Farmer,* VIII (July, 1871), 223, XIV (July, 1877), 224 and *passim.*

Angry that the College had done nothing for agriculture and fired by their hatred of militarism, the farmers concentrated their attack upon Jones and Parker. With considerable truth they pointed out that the two non-Marylanders cared little for farming, that they had budgeted $5,000 annually for mathematics and $600 for agriculture. Critics accused the College of "seducing" their sons away from the farm and catering to students who "wish only to *escape* the farmer's vocation." Vehemently they complained that the College did not provide for "the *ordinary* education of children." Jones and Parker could only reply that it was more democratic, not less, to provide farmers' sons with "book-learning like the sons of any other class"; that the students themselves refused to take the agricultural courses offered; and that colleges were meant to teach leadership rather than provide ordinary education for children. But the farmers were not listening to arguments; they demanded Jones' scalp.[32]

When the president, with the trustees' consent, raised his salary from $1,500 to $2,500 annually, cries went up of "mismanagement of finances," "corruption," and "fraud." In May, 1875, a number of the trustees succeeded in calling a meeting which the president and a number of his supporters could not attend. With a bare quorum present, they rammed through a resolution condemning his militaristic program, his "neglect of agriculture" and his "general waste and extravagance," and asked for his resignation. Jones accepted the verdict, and departed with an eloquent defense of his administration. Two months later a full assembly of the trustees appointed Captain William H. Parker to continue a program identical to that of his predecessor.[33]

At almost every meeting of the trustees and every session of the general assembly the brave and hounded president fought off his enemies. In 1876, following the dismissal of venerable old Nicholas B. Worthington, one-time acting president of the institution, Parker withstood a typical attack. His enemies, William B. Sands, George H. Calvert and Allen Bowie Davis, launched a proxy fight to dislodge him.[34] His supporters, including James H. Earle and Allen Dodge, won the fight partly as a result of a widely quoted verse:

[32]*American Farmer*, IV (May, 1875), 198-202; VI (August, 1877), 278-279; VII (February, 1878), 77-80; *Maryland Farmer*, XII (May, 1875), 164-165; XIX (February, 1882), 61; XXVI (October, 1889), 290-291.

[33]*Baltimore American*, 25 January 1875; 15 May 1875; 10 June 1875; 14 September 1875; *Maryland Farmer*, XII (May, 1875), 165-167; XII (August, 1875), 243; XIV (November, 1877), 35-352; *American Farmer*, IV (May, 1875), 191-193.

[34]*Maryland Farmer*, XII (May, 1875), 165-167; XIV (September, 1877), 286-290.

> Give EARLE the proxy for your stock,
> The College stands upon a rock.
> Commit it into CALVERT'S hands,
> The College falls—it rests on SANDS.
> Just look you'll find in Holy Writ,
> A cure precisely that will fit;
> The question now for one and all,
> Is "shall it stand or shall it fall?"[35]

More serious were the attacks from the public and the general assembly. When further state aid was denied in 1882, it appeared doubtful that the College could endure. The valiant president raised tuition fees and reduced his own salary, but the fall enrollment was down to less than fifty. Tired of a battle he could not win and knowing that the last hope for the school's revival lay in his departure, in September, 1882, Parker submitted a gracious letter of resignation, suggesting that it was time for him to seek adventure elsewhere. Off he went as United States consul to Korea.[36]

A few of the stockholders, including George H. Calvert and Allen Bowie Davis, suggested that liquidation of the College assets would be profitable to the old shareholders, while some farmers suggested full state confiscation, sale of the land, or the refurbishing of the building as a public high school or an experiment station. Still, Jones and Parker had earned the respect of those who knew them, many old students rallied and the trustees determined to hold on. Early in 1883 they found another able man who was willing to try his hand at the presidency.[37]

Augustine J. Smith with his courtly manners and florid language was almost the caricature of the southern gentleman. Possibly the trustees saw themselves in him. A Virginia gentleman who had made a fortune as a sugar factor, Smith was ideally suited to impress the rural countryside. Popularity was his prime educational policy, and he promised to "cover the state with letters and speeches" to "reestablish the college in public confidence."[38] He began with

---

[35]*Ibid.*, XIV (October, 1877), 322; see William B. Sands to James E. Earle, 10 May 1877, Earle Papers, McKeldin Library.

[36]*Report of the Board of Trustees . . . 1882* (Annapolis, 1882), 6-14; *Laws . . . of Maryland . . . 1882*, Chap. 432; *Laws . . . of Maryland . . . 1888*, Chap. 326; *Maryland Farmer*, XIX (November, 1882), 367; *Baltimore American*, 12 October 1882.

[37]*Baltimore American*, 13 October 1882; 20 September 1883; *Catalogue, 1882-1883*, 4-18; *Seventeenth Annual Report of the State Board of Education* (Annapolis, 1884), [Document "M," House and Senate Documents], 9, 20; *Maryland Farmer*, XX (March, 1883), 92-93; XX (April, 1883), 128-129; *American Farmer*, V (January, 1876), 35; I (15 February 1882), 57; V (15 March 1886), 90-91; VI (1 July 1887), 199.

[38]*Maryland Farmer*, XX (March, 1883), 92-93; XXIV (July, 1887), 218.

beautiful finesse, consulting the editors of Maryland newspapers and farm journals about accepting the position. Soon he was everywhere, fathering the students, charming local grange organizations, flattering individual farmers and addressing the general assembly. He rewrote the College catalogue in ornate style, promising everything to everybody. To the farmers he pledged to substitute "a home-like atmosphere" for the prevailing militarism. To the trustees he agreed to uphold a traditional curriculum with respectable standards. To the students he promised better food, more comfortable beds, a better library, more "amusements" and "paternal counsel."[39]

Smith's popularity paid off eventually, but not during his own administration. With little financial support and no scholarships, enrollment continued to fall, and for three years there were no graduates. Playing entirely for the future, Smith closed the financial records of the College even to the trustees, put off creditors and accumulated a debt of over $15,000. When help failed to arrive as soon as expected in the form of new legislation, he was in trouble. Amid imputations of dishonesty, Smith pleaded ill health and resigned. For the remainder of the academic year 1887-1888 one of the trustees, Allen Dodge, served as acting president.[40]

During the entire fifteen years from 1873 to 1888 under Jones, Parker, Smith and Dodge the institution had reeled from the attacks of the farmers. Despite imaginative leadership, it had produced only thirty-eight graduates, scarcely more than during the years of war, reconstruction and indifference. The College had still not found the bridge between higher education and the people, but just as the Morrill Act of 1862 had pointed the way, new legislation including the Hatch Act of 1887 would lead the way.

The People's College

While most American land-grant colleges staggered under agrarian attacks during the 1870's and 1880's, and while a few of the stronger institutions quietly carried on research, both the hostile farmer and

[39]*Ibid.*, XX (April, 1883), 128-129; XX (May, 1883), 133-134; XXI (February, 1884), 65-68; XXI (March, 1884), 95-97; *Catalogues, 1883-1884, 1884-1885, 1885-1886;* Augustine Jacquelin Smith, *The Necessity for Agricultural Education* (Washington, 1883), 3-15.
[40]*American Farmer,* V (15 March 1886), 90; VI (15 May 1887), 139; VI (1 July 1887), 199; *Maryland Farmer,* XXIV (July, 1887), 218; *Washington Star,* 15 January 1884; *Washington Republican,* 15 January 1882.

the indifferent businessman began to see a use for the beleagured institutions. By the 1880's the farmer was beginning to make large demands on the politicians. With growing anger he was calling for sweeping legislation to control the railroads, break the trusts, lower tariffs, create inflationary money and establish a graduated income tax. Among his lesser demands, he was calling for government agencies to police the distribution of such products as the fertilizer which he had to buy from the businessman and to regulate the practices of the trusts which bought his produce. Moreover, he wished the government to find him more profitable crops to grow, and possibly the land-grant colleges might perform some of these functions. To the conservative businessman, horrified at many ideas of the farm organizations, it seemed prudent to yield to specific demands in an effort to buy off the more radical ones. Why not let the little land-grant colleges supervise the sale of fertilizer? What could be easier than giving them a few million dollars to experiment with new crops?

For the Maryland Agricultural College a new role began, unglamorously, with the State Fertilizer Law of 1886. Cheated and bewildered for years by unscrupulous manufacturers who advertised inferior and even worthless brands of fertilizer, the farmers petitioned the general assembly for $1,700 annually for a state official to inspect the various brands and publicize the results. It was a modest request, and the legislature readily approved what may have been the first piece of agricultural legislation in Maryland since the war. For lack of any other established agency, the legislature assigned the fertilizer inspector to work under the direction of the College president. It was the beginning of a code of farm legislation far larger than anyone realized.[41]

The really important legislation, however, the legislation President Smith had been counting on, came just as he resigned—the federal Hatch Act which created agricultural experiment stations. Several states already operated such stations primarily to test brands of fertilizer and seeds, and a number of Maryland farmers had suggested that the College be put to similar use. When Congressman William Hatch of Missouri requested a paltry million dollars to support experimentation, both political parties outdid themselves to appear the farmers' friend. The bill promised $15,000 annually to one station in each state, a sum considerably more than the total

[41]*Laws . . . of Maryland . . . 1886*, Chap. 477.

budget of the Maryland Agricultural College. The trustees promptly offered the College farm and the Rossborough House for use by the experiment station, pointing to the mutual aid which the College and the station might provide for each other. Desperately the trustees fought off attempts to attach the station to Johns Hopkins University or to establish it in place of the College. The general assembly agreed to join the two, and within a year the station was in operation spending its first $15,000 in experiments on the College campus. Officially the two institutions were separate, but the governor appointed identical trustees for both, and soon even their budgets were entwined.[42]

The trustees even filched their next president from the experiment station. As soon as they learned that the well-known Henry C. Alvord had undertaken the job of director of the station, they asked him to take over as president of the College as well. Alvord agreed, accepting both positions and both salaries.

Almost everything about Alvord pointed toward a new era. His eight predecessors were Confederate veterans, but here suddenly was a Massachusetts man, a former major in the Union army. Although he had no college degree—and never really thought much of one—he was a scientist of national reputation, a specialist in dairying, the author of four books and a score of articles. Professor in the Massachusetts Agricultural College and chief founder of the American Association of Land Grant Colleges before he came to Maryland, he subsequently served as president of Oklahoma Agricultural and Mechanical College and as head of the dairy division of the United States Department of Agriculture. Most of all he represented the new era as an administrator. He acquired a secretary, an expense account, a typewriter and a telephone. A man who was systematic, calculating, and exact, he would have been more admired by his successors than by his predecessors.[43]

Alvord liked to call the institution "The People's College" which

[42]Arthur J. Klein, *Survey of Land Grant Colleges and Universities*, 2 vols. (Washington, 1930) , I, 23-33; Ross, *Democracy's College*, 177-182; *Maryland Farmer*, XXI (February, 1884) , 65-66; XXIII (April, 1886) , 125-128; XXIII (May, 1886) , 148; *Report of the Board of Trustees . . . 1888-1889*, 27-28, 39-46; *Baltimore American*, 27 October 1888.

[43]Alfred Charles True, "Henry Elijah Alvord," *Dictionary of American Biography*, I, 238-239; Department of Agriculture, Personnel Records, National Archives, Washington, D. C.; Records Office of the Secretary of Interior, National Archives, Washington, D. C., RG 48, P and M Division, LR, Box 98-106; *Report of the Board of Trustees . . . 1888-1889*, 7; *Baltimore American*, 13 March 1888; 17 May 1888; *Maryland Farmer*, XXV (April, 1888) , 101-103.

meant that service to the farmer was more important than standards for the students. In place of the former entrance requirements of Latin, algebra and history, he substituted a perfunctory oral examination in "reading, spelling [and] common-school arithmetic." Abolishing the preparatory school long conducted for poorly qualified students, he suggested that students might enter the College with little restriction as to age. He ended the engineering course and announced that every student would earn the "strictly agricultural" B.S. degree. Taking the "practical results" from agricultural studies being conducted over the country, he built the curriculum around horticulture, botany and breeding. Chemistry, he apologized, meant only "agricultural analyses"; physics meant the study of light, heat and electricity in "their economic applications"; mathematics meant measurements, surveying, roadmaking, drainage and construction. As for other subjects, English emphasized the ability to write business letters, the optional course in foreign languages concentrated on translations of agricultural journals and history emphasized "the privileges and duties of citizenship."[44]

Everything seemed to fall into Alvord's lap. Following the Fertilizer Act of 1886 and the Hatch Act of 1887, in the next year the general assembly restored its $6,000 annual appropriation and established scholarships to pay expenses for twenty-eight students. In 1890 another federal bonanza came, the greatest yet, with the Second Morrill Act. Still trying to appease farm discontent, a conservative Congress appropriated $15,000 for technical education to each of the land-grant colleges to be increased at the rate of $1,000 a year until the annual grant reached $25,000. That sum was to be continued permanently. The Second Morrill Act was probably the first national legislation in American history providing education "without distinction of race or color." The trustees, consequently, granted about one-fifth of the money to Morgan College of Baltimore, to be spent for its Normal and Industrial Branch at Princess Anne on the Eastern Shore.[45]

As money flowed into the College treasury, Alvord basked in the farmers' approval. In five years the College budget increased 500 percent, from about $10,000 in 1887 to $50,000 in 1892. Looking for ways to spend the money, Alvord eliminated tuition entirely,

[44]*Report of the Board of Trustees . . . 1888-1889*, 5-9, 18-19, 30; *Catalogue, 1891-1892*, 6; *American Farmer*, IX (March, 1890), 72.

[45]*Laws . . . of Maryland . . . 1888*, Chap. 481; Ross, *Democracy's College*, 177-182; *Report of the Maryland Agricultural College . . . 1890* (Baltimore, 1890), 4-6.

reduced student living expenses to $180 a year, increased the faculty from six to twelve—of whom seven were in agriculture—and hastily built a fashionably ugly, two-story Victorian structure with a silo-like turret to serve as a library and gymnasium.[46]

Despite prosperity, however, Alvord still faced one stubborn fact: most students did not want to study agriculture. Parents might like the curriculum, and the study was indeed approaching academic respectability, but most young men went to college to escape the farm. Despite the free tuition and the expanded faculty, enrollment in 1892 was scarcely more than when Alvord arrived and only half of what it had been a decade earlier. By counting his entire student body, Alvord liked to boast that Maryland had more agricultural students than Cornell, Pennsylvania State or Wisconsin, but he seemed not to realize that the success of those institutions lay in their having evolved, in varying degrees, into state universities that did not require agriculture. Alvord had made a major contribution with his concept of the "People's College," but he scarcely understood what students wanted. He made the mistake of listening to what their parents said the young men wanted.[47]

For all the promise of revival, the College had not quite made the transition to the modern world. The trustees were impatient at the lack of growth and some lamented the decline in standards. Irreconcilable enemies pointed out that the College received over $10,000 for each graduate it produced. When Alvord was unable to settle a petty faculty squabble, the trustees came in to mediate.[48] Alvord appealed "confidentially" to alumni and even to students to write letters supporting him: "I understand that writing such a letter is *your proposition*—not mine," he pleaded. "I only offer suggestions."[49] Such awkwardness only made matters worse, and in July, 1892, the trustees announced his resignation.[50] In almost thirty years since the war, ten presidents had tried to rescue the battered little College on the hill, and still it had not grown since Calvert's day.

[46]*Report of the Maryland Agricultural College . . . 1891* (Baltimore, 1892) , 4-6; *Report of the Maryland Agricultural College . . . 1893* (Baltimore, 1894) , 30-31.

[47]*Report of the Maryland Agricultural College . . . 1890,* 7; *Report of the Maryland Agricultural College . . . 1891,* 6.

[48]*American Farmer,* IX (15 June 1890) , 170; *Maryland Farmer,* XXVII (19 March 1890) , 190; XXVII (14 May 1890) , 328-329; XXVIII (July, 1891) , 20-21; XXVIII (September, 1891) , 28-30; XXIX (April, 1892) , 25-26.

[49]Henry E. Alvord to Fletcher P. Veitch, 30 May 1892, Veitch Papers, McKeldin Library.

[50]*Maryland Farmer,* XXIX (July, 1892) , 38; XXIX (August, 1892) , 26-32.

Student Life

Enemies of the College were especially angered by its dilapidated appearance. Visitors usually arrived by one of the ten daily trains from Baltimore or one of the ten from Washington. They found themselves at College Station, an unscheduled stop in a desolate marsh, and unless someone met them they walked the three-quarters of a mile to the College. Visitors before the war crossed some of the best-kept fields in the state, but Calvert's heirs had allowed most of the plantation to fall into ruin. Although this land did not belong to the College, people judged the institution by its surroundings, and fields of brambles set the stage in the 1870's and 1880's just as chaotic urbanization does today. During Alvord's administration the area began to look better. A Washington real estate developer drained the land and subdivided it into streets and village lots, and in 1890 the name was changed to College Park. A little railway station appeared with a telephone connection to the campus. The College donated trees for the town and helped to finance a plank walk from the station to the campus.[51]

Beside the muddy turnpike stood the Rossborough House, residence of the farm manager and headquarters of the 286-acre College farm. Until the experiment station came, it looked like a thousand other Maryland farms, with chickens clucking around the porch in front, and tumbled-down sheds, the privy and the unpainted barn behind. Also at the rear was a brick building which served as a laundry until about 1890 when it was converted into a chemistry laboratory. On special occasions, such as commencements, the more energetic presidents saw that the outbuildings were whitewashed. Around the farm rotting rail fences let the pigs out, and the poorer fields grew up in weeds. About sixty acres were cultivated, producing such crops as corn, wheat, oats, potatoes and cabbages. There was a sizable garden and a good orchard. The College owned about a dozen head of cattle, two mule teams, several dozen pigs and sometimes a small herd of sheep. The farm manager spent about $1,500 annually for seed, fertilizer, labor and repairs and supplied much of the food for the students and faculty.

[51]*Baltimore American,* 13 April 1871; *Maryland Farmer,* XXV (April, 1888), 101-103; XXIX (August, 1892), 26-28; *Report of the Board of Trustees . . . 1888-1889,* 8-11.

Neighborhood sales almost paid for the next year's seed and fertilizer.[52]

The main College building, the five-story mustard-stucco structure Calvert built, stood in the midst of a beautiful grove of cedars, oaks and elms. At the edge of the grove in front of the building was a well-beaten parade ground, a tall flag pole and a half dozen artillery pieces. If the visitor were sufficiently important, the cadets were mustered there, standing at attention in high-collar gray uniforms. Behind the College, and out of sight, were three sharecropper cabins. The cropper families cultivated about forty acres, turning over a portion of their crops to the College, or else doing chores and janitorial work as payment for use of the land. On a hill two hundred yards north of the College stood the well-kept house of the president. To visiting farmers it was the one building that looked a little too fine.[53]

Seeing the students lined up, their long hair parted in the middle and billowing out under their caps, the modern visitor would have noted their youth. Most were too young for the beards which were fashionable in the professional schools, for the prep school accepted students at twelve years of age, and College freshmen were usually fifteen.[54]

Most students came from farm families, and many were related to the trustees. Fifteen or twenty came from Prince George's County; about forty others were from various part of the state; six or eight came from surrounding states or from the District of Columbia. When Jones and Parker conducted their military prep school many more came from as far away as New England or California.[55] The students who had been sent by their parents to study agriculture probably disliked the College. About half left before completing the first year, and only a sixth of them graduated. Others, knowing what the institution offered, seldom intended to return to the farm. President Jones admitted that, except for the freshman class, every

[52]"Maryland Agricultural College Journal, 1858-1873," bound MS., McKeldin Library; Account Books, 1873-1888, bound MS., McKeldin Library; *Baltimore American*, 20 September 1883; *Report of the President of the Maryland Agricultural College to the Board of Trustees . . . 1875* (Baltimore, 1875), 5-6; *Report of the Board of Trustees . . . 1888-1889*, 23-28; *Report of the Maryland Agricultural College . . . 1891*, 17-22.

[53]*American Farmer*, VI (July, 1877), 246-249; *Catalogue, 1891-1892*, 5-15. See pictures in *Report of the Maryland Agricultural College . . . 1893* (Baltimore, 1893), *passim*.

[54]"Register of Students, 1856-1906"; *Catalogue, 1874-1875*, 26; *Catalogue, 1886-1887*, 26; *Catalogue, 1891-1892*, 6; *American Farmer*, V (January, 1876), 27-28.

[55]"Register of Students, 1858-1906"; lists of students, their place of residence and name of guardian are listed in most of the annual catalogues.

student he knew dreamed of a career in the city.[56] Parents had to sacrifice for their son's education. Throughout most of the period expenses for tuition and board totaled about $250 a year; a dress uniform with two shirts, a fatigue uniform and a Confederate cap cost about $30 more.[57]

A stern regime of rules and threats governed daily life, restraining the youthful rebellion that seemed to hover beneath the surface. Professors, judged as disciplinarians more than as scholars, must have blanched at the prospect of controlling students without the military system. Many defended the semester-long freshman hazing as an essential outlet for youthful vigor. The College catalogues dwelt upon the standard rules against drinking, smoking, gambling and cutting classes, but they also concerned detailed rules for children about marking on walls, running up stairs, leaving rooms during study hours, loud talking and even weekly baths. Most professors were ready and able to hand out a healthy walloping when the occasion demanded.[58]

When reveille sounded at half past six each morning students dashed down for prayers and breakfast. At half-past seven they stood by their beds, ramrod straight, for daily inspection. From eight until twelve they attended the first four "recitations" of the day. Although some variation existed for different levels of study and for students emphasizing different fields, about half the students attended the same class at the same time. What a professor did not cover in one year, he would get to the next. At noon came an hour of military drill, and at one o'clock the main meal of the day. Meals were plain, substantial and southern: pork, cornbread, turnips, potatoes, fresh vegetables and fruit. From two until four came two more recitations. Then until six many students worked for the farm manager receiving about ten cents an hour to help pay their board; others lounged about, studied or perhaps played "base ball" —a frivolity frowned upon by officials. Supper came at six, after which were prayers again, and from seven until ten o'clock cadets were restricted to their rooms for study. The two-semester academic

[56]*Maryland Farmer*, X (June, 1873), 177; also, *Catalogue, 1888-1889*, 13.

[57]*Report of the Board of State School Commissioners Showing the Condition of the Public Schools of Maryland* (Annapolis, 1872) [Document "U," House and Senate Documents, 1872], 16, 34; annual *Catalogues, passim; Annual Reports of the State Board of Education, passim.*

[58]*Baltimore American*, 24 February 1880; *Maryland Farmer*, XXIII (December, 1886), 356; *Catalogue, 1872-1873*, 19-20; *Report of the President . . . 1875*, 5; *Catalogue, 1888-1889*, 25; "Class History," *Reveille, 1897* [Student Annual] (Baltimore, 1897), 27-51.

year lasted from mid-September to late June, with two days off at Thanksgiving, two at Easter and about a week at Christmas.[59]

The pattern of daily life was never as harsh as the rules would indicate, for young boys could always find time for relaxation and friendships to soften the military discipline. When parents saw fit to withdraw their sons for weeks or even months to work at home, they generally fitted back into the College schedule without penalty. Several times each year they held dances, sometimes with costumes and Chinese lanterns, which often lasted until almost dawn. The College had its own band and glee club, and at least one literary society was always active. For students who behaved themselves during the week, Saturday afternoons and Sundays were free for church trips into Washington or for visits to their homes; and the presidents knew the students did not spend all that time in church.[60]

The most deadening part of College life concerned things intellectual. Although Maryland's feints toward science and electives sounded progressive, the methods of instruction were antedeluvian. Classrooms were called "recitation rooms" where professors tirelessly drilled the boys in a fixed body of facts. Examinations concerned the names of state capitals, the chronology of battles and the conjugation of verbs. Even in science where the laboratory slowly replaced recitations, emphasis was still on memorizing formulae, periodic tables and botanical names. Most professors believed that controversy was hostile to efficient learning, that boys were to be shielded from the issues of Darwinism, imperialism and populism which were boiling outside the College. The library did not subscribe to a newspaper, and students were forbidden to read contemporary novels. The Mercer Literary Society, forbidden to consider "upsetting questions," debated instead such topics as "Self-Reliance" and "The Importance of Scientific Agriculture." The ivory tower was cold and sterile. A professor with ideas had better return to his job and quiet the boys on the fourth floor.[61]

The festive event of every academic year, far greater than at

---

[59]Details varied from year to year. This particular schedule is taken from *Report of the President . . . 1875*, 9-11. See annual *Catalogues, passim; Maryland Farmer*, XIX (May, 1887), 146.

[60]*Reveille, 1897*, 66-72 and *passim; Report of the Board of Trustees . . . 1882*, 7; *Baltimore American*, 22 February 1889.

[61]Richard Hofstadter and C. DeWitt Hardy, *Development and Scope of Higher Education in the United States* (New York, 1952), 17-28; Arthur Meir Schlessinger, *Rise of the City, 1878-1898* (New York, 1933), 202-216; *Catalogue, 1892-1893*, 12, 21-23, 44-48.

present, was the three-day commencement ceremony. Despite the widespread dislike of the institution, the governor usually attended along with the chief legislative leaders, trustees, delegations from the Grange, newspaper reporters and hundreds of relatives. On Sunday morning a Methodist or Episcopal bishop delivered the baccalaureate sermon, and the afternoon was given over to musical concerts—perhaps by a special choir brought out from Washington to perform with the College glee club. Monday was devoted to military drills, student orations and dramatic productions. Although the public examination disappeared after the Civil War, the commencement oration, on such topics as "Improvement" or "Agriculture," was still the high point of every boy's college career. Lower classmen performed one-act plays, sometimes in a foreign language. Finally, on Tuesday, crowds gathered in the low-ceiling basement chapel, which was elaborately decorated with bunting and flags, boughs and evergreens, muskets and swords. An orchestra played. The president awarded gold and silver medals for deportment, for high scholastic averages and for essays on agriculture. One incredulous visitor observed that "more than half of the student body received medals." The governor or a visiting dignitary spoke interminably about buckling on armor for the battle of life or about the happy rewards of rural living. The ceremonies went on even when there were no graduates, but if two or three received degrees they were greeted with applause, cheers and traditional bouquets. The graduates and their families had supper at the president's home and in the evening came the commencement ball, the climax of all the festivity. For the ball in 1878 President Parker arranged a long-remembered surprise: attending as guest of honor was beautiful Lotta Crabtree, the most famous actress of the day.[62]

Of the seventy graduates from 1865 to 1892, about one-third made their careers in Baltimore, and another third moved to Washington, New York or other cities outside of Maryland. The great majority emerged as prominent local citizens, while almost a quarter went on to obtain advanced degrees and two obtained recognition by inclusion in *Who's Who in America*. These were Fletcher P. Veitch, a government chemist, and Francis P. Soper, a school superintendent. The record of the graduates verifies the charge that the College

[62]Charles W. Melick (of the Experiment Station) to E. A. Ross, 14 September 1907, Ross Papers, State Historical Society of Wisconsin (copy in Maryland Room, McKeldin Library); *Baltimore Sun*, 26 June 1878; *Baltimore American*, 20 June 1889; *Maryland Farmer*, XIII (August, 1876), 261; XVI (July, 1879), 162; XVIII (August, 1881), 255.

led away from the farm. Indeed, both in modesty and eminence, the record typifies the work of the land-grant colleges in the era they found most difficult.

14 businessmen
8 doctors
8 lawyers
7 government workers
6 engineers
3 educators
2 farmers
1 clergy
1 army
20 unknown[63]

Like most of the land-grant institutions, the Maryland Agricultural College had not quite found its place in the era or in the state. Despite able leaders, bold experimentation and endurance, it had not come to terms with the ruthless, practical, egalitarian forces of the day. Despite federal aid and half-ownership by the state, it remained simply another struggling private institution. Nevertheless, if impatience, crassness, disorganization and even irresponsible anti-intellectualism were part of the American democracy, so was self-assurance, idealism, a faith in education and an ability to find practical answers to growing needs. Gradually the College was adjusting to democracy and coming to represent its virtues.

[63]C. G. Church and Ruben Brigham, eds., *Alumni Record of the Maryland Agricultural College, 1914* (Baltimore, 1914), 11-35.

9

Professional Schools in an Industrial Age

While the land-grant colleges languished, American professional education was nearly overwhelmed by the proliferation of schools. State licensing regulations collapsed under the surging demand for professional specialists plus the laissez faire political philosophy, so that degree mills, each promising an easier degree than the other, sprang up to bid for students. Professional education deteriorated into vocationalism, responsible proprietary schools often became rankly commercial and cutthroat competition drove standards to their lowest depths. By 1890 it was generally easier to obtain a degree in medicine, law, dentistry or pharmacy than it had been a half-century earlier.[1] Of course, not every school auctioned off its degrees and its reputation. In professional education, as on the undergraduate level, a few giants, such as Harvard and the Johns Hopkins, quietly went their way establishing totally new kinds of standards and laying the basis for a return to sanity by the others.

[1]See Arthur Meier Schlessinger, *Rise of the City, 1878-1898* (New York, 1933), 216-218; Abraham Flexner, *Medical Education in the United States and Canada . . .* (New York, 1910), 3-19; Roscoe Pound, *The Lawyer from Antiquity to Modern Times . . .*

Maryland often seemed not only to reflect but also to exaggerate the prevailing trends in higher education. Its agricultural education, for example, was far ahead of most states before the Civil War; its promise during reconstruction was more glowing; and its burdens during the two succeeding decades were more depressing. Similarly, the state's professional schools had been leaders before the Civil War; their future in 1865 seemed especially brilliant; and their response to the industrial era, both for good and ill, was more dramatic than in almost any other state.

The Medical School and Its Competitors

After the Civil War, with many southern medical colleges unable to open, the South's rising generation looked to Baltimore for professional training. Recognizing its opportunity, the University of Maryland medical faculty spread its advertisements throughout the old Confederacy. "The University of Maryland is a Southern Institution . . . intimately connected with the future of the great Southern country," they boasted. "All the members of the faculty of the University belong to Maryland, Virginia, North and South Carolina, and many among them are names familiar to every Surgeon of the Confederate army." By 1871 the advertisements stated that students "of every state from Delaware to Texas" were in attendance—they could have said from New York to Texas—and with considerable truth claimed the University to be "the centre of medical instruction in these states."[2] The eighty-three-member graduating class of 1869, the largest the University had ever had, included more graduates from the old Confederacy than from Maryland and all the northern states combined.[3]

More important than high enrollment was the new group of

(St. Paul, 1953), 212-242; Robert W. McCluggage, *History of the American Dental Association* . . . (Chicago, 1959), 299-302.

[2]*Annual Circular of the School of Medicine, 1870-1871* [Titles vary; hereafter cited as *Catalogue*] (Baltimore, 1870), 5-6; *Catalogue, 1871-1872*, 3.

[3]Graduates and their place of residence are listed in the annual catalogues and in Minutes of the Board of Regents, 1869-1909 (bound MS. volume in medical school archives). There were 83 graduates in 1869, 47 in 1875, 53 in 1880, 73 in 1885, 111 in 1890, 55 in 1895, 65 in 1900, 96 in 1905, 85 in 1910, 72 in 1915, 50 in 1920. The unusual group of 1890 came just before a new 3-year course requirement.

professors who came after the war to form a distinct generation of leadership for the school of medicine. The first generation of physicians had dominated the institution from 1807 until the 1840's and had included Davidge, Potter, DeButts and Pattison, all of whom had obtained their training by way of Edinburgh with its theoretical approach to medicine. From the 1840's until the 1860's the second generation of leaders had included Smith, Ducatel, Dunglison and Roby. Chiefly from New England, they emphasized experimental laboratory methods. A third generation of notable physicians flourished from the 1860's until the 1890's. Chiefly from the South, since the University was able to attract almost any former professor from defunct southern medical colleges, most of them had obtained specialized training in France where the new emphasis lay in specialization and clinical observation.

Most famous of the new group was Julian John Chisolm of South Carolina, author of the classic *Manual of Military Surgery*. As professor of eye and ear diseases at the University from 1868 to 1896, he served as president of almost every national and international ophthalmological society of his day. Also from South Carolina came Francis T. Miles, professor of physiology and nervous diseases from 1869 to 1903, author of a dozen volumes on nervous diseases and president of the American Neurological Association. William Travis Howard from North Carolina served as professor of gynecology and pediatrics from 1866 to 1896; he invented a multitude of surgical instruments and was founder and first president of the American Gynecological Society. Richard McSherry of Virginia, least distinguished of the group, was professor of the practice of medicine from 1864 to 1885 and author of numerous books on popular medicine. Three Marylanders also joined the staff. Christopher Johnston taught surgery from 1864 to 1881 and was widely recognized for pioneer work in plastic surgery; Francis Donaldson covered the field of throat and chest diseases from 1868 to 1888; and Samuel Claggett Chew taught *materia medica* from 1866 to 1909. Finally, two men remained from an earlier generation, George W. Miltenberger who taught anatomy from 1842 to 1891, and William E. A. Aiken who taught chemistry from 1837 to 1883. The nine men averaged over thirty-two years of service at the University, and at least five of them—Chisolm, Miles, Howard, Johnston and Donaldson—were men of national and even international reputation. By the 1880's their ideas were becoming dated, but immediately after the war they brought vigor and fame to the University.[4]

The first important innovation of the new professors was to bring to the study of medicine an emphasis on specialization. While the unusual crowding of the profession in postwar Baltimore may have encouraged that trend, the University played an important role in leading American medicine toward the compartmentalization which was becoming the blessing and the curse of industrial life. For many years people at the school claimed that Howard's course in gynecology and pediatrics was the first true specialty ever taught in an American medical school. Far more important, the new professors revised all courses to give students a new and intensive introduction to such fields as neurology, ophthalmology, throat and chest diseases and the various branches of surgery.[5]

Developing specialties even further, and taking advantage of the medical talent flowing into Baltimore, the medical school in 1866 began an optional ten-week summer course of special studies. Differing entirely from the summer preparatory program offered in the past, the Summer School of Specialties was designed as advanced, or postgraduate, education for ambitious students. The $50 summer tuition fee included use of the University hospital wards and laboratories and lectures by members of the faculty and by outside specialists. In one year, for example, four of the regular professors lectured on orthopedic surgery, plastic surgery, venereal disease, ophthalmology and auscultation, while the noted southern physicians, Russell Murdoch and M. J. DeRosset, lectured on their specialties, diseases of the eye and of the kidney.[6]

The second great postwar change at Maryland, and for that matter in all the best American medical schools, was an expansion of the French technique of clinical teaching. By the mid-nineteenth century the world's medical center had shifted from the lecture halls of Great Britain to the hospital clinics of Paris, and by luck or design five of the new professors—Chisolm, Miles, Johnston, Don-

[4]See Eugene Fauntleroy Cordell, *University of Maryland* . . ., 2 vols. (New York, 1907), I, *passim* for biographical sketches.

[5]Richard Harrison Shryock, *Development of Modern Medicine* . . . (New York, 1947), 382; Cordell, *University of Maryland*, I, 245-246; *Catalogue, 1867-1868*, 11; *Catalogue, 1893-1894*, 5.

[6]Cordell, *University of Maryland*, I, 245-246; *Baltimore American*, 15 March 1866; *Catalogue, 1866-1867*, 7; *Catalogue, 1869-1870*, 11-12; *Catalogue, 1880-1881*, 6-12; Minutes of the Faculty of Physic, 1869-1896 (bound MS. volume in medical school archives), 1 May 1869; 27 March 1879; 3 April 1880.

aldson and Chew—arrived at the University fresh from postgraduate work in Paris and crusading for the expansion of clinical teaching. Soon after the war the faculty finally abolished the old thesis requirement for students. Parallel reading and even lectures were pared down, and students were required to spend at least three hours a day in the various clinics. The clinical emphasis was especially apparent in obstetrics. The students of 1810 heard lectures; those of 1850 practiced on manikins and watched a professor attend one or two deliveries; and the student of 1890 submitted notes on at least ten patients whom he had attended in consultation with a professor through prenatal to postnatal care. The clinic had almost entirely replaced the old apprenticeship, thus gradually shifting practical bedside training from the beginning to the end of a student's training period. Clinical training was the bridge between the old apprenticeship and the modern internship and residency.[7]

While the University had pioneered with its teaching hospital in the 1820's, its facilities were inadequate to meet the demands of the new French training, and clinical expansion became the faculty's greatest postwar project. Although it was difficult for the state to aid a hospital so entwined with the personal profits of the professors, in 1868 the general assembly appropriated $2,500—a sum gradually increased to about $5,000 annually—on the condition that the hospital provide continuous free service to one patient from each county and legislative district of Maryland, and that it give free tuition to one student from each county and district.[8] In 1870 the professors spent about $6,000 of their own money to add a small wing to the hospital, and in 1874 the assembly appropriated $30,000 for remodeling and expansion. To the buildings on Lombard Street, completed in 1822 and 1852, the faculty added elevators, hot water and inside bathrooms; in addition they built a narrow, three-story brick wing along Greene Street. By 1880 the hospital had 95 beds, plus living space for 24 interns and 11 nurses.[9] Students clamored for the opportunity to serve a six-month stint as intern, living and working in the hospital. These who won the privilege paid about $100 for board;

[7]Shryock, *Modern Medicine*, 151-191; Minutes of the Faculty of Physic, 15 April 1869; 22 May 1871; 23 May 1887 and *passim; Catalogue, 1869-1870*, 8, 10-14; *Catalogue, 1890-1891*, 3-8; Cordell, *University of Maryland*, I, 294; *Maryland Medical Journal*, VIII (November, 1881), 334.

[8]*Laws of Maryland . . . 1868* (Baltimore, 1868), Chap. 410.

[9]*Ibid., 1874*, Chap. 266; Minutes of the Faculty of Physic, 12 June 1874; 23 September 1874; *Baltimore American*, 4 October 1875. For a full description of the hospital see *Maryland Medical Journal*, XXII (December, 1881), 175-176.

graduates received free board and about $100 for their services.[10]

In 1870 the University helped its ophthalmology professor, J. J. Chisolm, to finance a separate, twenty-bed eye and ear infirmary for his teaching. Neither he nor the University could afford the operating costs, and a few years later he persuaded the Presbyterian Church to take it over and expand it as the Presbyterian Charity Eye, Ear and Throat Hospital.[11] Finally, in 1887 various women's clubs contributed about $8,000, to which the faculty added $4,000, to buy a nearby three-story house to serve as a free lying-in hospital for expectant mothers.[12]

When the additional facilities still failed to fill the teaching needs, the faculty turned to out-patient clinics. In 1866 it created an "Out-Door" obstetrical department that provided free faculty and student attendance at the homes of patients who registered at the hospital.[13] Two years later the faculty established an extensive dispensary, or out-patient department, that included a large room in the hospital where groups of students under a staff supervisor were on duty during certain afternoon hours to provide free drugs and advice for anyone who walked in from the street.[14] Since this was so clearly a public service, the government of Baltimore appropriated varying sums, usually about $4,000 annually, to help support the clinic.[15] While the agricultural colleges waited until public service functions were forced upon them, the new teaching methods in medicine guided the medical school into the type of public service that eventually became an important function of the modern state university.

As government and charity hospitals expanded after the war, the University obtained teaching privileges in them. With the development of anesthesia and antiseptic procedures, hospitals became places for getting well instead of places to die. The middle class began to patronize and support them so that within a decade of the war's end,

[10]Minutes of the Faculty of Physic, 14 October 1870; 20 January 1871; 18 February 1875; 13 December 1876; Catalogues, passim.
[11]Minutes of the Faculty of Physic, 8 April 1870; First Report of the Board of Managers of the Presbyterian Hospital (Baltimore, 1880), 1-3.
[12]Baltimore Sun, 5 February 1887; 3 March 1887; 9 April 1887; Minutes of the Faculty of Physic, 26 February 1887; Maryland Medical Journal, XXIII (July, 1890), 259-266.
[13]Eugene Fauntleroy Cordell, Medical Annals of Maryland, 1799-1899 (Baltimore, 1903), 708.
[14]Catalogue, 1868-1869, 12; Minutes of the Faculty of Physic, 8 March 1869; 15 April 1869; 3 March 1870.
[15]Report of the City Comptroller . . . 1869 (Baltimore, 1870), 636-637. See complete file of these Reports, especially, 1870, 41-42; 1871, 40; 1872, 48; 1878, 47-49; 1890, 76-79.

Baltimore hospital facilities had increased tenfold. During that period the city opened the 1,000-bed Bay View Hospital, one of the largest in the world. Other government and religious agencies opened City (now Mercy) Hospital, Hebrew (now Sinai), Marine, St. Agnes, and St. Joseph Hospitals. With each of these the school of medicine drew up different agreements almost every year. In some instances the hospital provided laboratory facilities or used those of the University; in others the hospital required, or permitted, the University to appoint a given number of graduates to serve a one-year residency; in still other instances the hospital required or permitted the University faculty to serve on its staff. Independent Baltimore physicians were frequently drawn into the agreements, being required or permitted to work with the students as "Clinical Professors." Frequently a few hundred dollars changed hands between the University, the hospitals and the private physicians; but essentially the public, the hospitals, the medical profession and the University had become interdependent. The modern industrial world had grown complex. No longer was the College of Medicine a self-contained or even a clearly definable unit.[16]

For the medical school, however, the entire clinical program was the beginning of troubles, most immediately because of the costs involved. By 1869, with the hospital running a deficit of $5,000 annually, the faculty reported that the situation was "desperate."[17] In frustration it blamed the long-suffering Sisters of Charity for extravagance in directing hospital affairs, but when the professors attempted to run the hospital themselves and to employ private nurses the deficits only increased.[18] The United States Navy, which occasionally utilized several private infirmaries in the area, withdrew its seamen from the University hospital, charging that its neglect of patients had reached "scandalous" levels.[19] Anxiously the faculty petitioned another Roman Catholic order, the Sisters of Mercy, to undertake the direction of the hospital, and the University absorbed

[16]Shryock, Modern Medicine, 346-347; Florence Meda Gipe, "Development of Nursing Education in Maryland" (Ed. D. dissertation, University of Maryland, 1952), 302-336; Minutes of the Faculty of Physic, 15 April 1869; 9 April 1870; 27 March 1885; Catalogue, 1890-1891, 4-8, 13; other Catalogues, passim; Cordell, University of Maryland, I, 120.

[17]Minutes of the Faculty of Physic, 7 December 1869; 2 March 1871; 29 May 1872; 18 June 1873.

[18]Ibid., 25 May 1876; Arthur J. Lomas, "As It Was in the Beginning: A History of the University Hospital," Bulletin of the School of Medicine, University of Maryland, XXIII (April, 1939), 206-207.

[19]Minutes of the Faculty of Physic, 3 June 1873; 14 May 1880; 22 May 1880.

the deficits by decreasing appropriations for salaries and teaching equipment.[20] By taking the initiative in founding the hospital and by entwining its finances with their own, the professors, like the Agricultural College stockholders, actually kept away substantial outside aid. To keep the hospital in operation the faculty economized by allowing the classroom building to go without paint for forty years.

Far more serious than hospital expenses, the University's outpatient clinic and its arrangements with public hospitals had opened the way for competition. By obtaining a few thousand dollars from the city and state governments for hospital and clinical support, the University unwittingly gave other groups of physicians the right to finagle for public aid for rival schools. By obtaining the use of public hospitals for clinical study, the University pointed to free facilities for all their rivals. Ten new medical schools appeared in Baltimore from 1865 to 1900, each contending for a share of the money and the enrollment that once went to the University.

First of the competing institutions, and typical of the rest, was that established by Edward Warren, the able ante-bellum professor at the University who had resigned to join the Confederacy. Within a few weeks of the surrender he was back in Baltimore unreconstructed, destitute and bitter. Furious at the University for admitting northern troops to its hospitals during the war, he demanded his old professorship of surgery. When the University replied that the post had been filled, he swore to destroy the institution he once had loved. Joining with other destitute former Confederate physicians, Warren scraped together $2,000 for secondhand equipment, and in 1867 reopened the long-dormant Washington Medical College—the school operated briefly in the 1830's by another embittered Maryland professor. University officials complained that Warren was intent upon "a scheme for personal revenge" and that his facilities and instruction constituted "a comedy—a comedy of errors." Replied Warren grimly, "the clinics of the *vieillard* of the University remind me of tragedies—they always culminate in a death."[21]

Warren set his tuition fee at $120 for northerners, a figure higher than the University's, but for "residents of the late slave-holding

[20]*Ibid.*, 24 September 1880; 8 March 1876; 22 May 1877; also, 14 December 1869; 16 May 1889; 8 October 1889; 15 December 1889; 28 January 1891.

[21]Edward Warren, *A Doctor's Experiences on Three Continents* (Baltimore, 1885), 363-364.

States" the amount was $50, half that of the University. His catalogue spoke of "the late war for truth and Southern liberty," offered special favors to "wounded and disabled soldiers" and promised a haven "where every *white* man . . . can think and speak and act according to the dictates of his conscience, without fear of bayonets."[22] A number of students from the University, including many in scholastic difficulties, were attracted by his lower fees, his four-month school term and his reputation for never failing students. Far surpassing the University in his appeals to Confederate sympathizers, Warren appealed to the rabid southerners in the legislature who gave him appropriations as an act of defiance. In 1868 he received $15,000 from the assembly and thereafter about $6,000 annually from the state and city.[23]

As his school's reprehensible standards became evident and as sectionalism faded, Warren resigned in 1872 to found still another institution, the College of Physicians and Surgeons of Baltimore. By offering tiny salaries and flattering titles to a large number of physicians, each of whom would teach only one hour a week, he secured widespread support from the city's medical profession. Soon, however, he abandoned this school also to become surgeon general to the Khedive of Egypt. But the many physicians associated with the institution used their influence to secure large grants from both state and city and, since the free bestowal of the title of professor was the chief means of paying the staff, tuition could be held below that of the University. Later, under able leadership, the College of Physicians and Surgeons acquired respectable quarters and attained moderately high standards.[24]

Eight other medical schools gouged into the University's enrollment with various special appeals, and various gradations of reputability and avarice. The Baltimore Medical College appeared in 1881, condemning Darwinism and boasting that it was a "Christian College." After the University decided in 1882 that it would be "indeli-

[22]*Annual Announcement of the Washington University School of Medicine, 1868-1869* (Baltimore, 1868) , 9; *Annual Announcement . . . 1869-1870,* 5-9.

[23]Genevieve Miller, "A Nineteenth Century Medical School: Washington University of Baltimore," *Bulletin of the History of Medicine,* XIV (June, 1943) , 20-29; *Laws of Maryland . . . 1868,* Chap. 246; *Laws of Maryland . . . 1874,* Chap. 266; *Report of the City Comptroller . . . 1870,* 41-42; also, *1871,* 40; *1878,* 47-49; *1890,* 76-79.

[24]Miller, "Washington University," 27-29; Bernard C. Steiner, *History of Education in Maryland* (Washington, 1894) , 289-296; Record Book of the College of Physicians and Surgeons, 1872-1891 (bound MS. volume in medical school archives) .

cate" to admit women,[25] a well-intentioned group of physicians opened the Women's Medical College of Maryland. If its facilities were meagre, its integrity was high, and it was probably the only proprietary competitor that the University welcomed and encouraged. The Baltimore University School of Medicine opened in 1884 without facilities or standards; the Atlantic Medical College of 1890 was begun by three professors who had failed to obtain medical licenses; and the Maryland Medical College of 1898 sold degrees to students who had been rejected everywhere else. When in 1900 the University refused to accept Negroes,[26] the Maryland Medico-Chirurgical and Theological College of Christ's Institution was founded to provide for them; and finally in 1913 came a weird establishment called the Maryland College of Eclectic Medicine.[27] The University of Maryland created a faculty committee to gather "information in regard to the irregular practices of the other medical colleges in this city."[28] The data could only be discouraging; unfortunately, irregular practices were likely to be a sign of prosperity for the rivals.

While the multitude of competing institutions in Baltimore and throughout the country served to depress standards and to decrease the enrollment of the University, a totally different influence came from the great new Johns Hopkins Medical School. Early in the 1880's Hopkins announced hitherto unheard-of standards, and in 1889, when the University of Maryland hospital was worth $90,000, Hopkins opened one worth $3,000,000.[29] With the entrance of its first medical class in 1893, the Hopkins faculty pointed the way for the entire world. Medical education generally, and the University of Maryland particularly, began to revive through the Hopkins leadership. Maryland quickly discovered that the new school was an ally rather than a threat, that it was eager to destroy unscrupulous institutions and to block out expanded roles for those that were reputable. Nevertheless, Hopkins had also seized the last semblance of leadership from Maryland, even on the local level. By the 1880's the

[25]Minutes of the Faculty of Physic, 17 September 1872; 26 February 1887.

[26]*Ibid.*, 24 April 1872; 8 October 1889; *Baltimore American,* 15 October 1889.

[27]For information on these schools see Steiner, *Education in Maryland,* 297-303; Flexner, *Medical Education,* 234-239; Gipe, "Development of Nursing," 344; Catalogues of the schools; see schools by name in "Vertical File" of the Maryland Room, Enoch Pratt Free Library, Baltimore.

[28]Minutes of the Faculty of Physic, 19 September 1887.

[29]Shryock, *Modern Medicine,* 348 and *passim;* Flexner, *Medical Education,* 28-29 and *passim;* John C. French, *History of the University Founded by Johns Hopkins* (Baltimore, 1946); Bertram M. Bernheim, *The Story of Johns Hopkins* (New York, 1948), 35-36, 52, 122-127.

once-fresh ideas of the University were commonplace. It had become "the old school."

Although the University's standards remained substantially higher than those of its other competitors, enrollment and salaries fell during the 1880's and debts and enemies increased. Despite all the growing complexity of medicine, the University was powerless to raise entrance requirements to a high school level, and the entire medical course was still crowded into two six-month terms, a standard set long before the war. A brilliant graduate of 1880 and subsequently a professor at Johns Hopkins, recalled the drabness that had settled over the institution:

It was not only the long semicircular wooden ledge on which we were to sit,—but the students! Coming in strangers from remote country districts, and intent on economy, the boys wore their oldest clothes in class. The very oldest clothes of a country youth, with a certain amount of negligee added, did not brighten up a room or give it style. . . .

The course was for two years, and the lectures of the first year were repeated in the second. A professor might write out for himself a course of lectures when he entered upon his chair, and read them year by year to his classes in the great amphitheatre class room for the rest of his life, with such little additions and corrections as occurred to him as the years rolled by. The second year the students knew all the anecdotes and rhetorical flourishes by heart, having applauded them the winter before. Professor Howard was particularly given to poetic flights. There was one about 'feeling the pulse of the morning dew' which he declaimed with so much feeling that the class, even when they were expecting it, drowned the next sentence with wild applause—which always pleased him very much.[30]

In an innocent way the University of Maryland had provided tragic leadership into a dilemma which faced all of American medicine. As one of the oldest and finest proprietary institutions, it had provided a model for its competitors. During the late 1860's and 1870's its prosperity, its outstanding faculty and its development of specialties and clinics all displayed an admirable adjustment to the postwar world. Yet its efforts only seemed to stimulate rivalry and lower standards. Like academic people everywhere, the professors were not at ease in the world of business competition. Somehow it had almost swallowed them.

[30]Allen Kerr Bond, *When the Hopkins Came to Baltimore* (Baltimore, 1927), 44, 47. There is another description of student life in *Maryland Medical Journal*, XX (April, 1889), 469-474.

The Law School Restored

The ante-bellum lawyer seemed to be either a statesman or a shyster with little middle ground between. The statesmen, pre-occupied with philosophical interpretations of constitutionality and natural rights, were the leaders of their age: Marshall, Adams, Jefferson, Calhoun and Webster on the national level; and Luther Martin, Reverdy Johnson, William Wirt and Roger B. Taney in Maryland. On the other hand there were fast-talking tricksters, widely despised and profiting from the misfortunes of others, the hated bill collectors, land speculators and defenders of petty criminals. Neither group had much formal legal training. The statesman-lawyer had generally attended college, taking the traditional undergraduate course in the theory and history of law; but efforts to institutionalize this type of legal training, such as David Hoffman's school, had usually failed. The shyster-lawyer had generally served a brief apprenticeship under a man after whom he had modeled himself.[31]

In the postwar world, however, a complex industrial society had little place for either the philosopher-statesman or the ignorant pettifog. The philosophical study of jurisprudence and the apprentice system became equally outdated. Instead, an immense need arose for knowledgable lawyers who knew how to sue railroads and manage trusts, to draw up contracts and calculate taxes, to handle bankruptcies and supervise stock issues. The revived School of Law of the University of Maryland was exactly what the era demanded—an efficient how-to-do-it night school that did not cost much, did not require much time, and the completion of which would be a reasonable guarantee of a profitable business career.

The University law school typified the practical kind of legal education that sprang up over the nation after war. Two or three prominent lawyers agreed to deliver a series of lectures after business offices had closed, and ambitious young men seized the opportunity to enroll for them. After a few years the students were loosely screened and admitted to the bar. No one felt particularly responsible for the lectures, either in maintaining standards or making money from them. Such a school had no particular life of its own and was little more than its classes. There was practically no collegiate atmosphere or alumni fellowship and no sense of providing

[31]Pound, *The Lawyer from Antiquity to Modern Times*, 177-187.

the leadership for a profession or of guiding the evolution of law.

Yet the schools filled a greater role than anyone expected. As practical, part-time afternoon or night schools they provided an opportunity for old-fashioned shopkeepers to become modern businessmen and for clerks to become professional lawyers. The University law school did not provide academic education in its noble scholarly sense, but at once it gave something more and less. Along with many similar institutions it was shaping not only the American legal profession, but also American capitalism and democracy. In fact, the new law schools succeeded in doing for a small class of city people what the Morrill Act had so far failed to achieve for the farmer.[32]

The revived law school appeared without plan or fanfare, and a few years later no one could even remember who suggested that it reopen. Probably Professor Christopher Johnston of the medical faculty suggested to Judge George W. Dobbin, a student of Hoffman's, that the medical school would gain in prestige if a law school were again associated with it.[33] At any rate in October, 1869, the judge called into session the University's long-inactive board of regents, which included the medical faculty and the honorary professors of divinity, arts and sciences and law. With John Pendleton Kennedy still presiding as provost, the regents endorsed the law school's revival and filled vacancies in the honorary faculty with men interested in teaching. If nothing else, the reestablishment of the school served to reactivate the central administration—such as it was —of the University.[34]

At first most of the teaching faculty came, like many of the medical professors, from the large body of prominent, unemployed Confederate refugees. During the first year there were only two instructors—Judge John A. Inglis, formerly of the Court of Appeals of South Carolina, and Judge Robert N. Martin of the Baltimore Superior Court. Both resigned within a year and were replaced by Judge Alexander H. Handy, once Chief Justice of Mississippi, Richard M. Venable, former professor at what is now Washington and Lee College in Virginia, and John Prentiss Poe, an ambitious Princeton graduate and young Baltimore lawyer. Poe retained his post for thirty-nine years, making the school practically his own.

Provost Kennedy and most of the medical faculty attended open-

[32]Alfred Zantzinger Reed, *Training for the Public Profession of the Law* . . . (New York, 1928) , 169, 193-202, 273-322.

[33]*Baltimore American*, 6 January 1870; 29 February 1884; Cordell, *University of Maryland*, I, 348.

[34]Minutes of the Regents, 13 October 1869.

ing ceremonies for the first law school class on February 1, 1870, at five o'clock, after downtown offices had closed. About twenty students were present, including several young members of the bar eager to establish contact with the well-known professors.[35] The class met on Mulberry Street in a room of the old arts and science building, most of which was rented out as a warehouse. The first academic year of the two-year course lasted only four months, but the second year ran from October to June with the fee set at $100. On Monday, Wednesday and every other Friday afternoon, Professor Martin lectured on his subjects: the Constitution, real property, rights of persons, crimes and torts, pleading and practice. On Tuesday, Thursday and alternate Fridays, Professor Inglis lectured on contracts, domestic relations, equity and evidence. On Saturday mornings the professors alternated at presiding over moot courts in which the students argued hypothetical cases. In addition, during the term students were supposed to read three or four textbooks and make periodic visits to the various courts in the city.[36]

The professors emphasized the professional character of the school by holding its first commencement in June, 1871, in the district court house. Only six students had lasted through the first-year course, and by prearrangement the court agreed to waive the perfunctory examination and admit them all to the bar. Most of the regents and many members of the bench and bar attended the brief ceremony, taking advantage of the occasion to award the venerable Reverdy Johnson an honorary degree. Still, it was not a commencement in the usual sense, for there were no sentimental songs, no bouquets and no speeches. The LL. B. degree and admission to the bar were not so much the final steps in a young man's education as the first step in his career.[37]

The school grew steadily. In 1872 the professors separated the two classes, meeting the first year students at five o'clock and the seniors at six. That year the number of graduates began to increase rapidly because the faculty allowed certain students to take the junior and senior classes simultaneously and graduate after a single eight-month term. Also in 1872 the general assembly gave the institution a boost by exempting graduates from the state bar examination. The ex-

[35]*Baltimore Sun*, 3 February 1870; 4 February 1870; 5 June 1871; *Baltimore American*, 29 February 1884.

[36]*Baltimore American*, 6 January 1870; 8 October 1872; 9 February 1876; *Catalogue of the Law School of the University of Maryland, 1870-1871* [titles vary; hereafter cited *Catalogue*], (Baltimore, 1870).

[37]*Baltimore Sun*, 5 June 1871; *Baltimore American*, 5 June 1871; also William Cabell Bruce, *Recollections* (n.p., 1931), 94-104.

emption was repealed in 1876, but re-enacted for the period of 1888 to 1899.[38] Soon the professors fell into the regular pedagogical procedures of the era. They devoted part of each day's lecture to "catechizing" the students; they required written examinations twice each year; they introduced a thesis requirement for graduation; and to provide incentives they offered three $50 prizes, one to the student who did best on the examinations, one for the best thesis and one for the best performance in the moot court. Throughout the late nineteenth century educators believed they were being progressive in substituting prizes for the earlier birch rod persuasion. On their own the law students organized quiz clubs and also formed the Inglis Literary Society.[39]

The number of graduates increased from about twenty a year in the late 1870's, to thirty in the 1880's, to more than forty in the 1890's. Soon the enrollment was too large for the dilapidated old building on Mulberry Street, and the University regents agreed to sell the building for $26,000 and to divide the sum equally between the medicine and law schools. The law professors contributed an additional $13,000 to their share of the funds and obtained permission to erect a building on Greene Street in the front yard of the medical school. The small church-like structure, completed in 1884, contained a lecture hall, offices and a library. For the first time two schools of the University were operating on the same campus.[40]

Along with the growing enrollment, the school's standards and reputation also increased. In 1880 John Prentiss Poe published a widely used two-volume textbook, *Pleading and Practice in Courts of Common Law*, which went through five editions during the next fifty years, spreading his renown so that by the 1890's at least a third of the students were from outside Baltimore, and a few were from other states. The faculty added a third year of classes in 1884, and while students could still graduate in one year almost all of them took at least the two-year course. Mere registration did not guarantee a degree, for the faculty regularly failed about ten percent of the students in each class.[41] As yet there were no formal entrance re-

[38]*Catalogue, 1872-1873*, 7; *Laws of Maryland . . . 1872*, Chap. 91; also *Laws of Maryland . . . 1876*, Chap. 264; *Laws . . . 1888*, Chap. 204; *Laws . . . 1898*, Chap. 139.

[39]*Baltimore American*, 8 October 1872; Samuel J. Fisher, "Recollections of the Law School," *Baltimore Sun*, 5 April 1959; *Catalogue, 1872-1873*, 7; *Catalogue, 1882-1883*, 11-18.

[40]Minutes of the Regents, 20 June 1883 and *passim*; *Baltimore American*, 29 February 1884.

[41]All matriculants and grades are recorded in an Examination Book (bound MS. volume in the law school archives); also Minutes of the Regents, *passim*.

quirements; but a quarter of the students were college graduates, a considerably larger proportion than in any of the other professional schools. To encourage students to take preparatory college courses and to establish a connection with the prestigious Johns Hopkins University, the law school agreed to accept that institution's graduates free of charge in exchange for which Hopkins agreed to enter law students in certain of its classes at reduced tuition charges.[42]

Soon a multitude of up-to-date subjects entered the curriculum—sales, suretyship, corporations, insurance, copyrights, bills and notes, commercial law, international law, shipping and admiralty—and occasionally the University was among the first to offer them.[43] By 1890 two-thirds of the lawyers entering the bar in Maryland, plus a host of businessmen, had attended the University law school.[44]

Every triumph of the school unfortunately brought closer the dire threat of competition. By 1890 it had an enrollment of about one hundred students, each paying a fee of $100. annually, a total income of $10,000. About $5,000 went for operating expenses—the building, a janitor, catalogues, diplomas and the library—leaving $7,000 to be divided among the seven professors. Poe took two shares since he accepted all the administrative duties; others who taught only once a week took fractional shares, but generally a professor who delivered three lectures a week for eight months received about $1,000. Although not spectacular, the profit inevitably tempted other lawyers to think of offering similar lectures.[45]

Another factor which simultaneously marked the University's success and stimulated its competitors was the personal career of John Prentiss Poe. The school required only a fraction of his enormous energy, and soon he was emerging as a major political power—many people termed him a political boss—of Maryland's highly conservative Democratic Party. From time to time he was on the city council, the state school commission, president of the state tax commission, member of the state senate, state attorney general and, in 1904, chief author of the national party platform. An outspoken party man and an advocate of business interests and Negro disfranchisement, he won powerful enemies who identified the law school with his conservative

[42]Catalogue, 1884-1885, 15-16; Catalogue, 1890-1891, 11.
[43]Reed, Training for Law, 273-306 and passim.
[44]Baltimore Sun, 5 February 1895.
[45]Exact figures on income are not available for these years. See, however, Minutes of the Law School, 1906-1913 (bound MS. volume in law school archives), and Minutes of the Regents, passim.

views. Liberal Democrats and Republicans were drawn together to oppose Poe, the law school and the conservative control of the state. The rival group established two new law schools in Baltimore and in 1895 succeeded in breaking temporarily the conservative Democratic stranglehold on state politics.[46]

The first rival, the Baltimore University School of Law, was originally sponsored by misguided professional educators bent on furthering vocational opportunities for Baltimore schoolboys. Easily they secured a sizable faculty of attorneys composed about equally of reputable political opponents of the University and lawyers eager for the lecture fees. The school opened in 1890 and attracted a large class, for its tuition was half that at the University. Ten years later, in 1900, the best of the professors seceded to found still another institution, the Baltimore Law School, and while it kept its fees low, its standards were higher than those at the University. With the three schools serving to weaken each other, the general assembly reinstituted a state board examination for all lawyers entering the bar.[47]

While competition and the profit motive were potential dangers for education, they characterized the industrial age and initially created the law school. If its graduates lacked the nobility of John Marshall's day, they also lacked the pettifoggery of the earlier era; if legal education lacked the excellence of Hoffman's school, at least the new system worked. By the 1890's, however, the time had come to move from a vocational to an academic discipline, to teach the theory as well as the practice of law, and to provide leadership as well as training. Poe and a few others were becoming vaguely aware that the University of Maryland School of Law needed the guidance of a real university.

The Dependence of Dentistry

By 1865 both Chapin Harris and Horace Hayden, the founders of the Baltimore College of Dental Surgery, were dead; but their school

---

[46]*Report of the Fifteenth Annual Meeting of the Maryland Bar Association . . . 1910* (Baltimore, 1910), 203-209; *Baltimore Sun*, 9 August 1906; John R. Lambert, *Arthur Pue Gorman* (Baton Rouge, 1953), 347-348, 355; *Terra Maria* [Student Annual], I (1905), 341; II (1906), 120.

[47]*Baltimore Sun*, 1 July 1890; Steiner, *Education in Maryland*, 316-317; *Annual Catalogue of the Baltimore University School of Law* (Baltimore, 1900); *Annual Catalogue of the Baltimore Law School, 1905-1906* (Baltimore, 1906).

remained a monument, the world-wide leader of its profession. Its faculty dominated the American Dental Association, its alumni were powerful in the half-dozen other dental colleges which had emerged throughout the country and its publications dominated the practice of dentistry in America and Europe. After the Civil War the graduating class quickly rose from its wartime low of nine to its normal level of thirty students annually. Eighty percent of them were from outside the state—North as well as South—and ten percent, many of them with medical degrees, came from Europe to carry back to the old world the dental techniques of the new. America's best known medical historian, Richard H. Shryock, forgetting such contributions as the Declaration of Independence, has called this "the first instance in which the transit of culture between the two continents was reversed."[48] With a modesty that bespoke self-confidence, the Baltimore College catalogues contained not a line of self-advertisement, but actually encouraged other institutions, outside of Baltimore at least, for the welfare of the profession.[49]

The Baltimore College of Dental Surgery had achieved its position largely because Hayden and Harris had fought to a standstill the ancient question of whether dentistry was a theoretical medical science or a practical mechanical art. They came to the obvious conclusion that dentistry was both, that it should be taught separately from medicine but should maintain close contact with a medical school and that it was a "DISTINCT PROFESSION" apart from medicine yet not a whit inferior to it. Their dental college maintained standards of admission, fees, length of study and general requirements equal to those of any medical school in the country. The proportion of dental students who passed final examinations was considerably smaller, relative to the number who began the course, than the number of medical students who passed in the College of Medicine.[50]

By the 1870's, however, the inevitable competition came to the Baltimore dental school, a rivalry intensified by unreal arguments between science and art, and costing the college its eminence. The first local rival was the Maryland Dental College which appeared in

[48]Shryock, *Modern Medicine*, 339. Dental school catalogues regularly list the graduates, their degree and their home.

[49]See McCluggage, *American Dental Association*, 155-171 and *passim*; *Annual Circular and Catalogue of the Baltimore College of Dental Surgery, Session 1867-1868* [hereafter, *Catalogue BCDS*] (Baltimore, 1867).

[50]*Catalogue BCDS, 1867-1868*, 3 and *passim*.

1873, establishing vague connection with the disreputable Washington Medical College. The older dental faculty grumbled that the new group was essentially mercenary, that its dean was bitter about his rejection for a position in the older institution and that it over-emphasized the mechanical side of dentistry. At first the new group respected standards and did not attempt to attract students by fee cutting, but unwittingly competition tore open theoretical argument and plunged dental education into a malestrom of commercialism and vocationalism.[51]

From the 1870's until about 1900 the debate raged, setting dentistry back by a generation. Should dental schools emphasize text-books, physiology, mouth diseases and saving teeth? Or should they emphasize clinical study, metallurgy, mechanics and replacing teeth? Modern dentists accept the obvious Hayden-Harris solution, but as the battle raged in the late nineteenth century dental schools tended to become either departments of medical colleges where dentistry was regarded as an inferior specialty of medicine, or independent schools for glorified apprentice training. In either case, dependent on medicine or totally independent, the dentist acquired a sense of inferiority to the physician from which he has still not entirely recovered.[52]

Guilty as anyone in raising the either-or question was the able Samuel Gorgas, graduate of the University's medical and dental schools, editor of the powerful *American Journal of Dental Science* and Harris' heir as dean of the Baltimore College of Dental Surgery. Originally Gorgas held to the medicine-and-mechanics position, but as competing institutions began to emphasize dentistry-as-mechanics, he retreated into the equally dangerous and dogmatic camp of dentistry-as-medicine.[53] Vigorously he denounced "the tendency of Students, particularly American Students, to substitute PRACTICE for STUDY";[54] carefully he built his faculty so that every professor had the M.D. degree in addition to dental training; and eagerly he

[51]Steiner, *Education in Maryland*, 305; *Annual Circular and Catalogue of the Maryland Dental College* (Baltimore, 1874), 4; *Catalogue BCDS, 1873-1874*, 4.

[52]McCluggage, *American Dental Association*, 155-172; T. W. Brophy, "Dental Education," *Transactions of the American Dental Association* . . . (1881), 173-174.

[53]For Gorgas' philosophy see *Catalogues BDCS, 1865-1882*, and *Catalogues* of Dental Department of the University of Maryland, 1882-1914; also editorials of the *American Journal of Dental Science*, 3rd Series, 1866-1902, especially I (May, 1867), 425-432; also article by Gorgas in *History of Baltimore, Maryland, from Its Founding* . . . (n.p., 1898), 507-512; T. O. Heatwold, "Abbreviated Biography of Ferdinand J. S. Gorgas" (MS. in Pamphlet File of Health Sciences Library, Baltimore).

[54]*Catalogue BCDS, 1866-1867*, 4.

worked for closer ties with the University medical school. In 1871 and again in 1872 Gorgas formally petitioned for the acceptance of the Baltimore College of Dental Surgery as an integral part of the University. The physicians hesitated, not through any disdain for the dentists, but for fear of splitting dentistry apart.[55]

Gorgas continued the negotiation, if not to merge the two institutions then to create an entirely new dental school as a department of the College of Medicine. At one point he appeared willing to allow one of the regular medical professors to serve over him as head of a dental department.[56] To the physicians the idea grew increasingly attractive. It fitted their emphasis on specialties and offered opportunities for increased income to those professors who might serve on both the medical and the dental faculties.[57] Possibly they became willing to gouge into the dental college profits since everyone seemed to be gouging into theirs.

Finally, in April, 1882, the University announced the creation of the third dental school in Baltimore, the Dental Department of the University of Maryland School of Medicine. Gorgas resigned from the Baltimore College of Dental Surgery, and carried with him to the new school the well-known and widely published James H. Harris— no relation to Chapin Harris—as his first assistant. The two men received seats on the University board of regents, but every other member of the dental department came from the medical faculty. Students studied chemistry, *materia medica*, physiology, surgery and anatomy, usually in the same classes with the medical students. In addition they took two special courses under Gorgas and Harris.[58]

The University provided its new department with good quarters. Borrowing about $6,000 against prospective dental student fees, the physicians constructed a plain two-story structure crowded behind the main University building. Opened for the fall session of 1882, it was considerably expanded three years later. On the first floor was a dental laboratory with a locker for each student; on the second was a free clinic or "Dental Parlor" containing twenty-five dental chairs, each equipped with an electric battery to power the drills and

[55]Minutes of the Faculty of Physic, 25 April 1871; 9 May 1871; 16 December 1872.
[56]*Ibid.*, 26 April 1882.
[57]*Ibid.*, 8 April 1882; 15 April 1882.
[58]*Ibid.*, 26 April 1882; *Announcement of the Dental Department of the University of Maryland, 1882-1883* [hereafter cited *Dental Department Catalogue*] (Baltimore, 1882); Cordell, *University of Maryland*, I, 384-387; *Dental Register*, XXXVI (June 1882), 312; F. J. S. Gorgas, "The History of the Dental Department" (MS. dated 1907 in possession of Professor G. P. H. Foley of the School of Dentistry).

equipment. The University saved the expense of lecture rooms and of chemical and anatomy laboratories by allowing the dental students to use those of the medical college. Although less extensive, the quarters resembled those of the Baltimore College of Dental Surgery at Lexington and Eutaw Streets.[59]

While Gorgas spoke eloquently for high standards, he assured a high enrollment for his new department by offering the easiest dental degree in Maryland. Students could obtain credit for one year's study by working at their leisure in the dental clinic and could then obtain their degree after a single term of class work.[60] The following year the Baltimore College of Dental Surgery cut its standards accordingly, and the downward spiral seemed to have begun.

With the danger apparent to everyone the dental colleges tried desperately to halt the slide. In 1883 they formed the Maryland State Dental Association, and the following year obtained state legislation requiring all dental college graduates to take a licensing examination.[61] The Baltimore dental colleges agreed to abide by the recommended standards set by the National Association of Dental Faculties, so that by 1886 they had not only returned to the two-year requirement, but also had moved ahead of medicine in establishing a graded curriculum with different courses for the junior and senior years. By 1889 dentistry was a year ahead of medicine in requiring an entrance examination to prove the "equivalent" of a high school education. Fees were frozen at $120 annually, and the term was set at five and a half months only slightly below reputable medical school requirements. In 1895 a fourth dental school appeared, the Dental Department of the Baltimore Medical College, and even it pretended to abide by the national standards.[62]

Superficially the dental schools seemed to have weathered the age of competition better than medicine. Their standards were almost as high as in 1860. The Baltimore College of Dental Surgery relied on its earlier fame, and the University Dental Department relied on Gorgas' renown, so that by the 1890's each boasted about sixty grad-

[59]*Dental Department Catalogue, 1882-1883*, 4; Cordell, *University of Maryland*, I, 388-389.

[60]*Dental Department Catalogue, 1882-1883*, 10-13.

[61]J. Ben Robinson, "Highlights in the History of the Maryland State Dental Association," *Journal of the Maryland State Dental Association*, I (1958), 5-17; *Laws of Maryland . . . 1884*, Chap. 150.

[62]*Dental Department Catalogue, 1885-1886*, 3; *Dental Department Catalogue, 1889-1890*, 11; *Catalogue BCDS, 1885-1886*, 11; *Annual Announcement of the Dental Department of the Baltimore Medical College* (Baltimore, 1896), 12.

uates annually. Even the mechanical-or-medical dispute faded with a general victory for medical orientation when the Baltimore College drifted into alliance with the College of Physicians and Surgeons which Warren had founded after the Civil War.[63]

In a deeper sense, however, the age had cost the dental schools their sense of leadership and pride. Preoccupied with competition, they promoted themselves rather than the profession. With too little time for service or scholarship, they advertised dentistry as a profitable vocation. With medical men dominating dental education, students wondered if they were able enough to become "real" doctors. The four Baltimore dental schools maintained an uneasy alliance, holding their own until they could find guidance back into the true academic fold and true professionalism.

The Independence of Pharmacy

While dental education suffered from subservience to medicine, pharmacy fell into trouble from exactly the opposite direction. By establishing a fierce independence from medicine on one hand and from drug manufacturers on the other, the pharmacists almost cut themselves off from the academic world to become dispensing clerks. Both dentistry and pharmacy had become professions in the 1840's, but by the end of the century both had backed away from truly professional character—dentistry because it spread itself too broadly, and pharmacy because it restricted itself too narrowly. Just as dentists today suffer as poor relatives of medicine, pharmacists still suffer under the stigma of being store clerks.

Maryland pharmacists had long benefited from a tight professional organization, although they were slow to define its boundaries. Using ing the word "college" in the medieval guild sense, the Maryland College of Pharmacy was the Baltimore guild of practicing apothecaries of which the teaching institution was only a part. Members of the faculty who happened to be physicians or wholesalers were not officially members of the college, but received special invitations to attend commencement ceremonies.[64] Because of its close professional organization the school never faced competition. It could

[63]Catalogue BCDS, 1882-1883, 7, 14.
[64]Minutes of the Maryland College of Pharmacy, 1840-1872 (bound MS. volume in the School of Pharmacy archives), 30 July 1840, and passim.

raise standards at will and in 1864, a half century before most other Baltimore professional schools, the pharmacists were strong enough to deposit all tuition fees in a central treasury and place all their professors on salaries. From their tightly knit group they formed in 1871 the first active alumni organization associated with any branch of the University.[65]

Their tight organization benefited the pharmacists as long as they maintained close alliance with both physicians and manufacturers. In the decade after the Civil War, relations among pharmacists, physicians and drug manufacturers may have been closer in Maryland than in any other state, allowing the pharmacists, like the physicians and dentists, to provide national leadership. The physicians led by introducing the French emphasis on specialties and clinics, the dentists by combining medical and mechanical training and the pharmacists by associating with medicine and industry. The druggists' alliance with medicine was particularly evident in education where the school of pharmacy was practically a part of the College of Medicine. Their alliance with industry was evident in the number of graduates, notably Alpheus P. Sharp and Louis Dohme, who became outstanding industrial chemists. Ambitious students, already successful in medicine or industry, attended the school of pharmacy to further their own professions. When the school needed a new laboratory building in 1876, both physicians and industrialists helped to finance it.[66] With the support of physicians and of manufacturers who would normally have opposed them, in 1870 the pharmacists of Maryland obtained the first effective laws in the nation to regulate the sale of drugs. The legislation required all retail druggists, first those in Baltimore and later all in the state, to pass an examination before the Maryland College of Pharmacy. Informers divided equally with the college the $50 fine imposed on violators.[67]

The alliance gave strength to the pharmacists as they attempted

[65]Ibid., 6 October 1864; 5 June 1871. Also American Journal of Pharmacy, XLIII (July, 1871), 329. The Maryland College of Pharmacy made official announcements, and frequently published its minutes in this journal.

[66]American Journal of Pharmacy, XLVIII (November, 1876), 521-522; Charles Schmidt and B. Olive Cole, "History of the Maryland College of Pharmacy and the School of Pharmacy, University of Maryland, 1841-1946" (bound MS. volume in School of Pharmacy archives; published in part in Steiner, Education in Maryland, 305-316), 19-21. A picture of the building is in the pharmacy catalogues, 1876-1886.

[67]Edward Kremers and George Urdang, History of Pharmacy, A Guide and a Survey (Philadelphia, 1940), 197-198; Minutes of the Maryland College of Pharmacy, 19 March 1868; 17 March 1870; Laws of Maryland . . . 1870, Chap. 104; also, Laws . . . 1872, Chap. 414; Laws . . . 1902, Chap. 179; Laws . . . 1920, Chap. 525.

to raise educational standards immediately after the war. In 1870, in cooperation with the University, they called a convention in Baltimore of the seven other American schools of pharmacy. This convention, which eventually led to the American Association of Colleges of Pharmacy, established national standards of a four-year apprenticeship, a two-year pharmacy course and a twenty-one-year age minimum for all graduates.[68] Two years later pharmacy became the first school associated with the University to require written entrance examinations and stood alone in urging other professional schools to adopt them.[69] For medical students wishing to take pharmacy courses, the guild equipped a special laboratory and employed an outstanding German professor who had recently migrated to Baltimore, William Simon, the first Ph.D. associated with any branch of the University.[70]

Despite harmony and progress, however, the happy relations began to break down in the 1870's, first with medicine and then with industry. Inevitably some physicians sold drugs directly to patients, and inevitably some pharmacists suggested cures to customers, and each group accused the other of encroaching on its domain. In addition, pharmacists occasionally discovered errors in the physicians written prescriptions, and occasionally made errors in filling them. Doubtless each side exaggerated the number of mistakes made by the other, but a mutual sense of their own superior knowledge and perhaps a mutual fear of their own guilt added acrimony to the disputes. In 1873, after a series of clashes, the pharmaceutical and medical societies of Maryland officially censured each other. By the end of the decade students from one college were no longer welcome in the classes of the other.[71]

Similarly the pharmacists fought with the manufacturers, particularly as prepared drugs cut increasingly into the retailers' profits. They lashed out at "the pressures," "the huckstering," and the "pattented nostrums" of the manufacturers on whom they were so dependent and blamed them for a growing profit squeeze. In 1878

[68]*American Journal of Pharmacy*, XLII (November, 1870) 488, 500-504; Minutes of the Faculty of Physic, 23 April 1870; *Baltimore Sun*, 15 September 1870.

[69]Minutes of the Maryland College of Pharmacy, 2 July 1872; *American Journal of Pharmacy*, XLV (November, 1873), 514; Schmidt and Cole, "History of the Maryland College of Pharmacy," 10.

[70]Minutes of the Maryland College of Pharmacy, 10 October 1872; Cordell, *University of Maryland*, I, 425-426, 435-436.

[71]*American Journal of Pharmacy*, XLV (February, 1873), 88-89; XLV (July, 1873), 328-329; XLVI (January, 1874), 40. For other examples of this dispute in Maryland, see *ibid.*, XLIII (April, 1871), 149-151; LI (September, 1879), 478-479.

the Maryland guild declared that manufacturers were no longer welcome as members, and no longer eligible to receive degrees in the College.[72] Cut off from both medicine and manufacturing, the pharmacists' tight organization became restrictive, narrowing its horizons and the service it could perform as a profession.

As pharmacy broke away from medicine and industry, its four-year apprenticeship became an exploitation of students rather than a service to them. Pharmacists began to speak frankly of using the apprenticeship to "limit the numbers in the profession," and to allow the proprietor to be "free to leave the store." Apprentices received a rigidly set pay, ranging from $75 for their first year to $150 for their fourth. If the apprentice lived with the pharmacist, the cost of his board was substracted from his meager wage, and often he ended up paying his employer.[73]

As was the case with the other professional schools, the College of Pharmacy enjoyed a measure of prosperity while it drifted toward vocationalism. The number of graduates increased from about fifteen each year in the 1870's, to about thirty in the 1880's, to about forty in the 1890's. The annual term expanded from six to eight months, fees rose from $50 to about $80, and classroom instruction increased from about nine hours a week to about fifteen. Among the faculty three men wrote textbooks which brought them national recognition—William Simon, David M. R. Culbreth and Charles Caspari. Caspari was one of the two or three most highly regarded pharmacists of his time.[74]

As was the case also with other professional schools, pharmacy overcrowded its profession and increased its facilities with little thought of the consequences. In 1886 the pharmacists tore down their little building on Aisquith Street and borrowed $35,000 to replace it with a huge, three-story structure, probably the finest pharmacy school building in the country. But just as medical, legal and dental education overexpanded through competition, so the phar-

---

[72]*Ibid.*, XLIV (September, 1872), 423-424; also, XLIII (November, 1871), 481-485; LII (February, 1880), 123-124; *Annual Catalogue of the Maryland College of Pharmacy . . . 1878-1879* [Hereafter *Pharmacy Catalogue*] (Baltimore, 1878), 8; *Pharmacy Catalogue, 1890-1891*, 29.

[73]*American Journal of Pharmacy*, XLIII (December, 1871), 532-535; *Pharmacy Catalogue, 1873-1874*, 29.

[74]Simon, *Manual of Chemistry* (Philadelphia, 1884) and twelve subsequent editions; Culbreth, *Materia Medica and Pharmacology* (Philadelphia, 1896) and six subsequent editions; Casperi, *Treatise on Pharmacy . . .* (Philadelphia, 1898) and eight subsequent editions. For biographical sketches see Cordell, *University of Maryland*, I, 420-454; *Remington's Practice of Pharmacy* (Easton, Pa., 1961), 45.

macists discovered when the note came due that they had over-expanded by their own actions.[75]

The Beginning of Nursing

Even the profession of nursing emerged at Maryland from the harsh economic realities of the industrial age. Called into existence by the medical professors rather than by nurses themselves, the Nurses Training School was designed to obtain the cheapest possible labor to run the hospital. The doctors erred, however, in hiring the formidable Louisa Parsons to head the program. She had in mind something quite different from menial service.

Since 1823 the University medical professors had benefited more than they realized from the ancient and honorable tradition of nursing in the Roman Catholic countries, brought to Maryland and to them by the Sisters of Charity and the Sisters of Mercy. The doctors must have reflected the prevailing feeling in Protestant countries that nursing was a job for servants. They claimed that the nuns were insubordinate and extravagant in running hospital affairs. While the Sisters cheerfully made endless sacrifices for their patients, there was a limit to the abuse they would take from students and professors. In 1889, by mutual agreement, the nuns and the doctors terminated their sixty-six year association.[76]

During the middle of the nineteenth century, meanwhile, the great Florence Nightingale launched a movement of epic quality and one that the doctors did not fully comprehend. The brilliant, charming English lady founded a new profession which began the transformation of nursing from a religious service to a scientific discipline and from menial servitude to eminent respectability. Organizing a unit of thirty-eight nurses for service in the Crimean War of 1854, she built a hospital base at Scutari where her heroic service won the almost pathetic devotion of 10,000 troops. Returning to England with the highest decorations of the British Empire, she established at St. Thomas' Hospital, London, the Nurses Training School which became a model for others that followed. She demanded intense training, high academic standards, feminine super-

[75]Schmidt and Cole, "History of the Maryland College of Pharmacy," 20-21, 5-6.
[76]Minutes of the Faculty of Physic, 25 May 1876; 10 September 1889; *Baltimore American*, 15 December 1889.

vision, firm discipline and rigid separation from the duties of the physician. One of the first respectable professions open to women, nursing was a triumph for feminism as well as for humanity and it attracted vast enthusiasm among women of the finest type. The doctors at Maryland tried to tap the new enthusiasm, believing they saw in student nurses a more pliant kind of hospital help.[77]

To supervise the program the professors employed the stern, militaristic English woman, Louisa Parsons, trained at St. Thomas Hospital by Florence Nightingale herself. Miss Parsons had served with the British troops in Egypt, and, like her teacher, had received high military decorations. Coming to America she served temporarily as the first superintendent of nurses at Johns Hopkins Hospital and first head of the Hopkins Nurses School which opened just a few months before the one at the University of Maryland. It was typical of Louisa Parsons, however, that she should move from her established position to accept a new challenge. At Maryland the physicians' concept of nurses training was medieval. They paid the new superintendent $600, half her Hopkins salary, and expected her to serve in the wards with her students for twelve hours a day.[78]

Miss Parsons was cleverer than her employers. Blandly she accepted all of the doctors' provisions with only a single one of her own: she demanded a fine $10,000 building for her students to replace their living quarters in the hospital. Her request seemed excessive, but believing that some of the money could be raised by public contributions, the doctors immediately began the construction of a three-story structure behind the hospital. After investing so much money they were trapped. They could not abandon the Training School, and the nurses' demands had just begun.[79]

The school opened in December, 1889, with grim offerings to its students. Compelled to sign a contract which bordered on indentured servitude, they were bound for two years with four weeks of vacation each year. The girls cared for patients, prepared the meals and served as charwomen. Seven days a week they worked two twelve-hour shifts, from seven to seven, with two hours off for church on Sunday mornings and two hours off for "exercise" one afternoon a week. In return they received free board and a wage of $8 a month.

[77]Cecil Woodham-Smith, *Florence Nightingale, 1820-1910* (New York, 1951); Richard H. Shryock, *The History of Nursing* . . . (Philadelphia, 1959).

[78]Minutes of the Faculty of Physic, 24 February 1893; Ethel Johns and Blanche Pfefferkorn, *The Johns Hopkins Hospital School of Nursing, 1889-1949* (Baltimore, 1954), 30-32; Gipe, "Development of Nursing," 92-97.

[79]Minutes of the Faculty of Physic, 12 December 1889; 5 July 1890; 28 January 1891.

As additional payment, the faculty agreed that one of the physicians would deliver one or two lectures a week to off-duty nurses, and that Miss Parsons was free to teach the girls what she wished after her duty hours.[80]

Surprisingly, perhaps, but indicative of the strength of the nursing movement, there were always plenty of applicants for the school. By 1895 there were thirty-two students enrolled and by 1905 there were fifty-five. The University did not award degrees to the girls and never considered them as true graduates; but beginning in 1892 they held a modest commencement ceremony in the hospital, and eight girls were authorized to call themselves "Graduates of the University of Maryland Faculty of Physic Training School for Nurses."[81]

Louisa Parsons worked valiantly to build academic standards and academic spirit. She established a month-long probationary period, instructed her charges tirelessly, created marks of rank among the various classes and encouraged student clubs, teas and even dances. She adopted a smart, distinctive uniform, designed by Florence Nightingale and made by the students. It consisted of a long, gray and white chambray dress, a white apron with a square white bib, black stockings and high black shoes, and a flat, white-laced Nightingale cap of which the students were particularly proud. With their own class colors, songs and traditions, the students possessed a greater sense of unity than any other school within the University.[82]

Two years after launching the school, Louisa Parsons left Maryland, perhaps because she believed her work was done, or perhaps in frustration at being unable to move faster. She returned to England for a time, but soon was serving American troops in Cuba during the Spanish-American War and, later, British troops in South Africa during the Boer War. Her funeral in 1916 was a magnificent display of British military pomp.

> The coffin was carried to the Church on a gun carriage—a company of soldiers, buglers, and a firing party—rifles fired over the grave and

[80]Gipe, "Development of Nursing," 246, 237; Jean Louise Bloom, "Development of the University School of Nursing" (MS. dated 1947 in Vertical File, Health Sciences Library, Baltimore), 5-14; *Baltimore Sun*, 4 May 1892; *Bulletin of the Nurses Alumnae Association*, V (April, 1925), 15-20.

[81]*Baltimore Sun*, 4 May 1892; Gipe, "Development of Nursing," 96.

[82]*Therapeutia* [Student Nurses' Annual, 1905; the title is in Greek characters]; Bloom, "Development of the School of Nursing," 5-14; Lillie R. Hoke, "The Maryland University Graduate Nurses' Cap," *Bulletin of the Nurses' Alumnae Association* (1940), 21.

the 'Last Post' sounded by the buglers. . . . It was immensely impressive . . . and the roadside [was] lined with people far and near.[83]

Of all of her accomplishments she must have considered the Maryland Training School her greatest, for her will provided that most of her estate—about $10,000—should go to the University of Maryland Nurses Alumnae Association.[84]

The nurses' struggles with the medical school continued long after Louisa Parsons left, and a multitude of her successors resigned in anger or disappointment.[85] The school of nursing remained the weakest of the University's professional schools, but its founder had endowed it with the noblest motives, the greatest spirit and the strongest drive for self-improvement.

From 1865 until well into the 1890's the harsh economic realities of the industrial age rather than the love of scholarship dominated the professional schools associated with the University of Maryland. In one sense those realities served the University, allowing the professional schools to succeed where the land-grant colleges had so nearly failed. Harsh realities permitted the medical school to obtain an outstanding faculty and a large enrollment from the destitute South and led it to introduce specialties and clinics which pointed toward the future. Economic pressures allowed the dental and pharmacy schools to prosper despite their ideological disputes. Economic needs re-established the law school and created the school of nursing. In a larger sense, however, the age threatened the University. Vocationalism, commercialism, competition and the necessity of placing economic needs above those of scholarship weakened all of the schools. In each of them, fortunately, the more astute professors recognized the urgent need for reform, for scholarship and for the ideals and goals of a real university.

[83]Letter of Mrs. William Osler to William Osler, 11 November 1916, cited in Harvey Cushing, "Louisa Persons . . .," *Bulletin of the Nurses' Alumnae Association*, III (April, 1923) , 10; also *Baltimore Sun*, 3 December 1916.
[84]There is a copy of this will in the archives of the Nurses' Alumnae Association, Baltimore.
[85]Minutes of the Faculty, 1891-1913, *passim;* Gipe, "Development of Nursing," 95.

10

The Agricultural College in a Reform Age

During the age of reform, from about 1890 to 1920, the land-grant colleges emerged into the forefront of American life. First as public service institutions supplying the agrarian-Populist demands for expanded governmental services, and then as educational institutions relating scholarship to the everyday needs of daily life, they symbolized and sometimes guided the reform spirit. College research agencies sought for ways of guaranteeing rural prosperity; college regulatory agencies supervised the farmers' crops, inspected the goods they bought and policed the warehouses at which they sold; college educational agents demonstrated contour plowing, taught wives to bake pies, organized younger children into 4-H clubs and persuaded older ones to go to college. The service agencies infused their philosophy into college education also. From embattled little military schools the land-grant institutions emerged into expansive, democratic universities. Football, fraternities, pennants, cheers and coeds appeared. The spirit of Theodore Roosevelt and Woodrow Wilson—the slightly naive spirit of four-square manly virtues and moral enthusiasm—reached its peak on the American campuses.

228

Gradually the Maryland Agricultural College was becoming more influential than Charles Benedict Calvert ever imagined. From the past it retained its small college tradition, out-of-date by itself, but warm and humanizing and still requiring attention to character and values. From the endowed universities came the newer tradition of scholarship and academic freedom, requiring attention to the frontiers of knowledge. From the reform movement came a tradition of democratic, utilitarian education and public service requiring attention to life outside the cloistered halls. Sometimes the influences conflicted, but generally they made accommodation for each other. There was one other important academic tradition—that of professional education. Increasingly men suggested that the Baltimore professional schools and the land-grant institution belonged together.

The Agricultural Agencies

Just as rural distress inspired reforms which culminated in the agricultural colleges of the 1850's, so it inspired the movement for agricultural agencies which gravitated around the land-grant colleges near the end of the century. Crushed by the industrial world, compelled to purchased expensive machinery and move from subsistence to cash crops, the farmer fell deeper into debt. From 1870 to 1895 farm tenancy in the United States increased 20 percent, and farm mortages increased 30 percent. Forced to sell his produce in an open market in competition with every other farmer and compelled to buy in a closed market from manufacturers and transportation trusts which could fix prices, the average farmer's income declined 40 percent.

While the distress and the resulting reform movement of the 1850's centered in the middle Atlantic states, the movement of the 1890's centered in the middle west. In the farm belt, local Granger laws appeared in the 1870's concerned particularly with regulating the railroads; the Greenback Party flourished in the 1880's concentrating on inflation as a panacea for the farmer's woes; and the Populists appeared in the 1890's obtaining hundreds of state laws to deal with every imaginable problem. In increasing measure the farm belt movements strengthened the mid-western land-grant colleges, giving them the public service functions which Maryland obtained later. Of the ten strongest land-grant colleges in 1895, eight were middle western.[1]

Federal legislation also tended to come earlier and reach further than legislation in Maryland. Pressured or frightened by western farm demands, Congress had approved the Hatch Act of 1887 creating experiment stations, and the Second Morrill Act of 1890 providing direct appropriations to the land-grant colleges. By the turn of the century the reform initiative passed to the major political parties under Theodore Roosevelt, William Howard Taft and Woodrow Wilson, all of whom strengthened the agencies associated with the land-grant colleges as a means of aiding the farmer. Six major acts, each with substantial appropriations, carried broad implications for the colleges and even broader implications for the American economy and government:[2]

1887　Hatch Act. Maryland Experiment Station established; obtained $15,000 annually.

1890　Second Morrill Act. Maryland obtained $25,000 annually for College; funds for Negro education provided.

1906　Adams Act. Maryland Experiment Station obtained additional $15,000 annually.

1907　Nelson Act. Maryland obtained $25,000 annually for preparation of agricultural and mechanical teachers.

1914　Smith-Lever Act. Maryland obtained $50,000 annually for farm and home demonstration agents. State matched appropriation.

1917　Smith-Hughes Act. Maryland obtained $20,000 annually for preparation of vocational teachers.

While neither the farmer nor the reform spirit ever dominated politics in Maryland, the farmer collected favors from both political parties. No Greenback or Populist delegate ever served in the general assembly, and no gubernatorial administration could be classified as part of the national reform movement. The conservative philosophy even dominated the Maryland farm organizations which generally expressed more enthusiasm for lower taxes than for expanded social services. In 1896, for example, the *Maryland Farm*

[1]Edward Danforth Eddy, *Colleges for Our Land and Time: The Land-Grant Idea in American Education* (New York, 1957), 82-147; U. S., *Report of the Commissioner of Education for the Year 1895-1896* (Washington, 1897), 1293-1295.

[2]Arthur J. Klein, *Survey of Land Grant Colleges and Universities* (Washington, 1930), 23-33.

Journal declared that the farmer's greatest national problem was the "vast bureaucracy" of the Cleveland administration.[3] Committed to neither political party, the Maryland farmer provided the balance of power for both, so that his moderate requests became virtual demands which Democrats and Republicans outdid themselves to champion. Although state legislation included smaller appropriations than the federal laws, it gave the College officials powers that reached out over every citizen:[4]

1886 Inspection of fertilizer sold in the state.

1888 Live Stock Sanitary Board. Control of disease among farm animals. About $50,000 spent annually by 1920.

1891 College helped to sponsor Princess Anne Academy for Negroes.

1892 State Weather Bureau, later separated from College.

1896 State Economic and Geological Survey.

1896 Farmers' Institute. To disseminate information among farmers; largely replaced by Smith-Lever Act.

1896 Inspection of nurseries and trees sold in state.

1898 State Horticultural Department. For control of insect pests and plant diseases. About $10,000 spent annually by 1920.

1900 Inspection of feeds sold in state.

1902 State begins appropriation for Experiment Station; $40,000 annually by 1920.

1906 Inspection and control of tobacco sales.

1906 State Board of Forestry, later separated from College.

1908 College trustees made State Board of Agriculture.

1912 Inspection of seeds sold in state.

1912 State Biological Laboratory to manufacture serums and insecticides for farmers.

1914 Ridgely Sub-station added to Experiment Station.

1916 Inspection of honey bees.

1916 State takes over full control of College, changes name to Maryland State College.

1916 Control grading and marketing of fruit.

1920 Consolidation of University of Maryland.

---

[3]*Maryland Farm Journal,* XXXIII (July, 1896), 43-44; XXXIII (August, 1896), 43-44; XXXIII (September, 1896), 43; Morris L. Radoff (ed.), *The Old Line State . . .* 3 vols. (Baltimore, n.d.), I, 105-130.

[4]*Laws of Maryland,* 1886-1920; University of Maryland, *Laws Relating to the Board of Regents . . .* (University of Maryland, Official Publications, [1930]), Vol. XXVII, No. 10.

Evolving in a conglomerate manner and their authority often overlapping, these various agencies gravitated around College Park, tacitly acknowledging the president of the institution as coordinator and director. From 1892 to 1920 the three college presidents— Richard W. Silvester, Harry J. Patterson and Albert F. Woods—made their greatest contributions not as academicians but as farm leaders, working for the proper types of legislation and administering the new agencies which emerged. Although the federal and state legislation passed without over-all plan or goal, it fell into four broad areas—research into farm problems, control over the rural economy, dissemination of information to the public and administration of the program.

Research fitted most naturally into the traditional role of an educational institution. With Charles B. Calvert's ante-bellum experiments on the College grounds, the institution claimed to have conducted the first agricultural research in the country. During and after the Civil War experimentation was forgotten, but with the establishment of the federally-supported experiment station of 1888, practical agricultural research again became a major function of the institution. With headquarters at the Rossborough House, the station built dozens of barns, sheds and greenhouses and soon was utilizing most of the College grounds for experiments. The state almost matched the federal appropriation for the experiment station, and just before World War I purchased an additional experimental site at Ridgely on the Eastern Shore.[5]

The experiment station concentrated on practical research, measuring the profits of different crops and testing varieties of seeds, cuttings, fertilizers, insecticides and farm machinery. Under the long, able direction of Harry J. Patterson, Maryland won particular recognition for developing new varieties of tobacco and strawberries, for work in soil analysis, entomology and dairy feeds and for pioneering in the control of hog cholera and of San Jose scale in fruit trees. Coordinating its work with other research throughout the country, the station published scores of free bulletins each year, keeping the farmer up to date on the latest discoveries, showing him the most economical design for barns and providing him with

[5]*Bulletin No. One of the Maryland Agricultural Experiment Station . . . June 1888,* 5-12; *Annual Report of the Maryland Experiment Station . . . 1888; Annual Report of the Maryland Experimental Station . . . 1903,* xv-xxx; *Annual Report of the Maryland Experiment Station . . . 1915,* xix; *Maryland Farmer,* XXXIII (July, 1896), 30-31.

the names and addresses of firms which sold the most reliable varieties of seeds.[6]

Other highly practical research activity included the State Weather Bureau, originally established to aid the farmer. The State Geological and Economic Survey, supervised jointly by the Maryland Agricultural College and the Johns Hopkins University, mapped the state to locate wells and plan roads, to help the farmer adapt crops to his particular type of soil and to establish equitable values for different types of farm land. In the broad area of economic and sociological research into such problems as marketing and patterns of rural family life, Maryland tended to lag behind many other states.

Officers of the College liked to estimate the cash value of each piece of research—the number of cattle that had been saved by a new vaccine, for example, or the increased profit of a recommended variety of corn. The figures always seemed to prove that Maryland farmers gained many millions of dollars from the relatively few thousands spent on research. By 1920, the College supervised the expenditure of about $100,000 annually for the various agricultural research agencies.[7]

The College's second broad area of public service involved controls over the rural economy, especially over the products which the farmer bought and sold. Beginning in 1886 with the State Fertilizer Law, other legislation empowered the College to inspect nurseries, livestock and poultry feeds, honey bees and all types of seeds used by farmers and gardeners. College agencies established standards for the grading of fruit and tobacco sold in the state. Inspectors guaranteed honest and complete labeling, prohibited the sale of inert or diseased products and publicized the results of comparative tests between different brands. Largest of the agencies was the Live Stock Sanitary Commission which enforced laws of innoculation and quarantine, regulated the transportation of animals into and out of the state and, when necessary, spent huge

[6]Alfred Charles True and V. A. Clark, *The Agricultural Experiment Station in the United States* (Washington, 1900), 247-253; *Annual Reports of the Maryland Experiment Station . . . 1888*, ff.; *Annual Reports of the United States Department of Agriculture . . . 1888*, ff.

[7]*Report of the State Weather Service Commission . . . 1893*, ff.; *Maryland Geological Survey*, 14 vols. (Baltimore, 1897-1941) I, 2-27; *Maryland Geological Survey, Report on the Highways of Maryland* (Baltimore, 1899), 27-30; Eddy, *Colleges for Our Land*, 124-139; *Annual Report of the Maryland Experiment Station . . . 1921*, xiv-xvi.

sums slaughtering diseased animals and reimbursing farmers for their loss. The State Biological Laboratory watched over slaughterhouses and veterinarians, advised farmers on serums and insecticides and frequently offered free supplies. The State Board of Forestry protected state parks and roadside trees and established rules for timbering and conservation. The State Dairymen's Association, supervised by the College, regulated the sale of all milk products.

Such police services often lay far from the traditional functions of higher education, but in the eyes of men who had never trusted colleges they brought great credit to the institutions. The landgrant colleges had become a catchall government functionary, assigned whatever services fell outside the scope of the established branches. Almost all of the control services stemmed from state rather than from federal legislation. By 1920 the control agencies associated with the College were spending almost $100,000 annually, about the same as the research agencies.[8]

The third College service, the dissemination of knowledge to the public, possessed the largest budget and carried the largest implications, since it involved no less than molding the attitudes and daily life of the rural community. Beginning with the printed reports of the experiment station, the dissemination service attained independent status in 1896 with the establishment of the farmers' institutes. Designed as a series of informative lectures, the institutes were directed by energetic William L. Amoss, who was soon contacting every community. He persuaded the College president to require professors to spend their summers lecturing over the countryside and the experiment station staff to travel during the winters. Farmers were deluged with talks, conferences, displays, fairs, contests, prizes and personal mail. Amoss even rented a boat to tour the Chesapeake bayside area with farm information and purchased a railroad car which the railway companies usually hauled free of charge. During droughts, blights or marketing crises, the railroad car sped through the state, stopping only momentarily for agents to thrust pamphlets at the farmers and shout advice. Amoss also organized hundreds of 4-H clubs to teach young people to love the farm and to follow the advice of experts.[9]

[8]*Report of the State Live-Stock Sanitary Commission . . . 1893* and ff.; *Report of the Maryland State Board of Forestry . . . 1906 and 1907* and ff.; *Biennial Report of the Maryland State College of Agriculture . . . 1917 . . . 1919 . . .*, 97-157.

[9]See large collection of correspondence, pamphlets and clippings in William L. Amoss Papers, McKeldin Library. Also, *Report of the Director of Farmers' Institutes . . . 1898,*

As funds from the federal Smith-Lever Act became available for farm and home demonstration agents, the entire dissemination program became known as the Extension Service. Under the direction of Thomas B. Symons, Maryland's program was recognized as one of the finest in the country. A small army of highly trained, well-paid professional agents—generally two men and one woman for each county—covered the rural areas, regularly visiting every farmer. Utilizing the Smith-Hughes funds, the Extension Service established contact with public school systems, providing outlines for special courses and specially trained teachers for elementary courses in agriculture, shop work and home economics.[10] With the coming of World War I, President Wilson appropriated defense funds to the land-grant college extension services to help mobilize the nation's unskilled manpower. The Maryland Extension Service established scores of night schools over the state to provide agricultural and mechanical training for farm and factory laborers.[11]

The Extension Service made a special effort to reach Negroes through public schools, through special Negro agents and especially through the little academy in Somerset County. That institution, founded by the Methodist Church in 1886 as the Delaware Conference Academy for Negroes, had come gradually under the control of Morgan College, a private Negro institution in Baltimore, and its name had evolved into Princess Anne Academy. In 1891, after the federal government stipulated that a portion of the land-grant money go to Negro education, the Maryland Agricultural College began making regular appropriations to Princess Anne Academy for training in blacksmithing, shoemaking, carpentry, bricklaying, farming and home economics. About 150 students attended annually, usually paying their fees and board by working in the institution. Not until 1927 did it offer college level work. Although the Maryland Agricultural College offered little supervision, it kept the appropriation to Princess Anne above the minimum required by the land-grant acts.[12]

---

ff.; *Baltimore Sun,* 9 March 1895; 11 December 1896; 7 February 1897; 19 January 1911; 5 February 1911; 10 February 1911; 3-4 June 1911.

[10]*Annual Report of the Maryland Agricultural Extension Service . . . 1915,* ff.; *Biennial Report of the University of Maryland . . . 1919 . . . 1921,* 70-98.

[11]*Annual Report of the State Board of Education . . . 1904,* 135-143; *1918,* 62-90; *1920,* 88-98; *1922,* 144-160; *Maryland Farmer,* XXXI (December, 1894), 37-38; also see, E. A. Miller, *Elementary Vocational Agriculture for Maryland Schools* (Maryland Agricultural College Bulletin [1915]), Vol. XII, No. 8.

[12]"Morgan College and the Maryland Agricultural College," in Records Office, Secre-

The Extension Service began the first summer schools at College Park in 1910, not for regular students but for farmers, farm wives and farm children who were enticed to attend, usually free of charge, for special "courses" of three days, a week, three weeks or two months. A variety of courses provided special instruction for rural ministers, rural teachers, rural canners, rural dressmakers, rural roadbuilders or rural farm agents.[13]

No one could measure the value of the land-grant colleges' dissemination of knowledge. The extension program was democracy in action, helping the farmers who constituted the most oppressed segment of the economy to find a place of dignity in the modern world. It was also a new undertaking for higher education and one that not only won the farmers' loyalty to the colleges, but also provided the institutions with a more democratic spirit. In cash terms the Maryland extension program by 1920 cost about $180,000 annually.[14]

The fourth subject covered by the mass of legislation concerned the administration of the Maryland Agricultural College and its multitudinous agencies. As research, control and dissemination services grew, the general assembly worried about their organization. While the College unofficially coordinated these government agencies, lawyers pointed out that private stockholders still owned half-title to the institution and named five of its eighteen trustees. Theoretically, the trustees could act contrary to the will of the state and, theoretically, the stockholders could vote themselves dividends from the state's money or liquidate the institution and claim half the assets. In the canal building fiasco before the Civil War and in the railroad embroglio after the war, individuals had profited scandalously from similar public appropriations. The combination of private ownership and public appropriation had created tragic dilemmas for the Baltimore professional schools and for decades

tary of the Interior, National Archives (Record Group 48, Patents and Miscellaneous Division, Box 98); *Baltimore Sun,* 13 October 1900; *Annual Report of the Maryland Agricultural College . . . 1895,* 85-86.

[13]*Baltimore Sun,* 22 August 1906; *Biennial Report of the Maryland Agricultural College 1914-1915,* 11; *Biennial Report of the Maryland State Board of Agriculture . . . 1916-1917,* 19, 44-45; *Summer Training School for Rural Teachers* (Maryland Agricultural College Training Bulletin [1915]), Vol. XII, No. 1; *Short Coure in Agriculture, Horticulture, Poultry Husbandry and Domestic Science* (Maryland Agricultural Bulletin [1914]), Vol. XI, No. 4; *Country Life Conference of Ministers* (Maryland Agricultural College Bulletin [1914]), Vol. XI, No. 2; *Maryland Farmer,* XXXIII (September, 1896), 13-15.

[14]*Biennial Report of the University of Maryland . . . 1919 . . . 1921 . . .,* 42-55, 70-98.

had made the Agricultural College the object of small farmer hostility. By the 1890's the farmers trusted the stockholders, and the shared ownership was generally forgotten; but occasionally urban opponents pointed to the legal snarl as a means of opposing the growing appropriations for agriculture.

College and state officials agreed on a solution as ingenious as the problem was complex. In 1902 the legislature made its annual appropriation to the College in the form of a loan with the College property as security. Four years later, insuring approval of the maneuver with a kind of conspiratorial wink, the assembly named the College trustees as the State Board of Agriculture. Then, taking its time, in 1914 the legislature asked for repayment of the loan. Obviously this was impossible. By foreclosure on the mortgage the private claims were wiped out—without protest from the stockholders—and the state became sole owner of the institution. Finally, in 1916 the assembly reorganized the trustee structure, creating a nine-man body appointed by the governor to serve jointly as the board of the College and as the State Board of Agriculture. The trustees' terms of office were staggered so that one expired each year. The College president served as executive officer "to give direction to the work of the Institution in all of its departments." Eventually certain "departments," such as the weather bureau, became independent, but the act of 1916 remains the basic law governing the institution.[15]

Emerging from federal and state legislation without rancor or fanfare, the agricultural agencies contributed more to the state than anyone quite realized. Although many other factors were involved, they played a substantial role in raising Maryland's farm income from $25,000,000 in 1890 to $40,000,000 in 1910 to an astonishing $110,000,000 in 1920. Again while other factors were involved, the agencies also played a part in pointing toward the strange phenomenon of agricultural overproduction after 1920. Most important of all, perhaps, the agricultural agencies contributed to the transformation of the College itself. The institution at College

[15]*Laws of Maryland . . . 1902*, Chap. 625; *Laws of Maryland . . . 1908*, Chap. 161; "Report of the Maryland Agricultural College," *Journal of Proceedings of the House of Delegates of Maryland . . . 1914*, 336-408; *Laws of Maryland . . . 1914*, Chap. 128; *Laws of Maryland . . . 1916*, Chap. 372; *Report of the Committee on the Maryland Agricultural College to the City-Wide Congress* (Baltimore, 1913), 4-15; *Biennial Report of the Maryland State College of Agriculture . . . 1917 . . . 1919*, 7-10, 80; *Baltimore Sun*, 22 March 1912; 25 November 1913; 10 April 1914; 24 September 1914; *Baltimore News*, 7 April 1914.

Park was ready by 1920 to move laterally into nonfarm activities and vertically toward university status.

The College as an Agricultural Agency

For twenty quietly prosperous years, from 1892 to 1912, the Maryland Agricultural College served much like one of the agricultural agencies growing up around it, providing the farmers' sons who came its way with a practical, vocational education. A multitude of presidents had failed by trying to push the institution beyond the immediate needs of the rural community, but the patient Richard W. Silvester succeeded by sensing exactly what the farmer wanted and then identifying the institution with those wants, however modest they were. The little College did not spring suddenly to life, but like the farmer himself it turned slowly back into the mainstream of American life.

Richard W. Silvester grew up on a Virginia farm, studied agriculture at the Virginia Military Institute during reconstruction and, as principal of Charlotte Hall Academy in St. Mary's County, Maryland, transformed that little academy into a practical farmers' school. In 1892 the trustees of the Maryland Agricultural College elected him without enthusiasm to replace the well-known but inept Henry C. Alvord. Silvester was the first president of the College with no grand schemes to make it famous, but he and the farmers understood each other and by following his agrarian instincts in an age of growing agrarian power, he served longer than all his predecessors. A slow, hard-working, well-intentioned Victorian, his deepest philosophy concerned the nobility of agrarian life. Intellectually he argued that farming "is the vocation on which all prosperity rests"; emotionally he called it "the loveliest of all professions on the face of the earth"; and almost religiously he maintained that it "brings men into contact with that mysterious principle of life, that essence of God in the world."[16]

As for his educational philosophy, Silvester was most concerned with serving the rural people who had never imagined sending their

[16]*Maryland Farmer*, XXIX (September, 1892), 17; XXXII (June, 1895), 14-19; XXIX (August, 1892), 32; XXIX (November, 1892), 17-23; XXX (January, 1893), 21-22; *Baltimore Sun*, 4 March 1906; *Reveille, 1900* [Student Annual], 8-9; *Reveille, 1917*, 15-16.

sons to college. Deliberately seeking the farmers' views on education, he liked to call the institution "A College for the Farmer's Boy." In practice the program was much like Alvord's "People's College." Concentrating on economy, Silvester further reduced the fees and board, expanded the scholarship program and combined class assignments with experiment station work for which he could pay the boys about fifteen cents an hour. The College catalogues boasted that students could obtain an education as cheaply as they could live at home. As late as 1912 the average student spent less than $120 a year for fees, books, board and laundry.[17]

Unconcerned about traditional academic standards, Silvester promised that "no efforts will be spared to make the transition from high school or grammar school a possible one." For students who had difficulties in grammar school, Silvester provided a "sub-collegiate" program and even a prep-school program below that. For those students who objected to preparatory work of any sort, there was a special ten-week course, begun in 1896, and a special two-year course, begun in 1898, that offered certificates which the students could call degrees. Better a ten-week vocational course than none at all. Of the 415 students enrolled at the College in 1912, only 134 were working toward an academic degree. Students who had graduated from one of the better high schools in the state usually entered the College as sophomores or, occasionally, even at the junior class level.[18]

In an institution designed for the public instead of for the scholar, the professor's place was lowly. Expected to spend up to thirty-six hours a week in the classroom and to devote the summer months to traveling for the extension program, a full professor in 1912 received a maximum salary of $1,800 annually. Although the College began offering graduate work in 1900, Silvester never had more than one Ph.D. on the staff. As for faculty tenure or academic freedom, the concepts had no meaning. Each professor was reappointed annually, and there was no protest when the president dismissed a professor in mid-term "due to some uncomplimentary remarks made by him about Governor Lowndes."[19]

[17]*Baltimore Sun*, 16 June 1898; *Maryland Agricultural College Catalogue, 1897-1898* [Hereafter cited *Catalogue*], 19-20; *Catalogue, 1912-1913*, 118-119.

[18]*Annual Report of the Maryland Agricultural College . . . 1895*, 21-28; *Catalogue, 1896-1897;* 10, 17; *Catalogue, 1898-1899*, 11; *Catalogue, 1902-1903*, 46; *Catalogue, 1912-1913*, 109-139.

[19]*Catalogue, 1900-1901, 23;* "Report on the Maryland Agricultural College," *Journal of House of Delegates . . . 1914*, 385-391; *Baltimore Sun*, 15 October 1898.

Silvester offered students their choice of two practical programs, agriculture or engineering. All of the ten-week and two-year students were limited to agriculture, and about half of the regular students accepted it as their major. Although the short courses were often superficial, basic research emanating from Cornell, the midwestern institutions and especially from the experiment stations was rapidly transforming agriculture into the legitimate scientific and professional discipline its advocates had long promised. By 1900 the vague courses in botany, chemistry and geology had given way to technical and highly practical courses in dairying, horticulture, field crops, pomology and vegetable culture.

Actually agriculture was becoming a more academically respectable subject than many of the students realized. Despite the growing farm prosperity and the ringing words of Silvester, the hayseed stigma remained. Agriculture majors became so accustomed to being called rubes that they named the president of the campus agricultural club the "High Clodhopper" and listed its members as "Rustics." Until about 1900 many agricultural majors returned to the farm, but during the twentieth century the great majority went into some type of research or extension work.[20] Perhaps the most outstanding agricultural graduates were W. W. Skinner, class of 1895, and Henry C. Sherman, class of 1909, both of whom won national recognition for their scholarship in the field of agricultural chemistry.

The other practical professional program was engineering which expanded from one part-time instructor in 1892 to eight instructors in 1912. At first Silvester soft-pedaled engineering, calling it "Rural Roadbuilding," "Farm Drainage," or "Farm Machinery"; but as students persuaded their parents to let them leave the farm, the president eventually admitted that the College was training technologists headed toward the city. Engineering, like agriculture, had its difficulties in emerging to academic respectability, and well into the twentieth century students spent much of their time studying blacksmithing, carpentry and mechanical drawing. Gradually, however, able professors like Harry Gwinner and Thomas H. Taliaferro began to establish the bridge between mechanics and physics and to separate the subject into such technical fields as civil, mechanical and electrical engineering. The engineering program produced

[20]*Catalogues, 1892-1912, passim; Reveille, 1900*, 124; *Reveille, 1908*, 171-172; *Reveille, 1914*, 147.

some of the most outstanding graduates the institution has had. These included Harry Clifton Byrd, class of 1908, who became president of the University of Maryland; Hershel Allen, class of 1910, who built bridges over the Chesapeake Bay and the Delaware River; William P. Cole, 1910, who served in Congress for fifteen years and became a United States judge; Millard E. Tydings, 1910, who served in the United States Senate for twenty-four years; and Charles M. White, 1913, who served for many years as president of the Republic Steel Corporation.[21]

Silvester eliminated liberal arts almost entirely. In 1912 when there were twelve instructors of agriculture and eight of engineering, the College employed only two instructors for the entire areas of English, history, languages, philosophy, economics and the social sciences. The catalogue listed only two courses in literature, and the one most frequently offered was "Farm Literature." Listed also were one course in history and two in civics, while in mathematics "Bookkeeping" was for many years the most popular course. Head of the liberal arts division was Silvester's vice-president, Thomas H. Spence, who insisted that the humanities and even the sciences must be "rigidly subordinated" to more practical subjects. He defended the liberal arts as useful for "training the mental faculties," as an aid in making speeches and writing letters and useful in providing farm boys with a measure of "refinement"; but he seldom suggested that culture had distinct values for its own sake. The College library, located on the second floor of the gymnasium, was open most of the day by 1912, but its total budget for new books seldom reached $500 annually. Although the emphasis on practical courses and laboratories had finally broken down the old system of recitations which had so long handicapped education, the new technological training included its own brand of anti-intellectualism.[22]

Silvester's administration coincided with a cult of manliness and militarism then sweeping the country, and even the farmers who

[21]*Catalogues, 1892-1912, passim; History of the Mechanical Engineering Department* . . . (Maryland Agricultural College Bulletin [1909]), Vol. V, No. 5. Sometimes a separate "Scientific Course" existed, a sort of amalgam of Agriculture and Engineering. For outstanding graduates, see University of Maryland Alumni Office records and *Who's Who in America* (Chicago, 1899, ff.).

[22]*Maryland Farmer,* XXX (January, 1893), 21-22; XXXII (July, 1895), 26; *Reveille, 1897,* 18; *Reveille, 1900,* 14-17; *Baltimore Sun,* 21 April 1913; *Catalogue, 1902-1903, 33* 38-41; *Catalogue, 1910-1911,* 78-79; *Catalogue, 1911-1912,* 14-16, 47-48, 85, 101-107; *Biennial Financial Report of the Maryland Agricultural College . . . 1906,* 8; *Biennial Report of the Maryland State College of Agriculture . . . 1917 . . . 1919 . . .* 25-26, 65.

had once despised the College's military system began to thrill to martial music. Scholars at the turn of the century were relating physical strength to Darwinism, newspapers called pridefully for American military preparedness against an unidentified enemy and Theodore Roosevelt invited prize fighters to spar with him in the White House. Silvester adopted the title of "Captain," and welcomed the spit-and-polish officers which the War Department sent to drill the land-grant college students. Although he increased the drill time to almost two hours a day, rivalry between the three military companies on the campus became so intense that voluntary drills occupied much of the students' extracurricular time. Increasingly the student officers assumed responsibility for campus discipline. Beginning in 1896, the War Department sponsored a two-week summer encampment for Maryland students at secluded spots along the Eastern Shore and accepted picked graduates for service as regular army officers. When the Spanish-American War came in 1898 Silvester encouraged student enlistment, and when a half-dozen veterans returned the following year they were regarded as the campus heroes.[23]

Curiously, perhaps, the military revival at the turn of the century coincided with a wave of religiosity that swept American campuses. The Young Men's Christian Association appeared at Maryland in 1893 and soon became the most active student organization. Silvester also allowed students to lead the daily chapel devotionals which lasted until 1918, and the literary societies introduced their debates with prayer. Possibly the religious emphasis was compensation for the displacement of character building as a primary function of the curriculum, or perhaps it was related to the sense of moral improvement that characterized the reform age.[24]

Indeed, there may have been a common theme linking reform, manliness, good citizenship, militarism, religion, sportsmanship and athletics. In any case, physical education and intercollegiate athletics were other powerful new influences at Maryland about the turn of the century. Although College officials tried to merge physical education and military training, the War Department seemed to sense a rivalry between the two and particularly opposed

---

[23]*Reveille, 1897,* 19, 53-54, 88-92, 101-104; *Reveille, 1899,* 17-22; *Maryland Farmer,* XXXII (July, 1895), 36; XXXII (November, 1895), 43-44; *Baltimore Sun,* 29 June 1910; *Catalogue, 1910-1911,* 73-79.

[24]*Catalogue, 1893-1894,* 18, 44; *Reveille, 1901,* 120; *Maryland Farmer,* XXXII (July, 1895), 47.

intercollegiate athletics. By the end of Silvester's administration athletics were becoming increasingly prominent and military influence was sharply on the wane.

Informal campus baseball and football games had been played since the Civil War, and inevitably boys from one institution began challenging those from another. The College's first recorded intercollegiate game occurred in 1888 when a baseball team, mostly of students, traveled to Annapolis to defeat a group from St. John's College and another from the Naval Academy. Two years later a football squad with many students from the College lost matches with high school teams from Sandy Spring and Laurel.[25] The first official team, however, was a football squad organized in 1892 by a student in the junior class, Sothoron Key. The two-game season was disastrous with a 58-0 loss to St. John's and a 62-0 defeat by Johns Hopkins, but the humiliation aroused the College. Almost immediately the trustees became the most enthusiastic athletics fans, appropriating $5,000 for a new gymnasium, while a faculty member volunteered to serve as coach. Early in 1893 a professor of physical culture appeared on the campus to begin the first regular classes in the subject. Later that year a baseball team appeared, track and tennis came in 1894 and basketball in 1905. In 1903 the College employed tough John Markey of Frederick as coach for its various teams. Coaches had to be tough then, for they were expected to play and, occasionally, neighborhood thugs were enlisted on the team.[26] The students complained bitterly, however, about one game with the University of Maryland in Baltimore:

This was the hardest fought game in which we participated, and should have been ours by a score of 6 to 0, but our opponents took advantage of the approaching darkness when we were within two yards of their line, and allowed three extra men to take places in the line.[27]

During the first ten years, when Maryland played most of the colleges in the state and surrounding area, as well as many of the high schools, its won-lost record was about even. In 1905, however, a curly-headed lad, Harry Clifton Byrd, entered the College from the Eastern Shore. For three years he led the institution to victories in every sport and over almost every opponent except the formidable

[25] *Athletic Number* (Maryland Agricultural College Bulletin [1915]), XII, No. 2, 1.
[26] *Reveille, 1897,* 76-82; *Reveille, 1900,* 84; *Athletic Number,* 1-15.
[27] *Reveille, 1897,* 80.

Johns Hopkins. Byrd graduated three years later, but just before Silvester resigned in 1912 he appointed the former sports hero as coach. That year the Maryland "Aggies" beat Hopkins in football for the first time.[28]

Silvester liked to point to new buildings as the measure of his long administration, and they were numerous if esthetically undistinguished. When he arrived there were only three buildings—the Rossborough House, the barracks and the president's house—plus some barns and tenant houses. By 1912 he had spent about $165,000 for renovations and buildings, creating a great horseshoe complex with the present Morrill Hall at the top of the curve:[29]

1893   Gymnasium and Library. Two-story brick; north of Morrill Hall; cost about $5,000; razed 1958.

1894   Mechanical Engineering. Two-story brick mansard; site of west wing of Taliaferro; about $10,000; razed 1961.

1897   Chemical Building, later McDowell Hall. Three-story brick; west of Mechanical Engineering; about $10,000; razed 1958.

1898   Science Hall, now Morrill Hall. About $24,000.

1901   Infirmary, now Home Management Center. About $5,000.

1904   Administration Building. Five-story gothic; southeast of Morrill Hall; about $35,000; burned 1912.

1909   Engineering Addition, now east wing of Taliaferro. About $23,000.

For all of Silvester's agrarian agencies and for all of the school's spirit and buildings, the little Maryland Agricultural College was still lonely there on the hill in 1912 and still awaiting a spark to propel it into the present. The increase in collegiate enrollment from 75 to 134 was hardly impressive for a twenty-year-period of growing farm prosperity. Although most of the institution's enemies had disappeared, many people regarded it indifferently as another agricultural agency, an educational branch of the government's farm program for rural boys who could not afford, or qualify for, admission elsewhere. Its vocational bent however sound, and its

[28]*Reveille, 1906*, 48, 132; *Reveille, 1908*, 31, 123-125; *Reveille, 1913*, 108-114; *Athletic Number*, 12-15.

[29]*Biennial Financial Report of the Maryland Agricultural College . . . 1912*, 11-12; *Catalogue, 1912-1913*, 15-17; also, *Annual Reports, 1892-1912, passim; Baltimore Sun*, 9 December 1893; 15 April 1895; 15 June 1895; 15 March 1899; 7 June 1903; 18 June 1904; 4 March 1906; 9 May 1908; *Maryland Farmer*, XXXI (October, 1894), 27-28; XXXIII (October, 1896), 44.

boy scout virtues however true, remained far from the academic ideals of a later generation. Silvester, nevertheless, by patiently identifying the institution with the needs of the people had laid the basis for a renaissance, and his real triumph came in the guise of disaster. After the great fire of 1912 the College attracted the state-wide attention which it needed. The very process of rebuilding provided the fresh start, the new invigoration and the positive leadership which Silvester had never quite grasped.

The fire occurred on November 29, 1912, the day before Thanks-giving, at the peak of the holiday ball. A band from Wash-ington was present, the auditorium of the new administration building was gaily decorated with palms and bunting, and the guests were moving toward the banquet tables for the 10:30 supper that was being served during the first intermission. Someone announced that the outside rafters were afire and the crowd rushed through the doors to watch the flames, almost as if the blaze were a part of the festivities. Eagerly the boys rounded up fire hoses, the Hyattsville fire department arrived and everything was pleasantly exciting until the wind began to rise and the water pressure began to fall. Then—too late to save much—officials ordered the fire fighting to stop, and all hands to empty the building of furniture and rec-ords. Already the flames were licking the main building, the old barracks which Calvert had built a half century before. The railroad rushed fire-fighting equipment from Washington, but no one was at the station to unload it. In awe the crowd watched while the two largest buildings on the campus crashed into ruins. Every dormitory room was gone, half the classrooms and offices and most of the College records. The loss was appraised at $250,000 and for years people were certain that this was the greatest event in the institution's history. But it was important in a way they did not realize.[30]

The College and Higher Education

During the next eight years a valiant spirit combined with the mood of reform, and the nation's needs in World War I combined with the state's need for a unified system of higher education; together these forces propelled the burned-out College toward the

[30]*Baltimore Sun,* 30 November-4 December 1912; 27 December 1912; 4 January 1913; *Reveille, 1913,* 36, 98-105.

finest tradition of higher education. Spirit, at first, was almost all the College had. Silvester, brokenhearted at the disaster, announced his resignation. The faculty, nevertheless, rallied the students on the lawn on the Monday following the fire and determined to continue classes as usual in the remaining buildings and barns. Thomas H. Spence served as acting president. From all over the state people sent castoff clothing to the students, as if the College were a charity. Residents of College Park, Hyattsville and Berwyn volunteered to board the boys for the rest of the academic year.[31]

The matter of rebuilding the College caused people to re-examine its basic functions, and for the first time many began to catch a vision of its true potentiality. The public school system was finally reaching the most isolated areas, farmers were enjoying their greatest prosperity in a century and rural boys were ready to attend colleges in significant numbers. For newspapers and service clubs, establishing a respectable farmers' college suddenly became a fashionable reform enthusiasm. Actually, few caught the full vision. While many talked of an outstanding state-supported institution for the farmer, scarcely anyone realized that to be fully respectable it would have to be an institution of higher learning for everyone.

Important state organizations took up the cause. The powerful Maryland Grange called a special meeting to demand that the institution be rebuilt, not only as the head of the agricultural agencies but also as a top-quality institution of higher learning. The *Baltimore Sun* agreed that farmers could rightly expect the state to provide them with an outstanding professional education. At least a half-dozen Maryland towns expressed faith in the College's future with offers of free land and free buildings if the site were moved. Most important of all, the influential City-Wide Congress, a group of self-appointed Baltimore reformers, took up the cause as one of its special projects. Sharing the enthusiasm, Governor Phillips Lee Goldsborough personally visited Rutgers and Cornell to find, he said, "the leading agriculturalist in the country" to head the College.[32]

After three months of searching, the governor and the trustees

[31]*Baltimore Sun*, 1 December 1912; 4 December 1912.

[32]*Ibid.*, 6 December 1912; 4 January 1913; 15 January 1913; 18 January 1913; 18 February 1913; 28 February 1913; 17 February 1914; and *passim;* Leroy Stafford Boyd, *The Maryland Agricultural College—A Plea for Its Removal and Enlargement . . .* (Washington, 1912) ; Charles H. Stanley, *Facts about the Maryland Agricultural College* (n.p., 1913) ; *Report of Committee on the Maryland Agricultural College to the City-Wide Congress* (Baltimore, 1913).

concluded that a remarkably able agriculturalist was quietly at work in their own front yard—modest, unassuming Harry J. Patterson, director of the Maryland Experiment Station. Devoted to research rather than administration, Patterson acecpted the position reluctantly, and during his four-year administration, from 1913 to 1917, he may have been the unhappiest president in the College's history. A graduate of Pennsylvania State College and long associated with Silvester, his ambition was simply to rebuild the little institution that had burned and, hopefully, to expand its agricultural service agencies.[33]

Patterson's administration was surprisingly successful, however, because he was able to yield to ideas broader than his own. Eager to keep standards "democratic," he yielded when the faculty insisted on three years of high school for admission to the freshman class. Uninterested in the liberal arts, he yielded when the trustees doubled the staff in that field while maintaining the agricultural staff at about the same level. Like Silvester he measured success by new buildings and was distressed when the legislature put off his requests, but willingly he followed its lead toward university status. With the money received from fire insurance, he completed in 1914 the five-story Calvert Hall in the then fashionable neo-Tudor, high-school style, and in 1915 finished a horticultural building that was later used for many years by the Music Department. Patterson failed to get additional money for scholarships, but during his four years as president enrollment jumped from 134 to 220. As had happened before, the times were pushing the College along faster than its administration quite understood.[34]

The greatest change that Patterson witnessed was the collapse of the military system and the emergence of a new collegiate atmosphere. With dormitories gone and students enjoying the freedom of town life, the old militarism gave way to the self-expression and relaxation essential for the pursuit of ideas. Even when Calvert Hall was completed, the barracks-type life—with its endless inspections and calisthenics and precise schedules—could never be reinstituted. Uniforms disappeared, and by 1916 the entire military

[33]*Baltimore Sun*, 3 March 1913; 18 April 1913; 21 April 1913; *Reveille, 1914,* 192; *Reveille, 1915,* 8-10.

[34]H. J. Patterson, *Facts Concerning the Maryland Agricultural College* . . . (n.p., 1914); *Biennial Report of the Maryland State Board of Agriculture . . . 1917, passim; Baltimore Sun,* 21 April 1913; 20 February 1914; 1 June 1914; 28 July 1915; *Reveille, 1915,* 14-16; *Reveille, 1917,* 16-19; *Catalogue, 1912-1913,* 4-5, 109, 139; *Catalogue, 1917-1918,* 3-4, 118, 165.

system was reduced to a lecture and two hours of drill a week.[35]

The new collegiate spirit found expression in student publications which often displayed more independence than the College officials approved. A staid, faculty-controlled yearbook, *Reveille*, had appeared since 1897, and a semimonthly newspaper, *Triangle*, had been published for the alumni after 1910. Students gained control of both publications after the fire, changed the name of the newspaper to the *M. A. C. Weekly* and began to express their opinions boldly. Although sometimes childish in their views, the publications heralded a new vigor and excitement in college life. Actually student vision was frequently broader than that of the officials over them. Even the faculty felt liberated and began to talk of its rights and of academic freedom.[36]

Fraternities were another expression of collegiate spirit and, at least originally, an indication of growing maturity and independence. With students scattered throughout the community and military discipline gone, the fraternities were designed to foster self-discipline, fellowship and high academic standards. The first fraternities at Maryland were scholarship societies in which professors frequently served as officers. Gamma Pi was the first to be recognized on the campus in September, 1913—it became Sigma Nu in 1917; Alpha Phi came the following month—it became Kappa Alpha in 1914; Iota Sigma, now Sigma Phi Sigma, appeared in 1914 and was the first to have its own fraternity house; and Sigma Delta, the first sorority, was recognized in 1920. Eventually good times tended to overshadow self-discipline, and the College officials had to face irate citizens who claimed that the social clubs were undemocratic; but for most of the students before 1920 fraternities added a style and prestige to the College which it badly needed.[37]

If civilian clothes, student publications and fraternities bewildered Patterson, the ultimate came in 1916 when the trustees voted to admit Charlotte Vaux and Elizabeth Hook as the first coeds. With the American feminist movement at its peak, the Smith-Lever Act of 1914 exerted pressure on the land-grant colleges to establish home economics courses to train women to serve as agricultural home demonstration agents. Fascinated by the prospect of broader agricultural services, Patterson embraced the change and moved

[35]*Catalogue, 1916-1917*, 81-85; *Reveille, 1916*, 142; *Reveille, 1917*, 16-19; *Baltimore Sun*, 18 December 1916.

[36]*Reveille, 1915*, 148; *Triangle*, 14 October 1914; *M.A.C. Weekly*, 21 October 1914.

[37]*Reveille, 1914*, 160-167; *Reveille, 1915*, 137; *Reveille, 1920*, 340-344; *M.S.C. Weekly*, 8 February 1917. See "University of Maryland—Fraternities and Sororities," in Pamphlet file, McKeldin Library.

into town so that the president's house could be rebuilt to serve as a women's dormitory. Charlotte Vaux received a two-year certificate in agriculture in 1918, and two years later Elizabeth Hook became the first woman to receive a four-year degree at Maryland. By then over twenty coeds were on the campus.[38]

Even the surroundings changed during Patterson's administration as College Park suddenly emerged from obscurity into a United States Air Corps boom town. Soon after their flight at Kitty Hawk, Orville and Wilbur Wright sold their airplane to the Army Signal Corps. The Corps acquired land about a mile from the campus, and in 1909 the Wright brothers arrived to lay out the field and train the first pilots. Generally considered to have been the first graded and equipped airport anywhere, the field became the scene of experiments that impressed the world and thrilled the little College community. In 1911, H. H. ("Hap") Arnold, Chief of the Air Force in World War II, set a distance record with a 42-mile flight to Frederick. College Park experiments included some of the earliest tests of gunfire from airplanes, blind flight and aircraft radio. Flight training moved to larger quarters when the United States entered World War I, but meanwhile College Park had become a sizable village.[39]

Finally, the legislature strengthened the president's powers and changed the name of the institution from Maryland Agricultural College to Maryland State College of Agriculture. Patterson's intention was exactly the opposite. When the legislature in 1916 considered the administration of its many agricultural agencies, Patterson suggested a three-man head for the entire organization. The director of the experiment station, the director of extension and the president of the College would have equal voice in running the whole. This organization would allow Patterson to share his burdensome responsibilities and would further cement the three services for the cause of agriculture. To the legislature, however, the troica seemed needlessly complicated. With high praise for the modest president the assembly actually strengthened his authority over the agencies and, instead of confirming the agricultural foundation of the College, yielded to the appeals of students and alumni to eliminate the hayseed connotation by changing the name to Maryland State College. Patterson insisted that the additional

[38] Reveille, 1917, 116; Reveille, 1920, 281-283.
[39] Alfred Goldberg (ed.), History of the United States Air Force, 1907-1957 (Princeton, 1956), 4-7; William F. Lynd, "The Army Flying School at College Park," Maryland Historical Magazine, XLVIII (September, 1953), 227-241.

phrase "of Agriculture" be officially adopted, but usually the words were ignored. As Maryland State College the institution was ready to aim beyond its limited rural scope and to appeal to the cities as an educational institution for all citizens.[40]

In January, 1917, Patterson persuaded the trustees to let him return to the experiment station where the variables were easier to control. In the four years following the fire, the College had gained in popular support, the campus had been rebuilt and standards and enrollment were sharply up. The military atmosphere had given way to a spirit of freedom, athletics, songs and cheers, extracurricula activities, student publications, fraternities and coeducation. The rustic "Aggies" had become State College, vibrant with a life of its own. The governor, newspaper editors and many civic organizations wanted to help the trustees find the right man as Patterson's successor. After considering Edwin B. Craighead, president of Tulane, and Raymond A. Pearson, president of Iowa State, they finally decided upon the dean and acting president of the University of Minnesota, Albert Fred Woods.

Some would have called the young Dr. Woods the most promising candidate in the country for the position. He had held important posts in the United States Department of Agriculture, was a noted scholar, had been an advisor to international agricultural congresses and as dean and acting president at the University of Minnesota, he was considered one of the leading figures in the rise of that institution to the front rank of the land-grant institutions. The Maryland trustees, planning more ambitiously than they had since the days of Calvert, offered the brilliant Woods $10,000 annually, triple his predecessor's salary and double that of the state governor. Woods accepted the offer after a talk with the governor, and thereafter during his nine-year administration, dealt directly with the state officials, sometimes almost ignoring the trustees.[41]

While outside events all seemed to have benefited Patterson, Woods arrived at College Park at exactly the wrong time. As the country plunged into World War I, the sentiment for building an educational institution turned suddenly into sentiment for war. The government established policy, and a good college president

[40]*Laws of Maryland . . . 1916*, Chap. 372; *Biennial Report of the Maryland State Board of Agriculture . . . 1917*, 7-13; *Baltimore Sun*, 15 October 1914; 30 July 1915; 19 February 1916.

[41]*Baltimore Sun*, 23 July 1916; 4 August 1916; 21 September 1916; 20 January 1917; 31 January 1917; 3 July 1916; 4 October 1917; James Gray, *The University of Minnesota, 1851-1951* (Minneapolis, 1951), 228-236.

could only display his patriotism by following obediently. In the spring of 1917 as students rushed off to enlist, enrollment fell precipitately in all American colleges and at Maryland from 220 to 153. To keep students in school, in the fall of 1917 the government took over the loose military system of the land-grant colleges and created the Reserve Officer Training Corps—ROTC—which guaranteed commissions to all students who completed specified military courses along with their regular college training.

By 1918 Woods found himself commandant of a military camp. Convinced that the ROTC satisfied neither the army's immediate need for officers nor the students' desire for service, the government took over the land-grant colleges for the all-military Student Army Training Corps—SATC. Soldiers who qualified for college level work were assigned to the institutions to complete their education under military discipline and military pay. At Maryland the government rented dormitories to serve as barracks, and placed the faculty and administration under army command. About twenty civilian students continued to attend classes along with about two hundred troops. In addition, the Army Signal Corps rented a portion of the College grounds during 1918, built temporary barracks, employed some of the faculty and conducted a special radio school for about six hundred men. Besides the hundreds who were trained on the campus, over two hundred students and alumni went to war, and at least six gave their lives.[42]

Despite the interruption of the flowering collegiate tradition the College benefited from the war. By equalizing the quality of its ROTC and SATC units over the country, the army raised standards markedly at Maryland. Entrance requirements increased, the expenditure for liberal arts subjects almost doubled and engineering moved ahead into hydraulics, kinetics, materials testing, structural design and theory. Although the SATC allowed few students to complete their degrees, it introduced to higher education thousands of boys who would never have attended college otherwise, and who would return after the war to continue. In addition Maryland obtained construction priority to complete in 1918 a large four-story agricultural building, now called the Skinner Building. Also, the

[42]*Baltimore Sun,* 14 April 1917; *Biennial Report of the Maryland State College . . . 1917 . . . 1919 . . .* 7-9; *Reveille, 1918, passim; Reveille, 1920,* 40-45; *Catalogue 1918-1919,* 24-25, 155; *Catalogue, 1919-1920,* 185-199; *Students' Army Training Corps at the Maryland State College* (Pamphlet file, McKeldin Library); *M.S.C. Weekly,* 19 December 1918; 16 January 1919; "Gold Star List" (Typescript dated 1961 in President's Office); *Reveille, 1920,* 300-302.

army spent at least $50,000 for long-serviceable temporary structures and miscellaneous plant improvements which fell to the College after the war.[43]

Woods was the ideal president to take advantage of postwar change always with an eye to true academic ideals. In January, 1919, the SATC gave way to the more relaxed ROTC as the regular peace-time organization for military training. With many veterans back to complete their education, enrollment soared from 153 in 1917, to 302 in 1919, to an impressive 517 in 1920. With the state accustomed to large wartime expenditures, Woods took advantage of the atmosphere to increase the total education budget of the College from $150,000 in 1916 to about $450,000 in 1920.[44]

Most of all, however, Woods was concerned with organizing the College as an outstanding institution of higher learning. He was the first president to serve at Maryland whose own career had been in higher education, the first leader fully aware of the organization of a modern university. In 1919, as soon as demobilization was complete, he announced the creation of seven schools within the College, each with its own dean who was responsible for budget, quality and expansion:

School of Agriculture	Dean P. W. Zimmerman
School of Engineering	Dean Thomas H. Taliaferro, replaced by Dean A. N. Johnson, 1921
School of Arts and Sciences	Acting Dean Thomas H. Spence, replaced by Dean Frederick F. Lee, 1921
School of Chemistry (merged with Arts and Sciences in 1921)	Dean H. B. McDowell
School of Education	Dean Harold F. Cotterman
School of Home Economics	Acting Dean Agnes Saunders, replaced by Dean Marie Mount, 1920
Graduate School—including Summer School	Dean Charles D. Appleman

[43]*Biennial Report of the Maryland State College of Agriculture . . . 1917 . . . 1919 . . .,* 7-9, 42-80; *M.S.C. Weekly,* 16 January 1919.
[44]*Biennial Report of the Maryland State Board of Agriculture . . . 1917,* 114-135; *Biennial Report of the University of Maryland . . . 1919 . . . 1921,* 35-59; *Laws of Maryland . . . 1914,* Chap. 721; *Laws of Maryland . . . 1920,* Chaps. 487, 727.

The system of deans and of separate schools for the first time recognized the separation of liberal arts and professional education within the institution. It established the liberal arts as a basic core curriculum which could be expanded or contracted without weakening the professional subjects. The system guaranteed the status of nonagricultural subjects, gave to professional men in each area the initiative for raising their own standards and enrollment and established an organizational basis for unlimited expansion. Such miscellaneous subjects as ROTC and physical education, along with the library and the multitude of agricultural agencies, were established as divisions reporting directly to the president.[45]

Woods introduced many minor changes designed to improve the quality and tone of education. He abolished the preparatory school which lent an immature influence to the campus. He allowed students to "major" within certain areas of each school, and permitted a narrow choice of electives in addition to their majors. Four additional Ph.D.'s appeared on the faculty, and new courses came in languages, history, economics, biology, chemical engineering, journalism and home economics. Finally, into his own office as assistant to the president, Woods called the irrepressible football coach, the 33-year-old Harry Clifton Byrd, full of ideas and energy and idolized by the students. Perhaps this appointment was the most important event of all for the future development of the institution.[46]

Maryland State College was a typical land-grant college by 1920. Neither one of the strongest nor one of the weakest, it had evolved from the people and from the times rather than from any one man's insight or leadership. The people and the times had called forth the agricultural agencies which made Maryland State College powerful under Silvester; they called forth the collegiate spirit that emerged under Patterson; and they called forth the leadership toward university values which Woods represented. In the Old World and in America almost until the twentieth century, institutions of higher learning had been considered the repositories of ancient knowledge and the conservative backbone of society. A new land and a new era, however, gave higher education a social consciousness, a role of reaching out to serve and a dynamic forward motion. These new values—with both positive and negative implications—were the contributions of Maryland State College and of all the land-grant col-

[45]*Biennial Report of the Maryland State College of Agriculture . . . 1917 . . . 1919 . . .*, 7-67; *Baltimore Sun*, 12 April 1919; *Catalogue, 1919-1920*, 11-26.
[46]*Catalogue, 1919-1920*, 11-12, 25-29; *Reveille, 1920*, 43-46.

leges in the early part of the twentieth century. Even Woods was taken by surprise when the institution suddenly became the University of Maryland, but he—and his assistant—were ready to assume leadership in that field also.

11

The Professional Schools in a Reform Age

While agrarian-Populist reforms elevated the land-grant colleges, a related urban-Progressive spirit reconstructed professional education. From the excesses of laissez faire came mergers, professional organization and legislative control. The proliferation of competing proprietary institutions led to mergers in education as it had in business; the stronger combinations then joined with philanthropic foundations, such as those established by Carnegie and Hopkins, to build professional organizations with power to accredit educational institutions; and accrediting agencies joined with legislative reformers to obtain licensing laws which insured high professional standards. Within the professional schools the reform spirit became an academic spirit, and business values gave way to university values.

By 1920 the Maryland State College had acquired the tradition of public service and popular support, and the University of Maryland had re-acquired its tradition of high standards and scholarship. At that point the traditions and the two institutions merged to form the present University of Maryland.

Overexpansion and Organization

The American professions were as desperate by the 1890's as the farmer and in their desperation lay the glimmerings of reform. Their plight grew out of the grotesque overexpansion of the proprietary professional schools which the University of Maryland had so unwittingly fathered. The overexpansion glutted the professions, depressed standards and gave a mercenary overtone to the whole business of professional education. In medicine, for example, 157 American schools competed for students in 1890, while today, for a population three times as large, there are only 84 medical schools. In Maryland alone, seven medical schools in 1890 awarded a total of 455 M.D. degrees, more than double the number that two schools award today. Such competition for enrollment destroyed quality. Even at the University of Maryland, where standards were relatively high, a boy could begin medical training with less than one year of high school and could obtain his degree after two terms of less than six months each. Conditions were similar or worse in law, dentistry, pharmacy and nursing.

Expansion of a different sort changed the atmosphere within the University from a closely-knit group of individuals with a highly personal interest in the institution, to a loose association of many instructors more interested in the professions as a whole. From 1890 to 1920, while enrollment remained almost stationary, the medical school staff increased from 21 to 177, the law faculty grew from 12 to 28 and the dentistry staff from 8 to 30. The reason for the change lay in the decline of profits in teaching and the transformation of the faculty from a few who devoted most of their time to the institution to many who gave only a fraction of their time. The Maryland medical professors earned about $4,000 annually from their teaching in 1820, about $2,500 in 1870 and less than $1,000 by 1900; the leading professors in law, dentistry and pharmacy earned slightly less. Offering such incomes, the University attracted some of the finest men in the country until about 1870, and they in turn made the University the basis of their professional life. As that generation departed about 1890, however, most of the major chairs were taken by a number of men who were primarily practitioners teaching in their spare time.

While there was a note of sadness in the growing impersonality of the professional schools—which such men as Davidge, Hoffman, Hayden and Harris had nourished so devotedly—the faculty expansion broadened the base of education as well as the base of responsibility. If Maryland no longer attracted the outstanding teachers of the country, it did attract the combined wisdom of the outstanding practitioners of the state. Students particularly remembered men like R. Dorsey Coale, Randolph Winslow, John C. Hemmeter, L. McLane Tiffany and Thomas M. Ashby in medicine; Henry D. Harlan and Henry Stockbridge in law; R. B. Winder in dentistry; and Charles Schmidt in pharmacy. For such men the University was neither an ivory tower of scholarship nor a business proposition as it had variously been for their predecessors. Only incidentally did student fees supplement their incomes. Primarily they taught for the honor involved, for the consultation that came their way from former students and above all from a sense of public service to their profession. When service to the profession finally made it mandatory, they were able to yield control of the institution as their predecessors could have never done.

Overexpansion of the University's physical plant was another case of misfortune since it pointed toward bankruptcy, yet of good fortune since it pointed toward state control. Although enrollment was stationary by 1890, the faculty, full of the exuberance which characterized the age and eager to attract students, rashly pushed ahead with new construction. From 1890 to 1907 the University acquired about a dozen new buildings which later it could not afford to paint.

The building spree began with the $10,000 Nurses' Home of 1890, financed out of the hospital budget even while the hospital was being subsidized by student fees. The following year the faculty appropriated $4,000 from salaries to remodel Practice Hall, the old laboratory behind the main building. Just as it was completed the entire structure burned, and immediately the faculty appropriated $8,000 to build again. The professors began their most ambitious structure in 1896, tearing down most of the old hospital and replacing it with a handsome neo-Palladian building. The new five-story, 200-bed University Hospital, used today as the outpatient department, was paid for by about $20,000 in public contributions and by $70,000 in bonds which the professors sold to themselves, hoping to profit from future increased enrollment. A few years later the faculty bought six old residences and a church along Greene and Lombard Streets, close to the campus. In 1903 they obtained a $75,000 mortgage for a new, four-story dental and pharmacy building constructed behind the main medical building in a style vaguely matching their new hospital. Finally, in 1907, the law faculty purchased $15,000 in bonds to rebuild the front of their building in a similar style.[1]

Competing institutions were also overexpanding, paving the way for their bankruptcy and merger with the University. For new buildings the Maryland College of Pharmacy went $35,000 into debt; the College of Physicians and Surgeons borrowed $100,000; and the Baltimore Medical College, the Baltimore College of Dental Surgery and the Baltimore University each borrowed about $40,000. All of the buildings, and all of the debts, eventually fell to the University of Maryland. Except for one belonging to the College of Physicians and Surgeons, all of the off-campus buildings were sold for debt; but still the University's finances remained a hopeless morass. The medical school alone, without thinking of repaying the principal, expended from student fees about $20,000 annually in interest. According to an inventory made in 1920, the total assets of the University amounted to about $800,000, with a crushing debt of more than half that amount.[2]

While the midwestern land-grant colleges pointed the way out of the farmer's dilemma of the 1890's, the endowed private universities provided leadership for the renaissance of professional education. Old institutions like Harvard and Columbia began to assert themselves by the end of the nineteenth century, and vigorous new institutions like Johns Hopkins, Clark, Stanford and Chicago appeared. Made powerful and independent by large endowments, the universities broke boldly from the competitive race for enrollment to offer a truly superior graduate-professional training. Of all the endowed institutions, Johns Hopkins provided the most dramatic example, especially for the University of Maryland which was almost in its shadow.

While the public frequently imagined bitter rivalry between the two institutions, knowledgeable people at the University quickly

[1]Minutes of the Faculty of Physic, 1869-1896 and 1896-1913, bound MS. volumes in medical school archives, 12 June 1890; 20 July 1890; 28 January 1891; 3 December 1893; 29 April 1895; 9 June 1896; 16 July 1903; 2 June 1908; Regents Minutes, 1909-1920, bound MS. volume in medical school archives, 8 July 1903; 12 April 1907; 10 June 1907; Minutes of the Faculty of Law, 1906-1913, bound MS. volume in law school archives, 7 June 1907; 23 March 1911; *Hospital Bulletin*, II (June, 1906), 50-53; III (October, 1907), 141; see Catalogues for pictures of the buildings.

[2]Regents Minutes, 1909-1920, bound MS. volume in medical school archives, 30 October, 1919; 25 November 1919; *Bulletin of the University of Maryland School of Medicine*, V (October, 1920), 114-115.

learned that Johns Hopkins was their powerful ally. Designed to train a small, highly select number of students, mostly from other states, and to produce scholars rather than ordinary practitioners, Hopkins did not challenge the enrollment or the aims of Maryland. Of its first thousand graduates, Hopkins located seven hundred on the faculties of other institutions, and exactly eight in Maryland as practicing country physicians. The University, meanwhile, gave the state more than four hundred rural physicians from 1897 to 1920. Johns Hopkins was designed to aid the professions by strengthening such institutions as the University of Maryland.[3]

The astute Hopkins president, Daniel Coit Gilman, cultivated the University. He obtained financially profitable consulting positions for at least seven Maryland medical professors, refused to establish schools of law and dentistry partly for fear of antagonizing the older institution and generously awarded honorary degrees to its professors. In return, he accepted its honorary degree. The Hopkins medical faculty went out of its way to support University professors for offices in the state and local professional societies, provided that they supported high standards. In medicine, nursing and law the two institutions occasionally integrated certain courses, and during the 1920's they tried to administer jointly a school of business administration. Other proprietary institutions found the giant far less cordial, for Hopkins looked eagerly to their bankruptcy and to their consolidation as part of a state-supported University of Maryland.[4]

The bridge between overexpansion and the high professional standards of the endowed universities lay in professional organization. A characteristic of the reform age, organization seemed a reaction to the rampant individualism of an earlier generation. Americans, following the example of the business trusts, banded into interest groups, civic clubs, professional societies, social fraternities, alumni groups and reform associations of many sorts.

On the most immediate level, the spirit of reform and organization brought forth powerful alumni groups at Maryland—not juvenile, sports-oriented rah-rah societies, but highly practical organizations of

[3]John C. French, *History of the University Founded by Johns Hopkins* (Baltimore, 1946), 86, 204-205; Bertram M. Bernheim, *The Story of Johns Hopkins* (New York, 1948), 35-36, 52, 122-127, and *passim; Hospital Bulletin*, I (March, 1905), 10-11; XI (February, 1916), 209; *Bulletin of the University of Maryland School of Medicine*, V (December, 1920), 153; IX (April, 1913), 29; *Old Maryland*, I (March, 1905), 51.
[4]Minutes of the Faculty of Physic, 28 May 1889; 11 November 1890; *Catalogue of the School of Law of the University of Maryland, 1884-1885* (Baltimore, 1884), 15-19; French, *Johns Hopkins*, 20-21, 110, 232-236.

graduates eager to protect the value of their degrees. Although originally organized by the faculty in 1880, the University medical alumni association came to life in 1893 when it obtained a special act of incorporation authorizing it to collect and manage an endowment fund for the school. Most active in the society was Eugene F. Cordell, a passionately loyal alumnus who devoted his life to promoting the University and who may have aided the institution more during this reform age than any other individual. An outspoken advocate of high standards, of salaries instead of the fee system and of unification under a central University administration, Cordell was too critical of existing conditions and too impatient for reform to make himself popular with the professors. Although the faculty eventually allowed him to serve as librarian and part-time lecturer on medical history, he made his real contribution through the alumni.

The alumni of dentistry and pharmacy, although in existence earlier, became active about 1890; the nurses organized in 1895 and the lawyers, the least academically minded, in 1917. In each case the alumni took positive action to raise endowment, to obtain favorable legislation and to insure stricter admission policies and higher academic standards. Often their chief opponents were the conservative faculties. About 1900 the farsighted Cordell founded an overlapping University alumni association, designed to work for the unification of the professional schools under a state-supported administration.[5]

Professional organizations sprang up on the state level, assuming the professional leadership which the University itself had lost. The Maryland Pharmaceutical Association appeared in 1883 and a State Dental Association a few months later. About 1886 the Johns Hopkins physicians reorganized and invigorated the ancient Medical and Chirurgical Society. The Maryland Bar Association came in 1896 and a state nursing association in 1903. Generally the first objective of the societies was professional licensing, and between 1884 and 1904 the general assembly was persuaded to establish or greatly strengthen the state board examinations for each of the professions. Although doubtlessly motivated in part by a desire to restrict competitors and consequently to raise incomes in the professions, the

[5]Eugene F. Cordell, *University of Maryland, 1807-1907*, 2 vols. (New York, 1907), 123, 260, 433; Minutes of the Faculty of Physic, 9 June 1903; 5 June 1905; 6 October 1908; Minutes of the Alumni Association of the Law School, 1917-1934, MS. volume in law school library, Baltimore.

organizations also displayed a growing concern with standards. Since the reform-minded public generally supported restrictions on professional practice, the professional organizations obtained a state board of health and scores of laws regulating garbage, sewage, quarantine, water supply, food labeling, birth registration and mortality statistics. The Maryland Bar Association obtained a new Maryland law code, aid for indigent litigants and a general expansion—except for Negroes—of individual civil liberties. Most important for the University of Maryland, each of the professional organizations established an educational committee to work for higher academic standards, state aid and the elimination of ruinous competition between schools. The professional organizations were helping the University to regain the professional leadership it had lost.[6]

Most important of the new organizations, however, were the national professional associations which gradually assumed authority to accredit professional schools. Although national associations had existed for reading papers and exchanging views since the 1840's, not until the 1890's were they able to assert themselves over the professional schools, sometimes with ruthless vigor.

In medicine the origin of accreditation lay at the University itself, or at least with its bothersome alumnus, Eugene F. Cordell. Eager to jar reform sentiment into action but aware of his own unpopularity within the University, Cordell in 1889 persuaded a group of Hopkins physicians to call a convention of the Baltimore medical colleges. Representatives of six hostile, mutually suspicious institutions attended and contented themselves—as Cordell intended—with issuing a call for a nationwide assembly of medical colleges. With encouragement from the American Medical Association, delegates from 134 colleges met in Nashville the following year and created the Association of American Medical Colleges. With Cordell in the background as a motivating spirit, the meetings lasted intermittently for two years while the delegates debated proposals for self-imposed minimum standards. Every medical journal and almost every newspaper in the country took part in the debate. Finally, in the fall of

---

[6]See, *Laws of Maryland, 1884-1904, passim;* Eugene F. Cordell, *Medical Annals of Maryland, 1799-1899* (Baltimore, 1903), 716-732; William T. Howard, *Public Health Administration . . . in Baltimore, Maryland* (Washington, 1924), 53-150; *Reports of the Maryland Bar Association,* 1896-1920; J. Ben Robinson, "Highlights in the History of the Maryland State Dental Association," *Journal of the Maryland State Dental Association,* I (1958), 5-17; Florence Meda Gipe, "Professionalization of Nursing in Maryland" (MS. in Vertical File, Health Sciences Library, Baltimore).

1892 sixty-four institutions—including the University of Maryland—took the momentous first step, committing themselves to formal entrance requirements, expansion of courses from two to three years and a curriculum with different courses each year, graded according to difficulty. The step may have been the greatest single advance in the development of American medical education, for once established the association was stronger than any of its members and able to set standards as the majority saw fit. It steadily raised requirements, and by 1903 was able to send out inspectors to guarantee the compliance of its members. About 1906 it turned over most of its authority to the American Medical Association which created the Council on Medical Education to broaden inspections and move against the non-member institutions.[7]

Although the University of Maryland managed to keep abreast of the rising requirements of the association, it was unprepared for the Flexner Report bombshell of 1910 which recommended the complete abolition of proprietary institutions. Underwritten by the Carnegie Corporation and compiled in cooperation with the American Medical Association, the report became one of the famous documents in American education. Its brilliant author, Abraham Flexner, a Johns Hopkins professor, visited all medical schools in the country, compiling detailed and often shocking descriptions of the education which they provided. Recommending that over half of them be closed, he particularly scored the profit system in education. Since Maryland was the founder and one of the most successful examples of that system, it became the particular object of his wrath. Unless its professors could be placed on a full-time direct salary basis, he maintained, it should be closed with the others.[8]

Although the American Medical Association moved slowly, henceforth its policy was to destroy the proprietary schools. In 1910, basing its judgment largely on Flexner's findings, it first awarded accreditation ratings of A+, A, B and C to every medical school. The top rank was reserved for Johns Hopkins and about a half-dozen endowed institutions. The A ranking, which the University of Mary-

[7]*Journal of the American Medical Association*, XIV (June 7, 1890), 829-830; Eugene F. Cordell, "The American Medical College Association: Its Origin, Development and Present Status," *Maryland Medical Journal*, XXXIV (January, 1896), 217-221; Minutes of the Faculty of Physic, 18 November 1890; Fred J. Kelly, *et al.*, *Collegiate Accreditation by Agencies within States* (Washington, 1940), 65-72.

[8]Abraham Flexner, *Medical Education in the United States and Canada* . . . (New York, 1910), 5, 39, 236-239; *Hospital Bulletin*, VI (July, 1910), 90-92; VI (August, 1910); 115-118; VI (October, 1910), 149-151; *Old Maryland*, VI (July, 1910), 88 89.

land struggled to maintain, meant minimum acceptable standards, whereas B and C grades were varying terms of abuse for the unaccredited. Thereafter, Maryland's College of Medicine maintained its rating only by going farther into debt, and its days as a private institution were numbered. Cordell and the organization he instigated had sounded the death knell of the proprietary system.[9]

Similar national accrediting agencies appeared for the other professional schools, each one struggling with its own technical problems. The distinct character of law in different states caused law school associations to develop slowly, but in 1900 the American Association of Law Schools began setting standards, and in 1923 the American Bar Association began accreditation ratings. The National Association of Dental Faculties began in 1884, struggled over the relationship of dentistry to medicine, eventually profited from a Carnegie-financed report similar to Flexner's in medicine and by 1916 acquired power to accredit schools. The American Conference of Pharmaceutical Faculties became powerful about 1900. The nursing profession relied on statewide organizations until the Association of Collegiate Schools of Nursing appeared in 1935.[10]

Propelled by an awareness of desperate conditions, by the example of the endowed universities and by the spirit of the reform age itself, the American professions had created organizations stronger than any single educational institution. The University of Maryland had played a significant part in the growth of these organizations, even though they threatened its existence. Heroically it struggled to meet their demands and those of the times.

The Rise of Standards

Never before, and never since, did the quality of professional education change so radically as between 1890 and 1920. Once an institution joined the march of reform there was no dropping out to rest. The endowed institutions set the pace, and the laggards were pub-

[9]Annual rankings and changes in requirements are listed in the *Journal of the American Medical Association,* usually in the May issue; see also *Catalogues,* 1895-1920; Richard Harrison Shryock, *Development of Modern Medicine* . . . (New York, 1947), 347-353.

[10]Kelly, *et al., Collegiate Accreditation,* 79-92; William J. Gies, *Dental Education in the United States and Canada* . . . (New York, 1926); Alfred Zantzinger Reed, *Training for the Public Profession of the Law* . . . (Washington, 1921).

licly branded as disreputable. One by one the weak professional schools of the state merged or fell by the wayside, until only those associated with Johns Hopkins or the University of Maryland were left. Even for the University the pace was almost too great, for without an effective central administration each of its professional schools struggled alone, innovating as it went to keep up with the relentless march.

The School of Medicine, especially harrassed by disreputable competition, eagerly embraced the first reforms. In 1891, a year before the Association of American Medical Colleges established its requirements, the faculty agreed to adopt the association's proposed entrance examination as an expression of support. The examination lasted about one hour and included "higher arithmetic" and an English composition of 150 words "in the student's own handwriting." Actually the recommended examination also required a knowledge of Latin, but for a number of years, apparently by tacit agreement, all of the Baltimore schools seem to have ignored it. In 1892 the three-year graded curriculum began, meaning that students took about four courses a year instead of eight and attended three years instead of two. The combined impact of entrance examinations and strengthened courses was greater than most people had supposed. The number of Maryland graduates declined from 111 in 1890 to 50 in 1895. For the professors, however, the change was relatively easy since three years of fees from a smaller number of students still almost equaled two years of fees from a larger number.[11]

The pace kept increasing. In 1895 the association decreed a fourth year of courses which the University was forced to accept, even though some of its Baltimore competitors were no longer members of the association. By 1905 the association required the equivalent of a high school education for admission, and by 1918 it required two years of college. The medical school term, meanwhile, stretched from five-and-a-half months to seven months by 1902 and to eight months by 1916. The pinch was on.[12]

What hurt the medical school most, however, was the growing attack on the proprietary system. About 1905 the professors ceased selling tickets directly to students, but collected all fees into a central

[11]Minutes of the Faculty of Physic, 4 December 1889; 19 May 1891; 11 April 1892; 14 May 1892; and ff.; *Catalogue of the School of Medicine, University of Maryland, 1891-1892* (Baltimore, 1891), 4; also *Catalogues* for the years following.

[12]Minutes of the Faculty of Physics, 7 March 1894; 15 October 1894; 20 May 1895; 7 April 1903; *Catalogues, passim.*

fund and distributed the money among themselves as "salaries." To the tough-minded Flexner, the practice was still proprietary education with the added stigma of subterfuge. In 1912 the Association of American Medical Schools required members to maintain a minimum of four full-time salaried professors. Although some faculty members suggested withdrawal from the association, the alumni forced compliance a year later, before the association could undertake disciplinary action. The four full-time instructors, used chiefly in the laboratories, received from $1,500 to $3,000 annually, while the more prominent part-time professors who continued to hold the major chairs reduced their profits to make up the required sum. When the association raised the requirements to six full-time men, and then eight, the University still managed to keep apace, but by 1915 most of the other professors received nothing whatever.[13]

As expenses soared the physicians looked desperately for other sources of income for the institution. In an effort to make the hospital pay for itself, the University raised the rates for private patients from $4 weekly to $12, and finally to $40. By refusing charity patients unless the city or state paid for them, it forced those appropriations up to about $40,000 annually. In addition, the women's auxiliary contributed about $2,000 a year to the hospital, and student fees rose from $130 to $215 annually. Cordell attempted to tap alumni enthusiasm by setting a million-dollar endowment goal, but despite substantial gifts from several retiring professors the fund was a virtual failure by 1920, with less than $61,000 in hand. Eagerly the University approached the great new Carnegie and Rockefeller foundations, but always the answer was the same—there could be no contributions to an institution based on securing profits for its sponsors.[14]

As these alternatives failed one by one, the faculty approached the general assembly with a blunt proposition: either the medical school must have a direct state appropriation or it would have to close. As early as 1900 the members of the medical faculty admitted to themselves that the situation was "critical" and "desperate," and a few

[13]Minutes of the Faculty of Physic, 28 May 1901; 21 December 1910; 24 June 1912; 23 July 1915; 27 July 1916 and passim; Regents Minutes, 23 March 1911; 3 October 1919; 25 November 1919; and passim; Baltimore Sun, 8 June to 20 July 1910; 28 April 1912.
[14]Minutes of the Faculty of Physic, 19 October 1891; 21 April 1892; 4 June 1894; Catalogues, passim; Baltimore Sun, 25 March 1907; 31 March 1907; 23 January 1913; Old Maryland, passim; Hospital Bulletin, IV (February, 1909), 430-432; IX (July, 1913), 80-82; IX (October, 1913), 135-152; Bulletin of the University of Maryland Medical School, I (March, 1917), 219; V (October, 1920), 115 and passim.

years later they informed the public that "the handwriting is on the wall . . . [we] cannot much longer exist."[15] Difficult as it was for the state to subsidize a profit-seeking corporation, it could not let the institution close. In 1904 the assembly made its first direct appropriation of $5,000, mollifying the competing medical schools in the state by giving them the same amount. By 1915, as other schools merged with the University, the state raised its appropriation to $15,000 annually, and finally in 1920 to $42,500. Carefully the state kept the medical school just up to the standards of the accrediting agencies and just above bankruptcy. Significant profits from the institution had long been forgotten; proprietary education was fading away.[16]

While the pressures for higher standards threatened the proud old University of Maryland, they proved fatal to its competitors. Intense rivalry and sacrifice had bred bitter hostility between competing institutions; there were too many professors to be absorbed by mergers and the public clung to the American myth that there was something inherently sacred about competition. Still, as the American Medical Association's harsh publicity drove students from the weaker schools, they were left with the difficult choice of consolidation or bankruptcy.

For years the Baltimore Medical College had talked of union with the University, and in 1913 the American Medical Association sent a mediator to Baltimore with a flat mandamus: unless the merger proceeded both institutions would lose their accreditation within the year. "We must hurry," wrote one dean to the other, and painfully they shaped an agreement. The Baltimore Medical College sold most of its assets to cover debts and gave the rest to the University; the University acquired control of Maryland General Hospital for clinical teaching, accepted twelve members of the defunct faculty and bought off the contracts of the other professors. Both schools set about reconciling their alumni and students to merging with an institution they had learned to despise.[17] Two years later, in 1915,

---

[15]*Hospital Bulletin,* VII (May, 1911) , 53; also, *Hospital Bulletin,* VII (August, 1911) , 114-115; Minutes of the Faculty of Physic, 28 June 1904; Regents Minutes, 19 March 1913; *Baltimore Sun,* 29 July 1912; 6 February 1916.

[16]*Laws of Maryland . . . 1904,* Chap. 638; *Laws of Maryland . . . 1920,* Chap. 487.

[17]Minutes of the Faculty of Physic, 3 April 1906; 2 April 1912; 13 January 1913; 31 March 1913; Minutes of the Baltimore Medical College, 1912-1914, bound MS. volume, medical school archives; *Hospital Bulletin,* IX (April, 1913) , 27-36; X (June, 1914) , 55-56; XI (February, 1916) , 199-202; *Baltimore Sun,* 23 January 1913; 6 March 1913; 10 March 1913; 20 March 1913.

the College of Physicians and Surgeons joined the University under similar conditions. At first the unified institution used both plants combining only the freshman and sophomore classes, but within a short time they merged entirely. The University also acquired clinical control of the Mercy Hospital and, except for Johns Hopkins, was once again the only medical college in the state.[18]

The School of Law responded least effectively to the reform age. Both John Prentiss Poe who headed the school from 1870 to 1909, and Judge Henry D. Harlan who followed as dean until 1913, were deeply conservative men, basically unsympathetic to the entire progressive movement. Neither faculty, nor students, nor alumni felt the loyalty which other professional schools inspired. The faculty maintained such irregular relations with the American Association of Law Schools that the primary initiative for reform came from the Maryland Bar Association.

The law school took its first improving step in 1898 by requiring two years of course work for the degree, several years after medicine and dentistry had required three years. In 1911 the Baltimore University School of Law joined the Baltimore Law School, and two years later the combination joined the University of Maryland School of Law. Consolidation of the rival schools, however, appeared to be a means of raising student fees as much as raising standards, for most of the regular professors in each of the three institutions only reduced the number of lectures they delivered and continued to earn about $1,000 annually.[19]

Standards rose again about 1913 when the law faculty required a high school education for admission, ten hours of courses a week and three years of study for the degree. The faculty introduced an optional day school, but for many years the night classes remained considerably larger. Also about 1913 the institution made its first feints toward the case system of study which emphasized underlying legal principles rather than the trade school application of law.[20]

[18]Minutes of the Faculty of Physic, 2 February 1914; 15 April 1915; 25 May 1915; 7 June 1915; Minutes of the College of Physicians and Surgeons, 1912-1915, bound MS. volume, medical school archives; *Hospital Bulletin*, VIII (June, 1912), 71; XI (June, 1915), 62-68; XI (November, 1915), 153; *Baltimore Sun*, 21 February 1915; 1 June 1915.

[19]*Baltimore Sun*, 5 January 1911; 30 May 1913; 16 July 1913; Minutes of the Faculty of Law, 21 April 1913; 20 May 1913; 27 May 1913.

[20]*Transactions of the Maryland Bar Association . . . 1897* (Baltimore, 1897), 65-67; *Transactions . . . 1912*, 53-58; *Transactions . . . 1913*, 40-43; *Transactions . . . 1920*, 41-45; *Transactions . . . 1935*, 19-22; Catalogues of the Law School, 1890-1920; Minutes of the University of Maryland School of Law, 1906-1913, bound MS. volume in law school archives, 4 January 1911; 25 January 1911; 18 December 1911; 24 June 1912;

By 1920, however, the national accrediting agencies ranked all of Maryland's professional schools in the top 30 percent of their kind except the law school which was ranked in the bottom 30 percent. Ironically, it remained the most prosperous and self-satisfied school in the University and was the only one to oppose the movement for unification and state control in 1920.[21]

The dentists found it easier to agree on high standards than on the theoretical question of dentistry as a mechanical art or medical science. In 1885 the National Association of Dental Faculties, founded in large measure by the Baltimore College of Dental Surgery, required an entrance examination and a graded curriculum and in 1890 established a three-year course. The entrance requirement preceded that of the medical school by six years and the three-year course by two years. Medical standards began to surpass dental standards around the turn of the century when disputes tore apart the dental associations. By 1910, however, new subjects like bacteriology, orthodontia—malocclusion of teeth—and prosthesis—fitting of false teeth—began to attract attention and tended vaguely to encourage reconciliation in favor of the close association of dentistry with medicine. By 1918 the Dental Education Council had established a high school education for admission, an eight-month term and a four-year course for all accredited dental schools.[22]

The first merger occurred in 1913 when the Dental Department of the Baltimore Medical College joined the University of Maryland, but consolidation of the two largest institutions was particularly difficult since they represented the extremes of the ideological dispute. The old Baltimore College of Dental Surgery, emphasizing dentistry as an art, held the national associations to such high standards that in 1918 the University of Maryland Dental Department lost its accreditation on the basis of inadequate facilities. The University, meanwhile, spokesman of the merger of dentistry with medicine, won its point before the associations so effectively that the Baltimore

---

Minutes of the Alumni Association of the Law School, 20 September 1929 and *passim;* Regents Minutes, 9 December 1914.

[21]Reed, *Training for . . . the Law,* 441 and *passim; Hospital Bulletin,* VIII (August, 1912), 111-112; XII (March, 1916), 10; *Baltimore Sun,* 19 May 1935.

[22]Robert W. McCluggage, *History of the American Dental Association* (Chicago, 1959), 175 ff., also, Catalogues of the Baltimore College of Dental Surgery and of the University of Maryland Dental School, 1885-1923; Minutes of the Dental Department of the University of Maryland, 1889-1923, bound MS. volumes in dental school archives, Baltimore.

College of Dental Surgery lost its accreditation the same year on the basis of mistaken views. Both institutions lost enrollment fast, but when Maryland began to receive state aid, the other had to capitulate. When the merger actually occurred in 1923, however, there was some doubt about who had swallowed whom. The combined school, awkwardly called the Baltimore College of Dental Surgery Dental School of the University of Maryland, resembled in its faculty and philosophy the old Baltimore College of Dental Surgery more than the University's former Dental Department.[23]

Pharmacy was the only profession associated with the University that never faced the perils of competition, and as was the case with dentistry, its real problem was ideological. Controlled from the beginning by powerful city and state organizations, pharmacy in 1878 was the first to adopt a graded curriculum, and in 1885 it began an entrance examination. Its most important reform, however, was overcoming prejudice against medicine and drug manufacturers and eliminating the reactionary apprentice system which forced students into a long term of servitude in the drug store. The Maryland State Pharmaceutical Association divided in the 1890's as its younger members fought to rescue pharmacy from its blind alley as a trade and to elevate it again to the level of a profession. In 1896 the association allowed the school to drop apprenticeship as an entrance requirement and directed that classes be placed on a full-time, eight-month basis. Slowly the school expanded its appeal to students interested in medical and manufacturing research. New courses appeared, frequently as electives, in such subjects as physiology, urinary analysis, pharmacognosy, commercial pharmacy and business administration. By 1901 students could elect a two-year Ph.G.—Graduate in Pharmacy—degree, or a three-year Ph.C.—Graduate in Chemistry—degree.[24]

The most important step for pharmacy came in 1904 when the Maryland College of Pharmacy officially rejoined the University of Maryland from which it had grown. Crushed under debts from over-

[23]Minutes of the Dental Department, 3 July 1913; 9 May 1918; 6 September 1918; 6 September 1922; 15 January 1923; 13 January 1926; *Baltimore Sun*, 20 January 1923.
[24]*Maryland State Pharmaceutical Association, Annual Proceedings . . . 1895* (Baltimore, 1895) , 7, 11-18, 26-27, 51-52, 78-79; *Proceedings . . . 1896*, 19-23, 51-52; *Proceedings . . . 1897*, 36-38; Edward Kremers and George Urdang, *History of Pharmacy . . .* (Philadelphia, 1940) , 290-293 and *passim;* Catalogues of the Maryland College of Pharmacy, 1878-1904; Catalogues of the University of Maryland School of Pharmacy, 1904-1923.

expansion, plagued by declining enrollment resulting from its rising standards, pharmacy joined as a department in the medical school until 1915 when it became an independent school within the University. The pharmacy building was sold for debts, and five pharmacy professors were incorporated into the University faculty. Temporarily the merger was a blow to pharmacists' pride; but common quarters, common supplies and a related faculty were beneficial to everyone, and the close relationship to medicine placed pharmacy back in an academic atmosphere and in the mainstream of medical research where it belonged. By 1923 all entering students had a high school education and took the three-year course.[25]

Of all the professions nursing had the farthest to go in reaching academic respectability and the greatest obstacles to overcome. The first hurdle lay, not in competition from outside the University, but in convincing the medical professors that nursing was truly an academic discipline. Relying on their own enthusiasm, the nurses set out to prove the value of nursing education by teaching themselves and establishing their own standards. The powerful Louisa Parsons required an entrance examination from the time she established the school; in 1900 the nurses added a third year of work and required that 200 hours be spent in the classroom; four years later they instituted their own state board examinations; and in 1907 the superintendent employed a registered nurse whose primary duty was instruction. Finally, by 1918 the school required a high school education for admission, and classroom instruction was up to 300 hours.

The nurses were slower in overcoming their second obstacle, the severe labor conditions imposed on them by the doctors who desperately needed inexpensive hospital help. The nurses appealed to public opinion, and particularly to the women's auxiliary which helped to support the hospital. Frequently they threatened to abandon the University, leaving the doctors to scrub the wards. By 1913 they won a 56-hour work week, but this was lost when the doctors appealed to their patriotism during World War I. Not until 1920 did the physicians permit the nurses to return to an eight-hour day and grant nursing graduates the right to receive their certificates at the University commencement. Not until 1924 did any nurses receive the B. S. degree and then only those who completed a five-year program combining two years of college with three years of nursing.

[25]Minutes of the Faculty of Physic, 3 March 1903; 5 April 1904; 17 June 1904; Charles Schmidt and B. Olive Cole, "Short History of the Maryland College of Pharmacy . . ." MS. in School of Pharmacy archives, 2-7; *Hospital Bulletin,* IX (April, 1913) , 31.

In 1946 the school finally obtained full independence from the hospital and the medical school.[26]

With relatively few exceptions, however, professional standards rose from their all-time low about 1890 to almost their present levels by 1920. The age of reform set the basic structure and pattern of professional education. Since then most of the schools have added to their entrance requirements, medicine has confirmed its internship program, classroom instruction has increased, and all of the schools except law have added substantial postgraduate work. But after 1920 University of Maryland graduates belonged to the modern world, and the people they served were the ones to gain.

The University Spirit

The modern University of Maryland evolved from something more intangible than standards and mergers; it also grew out of a new enthusiasm for the institution and for education. The academic temper surging through American colleges was closely related to the progressive age, full of idealism and sentimentality, of fraternity and scholarship, of excitement about the importance of learning and about living life to its fullest. The cold business-age quest for a license to practice gave way to a glorification of University life.

People at Maryland began talking about University spirit during the 1890's as the student nurses arrived, as the building program got under way and as the faculty began to expand with younger men. The buildings were painted, the streets were paved and electric lights were installed. Students began wearing coats and ties to class, they sat in seats instead of perching along the backs of the benches and they ceased the ancient practice of spitting tobacco juice on the floors. Freshman hazing first became a problem, and the students initiated an honor system which lasted until 1916. The faculty gen-

[26]Florence Meda Gipe, "Development of Nursing Education in Maryland" (Ed.D. dissertation, University of Maryland, 1952), 95-99, 237-238 and *passim;* Announcements of the School of Nursing in *Bulletin of the Nurses Alumnae Association,* 1920 ff.; Virginia C. Conley, "History of the School of Nursing," MS. in archives of Nurses' Alumnae Association, Baltimore; Minutes of the Faculty of Physic, 1896-1913, bound MS. volume in medical school archives, 5 December 1899; 21 December 1899; 6 March 1900; Minutes of the Regents, 1909-1920, bound MS. volume in medical school archives, 3 January 1917; *Bulletin of the University of Maryland School of Medicine,* II (July, 1917), 101-102.

erally encouraged the new spirit, aware that it marked the institution's renaissance.[27]

Intercollegiate athletics has facilitated the development of many academic institutions, and at Maryland the new spirit was expressed in a football yell. In 1895 a medical student named Norfleet Gibbs organized a medical-dental-law school football team that defeated Baltimore City College twice and lost to St. John's. The uniforms were a motley array of padded clothes with the letter M painted on the shirts, but the players were immediately heroes, and for the first time the students in the various schools felt a sense of unity. Students and faculty formed an athletic association; the professors paid for real uniforms; teams of baseball, ice hockey, track and basketball appeared; and friends of the University began reading about the institution in newspaper sports pages. Since many of the University players were much older than regular college students, there was difficulty finding opponents at first; but the University's approximately even won-lost record soon attracted such schools as the Maryland Agricultural College, St. John's, Navy, Georgetown and, occasionally, such distant schools as Rutgers and North Carolina. The greatest sports rival was Johns Hopkins, and contests with it in any sport attracted throngs of students, faculty and alumni. When a dental department professor won a prize at a state exhibition for a set of plates made of maroon and black rubber, the University teams adopted those colors as theirs. Freshmen received a pamphlet of University cheers to memorize, and frequently faculty members led the cheers:

> Rif! Raf! Ruf!
> Rif! Raf! Ruf!
> University of Maryland!
> Is pretty hot stuff!!![28]

In addition to teams, fraternities and clubs of every sort appeared, usually with faculty participation, and often with substantial monetary contributions from it. The old secret Rush Medical Club was revived in 1890, and three years later some of the dental students

[27]*Hospital Bulletin*, II (June, 1906), 50; Minutes of the Faculty of Physic, 30 May 1893; 21 April 1898; 22 February 1899; *University Gazette*, III (March, 1917), 34; *Baltimore Sun*, 1 November 1910.

[28]*Bones, Molars and Briefs, 1897* [Student Annual] (Baltimore, 1897), 32-50, 91-94; *Bones, Molars and Briefs, 1898*, 63-64; *Bones, Molars and Briefs, 1904*, 180; Regents Minutes, 10 May 1904; Minutes of the Faculty of Physic, 1 March 1898; 22 September 1899; 27 April 1900.

joined the national Xi Psi Phi professional association. The YMCA became an especially active campus-wide organization, renting its own building adjacent to the University. Its avowed object was "social and moral cultivation" through the promotion of "college spirit, religious devotionals, and innocent games." A professor organized Phi Sigma Kappa social fraternity in 1897, and two years later Kappa Sigma appeared with its own fraternity residence house. There were banjo, mandolin and glee clubs, a secret Mystic M Club, a Gourmandizers Club with the motto "Two Beers and a Gorge," and a semisecret 700 Club devoted to pursuing "all forms of sin."[29]

Frivolous and serious campus publications appeared, beginning in 1897 with the student annual *Bones, Molars and Briefs.* Filled with sentimental high seriousness and rude insults to the faculty, the tone of the old annuals is incongruous today. A few years later Eugene F. Cordell began *Old Maryland,* a monthly journal dedicated to promoting the cause of a greater University. He vigorously championed high standards, mergers, endowment, university spirit, and faculty and alumni accomplishments. Just as vigorously he denounced the lingering fee system, the obstacles to state control and even the individuals who made errors in the operating room. The journal was frequently more bracing than the professors could take, and partly to answer Cordell and partly to publicize clinical findings, the medical faculty began its own monthly *The Hospital Bulletin.* The various publications kept the University aware of itself, and frequently provided lively copy for the Baltimore newspapers which, in turn, kept the state aware of the University.[30]

By anecdote and sermon the publications told of the thousands of University graduates who were useful citizens, and of the few who were famous. Almost everyone in Maryland knew of such law school graduates as Albert C. Ritchie, governor of the state, and John C. Rose, Federal judge, reformer and friend of Theodore Roosevelt. From medicine there was James Carroll, a national hero who lost his life in Cuba with Walter Reed in experiments to find a cure for

[29]*Bones, Molars and Briefs, 1897,* 55-67; *Bones, Molars and Briefs, 1899,* 73-88; *Bones, Molars and Briefs, 1900,* 41; Minutes of the Faculty of Physic, 7 November 1900; 5 February 1901.

[30]*Bones, Molars and Briefs,* 1897-1904, became *Terra Mariae,* 1905 to date; *Old Maryland,* 1905-1914, became *University Gazette,* 1914-1917; *Hospital Bulletin,* 1905-1916, became *Bulletin of the University of Maryland School of Medicine,* 1916 to date. Occasionally individual schools published a separate annual, and occasionally alumni groups, notably the nurses, published periodical bulletins. For the Cordell-Faculty dispute, Minutes of the Faculty of Physic, 5 June 1905; 6 October 1908.

yellow fever. Almost every American physician knew of the psychiatrists, August Hoch and George Rohe; the laryncologist, W. C. Jarvis; the ophthalmologist, Samuel Theobald; and the medical writer and professor, John C. Hemmeter. Best of all for University morale, practically everyone knew of J. Whitridge Williams who had risen to become dean of the medical school at, of all places, the Johns Hopkins University.[31]

A younger group of men, graduating from Maryland in the decades around the turn of the century, became outstanding later. They included surgeons William Wayne Babcock and George Eli Bennett; medical corps general Norman T. Kirk; United States judges W. Calvin Chestnut and Simon E. Sobeloff; United States Solicitor General Philip B. Perlman; United States Senator Millard E. Tydings; United States Ambassador David K. E. Bruce; pharmacist H. A. B. Dunning; and army nurse, Mary Gavin.[32]

The turn of the century stimulated a sense of destiny, self-examination and resolve on the Maryland campus. Four years later the heart of downtown Baltimore burned in one of the most costly fires in American history. The University was spared, and the vast expenditures for rebuilding the city invigorated the institution with a sense of the past and of the future. The most important reawakening, however, was the University's own centennial in 1907.

Two years of planning and thousands of dollars went into the centennial celebration. Cordell wrote a two-volume history of the University for the occasion, and the regents financed a lavish 300-page volume of centennial proceedings. The ceremonies culminated in the commencement of 1907 as more than a thousand visitors poured into Baltimore, including delegates from universities over the entire world. The *Baltimore Sun* called it "the greatest gathering of scholars and educators that Baltimore has ever witnessed."[33] On the first festive day, May 30, there were tours, speeches and luncheons around the flag-bedecked campus, a band concert and scores of class reunion banquets. The next day the faculty awarded 237 student degrees and 28 honorary degrees in the Lyric Theater. Observers were captivated by the Victorian display:

[31]All except Ritchie appear in Allen Johnson and Dumas Malone, eds., *Dictionary of American Biography*, 22 vols. (New York, 1946). In addition are listed Henry Rose Carter, James Ambler, Oliver E. Janey and Richard H. Thomas, all noted physicians.

[32]Records of the Alumni Office, College Park.

[33]*Baltimore Sun*, 25 March 1907. For a description of the event see John C. Hemmeter, ed., *The Centennial Celebration of the Foundation of the University of Maryland* (Baltimore, 1908) ; and *Baltimore Sun*, 30 May-4 June 1904.

With hundreds of electric lights sparkling in competition with the flood of daylight that streamed in through the windows, with decorations which for richness and beauty surpassed any scheme of adornment that has ever hung from the walls and galleries . . . [it was] one of the most imposing ceremonies ever held in the city.[34]

Still the ceremonies built up. That evening there was a banquet for 800 guests, and the presidents of Princeton and of Clark universities made major addresses. The following day the University officials, working anxiously for unification with St. John's College, played host to the crowd aboard a steamer to Annapolis, where the St. John's commencement provided more bands, banquets and speeches. Although the delegates received a good show for their travel, it was the University of Maryland and the people of Maryland who were most impressed. Each fall for the next ten years the University suspended classes for Academic Day, a sort of memorial to the great centennial celebration. The holiday provided parades and speeches about the importance of educational institutions in general and of Maryland in particular.

The new University spirit, like so much of the reforming zeal of the age, seemed to explode into patriotism when America entered World War I. Hurriedly the medical faculty organized a volunteer hospital base unit of 24 professors, 65 nurses and 157 students, plus a few outside volunteers, and amid statewide huzzas it sailed for France. To keep the professional schools operating, the government, as it had for the undergraduate college, organized the Student Army Training Corps allowing students to continue their education as cadet officers. Barracks appeared a few blocks from the University campus, and in the fall of 1918 almost every student wore a uniform and marched to class. The institution seemed carried away with the war fever. Fraternities closed, sports and publications almost ceased, standards were sharply reduced and the faculty introduced a compulsory course in War Aims. At least 175 alumni are known to have served in the war, plus the cadet officers; at least two alumni were killed.[35]

Although the war seemed to sap the University's reform enthusiasm, it also seemed to give most of its professors a larger perspective

[34]*Baltimore Sun*, 1 June 1907.
[35]*Ibid.*, 10 May 1919; also 24 June 1917; 26 July 1917; 11 April 1918; 10 March 1919; 27 April 1919; *University Gazette*, III (May, 1917), 112-115; IV (July, 1917), 131; *Bulletin of the University of Maryland School of Medicine*, I (May, 1917), 253-254, 278-279; III (October, 1918), 126; *Terra Mariae*, 1918; *Terra Mariae*, 1919; "World War I" in Vertical File, Health Sciences Library, Baltimore.

and a final willingness to yield their personal control to a central administration. The pressures of the accrediting agencies and of economic realities were harsher than ever, and the lack of leadership —such as Woods was providing at College Park—was more apparent. The only question was precisely how the state should take over.

The Politics of State Control

Outside of the University as well as within, there remained serious obstacles which had, after all, delayed the development of a true state university for so long. One could point to geographical and religious divisions within the state as explanations of the delay, or to the traditionally economy-minded state government or to the lack of educational leaders. A more formidable obstacle lay, not in the failure, but in the very success of the private institutions which had risen to take the place of a state university. The Johns Hopkins served the scholars, proprietary schools served the professions, the Maryland Agricultural College served the farmers, state normal schools provided teachers and such private institutions as Washington, St. John's, Loyola, Western Maryland, St. Mary's, Morgan and Goucher served for regular collegiate training. The general assembly had fallen into the peculiar custom of providing regular appropriations to almost all of these institutions. By 1912 Johns Hopkins alone received over $600,000 from the state, and by 1920 the legislature was doling out, in pork-barrel fashion, almost $1,000,000 annually to unregulated private, denominational and proprietary institutions. Each institution had a vested interest in the system. Each institution feared that a state university which might include it meant loss of independence, and that a state system which might exclude it meant the loss of its state subsidy. Generally the established colleges considered the idea of a state university unnecessary and socialistic.[36]

The University of Maryland's own charter was another obstacle to state control. Drawn up in 1807, modified in 1812 and tested in the courts in 1838 by Daniel Webster, the charter presumably could be altered only with the professors' unanimous consent. Few of the law professors wanted state control, and in medicine and dentistry

[36]*Hospital Bulletin*, II (September, 1906), 110-111; IV (April, 1908), 249; V (June, 1909), 70-73; *Baltimore Sun*, 23 March 1908; 1 June 1913.

one or two professors apparently preferred University bankruptcy so that they could claim their share of the property. The charter, moreover, provided no effective government to assume leadership of a state university. The board of regents was merely a confederation of the professors, and the unsalaried provosts were generally uninterested in the University. John Pendleton Kennedy, a dilettante by profession, served from 1850 to 1870; kindly Severn Teackle Wallis, a bachelor judge and poet, served until 1894 looking the soul of dignity at commencements; and Bernard Carter, a busy city lawyer who served until 1912, seldom found time to attend any University functions.[37]

The first step toward central administration and state control came in 1907 when Eugene F. Cordell masterminded a tentative merger between the University and St. John's College. Winning the support of the alumni associations of both institutions, Cordell appealed to Governor Edwin Warfield who promptly saw possibilities in a merger. The governor called in representatives from the University, St. John's and the Maryland Agricultural College. The College Park institution soon withdrew, preferring to ride the tide of agricultural development than to be involved in the university movement. After painful negotiations the other two institutions agreed to establish an advisory supergovernment which included the governor as chancellor, the provosts of each institution and a council of eight faculty members. During the next few years the supergovernment managed to integrate certain courses and even exchanged instructors so that students could combine their senior college year with their first year of professional study. St. John's called itself The Department of Arts and Sciences of the University of Maryland, and the two institutions held joint commencements in Baltimore. Still, the merger had no legal standing, the supergovernment had no budget and each school remained free to veto recommendations as it saw fit.[38]

For several years the two institutions seemed on the verge of complete union. In 1910 the general assembly expressed its approval of the merger by strengthening the power of the supergovernment and by adding other institutions to it. Since the other schools protested,

[37]Cordell, *University of Maryland*, I, 109-117.
[38]*Old Maryland*, I (May, 1905), 64-65; I (October, 1905), 132-133; II (February, 1906), 27; II (May, 1906), 67-69; II (October, 1906), 136-137; III (January, 1907), 8-9; Regents Minutes, 13 September 1905 to 26 May 1909; Catalogues of St. John's and the University, 1905-1920.

however, and since lawyers pointed to the violation of charters, the governor vetoed the bill. Two years later, in 1912, the University's titular president Bernard Carter died, and the University attempted to pump life into the union by naming Dr. Thomas Fell, the president of St. John's College, to serve as provost of the University of Maryland as well. To make his position real, instead of honorary as it had been in the past, the various schools in the University contributed $1,000 annually from student fees toward his salary. In addition to his presidency of St. John's, Fell spent three days a week in his Baltimore office campaigning for the final, legal union of the two institutions.[39]

The marriage seemed complete in 1914 when Fell persuaded the assembly to recognize the combined institutions as the State University of Maryland. The bill created a state-appointed board of regents, provided for a full-time provost and appropriated $20,000 as a beginning for the government of the institutions. The first blow came, however, when Fell declined the head position preferring to remain at St. John's. Other prominent educators also refused the position, and the death blow for the entire plan came when the regents accepted a purely political figure, William M. Maloy, the well-meaning sponsor of the state university bill in the assembly. Maloy generously agreed to serve without salary, but for St. John's College, the whole episode had turned unsavory. Fearing political involvement, the Annapolis institution withdrew from the plan so that the act never went into effect. The voluntary merger of 1907 remained technically in force, and Fell remained, without salary, as honorary provost of the professional schools. With the failure of the state university plan and the coming of the world war, however, each institution increasingly went its way. The state's history might have been curiously different if its capital, instead of College Park, had become the headquarters of the present day University.[40]

After the war, when the American Medical Association determined to end proprietary education once and for all, the University

[39]*Baltimore Sun,* 23 March 1908; 12 November 1909; 30 November 1909; 1 December 1909; Regents Minutes, 24 February 1909 to 28 May 1910; 23 March 1911; 1 May 1911; 19 June 1912; 25 September 1912; 2 October 1912; 19 March 1913; 21 May 1913.

[40]Regents Minutes, 6 January 1914 to 27 May 1914; 31 March 1915; 14 November 1916; 29 May 1917; and *passim; Hospital Bulletin,* IX (July, 1913), 80-82; IX (January, 1914), 201-219; X (April, 1914), 32; X (February, 1915), 203; *Baltimore Sun,* 28 July 1912; 22 August 1912; 19 November 1912; 1 June 1913; 15 January 1914 to 24 May 1914; 12 December 1914; 9 January 1915; 23 January 1915; 13 April 1915; *Laws of Maryland* . . . 1914, Chaps. 198, 791.

medical professors searched desperately for an undergraduate college to provide a base for a merger as a state university. Almost wearily the physicians tried again to revitalize the union with St. John's, but the proud little Annapolis institution, frightened by the University's debts, wanted nothing to do with it. The physicians faced further humiliation when Western Maryland College, a tiny Methodist institution, also turned down their plan.[41]

As a last resort in December, 1919, the officials of the grand old University of Maryland, hat-in-hand, approached the board of trustees of the Maryland State College.[42] To the professional men there was nothing inspiring about alliance with an agricultural and technological institution. To Albert F. Woods, on the other hand, there was nothing inspiring about assuming the University's crushing debts. Perhaps the only man who caught a vision of the future possibilities was the 31-year-old assistant president, Harry Clifton Byrd, who encouraged the president and the trustees to listen to the University's overtures.[43]

Various committees negotiated during January and February, 1920, but agreement between the two institutions had to come promptly if enabling legislation was to be passed while the general assembly was in session. Early in March, Judge Henry D. Harlan and Judge John C. Rose, both members of the law school faculty, drafted a proposed bill which made the Maryland State College trustees—which was also the state board of agriculture—the owner of all University property and debts and the sole director of all University affairs. The combined institutions were to be known as The University of Maryland. Although not a single representative from the professional schools was admitted to the board of trustees, that body was called the board of regents to perpetuate a historic name.[44] The trustees approved the draft bill on March 12, and named a committee "to take the necessary steps to have this Bill introduced in the House of Delegates and to do all that is necessary to have this Bill passed."[45]

The committee requested Millard E. Tydings to introduce the bill into the legislature. An honor graduate from the State College in

[41]Regents Minutes, 25 November 1919 and 1909-1920, *passim.*

[42]Minutes of the State Board of Agriculture, bound typescript volumes in archives of the University of Maryland Board of Regents, Baltimore, 12 December 1919.

[43]*Maryland State Review* [Student Newspaper], 5 November 1919.

[44]Regents Minutes, 6 March 1920.

[45]Minutes of State Board of Agriculture, 12 March 1920.

1910 and from the University law school in 1912, young Tydings was Speaker of the House of Delegates and already one of the most influential men in the state. He descended from the speaker's rostrum on March 15 to introduce the bill, and it was referred to both the judicial and education committees. A week later both committees reported favorably, and on March 30 the bill won final house approval by a roll-call 86-0 vote. It passed unanimously in the senate, and on April 9 was signed into law by another University graduate, Governor Albert C. Ritchie. The final wording was identical to the proposed draft by Harlan and Rose.[46]

Although "Speaker Tydings' Bill" passed with apparent ease, there was much potential opposition to the measure. Some legislators apparently feared that a private institution was profiting at state expense. Governor Ritchie, with more foresight than most of his contemporaries, blanched at the prospect of the staggering financial requests which he knew would be forthcoming.[47] Traditional conservatives, such as the *Baltimore Sun*, expressed doubt about the whole principle of state support for higher education.[48] Tydings and the officers of the two institutions may not have realized themselves the implications of the act, or they may have maneuvered skillfully to prevent legislators from raising troublesome questions.[49] In any case, the bill passed without fanfare, and at last a state university was born in Maryland. Within a few years, as Governor Ritchie feared, it would be gobbling up a huge portion of the state revenues. Within a few more years it would be one of the largest universities in the world.

Two months later Tydings was invited to speak at College Park. President Woods introduced him as a prominent alumnus, and Tydings spoke chiefly about farm problems. There was still little indication that either man fully realized what he had done.[50] President Woods' assistant, H. C. Byrd, did not speak.

[46]*Journal of the House . . . 1920* (Annapolis, 1920), 830-831, 1043, 1479-1480; *Journal of the Senate . . . 1920* (Annapolis, 1920), 1037, 1090, 1151; *Laws of Maryland . . . 1920*, Chap. 480.

[47]Albert C. Ritchie Papers (Hall of Records, Annapolis), 1924 *passim*.

[48]*Baltimore Sun*, 29 March 1920; 1 April 1920.

[49]Dr. H. C. Byrd indicates that the latter was the case. Interview, Annapolis, 10 November 1960.

[50]*Baltimore Sun*, 15 June 1920.

12

Jazz and Depression

Amidst the jazz and materialism of the 1920's, a mood of conservatism settled over American higher education. It was time for reaction against the public service and vocational training functions of a university and time for a deepening of the collegiate experience. Land-grant college democracy meant not only vocational opportunities for all, but also the right of all men to the education of a gentleman. University professionalism implied depth of learning as well as high standards and specialized knowledge. Such professors as Irving Babbitt of Harvard reaffirmed the humanistic values, calling for a basic core curriculum and recognition of the faculty as the heart of a university. Torn between materialism off the campus and the quest for humanistic education within it, the American student began to speak for himself. Veering from jazz-age gaiety to depression bewilderment, he epitomized the nation's mood.

The University of Maryland, like many other institutions, gained more than it lost in the conflicting currents. Despite the state's parsimony the institution grew rapidly, consummating its merger and strengthening its humanist base. Although President Albert F.

Woods was destroyed by the excesses of the jazz age, and President Raymond A. Pearson was destroyed by the cruelty of depression, the University found within its faculty and students a new self-assurance, an awareness of internal strength.

Consummating the Merger

Although the merger of 1920 was the logical culmination of decades and even centuries of educational development in Maryland, the institution still had to win the confidence of the state. With all of its history there was a newness about the institution, a sense of starting over. Slowly, carefully President Woods and his advisors drew their plans—plans for approaching the legislature, for reorganizing the administration, for strengthening the faculty and for altering the image of the institution. Their model—and the model for the University of Maryland ever since—was not the private eastern universities, but the state universities of the middle west. President Woods had read his Irving Babbitt and shared the enthusiasm for the humanities which the eastern universities represented, but such programs had to come in addition to, not in place of, those that already existed. The University would not de-emphasize its public service and technological training; it would build a strong liberal arts program in addition to them. It would be large enough for a multitude of different programs without compromise among any of them. In Woods' view, the debate between culture and agriculture was meaningless for no either-or question was involved. A state university properly included both.[1]

Both President Woods and Governor Ritchie had hesitated in transforming Maryland State College into the University of Maryland primarily because both men dreaded the political wars they knew must eventually be fought. Although it was easy for the general assembly to approve a merger, it was something else to accept the full responsibility for it. Several state universities in 1920 consumed a quarter of their state's budget; indeed, within just forty

[1]*Biennial Report of the University of Maryland . . . from September 30, 1919 to October 1, 1921* (University of Maryland Official Publications, vol. 19 [1921], no. 1), 7-21; Woods expressed his philosophy in some fifty speeches and articles each year. See bibliography and copies of many of these in Woods Papers, McKeldin Library, College Park. See especially speech dated 4 June 1932, Woods Papers, McKeldin Library.

years the University of Maryland would consume annually more than the entire state budget of 1920. In a decade of retrenchment, Woods had to convince a state dominated by one of the most conservative—and probably the strongest—governors it has had that the cost of a university was worthwhile. Like two white knights, one representing the University, the other representing economy, Woods and Ritchie faced each other for one of the greatest battles of their careers.

Woods and Ritchie were cool toward each other because they were so much alike. Men of towering ability and impeccable integrity, they could never get beyond an unyielding dignity in their association. Politically, Albert Cabell Ritchie represented the purest state rights philosophy since the days of Jefferson and Calhoun. First emerging on the national scene for his opposition to prohibition as an infringement on the states, he tirelessly attacked the Coolidge and Hoover administrations for their burgeoning bureaucracy and spendthrift policies. Handsome and aristocratic, he served as governor for an unprecedented four terms, from 1921 to 1935, and was a contender for the presidential nomination at each Democratic convention in that period. He reorganized Maryland's government along modern and efficient lines, instituted a civil service and a model state purchasing agency. He cleaned up the corrupt Baltimore police force, built roads and schools, helped private industry to build a vast power system for the state, maintained labor peace in an era of strikes and still reduced taxes by 30 percent.[2] The governor respected higher education, but as a graduate of the well-endowed Johns Hopkins University and a former student and professor at the once-prosperous University of Maryland law school, it was hard for him to admit that state funds needed to be committed to it. If public money had to be spent, then Ritchie wanted to be consulted personally on every expenditure and faculty promotion. To Woods the battle involved not only the growth, but the independence of the University.[3]

The first skirmish occurred in 1922 in the biennial session of the

[2] See Hamilton Owens, "Ritchie of the Free State," *American Mercury*, VII (March, 1926), 280-287; Harry Carter, "The Gentleman from Maryland," *North American Review*, CCXXXII (July, 1931), 43-48; Albert C. Ritchie, "Back to States' Rights," *World's Work*, XLVII (March, 1924), 525-529.

[3] Ritchie to Woods, 21 April 1920, Ritchie Papers ("Letters and Miscellaneous File #31") Hall of Records, Annapolis; also Ritchie Papers ("Governor's Correspondence, University of Maryland, 1920-1930 *passim*"), Hall of Records; Ritchie File, Woods Papers, Regents' Office, Baltimore; Interview, Mark W. Woods, 25 January 1962.

legislature when Woods launched a naive flanking movement to increase the University budget from $540,000 to $1,930,000 in a single leap. Winning the support of the governor's specially appointed Education Commission, but avoiding consultation with the chief executive, Woods sent the request directly to the legislature. Ritchie was justifiably disturbed to learn of the unexpected challenge to his carefully prepared budget and announced his forthright opposition. Angrily he pointed out that the University was asking the same appropriation for 2,000 students that the public schools received for 250,000. Although Wood's case was strong, he was not yet a match for the governor. Before the University president quite realized what had happened, the assembly adjourned, almost without debate on his request, after giving the institution only $793,000. Ritchie felt proud of his generosity and let the University know that it should be grateful. Woods knew, however, that his original request was unpadded and that if the University were to become strong even $1,930,000 was only a beginning. Reluctantly he retreated from his principle of low tuition in order to obtain the funds essential for high University standards.[4]

By 1924, with Woods and Ritchie both convinced that their positions were at stake, the University bill dominated one of the most headline-filled legislative sessions since the Civil War. Preparing a magnificently reasoned operating budget of $2,763,000 annually, Woods mobilized scores of citizen groups and all of Ritchie's enemies. While the budget was sound, however, the presentation again was questionable. Some of the requests were tied to local pork barrel bills as a means of obtaining support, and controversial items, such as salary increases, were so tied to essential appropriations, such as that for the University hospital, that their defeat practically meant throwing indigent patients into the streets. The maneuver ran according to plan, the University accepted minor cuts, the pork barrel legislation received substantial increases and the huge conglomerate appropriations bill passed by an easy margin.

That was what Ritchie was waiting for, and he sprung the trap. For the first time in Maryland history a governor appeared before the general assembly in mid-session, announcing his veto of the entire appropriations bill. Furthermore, since the University of Mary-

[4]*Baltimore Sun*, 1 September 1921; 5 October 1921; 27 November 1921; 2 February 1922; 16 March 1922; 2 June 1922; 27 May 1923; Regents' Minutes (Regents Office, Baltimore), 11 June 1921; Woods to Ritchie, 18 October 1921, Ritchie Papers ("Governor's Correspondence . . ."), Hall of Records.

land had proved to be a disruptive influence in economical government, he demanded that it be dissolved. Ritchie redrew the issue.
No longer was it a question of a bad appropriations bill. The question was simply between a state University and low taxes. To divide
University supporters he offered a deal: he would sign the requested
appropriations for the Baltimore professional schools if they would
agree to dissolution of the 1920 merger. Pork barrel bills fell by the
wayside as the state engaged in a full scale debate over the merits of
higher education. Newspapers, alumni and public organizations deluged the assembly with advice. Most eloquent of all was Woods, the
symbol, even for his opponents, of something fine in education. At
two o'clock in the morning of April 1, 1924, the Senate voted 16-13
to uphold the merger. The House concurred, voting the University
$927,000 for the following year and, to discourage a veto, promptly
adjourned *sine die*.[5]

Although Ritchie won the immediate appropriations fight, the
University was the long-run victor for it had passed the final test of
its right to exist as a state-supported institution. Ritchie acknowledged the University's victory, and soon included the institution in
his list of great accomplishments. Regularly he appeared at campus
gatherings and commencements, and his continued advice on details
of operations began to assume a decidedly friendly air. The state
had accepted its University.[6]

While the University was establishing its place in the state, Woods
worked to organize the proud and independent Baltimore professional schools into a central administrative system. He appointed
T. O. Heatwole, Dean of the School of Dentistry, to serve as the
Baltimore representative of the central University authority. Heatwole regularly met with College Park officials, and Woods regularly
met with the Baltimore Council of Deans to integrate the two centers. Pre-medical, pre-law, pre-dental, pre-pharmacy and pre-nursing
programs were established which required certain Baltimore professors to meet classes in College Park, and certain College Park classes
to attend lectures and laboratories in Baltimore. A renowned phy-

[5]Regents' Minutes, 10 October 1923; 3 March 1924; *Baltimore Sun,* 30 November-2
December 1923; 7-9 January 1924; 19 February-9 April 1924; 6 June 1924; Albert C.
Ritchie, *Governor Ritchie's Address to the Joint Session of the Maryland Legislature
. . . March 18th, 1924* (Pamphlet, Maryland Room, McKeldin Library) ; Ritchie Papers
("Governor's Subject File, University of Maryland") , Hall of Records.
[6]*Baltimore Sun,* 16 November 1926; 20 November 1926; 9 January 1927; *Diamondback,*
2 May 1928; Ritchie Papers, *passim* ("Governor's Correspondence . . .") , Hall of
Records.

sician, J. M. H. Rowland, became Dean of the School of Medicine. Ever mindful of extension work, the College Park officials encouraged the medical school to establish courses over the state to keep physicians up to date on recent developments. Comprehending the necessity for the professional schools to keep abreast of standards dictated by the accrediting agencies, Woods' administration ably represented the needs of those schools before the legislature, so that by 1926 the state appropriation for the Baltimore operations almost doubled the increase for College Park. On both campuses officials planned joint social functions and labored to promote a feeling of unity.[7]

Although the Baltimore schools were pleased in obtaining what they wanted from the merger, Woods never considered the union a total success. For one thing, he failed in his attempt to combine the Baltimore fees and appropriations into a common fund. The more prosperous schools, particularly law and dentistry, objected so strongly that the governor interceded to require that each budget remain separate. As a result, the University constantly negotiated loans and cut salaries in one school, while another flourished with a comfortable surplus. Woods also failed to gain from the Baltimore deans any real control over faculty appointments and was unable to halt the tendency toward in-breeding as the schools continued to select faculty members largely from their own graduates. The professional schools would agree to no common admissions policy, and never trusted College Park to supervise schedules, grades, examinations or classroom procedures. Even the joint commencements and social functions remained a little awkward for everybody, since students and alumni from one campus felt little kinship and only a limited respect for those from the other. Superficial unity and cordiality remained, but the central administration never quite succeeded in governing.[8]

[7]A. F. Woods, "The Reorganizations of the Medical School . . .," *Bulletin of the University of Maryland School of Medicine* . . ., V (December, 1920) , 143-167; XII (October, 1927) , 95; XVII (July, 1932) , 30-33; Minutes of the Deans' Council, Baltimore, 1920-1927 (Deans' Council File, Woods Papers, Board of Regents Office, Baltimore) ; Heatwole File, Rowland File, Harlan File, Kelly File, DuMez File in Woods Papers, Regents Office; also see these files in Wood Papers, President's Office, College Park; *Biennial Reports,* 1921-1926, *passim; Baltimore Sun,* 30 June 1920.

[8]Regents' Minutes, 23 September 1921; 8 April 1927; Ritchie File, Woods Papers, Regents' Office; Samuel M. Shoemaker to Ritchie, 10 December 1927, Ritchie Papers ("Governor's Correspondence . . ."), Hall of Records; Report of a Committee, Faculty Senate Minutes (Senate File, Pearson Papers, President's Office, College Park), 26 Novmber 1934; Interview, Myron S Aisenberg, 15 March 1962; *Baltimore Sun,* 6 March 1924; 9 April 1924; 14 April 1924. Baltimore fees were merged with the general University budget in 1927 (*Laws of Maryland . . . 1927,* Chap. 654).

College Park gained most from the merger, for Woods now had a mandate to transform the agricultural and technological institution into a university. The difference lay, not in size or even in the addition of professional schools, but in faculty, standards, curriculum and breadth of aim—enrichments often difficult to explain to taxpayers. Although deeply disappointed at the appropriations received from the legislature, Woods channeled the increases almost entirely into an internal strengthening of the institution. Desperately he cut out frills. From 1920 to 1926 the expenditures for furniture, office supplies, commencement programs and motor vehicles was cut in half, insurance policies lapsed and students complained about the food in the dining hall. For certain academic expenditures, however, Woods appeared almost extravagant. Faculty salaries soared from $162,000 in 1920 to $322,000 in 1926. The salaries of top professors tripled, and the budget for scientific apparatus and library books more than quadrupled.[9]

Faculty improvement remained the greatest single emphasis of President Woods to the extent that Yale, Chicago and other institutions never understood how he lured away some of their strongest men. For one thing he was willing to pay up to $7,500 for an outstanding professor. Beyond that, he offered them his vision of a great new university and a free hand in building their own departments for it. The number of Ph.D.'s at College Park increased from five in 1920 to twenty-five in 1926.[10]

Before the merger, when Woods was still building a technological institution, he revealed his faith in outstanding scholars by bringing in Percy White Zimmerman from Chicago as Dean of Agriculture, and Arthur N. Johnson from Harvard as Dean of Engineering. Along with them came Arthur G. McCall, head of geology and soils, and Charles O. Appleman, plant pathologist in the Experiment Station and later Dean of the Graduate School. After the merger, Woods intensified his search for able scholars in the established programs and for able organizers for new ones. Eugene C. Auchter came from Cornell to head horticulture, and Morris S. Kharasch from Chicago as professor of organic chemistry. William S. Small became Dean of Education, Herbert Maynard Diamond became Dean of Business and Adele Stamp arrived as Dean of Women. All

[9]*Laws of Maryland . . . 1920*, Chaps. 487, 727; *Laws . . . 1922*, Chap. 464; *Laws . . . 1924*, Chaps. 176, 280, 532, 212; *Laws . . . 1927*, Chaps. 345, 654. For a digest see "Statement of Receipts and Disbursements . . . 1920 . . . 1932," Pamphlet File, Maryland Room, McKeldin Library; also *Biennial Reports*, 1919-1927.

[10]*Biennial Report, 1919-1921*, 20-21; *Triennial Report, 1923-1926*, 18-24.

but Miss Stamp were Ph.D.'s, and all were, or were soon to be, listed in *Who's Who in America.*

Central to any university was basic work in arts and sciences, long neglected at Maryland during the period of vocational emphasis, but during the 1920's the fastest growing branch of the institution. To head the College of Arts and Sciences, Woods again looked for a powerful outsider and attracted a noted Yale sociologist and former United States consul in Peking, Frederick E. Lee. Too ambitious to be popular, Lee delighted in serving as Woods' hatchet man, ruthlessly sidetracking the professors he deemed unworthy and replacing them with brilliant new ones.[11] From Nebraska came Homer C. House to head the English department, and from Pennsylvania Adolph E. Zucker to head foreign languages. From Tufts came Arthur I. Andrews as head of history, and from Yale, George P. Murdoch to head sociology. All but House were recognized in *Who's Who in America.*

Dean Lee and his galaxy of new department heads set out to make the College of Arts and Sciences the heart of the University and the citadel of high standards. From 1920 to 1926 the Arts and Sciences faculty increased from 7 percent of the College Park total to 34 percent, and the number of students majoring in the College grew from 20 percent to 45 percent. Departments of philosophy, political science and sociology became independent from older departments. Chemistry, physics, mathematics and zoology were transferred from the Colleges of Engineering and Agriculture where they had been handmaids of technical training, to the College of Arts and Sciences where they were studied for their own sake. At the end of World War I, students in agriculture or engineering took only about four courses in basic subjects outside their own college, but by 1926 they took at least ten courses in the College of Arts and Sciences. These basic courses, once considered the easiest in the curriculum, became the most difficult, the accepted standard of measurement for the ability of students in the various professional areas.[12]

To evaluate educational programs in the University, Woods named an Educational Standards Committee, generally considered the strongest committee on the campus, and headed by Dean Lee, the strongest member of the faculty. The committee promptly scrapped

---

[11]Regents' Minutes, 15 September 1922; 6 January 1925; 20 March 1925; 22 May 1925; Lee File, Woods' Papers, College Park.

[12]*Biennial Report, 1919-1921*, 38, 59; *Biennial Report, 1921-1923*, 21, 41-42; *Triennial Report, 1923-1926*, 38-40.

the department of journalism and the department of library science, both of which seemed expensive and of questionable academic standing. Other areas were enlarged. The School of Engineering established an extension school of mines and so expanded its research facilities as to become an experiment station for the State Roads Commission. The School of Education expanded from elementary and vocational training to the training of secondary school teachers and administrators. Home Economics, a favorite of President Woods, added work in textiles, interior decoration and institutional management. In 1920 the Graduate School awarded its first M. A. degree in a field other than agriculture, and also its first Ph.D. degree.[13]

The College of Business Administration, a particularly fashionable subject in the 1920's, briefly became the largest within the University, but when Woods and the Educational Standards Committee became convinced that its standards were low, they abolished it. The subject began at Maryland in 1921 when a Baltimore Y.M.C.A. director, Maynard A. Clemens, persuaded the University to establish business administration as a night school, with the medical buildings as classrooms and Baltimore businessmen as part-time instructors. Soon over 600 students were enrolled for a conglomeration of courses in accounting, real estate, salesmanship, foremanship and a dozen other subjects. For most students and many professors it provided an evening's entertainment without much connection with university standards. To shore up the program, Woods convinced the Johns Hopkins University to join in sponsoring some of the courses and acquired an able dean, Herbert M. Diamond, to organize the operation. But Diamond may have been the first dean deliberately to abolish his own empire. He recommended that the entire work be transferred to College Park as a department in the College of Arts and Sciences, and in 1926 the College of Business Administration faded away.[14]

Far from frightening students or antagonizing the public, the rigorous standards at Maryland sent enrollment soaring. For the first time in almost forty years the University did not court popularity by promising easy admission or low fees, and for the first time it gained broad public respect. For most Marylanders it was a

[13]*Biennial Report, 1919-1921*, 14; *Biennial Report, 1921-1923*, 44-51, 54-56; *Triennial Report, 1923-1926*, 64-65.

[14]S. M. Wedeberg and Dudley Dillard, "History of the College of Business and Public Administration, University of Maryland, 1921-1961 . . ." (Pamphlet File, McKeldin Library), 1-22; *Triennial Report, 1923-1926*, 41-42.

prosperous decade, with college attendance fashionable as never before and with parents convinced that quality education guaranteed a superior livelihood for the future.

Only the farmer failed to share the prosperity, but even he had become convinced of the value of an education which led away from the farm. Vast agricultural improvements through the past decades, intensified by agricultural overexpansion during the war, resulted in a glutted market. The new farm plight marked a failure of the land-grant colleges which had increased production without an eye to the results. As the farmers faced the need to migrate to the city, however, and as land-grant institutions educated increasingly for urban occupations, the institutions began to shed the cow-college stigma which had long frightened away city students. Although enrollment in the College of Agriculture dropped almost by half, and the relative importance of the Experiment Station and the farm extension program also sharply declined, the total University enrollment, both from rural and urban areas, revealed the typical expansion of the era:

ENROLLMENT[15]

	1919-1920	1926-1927
College Park		
Agriculture	213	123
Engineering	108	234
Arts and Sciences	95	506
Education	59	131
Graduate School	13	99
Home Economics	2	46
	490	1139
Baltimore		
Law	346	452
Medicine	278	371
Dentistry	119	395
Pharmacy	77	277
Nursing	71	110
	891	1605

During Wood's administration the appearance of the campus changed less than the internal structure, but a few medium sized buildings appeared. In 1920 the $200,000 Baltimore Nurses' Home was completed, largely from contributions. The following year

[15]Biennial Report, 1919-1921, 67-68; University of Maryland Catalogue, 1927-1928, 258.

College Park acquired a small, $125,000 women's dormitory, known for many years as Practice House and razed in 1962; and a slightly larger men's dormitory, now Baltimore Hall. In 1924 came three buildings worth about $400,000: a dairy building, now part of Turner Laboratory; Ritchie Gymnasium now Annapolis Hall; and the old Byrd Stadium located east of the Baltimore Boulevard.[16]

Woods let others concentrate on the physical plant. For him, the capstone of his work came in November, 1925, when he announced to an excited faculty that Maryland had finally obtained membership in, and thus full accreditation by, the Association of American Universities. That same month Phi Beta Kappa, the world's most famous scholarship society, asked for pertinent facts before establishing a chapter at Maryland. Unfortunately for the University, Woods had already decided to resign. Phi Beta Kappa decided to wait.[17]

All That Jazz

The voice from Maryland, and from many campuses, that most fascinated the public during the 1920's came from the students. The very word "collegiate" ceased to mean a type of education and came to indicate a way of life, an ideal of insouciant gaiety. Perhaps America, in reaction against crusades to re-make the world, was more collegiate, even more sophomoric, than the college sophomore. The country's tastemakers idealized the behavior that they imagined existed on the campus, and frequently it was they, more than the students, who gave birth to the fads and stereotypes of the decade. Careful observers noted that carefree couples with pennants, hip flasks and raccoon coats were often prosperous alumni in search of youth. Public figures, such as F. Scott Fitzgerald, Mary Pickford and Jimmy Walker who liked to think of themselves as "collegiate" were, in fact, embarrassingly close to middle age. But whether the image really came from the campus or the public, college life had come to represent an ideal. With the country egging them on, the students set out to enjoy themselves.

[16]*Laws of Maryland . . . 1920*, Chap. 727; *Laws . . . 1922*, Chap. 464; *Laws . . . 1924*, Chaps. 280, 532; for a financial history of buildings see *University of Maryland Financial Report for the Fiscal Year Ended June 30, 1952* (College Park, 1953) , 113-122.

[17]*Triennial Report, 1923-1926*, 7; Minutes of the Faculty Senate (Faculty Senate File, Adele Stamp Papers, Maryland Room, McKeldin Library) , 4 November 1925; *Diamondback*, 10 November 1925.

The great change on the campus, especially at Maryland, was the flood of coeds. No longer were they oddities, sweet and demure on a pedestal, but aggressive, mannish and participants in everything. At College Park they numbered over 300 by 1929, and had graduated from every college in the University, including engineering and agriculture. They demanded membership in the Y.M.C.A., the debate team and the student government association, while organizing their exclusive Y.W.C.A., the women's debate team and the women's government association. The girls' rifle team took part in intercollegiate matches all over the country and became one of the most prestigious organizations on campus. There were also girls' teams in track, basketball, tennis, bowling, swimming and hockey.[18]

At the beginning of the decade University authorities established strict rules forbidding the girls to smoke and requiring them to be locked in their rooms by dark each evening, but angry protest meetings and petitions soon won them about the same freedom they have today. Disturbed by the apparent discrimination in the word "sorority," the coeds determinedly called their organizations "women's fraternities." In fads, looks and behavior they proclaimed their equality. Unbuttoned, flapping galoshes gave them the name of "flapper" that characterized the age. Their boundup chests, frizzy, bobbed hair, cloche hats, fur-collared coats and short, shapeless dresses live on in fashion infamy.[19]

If the coeds sometimes barbarized womanhood, they had a remarkably civilizing effect upon the men. Toward each other, the male students dropped the juvenile bravado that typified an earlier generation, and toward the coeds they cultivated a casual, sophisticated demeanor to replace the embarrassed country-bumpkin manner. No longer was it necessary for the academic regulations to spell out rules against boisterous rowdyism, such as scuffling and racing on the stairs. Hazing gave way to rat court—rabbit court for women—where freshmen who forgot their ties were sentenced to wear ties around their waists for a week, and those who failed to respond to a greeting were sentenced to sit silently in a tree for part of an afternoon. Gentlemanly behavior and dress became major pre-

[18]*Reveille, 1925,* 131-148; *Reveille, 1929,* 135-148; also *Reveille,* 1920-1930, *passim; Terra Mariae,* 1920-1930, *passim; Diamondback,* 1920-1930, *passim;* and especially *Maryland Mallet* (Campus humor magazine) , 1921-1922, *passim.*

[19]*Biennial Report, 1928-1930,* 12-13, 74-77, 82-87; *Student's Hand Book of the University of Maryland, 1925-1926,* 58-62 and *passim; Reveille, 1929,* 263-301 and *passim;* Student Life Committee File, Virginia Flanagan File, Academic Regulations File, Stamp Papers, McKeldin Library.

occupations of the fraternities, and haberdasheries became the chief advertisers in the *Diamondback.* No longer did men wear work clothes to class, for the fashion-dictated attire was a coat and tie, or an "M" sweater with knickers and loud golf hose.[20]

Even the professors changed. The alumni, remembering a faculty which championed hopelessly old-fashioned values, created the caricature of the absent-minded, fuddy-duddy professor; but students at Maryland often found the professor to be shockingly modern in his ideas and attitudes. He seemed to have evolved from an old school-teacher to a young scholar. His social status was low for the materialistic age did not esteem intellectuals, but relative to the whole economy his economic status was high. The typical full professor made about $4,500 annually and lived in a large College Park house which today probably is occupied by a fraternity. He had an automobile and a maid, and saved for an occasional summer trip to Europe.[21]

Although few very wealthy students attended Maryland, the prosperous times deeply affected student life. It was fashionable to have money; rich students boasted and poor ones tended to be secretive if they had to work part time for the money they spent so freely on week ends. While tuition and board rose from about $350 in 1920 to well over $500 at the end of the decade, still the students voted to add $25 to their fees to boost the athletic and student publication funds. Over 80 percent of the students belonged to fraternities by 1929, even with initiation fees as high as $150. At least two speakeasies and three lunchrooms flourished within walking distance of the campus. Student automobiles became a problem, and in 1927 the campus police issued their first parking ticket.[22]

With classes lasting into Saturday afternoons, the campus seemed more alive on week-ends than during the week. Dance committee chairmen took for granted that every male student owned a tuxedo, and attendance at major balls frequently exceeded the total College Park enrollment. In addition to numerous hops in fraternity houses, the *Diamondback,* during a single semester, counted nineteen dances

[20]*Academic Regulations and Other Information . . . 1928-1929* (Pamphlet, Maryland Room, McKeldin Library) ; *Diamondback,* 6 November 1923; 27 October 1925 and *passim.*

[21]*Diamondback,* 19 November 1929; 11 February 1935; "University of Maryland Budget for 1927-1928," Comptroller's Office, College Park.

[22]*Maryland State College Catalogue, 1919-1920,* 36-37; *University of Maryland Catalogue, 1929-1930,* 46-47; *Reveille, 1929,* 265-303; Minutes of the Faculty Senate (Faculty Senate File, Stamp Papers, McKeldin Library) , 5 May 1926; Interview, Adele Stamp, 8 February 1962; *Diamondback,* 6 December 1927; 23 October 1928.

in the gymnasium and four University dances in Washington hotels. The most elaborate affairs were held in the Willard Hotel where favors included gold-plated pen knives for men and sterling silver pendants for women. House parties, boat parties, campus movies, pep rallies, picnics, teas, hay rides and football trips added to the activity. Music seemed to be everywhere. There was a college orchestra, a glee club, combos, minstrels, operettas and concerts. While the Baltimore campus was quieter, its occasional hotel dances rivaled those of the undergraduates.[23]

Intercollegiate athletics reached a new zenith during the up-roarious decade, with every student expected at every game and repeating every complex cheer. Never was spirit so high or Saturday's hero so lionized. Professors dismissed classes before big games, and University authorities declared official holidays to celebrate unusual victories. The *Diamondback* boasted that Maryland was one of the most sports-minded institutions in the country.[24]

The recruiting of out-of-state muscle men had not begun, and there was little feeling that athletics brutalized things intellectual. Convinced that cleanly won victories enhanced classroom morale, University officials led the way in establishing the Southern Conference, designed primarily to expand intercollegiate contacts, but incidentally formulating far stricter athletic rules than existed a quarter century later. Even Dean Lee, with all his sternness about standards, did not protest as the coaching staff grew to eight men, more than any department in the College of Arts and Sciences. Indeed, the Baltimore schools testified to the value of intercollegiate sports, for most professors agreed that the schools had lost some of their old spirit when their teams disappeared in the merger. Since sports events were not yet attracting the huge noncollegiate crowds of a later day, the greatest criticism of big-time athletics was that they lost money. University officials hesitated to admit how much they lost, but to quiet the criticism and keep athletics out of the regular budget the alumni incorporated the Maryland Athletic Association which financed the teams from gate receipts, alumni contributions and special fees which the students levied voluntarily upon themselves.[25]

[23]*Diamondback*, 19 March 1929; 26 March 1929; 2 November 1922; 25 November 1924; 7 June 1926; 26 November 1929; *Reveille, 1925*, 175-180; *Reveille, 1929*, 122-132; *Baltimore Sun*, 17 November 1921; 20 November 1921; 19 March 1928.

[24]*Diamondback*, 13 November 1923; 23 March 1926; 1 March 1927 and *passim*.

[25]*Ibid.*, 6 October 1925; *Baltimore Sun*, 7 December 1923; 7 February 1926; 16 September 1928; 12 November 1928; 29 November 1929; 30 November 1928; 11 November

In football, by far the greatest sport on the campus, Maryland rose from a regional to a national power. With the team still nonprofessional, no one expected a perfect record or even a national championship; but victories included two upsets over Yale, one of the strongest teams in the nation, and others over powerful Princeton, Pennsylvania, Syracuse, Cornell and North Carolina. Playing some of the best teams, Maryland secured for the decade a record of 48 wins, 37 losses and 8 ties. Students at the still small, still largely unknown institution swelled with pride. All over the state many people, ignorant of the name of the University's president, learned to thrill at the exploits of the handsome coach. Other sports received due emphasis, and again Coach Byrd properly received the credit. At various times in the decade Maryland also claimed national championships in lacrosse, cross-country running and rifle shooting as well as conference or state championships in football, baseball, basketball, track, hockey and tennis.[26]

Even more than athletics, however, Maryland's long-famous May Day festivities seemed to symbolize the frivolous mood of the decade. On those occasions the campus turned out en masse, the band played jazz rhythms and scantily clad coeds acted nursery rhymes in pantomime and danced around the maypole. The age of childish innocence was far from over. For all the daring sophistication of the debate team in arguing about free love or the jokes about bathtub gin, polls showed Maryland students overwhelmingly in favor of prohibition. Still, there was also a reckless irresponsibility in the high spirits, a too-impatient revolt from the past which occasionally could be wild and dangerous.[27]

The irresponsibility exploded at Maryland in the disastrous Chi Omega affair which drove President Woods to his resignation and even threatened to destroy the institution. It began in the fall of 1922 when the campus sororities refused bids to a group of coeds they considered too "fast." The rejected girls knew why they had been turned down and set out to live up to their reputation. Violations of minor rules mounted, until finally in March, 1923, the desperate president suspended two of the trouble makers for the

1929; Byrd-Ritchie Correspondence, 1928-1929, Ritchie Papers ("Governor's Correspondence . . ."), Hall of Records; Athletics File, Pearson Papers, President's Office.

[26]For Record of teams, see *Reveille*, 1920-1930, *passim*.

[27]May Day File and May Day Scrapbooks, Stamp Papers, McKeldin Library; *Reveille*, *1929*, 146-148; Interview, Adele Stamp, 5 February 1962; *Terra Mariae*, *1928*, 326-330; *Diamondback*, 13 December 1927; 2 March 1926; 26 February 1929.

minor offense of smoking. Newspapers in Washington and Baltimore, hungering for salacious stories from the campus, gave the incident broad coverage and darkly hinted of far graver coed scandals.[28]

Two people were especially interested in the stories. One was Vivian Simpson, a brilliant, high-principled, rebellious coed who resented the University's making victims of the girls and saw basic principles of womens' rights at stake. The other was an aggressive female attorney from the midwest, Mary Love-Collins, who saw an opportunity for establishing another profitable chapter of Chi Omega, a national sorority that she represented. Miss Love-Collins roared into College Park, firing angry telegrams as she came.[29] Quickly she struck an alliance with Vivian Simpson, founded a chapter of Chi Omega at Maryland and invited every rebellious spirit she could find to join it. "The only way we can get anything around here," said one of the girls melodramatically, "is to stick together and as an organized body rebel against the rules."[30] Although the sorority had been established in total violation of University regulations, Woods hesitated to suspend the entire lot of girls since suspending two of them had begun the trouble.

Excited about their rights, bewildered and egged on by Miss Love-Collins, the rebellious coeds pressed the initiative. Secretly they drew up affidavits for a friendly newspaper reporter who on April 29, 1923, blazoned across the front page of the *Washington Post*, a story that shook the University's foundations. Calling the institution a "pajama paradise," it declared that University "officials," presumably including the impeccably proper President Woods, were actually seducing coeds:

> Several officials showed a decided tendency to get "mushy," according to the coeds, one of the men in question, according to an affidavit, entreating her to "kiss him."
> The same man, it is charged, on another occasion, with another woman student, entered a private office, and after securing the door suggested that they engage in what he termed a "petting party."

[28]Chi Omega File, Stamp Papers, McKeldin Library; *Baltimore Sun,* 17 March 1923; 28 April 1923.

[29]Mary Love-Collins to Woods, Telegram, 22 March 1923, Woods File, Stamp Papers, McKeldin Library; Mary Love-Collins to Ritchie, Telegram, 4 April 1923, Ritchie Papers ("Governor's Correspondence . . . "), Hall of Records; J. A. Garrett to Ritchie, 10 April 1923, Ritchie Papers ("Governor's Correspondence . . ."), Hall of Records.

[30]Testimony of Esther Williams in Virginia Flanagan File, Stamp Papers, McKeldin Library.

Another official, it is charged, after taking one of the coeds for a ride, stopped his car by the roadside on the pretense of letting the engine cool, and offered his companion a drink of whiskey from a bottle marked "rye". . . .

This official, it is also charged, on frequent occasions during the summer school term made up night swimming parties, to which the fairest of the coeds were invited. No male student of the University participated, it is said.

In a moment of facetiousness, if the terms of the affidavit may be taken literally, one official invited a fair coed and her roommate to a "spanking party" at an apartment house in Washington. . . .

The Board of Regents of the University has not acted. It has been concerned with building plans involving the expenditure of millions of the taxpayers money!

The University regents and the administration refused to reply to the charges, knowing that denials would only prolong the publicity, but the student body could not contain its outrage at an attack apparently directed against their respected president. The *Diamondback* rushed into print with an extra edition, shouting defiance with the first banner headline in its history: "UNPRINCI-PLED, UNFAIR, UN-AMERICAN," it cried, "THIS IS A DAM-NABLE MISREPRESENTATION." Calling a mass meeting at which no member of the faculty was present, the students passed resolutions condemning the Washington newspaper, praising the president and demanding immediate dismissal of the students who signed the affidavits. Only Vivian Simpson and one other student voted against the resolutions. Fully aware of the real issues involved, the students in their resolutions urged the administration not to yield to the "attempts of any 'Amazon-hued' sorority to gain recognition."[31] Since the *Washington Post* refused to reveal exactly which girls had signed the affidavits, any just discipline or even further investigation seemed impossible.

The administration had its own way, legal or not, of discovering who had signed the affidavits. Working closely with the board of regents, Woods waited quietly and just before the fall term began in 1924 he wrote to Vivian Simpson and Virginia Flanagan, stating that they would not be readmitted. When Vivian Simpson appealed, the president relented and allowed her to register provided she foreswore membership in Chi Omega. Although any other coed would have been intimidated long before, the strong-minded girl

[31] *Diamondback*, 1 May 1923.

refused to limit her associations and announced to reporters that she would take the case to court. Again the newspapers enjoyed a field day as a local judge probed into every detail of coed life.

By now the University's case was weak. If belonging to Chi Omega were grounds for dismissal, at least ten girls should have been dismissed long ago. Vivian Simpson's only specific misdeeds were so minor—such as using an iron in the dormitory against regulations—that they appeared ridiculous. Worst of all, the University did not wish to press the newspaper affidavits as slander, for while Woods' reputation was perfect the authorities had reason to fear some truth in the charges in the cases of certain other valuable officials. The result was that the University lost the case at exactly the moment that Governor Ritchie was demanding that it be dissolved for altogether different reasons. As the legislators walked into the state house to vote on the continued existence of the institution, Chi Omega officials handed them pamphlets accusing the University administration of moral turpitude. The University won the vote in the legislature, and it appealed and eventually won the case against Vivian Simpson. The Court of Appeals expressed the opinion that the affidavits given the newspapers were false, and ruled that a University must have discretion to select students as it sees fit for the general welfare. But for Dr. Woods, the episode could not be easily forgotten.[32]

People commented that the president suddenly seemed much older. "I used to look forward to going to the office," he said, "but now I have headaches and look forward to going home."[33] He remained a little over a year after the final court decision, prepared the budget requests for the 1927 legislature and saw the culmination of his work in the accreditation by the American Association of Universities. He was eager, however, to resign before the new general assembly began debate and a fine position awaited him as director of research in the United States Department of Agriculture. Meanwhile, Raymond A. Pearson, President of Iowa State College

[32]Chi Omega File, Virginia Flanagan File, Vivian Simpson File, Woods File in Stamp Papers, McKeldin Library; complete bound transcript of the case in Stamp Papers, McKeldin Library; Interview, Adele Stamp, 5 February 1962; *Baltimore Sun*, 24 October 1923; 9 February 1924; 20 March 1924; 28 March 1924; 20-21 May 1924; 5 December 1924; *Reports of Cases Argued . . . Maryland*, 146 (1924), 547-553; Scrapbook of newspaper clippings on the case, President's Office.

[33]Interview, Adele Stamp, 5 February 1962; also Maude McKenny to Woods, 13 March 1924, Woods Papers, McKeldin Library. President Woods' son, Mark W. Woods, is inclined to minimize the case as a factor in his father's resignation, emphasizing instead the attractive offer from Washington. (Interview, 9 February 1962).

had expressed great eagerness for the position at Maryland, and in February, 1926, the board of regents reluctantly accepted Woods' resignation, to take effect the following September. From 1926 to 1948 Woods remained one of the highest ranking members of the Department of Agriculture, but he seldom visited the campus.[34]

Depression Mood

Astute investors around the University might have pulled out of the stock market in time to prevent later losses, for an air of heavy depression began to settle over the campus at least two years before the 1929 crash. In part the gloom came from the farmer who did not share in the prosperity of the decade and from the University's agrarian agencies which were accused of fostering the incomprehensible new malady of overproduction. In part the campus gloom stemmed from Governor Ritchie's economy. Most of all, however, it seemed to emanate from the president's office where Woods' optimism and sense of expansion were replaced by the old-fashioned look and timid manner of Raymond A. Pearson.

Born on an Indiana farm, Pearson obtained his M.S. degree from Cornell where he eventually became professor of dairying. Cornell nominated him to serve as the New York Commissioner of Agriculture, and from there he went as president to Iowa State College. His administration at Iowa was far from happy, apparently marred by personality conflicts more than by substantive issues. The Maryland regents learned much later that his resignation at Iowa had taken place a full month before his new appointment and that it had not been entirely voluntarily.[35]

One of Pearson's difficulties lay in his lack of an educational philosophy, of anything he wanted to do with a university besides keep it running, and such an attitude on the part of an academic administrator is likely to be disastrous. Pearson's only conditions for coming to Maryland were a $15,000 salary, a personal expense account and an automobile and chauffeur. His inaugural address, instead of being a broad statement of policy, included an apology

[34]Woods File, Woods Papers, Regents' Office; Regents' Minutes, 9 February 1926.

[35]Earle Dudley Ross, *History of Iowa State College* . . . (Ames, 1942), 272-336; "Why Pearson Left Iowa" (Pamphlet, Pearson Papers, Regents' Office); *Baltimore Sun*, 14 November 1926.

for not yet knowing many people and a hope that critics would be tolerant of inevitable mistakes. He concluded with weak praise for his predecessor and a promise of moderation that seemed weaker still. "This University has been developed with a view to serve the principal needs of the State," he said. "It would be a mistake to be more ambitious."[36]

Pearson soon offered more concrete discouragement to ambitious University advocates by meeting with Governor Ritchie to negotiate, rather than to fight, for the large 1927 budget which Woods had prepared. Instead of a 100 percent increase in operating expenses for College Park and a $3,500,000 building fund, the new president quietly settled for an increase of 15 percent and $935,000 for buildings. Even he seemed momentarily discouraged as he came from the governor's office, admitting to reporters that Maryland was the only state in the nation in which budget appropriations for its University failed to match student tuition. Quickly, however, he remembered himself and added, "I am sure Governor Ritchie has done the best he can. . . . There will be no fight in the legislature. . . . It is not the purpose of the board of regents to spread out over the whole field of education."[37] Ritchie had found his man, and until the depression swept both of them from office they never disagreed publicly. During Pearson's nine-year administration, from 1926 to 1935, he helped the governor to hold state appropriations for College Park maintenance to within 20 percent of what they were when he took over.[38]

With academic improvement held in abeyance, Pearson slowly emerged as a building president, obtaining a total of almost $4,000,000 for new construction, but in large measure the initiative came from Ritchie rather than the president. The governor in his later years seemed to think of the University almost as a personal monu-

[36]"Inaugural Address," Personal File, Pearson Papers, President's Office; also Shoemaker File, Pearson Papers, President's Office; *Baltimore Sun*, 23 September 1926. Nelson A. Crawford, *A Man of Learning* (Boston, 1928), patterned after Sinclair Lewis' *Elmer Gantry*, was a popular satire about a university president. According to A. E. Zucker, a friend of Crawford, Pearson was the inspiration and model for the novel. (Interview, A. E. Zucker, 13 March 1962).

[37]*Baltimore Sun*, 16 November 1926; 20 November 1926; 9 January 1927.

[38]Pearson to Ritchie, 9 February 1927 and 7 May 1929, Ritchie Papers ("Governor's Correspondence . . ."), Hall of Records; *Biennial Reports*, 1926-1928 and 1934-1936, *passim; Laws of Maryland . . . 1927*, Chaps. 345, 654; *Laws . . . 1929*, Chaps. 132, 134; *Laws . . . 1931*, Chaps. 150, 253; *Laws . . . 1933*, Chap. 597; *Laws . . . 1935*, Chaps. 92, 548.

ment. His interest in construction on the campus was a sort of reward to the institution for holding down operating expenses and also a means of fighting the depression by creating construction jobs. Long overdue, a building program would have been Woods' next major emphasis. The dental school lacked the top accreditation rating because of inadequate facilities, some of the deans were without private offices and the coed dormitories were jerry-built World War I barracks. To make the best of his opportunity, Pearson worked tirelessly with alumni and citizen groups to obtain additional contributions. He relied heavily on the advice of such men as Samuel Shoemaker, W. W. Skinner and E. Brooke Lee, the financial and construction authorities on the board of regents. Proceeding leisurely and relying on professional architects for buildings and landscaping the officials usually obtained outstanding esthetic as well as functional results:

MAJOR CONSTRUCTION, *1928-1935*[39]

1928 Silvester Hall, originally called Chemistry Building—$225,000.
Dining Hall, wings added later—$300,000.
1929 Dental-Pharmacy Building, Baltimore—$258,000.
1930 Poultry Barns—$30,000.
1931 Heating Plant, College Park—$216,000.
1932 22 acres of land, College Park—$22,000.
Holzapfel Hall, originally Horticultural Building—$150,000.
Shoemaker Building, originally Library and Administration Building—$208,000.
Ritchie Coliseum—$181,000.
Preinkert Field House, originally Women's Field House, wings added later—$42,000.
St. Mary's Hall, originally Margaret Brent Hall—$176,000.
East wing of Francis Scott Key Hall, originally addition to Engineering Building—$92,000.
Law School and grounds—$200,000.
1934 University Hospital—$1,800,000.

The expanded, beautified campus paid off by raising both the ranking and the enrollment of the institution. Early in 1930 the law school finally obtained an A rating, and a few months later

[39]Campus File, Buildings File, E. Brooke Lee File, Shriver File in Pearson Papers, Regents' Office; Buildings File, Campus File, Pearson Papers, President's Office; Regents' Minutes, *passim; Biennial Reports, passim; University of Maryland Report for the Fiscal Year Ended June 30, 1952,* 113-122; *Diamondback* and *Baltimore Sun* usually contain building dedication ceremonies.

the dental school obtained the top A grade. The new hospital gave the medical school unsurpassed clinical facilities.[40] Additional dormitories helped to swell the total full-time enrollment from 2,734 in 1926-1927 to 3,487 in 1935-1936. As the depression deepened, however, the rise of college enrollments became alarming rather than encouraging, a sign of unemployment rather than love of learning. To avoid overcrowding the professions, the University generally, and the Baltimore schools especially, raised standards above normal levels.[41]

For the faculty, Pearson's construction program only made other economies all the more intolerable. Professors are traditionally skeptical of a building president, fearful that bricks and mortar are being paid for out of salaries. After Woods' disappointment in the Ritchie fight the faculty had remained passionately loyal, expecting increases for their departments in the subsequent 1927 appropriation; but Pearson ignored the implied committment and brusquely ordered the faculty "to restrict rather than extend the scope of work."[42] He also found himself unable to support the major library expansion or the new department of fine arts which Woods had promised, and as vacancies occurred in philosophy, classical languages and music, Pearson allowed those departments to die.[43]

Faculty discontent was present almost from the beginning of Pearson's administration. In 1927 the powerful Frederick E. Lee resigned, angrily denouncing Pearson's "secret conferences" with the governor in which he traded basic academic needs for new buildings. "In complete frankness," wrote Lee, "I would say that I left the University primarily because Dr. R. A. Pearson had become President of the institution." By the time the stock market crashed, at least a dozen other professors saw the vision that Woods had given them fade. They too turned in their resignations.[44]

As the economy spiraled downward the educational budget tight-

[40]*Biennial Report, 1928-1930,* 67-71; also Pearson to Ritchie, 7 March 1930, and J. Ben Robinson to Ritchie, 25 July 1930, Ritchie Papers ("Governor's Correspondence . . ."), Hall of Records; *Bulletin of the Medical School* . . ., XIX (April, 1935), 155-165, 196-197.

[41]*Biennial Report, 1926-1928,* 119; *Biennial Report, 1932-1934,* 36; *Biennial Report, 1934-1936,* 75-80; *Baltimore Sun,* 30 August 1932.

[42]*Biennial Report, 1928-1930,* 9.

[43]*Biennial Report, 1930-1932,* 7; *Biennial Report, 1932-1934,* 18-19, 25; Pearson to Byrd, 9 December 1933, Byrd File, Pearson Papers, President's Office; Pearson to Ritchie, 7 January 1927, Ritchie File, Pearson Papers, Regents' Office.

[44]Regents' Minutes, 13 May 1927; Lee to J. Marshall Mathias, 26 April 1935, Byrd File, Pearson Papers, President's Office.

ened more. In 1931 Ritchie requested the University to return 15 percent of its annual budget to the state treasury, and the harassed president announced that the money must come from salary and equipment cuts. Each year the construction budget grew larger as the governor tried desperately to create jobs, but despite the rising student enrollment the operating budget barely held its own. In 1933 Ritchie again requested a return of funds to the state, and again salaries fell. By 1935, with the College Park teaching loads almost double what they had been, another dozen professors had turned in their resignations.[45] Kharsch, Gordon, Andrews, Murdoch, Auchter, Zimmerman and McCall were among the more prominent who drifted away. Frederick E. Lee, looking back, calculated that while College Park enrollment doubled, "at least 24 faculty members with the Ph.D. have left the institution since Dr. Pearson became president in 1926, made up of deans, heads of departments and others of high rank . . . and in their places three professors with the Ph.D. have been appointed."[46]

Times were desperate everywhere and no one consciously blamed Pearson for that, but somehow his manner caused the faculty to feel that he was unsympathetic. Instead of fighting the budget cuts, he seemed to be in league with the governor by encouraging retrenchment. "In several of our departments," he volunteered, "some further increases [in budget savings] can be cared for, if necessary."[47] Some departments in the University, particularly the Baltimore schools, discovered that they could bully the president on budget matters; but when he yielded to pressure, or made deals, the secrets inevitably became known.[48] People were irritated by Pearson's old-fashioned high collar and his high buttoned shoes, by his automobile and chauffeur and by his habit of walking across the campus staring owlishly ahead without recognizing anyone. Professors talked about his long Florida vacations while he issued orders for faculty vacations to be curtailed, and about his interference with routine classroom affairs while he vacillated over important decisions. For the crisp resolution of problems the faculty and the

[45]Regents' Minutes, 25 March 1932; 17 June 1935; *Biennial Report, 1930-1932,* 9; *Biennial Report, 1934-1936,* 7-9.

[46]Frederick E. Lee, "The University of Maryland Episode," *School and Society,* XLII (13 July 1935), 63.

[47]*Biennial Report, 1930-1932,* 7.

[48]Regents' Minutes, 14 August 1934; 23 November 1934; 21 September 1934; 18 May 1934; 17 June 1935; Henry Holzapfel to Samuel M. Shoemaker, 19 November 1930, Shoemaker File, Pearson Papers, Regents' Office.

regents turned increasingly to the president's assistant, the happy and expansive "Curley" Byrd.[49]

While faculty morale crumbled, the student mood also changed, growing serious, searching, sometimes angry, and providing a greater threat than the faculty to an uncomprehending administration. Ballyhoo and nonsense suddenly became immature rather than sophisticated, fads and fashion became unfashionable and the flapper discovered she could more nearly equal men by being a woman. The men, no longer pretending to be rich, tore the velvet off their tuxedoes to wear them to class. Campus police discovered students sleeping in classrooms at night to keep warm. As fraternity membership declined, at least two groups sold their off-campus houses and moved into the dormitories.

During the 1930 football season the pep rallies lost their spark, attendance at games declined and even the students began to talk of de-emphasis.[50] That same year the *Baltimore Sun*, always leary of the ambitious, politically minded football coach, discovered that the football team had scheduled two games in a single day and let loose a barrage against big-time athletics.[51] Coach Byrd, however, either reflected the changed campus mood or cannily responded to it, for already athletic emphasis had shifted toward such intramural and participant sports as tennis, track and boxing. Two years later Byrd dropped his coaching activities to devote full time to administration.

Campus publications assumed new importance and by the mid-thirties were generally superior to anything they have been since. The *Diamondback* conducted tests and interviews to select reporters from an army of volunteers. A new literary and humor magazine, *The Old Line*, appeared. The College Park annual eliminated the military implication in its title by changing its name from *The Reveille* to *The Terrapin*, while the Baltimore schools continued with their annual, *Terra Mariae*. Student editorials evolved from insipid commentary about football games to forthright stands on the fundamental educational and political issues of the day. Not

[49]"Maryland: Most Faculty Down on University's President," *News-Week*, V (29 June 1935), 39; Interview Adele Stamp, 5 February 1962; Interview, A. E. Zucker, 12 March 1962; see Byrd File, Pearson Papers, President's Office; Regents' Minutes, 23 January 1931; *Diamondback*, 13 May 1935; 3 June 1935 and *passim; Bulletin of the School of Medicine* . . ., XVIII (October, 1933), 76.

[50]*Diamondback*, 29 March 1927; 22 January 1929; 29 January 1929; 14 January 1930; 28 January 1930; 7 December 1931; 8 February 1932; 5 December 1932 and *passim*.

[51]*Baltimore Sun*, 11 February 1930; *Diamondback*, 25 January 1932.

content merely to report student events, the editors covered meetings of the board of regents, pried secrets from faculty meetings and took stands on the deeply serious educational issues that they discovered.[52]

Student government became a far more serious concern as party loyalty and violent political campaigns divided the campus over issues which frequently reached outside the University. While the student government constitution of 1925 had airily declared its aim "to promote general student activities," the constitution of 1932 grimly proclaimed the determination "to learn the responsibilities of citizenship [and] take upon ourselves the burdens of Student Government."[53]

Just as May Day had symbolized the frivolity of the 1920's, so political clubs and occasional angry outbursts symbolized the serious depression mood. As northern schools became overcrowded many Jews arrived on the campus. At one time they comprised over half the medical school enrollment and opened the way on the campus for the acrid anti-Semitism which flourished abroad. After a winter dance in College Park in 1931, someone suggested that they "get" the Jews who had not been invited to the affair. No one was seriously injured in the resulting rock-hurling riot, but University officials began to talk of a "quota" on out-of-state students. Although the authorities took no formal action, the Jewish enrollment began to decline.[54]

Even more alarming to some University officials were the active Communist, Socialist, Liberal, Democratic and Republican organizations on the campus. The speakers they helped to obtain for the University—many of them such outstanding figures as Mrs. Franklin D. Roosevelt, Henry Wallace, Sumner Welles and Norman Thomas —now received louder applause than the coed beauty queens.[55]

[52]Faculty Senate Minutes, 8 December 1933; also 3 December 1931 and 1934-1935 *passim*, Senate File, Pearson Papers, President's Office; *Diamondback*, 7 November 1932; 13 February 1933; 6 March 1933; 3 April 1933 and *passim*.

[53]*Student Hand Book of the University of Maryland, 1925-1926*, 44; *The "M" Book of the University of Maryland, 1934-1935*, 30; see *Diamondback, passim*; also *Bulletin of the School of Medicine . . .*, XIV (January, 1930), 141-142; XVII (July, 1932), 38; XXI (January, 1937), 131-132.

[54]J. M. H. Rowland to Ritchie, 4 August 1932, Ritchie Papers ("Governor's Correspondence . . ."), Hall of Records; *Baltimore Sun*, 18 December 1931; *Diamondback*, 30 November 1931.

[55]Faculty Senate Minutes, 20 May 1931; 23 January 1933; 8 March 1933, Senate File, Pearson Papers, President's Office; *Baltimore Sun*, 12 March 1933; 11 April 1933; 9 November 1933; 5-6 March 1934; 13 April 1934; Interview Adele Stamp, 5 February

Convinced that radical ideas flourished around the Y.M.C.A., in 1934 President Pearson expelled the organization from the campus. His assistant wrote to other universities to discover how they handled the "liberal problem":

> During the current academic year we have had some difficulties which seem to have emanated largely from more or less radical sources. . . .
> Personally, I am convinced that a good deal of this is carried on through so-called "Liberal" or "Socialist" clubs. . . . Such propoganda in this section takes very definite forms such as attempts to break down the national defense, to bring into education a policy of refusing to bear arms for the country, social equality of the races, etc.[56]

Just as the social problems of the 1920's had exploded in the Chi Omega case, so political problems of the early 1930's found their way into two court cases which epitomized the University's difficulties in the depression decade. The first case opened the unmentionable race question. Since the graduation of a single Negro from the law school in 1885, segregation at Maryland had been a firm, unspoken rule. The University contributed money to Princess Anne Academy as the land-grant acts required, and in 1927 that little institution began four years of college level work; but as the depression tightened Pearson allowed instruction there to fall below high school standards, and its enrollment to fall to thirty-four students. In 1932 the regents somewhat guiltily established a fund totaling $600 from which Negroes could apply for tuition to out-of-state institutions.[57]

In 1934, however, a Baltimore Negro, Donald Murray, who had paid his way through Amherst, refused the pitifully small grant and sued to enter the law school. Murray, represented by the brilliant young attorney, Thurgood Marshall, won his suit, entered the University and four years later graduated with distinction.

1962; Interview, Virgil Lowder (Director of Christian Association at Maryland, 1930-1934), 6 February 1962.

[56]Byrd to Livingston Farrand (President of Cornell University), 23 March 1933, Byrd File, Pearson Papers, President's Office; also Interview, Virgil Lowder, 6 February 1962; *Old Line*, VI (March, 1936), 9.

[57]Regents' Minutes, 9 September 1932; 22 April 1935; *Biennial Report, 1926-1928*, 121-123; *Biennial Report, 1932-1934*, 114; *Biennial Report, 1934-1936*, 92-94; T. H. Kiah (Principal, Princess Anne Academy) to Ritchie, 21 February 1922, Ritchie Papers ("Governor's Correspondence . . ."), Hall of Records. The scholarship fund was raised to $10,000 to 1933 and $30,000 in 1937 (*Laws of Maryland . . . 1933*, Chap. 234; *Laws . . . 1937*, Chap. 506).

Officially the case opened all the University's professional schools to Negroes, but to avoid "indiscriminate" mixing, the legislature promptly increased the out-of-state scholarship fund to $30,000. To evade possible suits to enter the undergraduate schools, the legislature appropriated $100,000 so that the University could purchase Princess Anne Academy from Morgan College and bring it up to full collegiate standing. Murray's case and the flurry of legislative debate which followed it significantly aided the cause of Negro education, but only won new enemies for the University. On the one hand standing determinedly for reaction and on the other hand yielding to integration, the administration withstood a flurry of attack.[58]

The second court case, involving compulsory military training at Maryland, went all the way to the Supreme Court and became the most famous pacifism trial of the decade. Facts in the case were simple. Ennis H. Coale, a freshman at the University, was a Methodist who like many other students responded to the powerful anti-war sentiment sweeping the American campuses. In consultation with his minister, he and a sophomore friend, Wayne Lees, determined that the compulsory ROTC at Maryland constituted "a preparation for war," and respectfully requested permission to avoid it. Most students considered the training to be a kind of compulsory exercise and shared the administration's indignation at Coale and Lees for desiring to shirk the unpleasant. After some hesitation, the regents allowed Pearson to expel the boys.

When Coale and Lees announced their decision to sue the University to re-enter without taking ROTC, the entire country seemed to take sides. The Methodist Church, supported by editorials from such outstanding newspapers as the *Christian Science Monitor* and by resolutions of the American Association of University Professors, dispatched lawyers to aid the boys. On the University's side sat the ROTC, supported by editorials from the *New York Times* and by resolutions from the American Legion which declared that the case was part of "a carefully planned Communist campaign." The decision was as simple as the facts of the case. The Baltimore Court ruled in favor of the boys, stating that conscientious objectors could refrain from compulsory military training in colleges. The Court of Appeals ruled for the University, saying that such objectors could

[58]*Reports of Cases Argued . . . Maryland,* 169 (1935) , 478-489; "Admission of Negroes to the University of Maryland," *School and Society,* XLVI (11 September 1937) , 335; Regents' Minutes, 22 April 1935; *Baltimore Sun,* 21 April 1935; 7 May 1935; 19 June 1935; 25 September 1935; 16-17 January 1936; *Laws of Maryland . . . 1935,* Chap. 548.

obtain their education elsewhere. Finally, the Supreme Court read the arguments and rejected the case, thus upholding the Court of Appeals and the University.[59]

Most of the students and many of the faculty at Maryland hailed the decision, but like the Chi Omega and the Murray cases, it was a Pyrrhic victory. Few could take pride in the notoriety the University had received. Somehow the University appeared to stand for compulsion rather than academic freedom and for militarism rather than intellectual values. Pearson acknowledged to the regents that faculty morale was dangerously low.[60]

The Revolution of 1935

Although University people called it a revolution, Pearson's final overthrow stemmed from old issues and was revolutionary only in complexity, violence and repercussion. The president's downfall stemmed from his personality, from his apparent overemphasis on construction, from his neglect of the faculty, from the self-assertion of the students and the misfortune of overpublicized court cases, and from the whole bane of depression and an eagerness for a new deal.

A forewarning of Pearson's disaster may have come in November, 1934, when the four-term Governor of Maryland, Albert C. Ritchie was finally swept from office by the liberal Republican, Harry W. Nice. Rightly or wrongly, people believed that Ritchie was Pearson's defender, and they stood much less in awe of a Pearson-Nice alliance. In the old tradition the new governor called Pearson to his office in January, 1935, to request further cuts in the University budget, and in the old tradition the president obligingly agreed.[61] This time, however, a storm of protest arose from individual regents, from the faculty and especially from the students. J. Marshall

[59]Transcript, briefs and decisions of all courts bound in "Official Record of a Case to Compel the University of Maryland to Excuse a Student from Military Education" (McKeldin Library); *Reports of Cases Argued . . . Maryland*, 165 (1933), 224-239. For a sampling of the national press, *Literary Digest*, CVX (18 February 1933), 18-19; *World Tomorrow*, XVI (1 August 1933), 461-462; *Christian Century*, L (12 July 1933), 900-901; *Baltimore Sun*, 16 December 1934.

[60]Regents' Minutes, 15 February 1935; 22 April 1935; Pearson to George M. Shriver, 8 April 1935, Shriver File, Pearson Papers, President's Office; *Biennial Report, 1932-1934*, 18-19.

[61]Regents' Minutes, 18 January 1935.

Mathias, one of the ablest editors the *Diamondback* ever had, head-lined a "deal" between Pearson and Nice and launched a veiled attack against the president's entire administration. When Pearson moved to expel Mathias, Byrd and the regents pointed out that every factual detail of the editorials was scrupulously accurate, and that any offense taken to the generalities would be an admittance of guilt.[62] Actually, things were far worse than Mathias knew, for behind the scenes Dean J. M. H. Rowland quietly announced to the regents that the School of Medicine was in danger of losing its accreditation. Worse still, when the American Association of Universities announced that Maryland's rating was up for review, Dean Charles O. Appleman of the Graduate School wrote to the president stating bluntly that the institution had little chance of passing the re-evaluation.[63]

While rumors flew, knowing people watched the movements of two individuals in the background. One was the president's popular assistant, H. C. Byrd. From his seemingly casual remarks, the faculty and students assumed that he was on their side, that he believed in better academic standing and salaries rather than in buildings. Rumors circulated that Byrd had held secret conversations with government officials in Annapolis and Washington who had money to appropriate. Observers noted his Rooseveltian manner, confident and optimistic, as if he were only waiting to offer exciting new solutions to the depression mood.[64] Ostensibly he remained completely loyal to Pearson who now depended on him more than ever. Regularly the bewildered president scrawled across his letters, "What shall we do now, Mr. Byrd?" and the answers were able and conscientious.[65]

The other major person in the background was the former dean, Frederick E. Lee, now at Illinois, but in close touch with Maryland and frankly eager to return as president. Writing to Byrd, Lee

[62]*Diamondback*, 11 February 1935; Pearson to Byrd, 28 December 1934, Byrd File, Pearson Papers, President's Office; Byrd to Pearson, 31 January 1933, Senate File, Pearson Papers, President's Office; Byrd to Pearson, 18 April 1935, Byrd File, Pearson Papers, President's Office; Pearson to Mathias, 27 March 1935, *Diamondback* File, Pearson Papers, President's Office; Pearson to Shriver, 8 April 1935, Shriver File, Pearson Papers, President's Office.

[63]Regents' Minutes, 15 February 1935; Minutes of the Faculty Senate, 11 April 1935, Senate File, Pearson Papers, President's Office; Appleman to Pearson, 9 April 1935, American Association of Universities File, Pearson Papers, President's Office.

[64]Regents' Minutes, 22 April 1935; Pearson File, Pearson Papers, Regents' Office; Interview, A. E. Zucker, 13 March 1962; Interview, Adele Stamp, 5 February 1962.

[65]See Byrd File, Pearson Papers, President's Office; also Pearson to Shoemaker, 3 August 1926 and 4 June 1928, and *passim*, Pearson File, Pearson Papers, Regents' Office.

outlined a plan "to *get* Pearson" by exposing to the public certain facts about his administration. "The steps necessary to put through some such scheme, if you are interested, and think it worth a try, are outlined in Enclosure 3," he wrote. "The enclosed possible new item could break, or could be made to break NOW. . . ."[66] Disdainful of such conspiratorial procedures, Byrd loyally showed Pearson a copy of the planned attack, and meanwhile continued a casual, friendly correspondence with Lee.[67] Lee then began a correspondence with Mathias, editor of the *Diamondback*.[68] Much later, after the dust had settled, the exposed and discredited Pearson could not understand how Mathias obtained such specific information about his administration, and the exposed and embarrassed Lee never understood how Pearson obtained such specific information about the attack.[69]

The real explosion occurred on March 25, 1935, with a ringing front-page *Diamondback* editorial calling Pearson's nine-year administration "a catastrophe." With names and statistics, Mathias documented the "deplorably low" morale, "the wrecking" of the faculty and the reduction of certain departments to "mere sham." Here was the long-awaited rallying cry. The student government established a committee to support Mathias. Alumni, faculty and even public officials called on the regents to "impeach" the president.[70] Professor A. E. Zucker, head of foreign languages and possibly the most renowned scholar remaining at Maryland, supported the call to action with a resignation which was spread across the newspapers:

> The reason for my resignation is complete lack of sympathy for the president, especially his lowering of academic standards, his lack of interest in research, and his neglect of the library. . . .
> Academically, conditions have grown so bad under the present administration that even the undergraduates have complained about them. Despite numerous resignations during the past eight years there has been brought to our campus not one recognized scholar

[66]Lee to Byrd, 20 April 1935, Lee File, Pearson Papers, President's Office.

[67]Lee File, 1935, Byrd Papers, President's Office; Lee File, Pearson Papers, President's Office; *Baltimore Sun*, 29 May 1935; 21 June 1935.

[68]Copies of correspondence in Lee File, Pearson Papers, President's Office; Interview, J. Marshall Mathias, 13 March 1962.

[69]Lee, "The University Episode," 62-64; Pearson, "The Situation at the University of Maryland," *School and Society*, XLII (5 October 1935), 446-449.

[70]*Diamondback*, 1 April 1935; *Washington Post*, 26 March 1935; *Baltimore Sun*, 31 March 1935.

who enjoys even the mild distinction of being in "Who's Who." I believe this will long stand as an intercollegiate record for University presidents.

Though we have, perhaps, the very poorest library among all state universities in the country, yet recently its budget was cut in half. For eight years, with growing indignation I have watched the deterioration of this University which gave such fine promise under President Woods and Dean Lee.[71]

Pearson's last days were painful. As soon as commencement was over the board of regents sent questionnaires to the eighty-four tenure members of the College Park faculty, listing seventeen questions to be answered anonymously, yes or no. Soon the questions were being quoted in the newspapers: "Do you believe there is a lack of administrative ability on the part of the president?" "Do you believe there is a lack of confidence in the president or his ethics?" Of the fifty-five professors who answered, forty-nine expressed a lack of confidence, a desire for a change. When the regents interviewed the fourteen highest ranking members of the University staff every one expressed opposition to the president. On June 28, the regents offered Pearson two months salary and demanded his resignation. Adding insult to their demands, they voted seven to two that if the resignation were not in hand by noon, July 1, the president would be "relieved of his duties." The regents unanimously requested H. C. Byrd to serve as acting president.[72]

There were brief twinges of conscience about the episode. Actually, Pearson was fired largely for carrying out the policies of two powerful state governors and of the board of regents itself. The use of anonymous questionnaires, the lack of specific charges, the refusal to allow the president to hear or answer the attacks were all vaguely disquieting, and the sensitive chairman of the regents, George M. Shriver, quietly resigned. Obtaining an obscure position in the United States Department of Agriculture, Pearson tried to explain his case. Vainly he petitioned for an extension of his salary and a recognition of long-forgotten items from his expense account. Three years later he died, a thoroughly broken man.[73] "Shabby

[71]*Baltimore Sun,* 5-6 May 1935; 11 May 1935; 18 May 1935; *Diamondback,* 6 May 1935.
[72]Regents' Minutes, 28 June 1935; 10 July 1935; also executive sessions, 10, 17, 31 May 1935; 17 June 1935; *Baltimore Sun,* 28-30 May 1935; 1, 11, 17-25 June 1935; 29 June-5 July 1935; Lee, "The University Episode," 62-64.
[73]Regents' Minutes, 28 June 1935; 10 July 1935; 20 September 1935; Nice to Board, Nice File, Pearson Papers, Regents' Office; Pearson, "The Situation," 466-469; *Bulletin of the Medical School . . .,* XX (July, 1935), 70-71.

business," editorialized the *Baltimore Sun*, disturbed that Pearson's trusted assistant had somehow emerged to inherit his position.[74]

But in times of crisis history quickly buries its mistakes. The smiling, forward-looking "Curley" was in command, ready to harness for the University's welfare the vast faculty and student passion which had gone into his predecessor's overthrow. Students always felt like cheering when they saw him. Soon he caused everyone to forget the trials of the past.

[74]*Baltimore Sun*, 2 July 1935.

13

The Age of "Curley" Byrd

By 1935 American colleges and universities were again in ferment, unsatisfied with old compromises and sometimes more eager for change than concerned with the direction of that change. For almost twenty years—from depression to war to postwar affluence—institutions of higher learning veered off in contradictory directions. Some, like Chicago under Robert M. Hutchins and St. John's under Stringfellow Barr, experimented with great books and an almost medieval curriculum, while others allowed vocational specialization to reach the extremes of basketweaving and barkeeping. Minnesota emphasized life adjustment, Antioch pioneered a work-study program and Sarah Lawrence and Bennington abolished classes altogether. Expensive private institutions cultivated intellectual snobbery, while some of the huge state universities, operating like business corporations, turned out their products as if on an assembly line.

At College Park and Baltimore the change was largely quantitative as the once gallant little Maryland became the Terrible Terps. The president—almost everyone called him "Curley"—infused faculty and students with a thrilling sense of progress as he cashed in on vast New Deal construction projects, war-time training programs and especially the postwar enrollment boom. From 1935 to 1954 full-time enrollment at College Park and Baltimore rose from 3,400 to 15,700, the annual budget grew from $3,000,000 to more than $20,000,000, and the plant value soared from $5,000,000 to more than $65,000,000. When Byrd retired to run for governor, Maryland was one of the largest universities in the nation.

The rapid emergence of a giant university dramatized issues in higher education which made the president one of the most controversial figures of the day. Some were staggered by the financial burden of universities. When Maryland's enrollment approached 5,000 the *Baltimore Sun* declared flatly that "college education in America has been overdone."[1] Others disliked the implications of an "educational plant" as Byrd called it, with its standardized product, its highly centralized administration and its treatment of faculty as hired hands with wages set by the laws of the market place. Academically Maryland had to be judged by the standards of the finest universities in the world, and critics no longer had patience with arguments about growing pains. Other vast state universities faced similar problems, but Maryland's rapid rise, and the personality of its amazing president, made the institution a particular focus of controversy.

The Devil Hath Power

As a football star, observed one reporter, Byrd had been noted for tricky footwork, wide-open plays and the ability to come up smiling after a hard tackle. He had the hero's ability of turning the crowd's enthusiasm to the whole team while reminding people of his own magnanimity in the gesture. As president of the University these qualities sharpened. To students he was a superman who made Maryland great, to some of his faculty he was a dictator and an anti-intellectual, while to thousands of the small farmers served by his agricultural agencies he shared credit with the president of the United States for ending the depression. To the general assembly he was an irresistible seducer of public funds, to the *Baltimore Sun* he was a scheming empire builder and to himself

[1] *Baltimore Sun,* 12 September 1939.

he was a righteous builder of the American way. It was the day of
Huey Long and James Michael Curley, Franklin D. Roosevelt and
Douglas MacArthur; it was a day of powerful personalities, and
Harry Clifton Byrd was one of the most powerful men in Maryland
politics or in American education.[2]

Much of his power lay in his glamorous appearance and personal
magnetism. "The Devil hath power to assume a pleasing shape,"
said the College yearbook beneath his graduation picture, and many
years later national columnists called him "the handsomest figure
in American politics."[3] Coeds, farm wives and society ladies sighed
at his flashing smile, his athletic physique, his curly silver mane.
Long after he had retired from the University, even after he had
passed his seventieth year, high school girls who served as typists
in his Annapolis office hung mistletoe in the doorways and giggled
in expectation.

He loved people so sincerely that even hostile critics, if they
dared to talk with him, came away strangely charmed. He did not
toady to the views of others, did not catch them up in a great cause
and did not overwhelm or dominate; but somehow he was so warm,
so disarmingly frank and so righteously for anything that was right
that almost no one could withstand his personality. "If you can't
lead 'em, lick 'em," said Byrd, "if you can't lick 'em, join 'em; and
if you can't join 'em, seduce 'em."[4] While the editorial page of the
Baltimore Sun crackled with hostility, the editors found one reporter
after another falling under his spell. Finally, in 1937, they dispatched
to College Park the irascible H. L. Mencken, a man with a noted
resistance to charmers, but to their despair he concluded his articles
by suggesting, perhaps tongue-in-cheek, that the Johns Hopkins
University should be merged with the Byrd empire. "The thing to
do with a man of such talents," wrote Mencken, " is not to cuss
him for doing his job so well; it is far wiser, so long as hanging
him is unlawful, to give him a bigger and better one."[5]

Personally as well as publicly, Byrd's reputation combined acknowledged righteousness with suspected license. He shunned nico-
tine, alcohol and profanity; he collected Bibles and seemed to have

[2]Bob Considine, "Curley Byrd Catches the Worm," Saturday Evening Post, CCXIII (28
June 1941) , 14; Sidney Shalett, "Maryland's Busiest Byrd," Collier's, CXXVI (9 December 1950) , 33.

[3]Reveille [Student Annual], 1908, 31; Considine, "Curley Byrd," 14.

[4]Shalett, "Maryland's Busiest Byrd," 33.

[5]Baltimore Sun, 17 May-5 June 1937.

an apt Biblical quotation for every occasion. At the same time his good looks and freewheeling manner invited the kind of gossip, openly expressed in the *Diamondback,* which few college presidents could have withstood.[6] Divorced the year before he became president—a fact in itself enough to destroy many public figures—he made no secret of his liking for the companionship of pretty coeds, and as president he gaily escorted them to dances and made light insinuations about his amours at commencement exercises. He seemed to thrive on unsupported gossip. Girls involved in the stories were too flattered to deny them, and the president chuckled at the tattling and seemed to relish adding to it.[7]

Known almost everywhere by his nickname, he displayed a warm generosity and egalitarianism in personal contacts. Campus janitors, subsisting on depression wages, could expect a raise when "Mr. Curley" learned another child had come, and when a laborer's child was sick, the president was ready to reach into his pocket for a $10 bill. At pains to find jobs and scholarships for needy students, he kept no record of his personal loans to scores of them. Such stories are legion. During the 1920's a poor farm boy who worked as football manager to pay for his college board shared a room with the coach on a football trip. "Boy, is that the best suit of underwear you've got?" said Byrd. A week later, back at College Park, the boy discovered a bundle of new underwear in his locker, and at Christmas a $20 bill appeared in the same place. Too embarrassed to thank his benefactor, the boy much later became a prominent member of the University's staff.[8] As long as the campus was small enough to be influenced by personal contact, the president's popularity was assured.

Enemies always suspected ulterior motives. Eyeing his sharp deals for the University, they wondered about the millions of dollars in appropriations that flowed through his hands. In 1933, shortly before he became president, a shocked legislative committee learned that vice-president Byrd, in addition to his budgeted salary of $5,000, received an unlisted $4,000 as athletic director and $2,500 as coach, plus additional income as a sports columnist for the *Washington Star,* an officer of a local bank and a director of the College Park Realty Company. After careful and even hostile scrutiny, however,

[6]*Diamondback,* 1 May 1923; *Baltimore Sun,* 16 September 1930; 3 October 1930; 31 August 1934.
[7]Interviews with members of the faculty, 1959-1962.
[8]Interview with the person involved, 24 October 1961.

the investigating committee agreed that he was worth his full salary and more to the University, and that his nonacademic interests represented an imprudent overflow of energy, rather than a pecuniary indiscretion.[9] When he became president he relinquished all of his non-University interests and refused the house, car and chauffeur which the regents urged him to accept. Not until 1947 did they persuade him to raise his salary to a relatively modest $20,000 a year.[10] Byrd's home and his way of life were simple, and his personal financial jottings, strewn here and there through his private papers, were exceptional only for the extraordinary sums he gave away. Each year he received hundreds of letters from almost every racial and religious group in the state expressing thanks for the check he had sent them.[11] Whether the gifts arose from generosity or politics no one will ever know, and he is disarmingly frank in saying that he is not too sure himself.

Above all Byrd was a self-confident man with a record of triumphs that made self-confidence natural. He cultivated friendships with governors, senators, and occupants of the White House. Enemies called it egotism when he talked of the championships his teams would win, the millions he would obtain from the next legislature and the way "his" faculty would soon surpass Harvard's, but they were enemies because they feared he might succeed. Perhaps the greatest facet of his self-confidence, or egotism, was his absolute certainty that history would vindicate his entire career. His deepest philosophy supported this confidence: "No matter what may happen temporarily, right, in the long run, will survive and prevail," he said. "No matter what they may say about me, I always did what was right for the University."[12]

While critics conceded his sincerity and his love of the institution, many argued that he never knew what a university was, that he was basically anti-intellectual. He seldom displayed humility in determining a course of action, and he rarely used the fashionable academic words. English professors cringed at the slang and syntax of the one-time English instructor. The faculty noted that politicians,

[9][Milton L.] Veasey Report File, Pearson Papers, Board of Regents' Office, Baltimore; also *Baltimore Sun*, 10-17, 22-24 February and 29-30 March 1933.

[10]Minutes of the Board of Regents, 26 September 1947; this was raised to $22,500 in 1952.

[11]Byrd's personal and official papers are preserved in forty-eight 4-drawer filing cabinets in the attic of the Administration Building, College Park. See especially the Personal Files and the Contributions Files.

[12]Interview with Byrd, 16 November 1960; also Shalett, "Maryland's Busiest Byrd," 89.

generals and businessmen received honorary degrees and made commencement speeches more often than scholars. To many of the staff his political and educational views added up to contradictory attitudes rather than a coherent philosophy. Although professors are likely to be conservative or even aristocratic about academic excellence, they are frequently liberal, egalitarian and passionate defenders of civil liberties in regard to politics or academic administration. When Byrd seemed to reverse this pattern, the professors were alarmed. "College is not only for the intellectual," said the president. "In fact there are fewer jobs to be filled in our country by top intellectual types than by boys of fair academic proficiency who can get along with people."[13] Whether this revealed a profound difference of philosophy with that of the professors, or whether it revealed intellectual blindness, critics frequently thought that it indicated the latter. They talked condescendingly about a football coach miscast as a university president.

To the faculty these differences grew increasingly important as professors came to feel that they had no voice in determining policy. "I never take a step without consulting my men," said Byrd. "My philosophy about leadership is that a general shouldn't get too far out in front of his army, or he'll get shot."[14] But the professors did not fancy themselves "his men," the analogy of an army general violated the centuries old traditions which glorified the community of scholars, and some were not concerned whether or not he were shot. In 1948 Phi Beta Kappa refused to establish a chapter at Maryland largely because of "the autocratic powers" of the president and a faculty "which does not function at all as an academic body." In 1953 the Middle States Association of Colleges and Secondary Schools expressed dismay that the entire institution was simply "the lengthened shadow of President Byrd." The American Council on Education in 1947, and a private investigation made on Byrd's request in 1949 offered similar criticism.[15] The president, having

---

[13]Tim Cohane, "How Maryland Became a Football Power," *Look,* XVIII (2 November 1954), 54.

[14]Considine, "Curley Byrd," 48.

[15]Carl Billman [Officer of Phi Beta Kappa] to Byrd, 30 July 1948, Phi Beta Kappa File, Byrd Papers; *Evaluation Report for the Commission on Institutions of Higher Learning of the Middle State Association of Colleges and Secondary Schools . . . 1953* (Washington, 1953), 9; *Higher Education in Maryland, A Report of a Survey by the American Council on Education with Recommendations of the Maryland Commission on Higher Education* (Washington, 1947), 240-241; R. B. Stewart, "Administrative Problems and Procedures, University of Maryland, 1949," 3, mimeographed report in the President's

learned academic procedure in a small institution when personal contacts insured democracy, never acknowledged that an institution might grow too large for his method of administration. With his office always open to callers, he never understood the charge of autocracy and never understood why complex machinery should be created to make the right decisions which he was making anyway.[16]

But whatever people thought of Byrd, no one doubted his political wizardry. His skill as a lobbyist had first attracted him to Woods and Pearson; and as president he wheedled, bamboozled and charmed more people out of more money than anyone in the state's history. Corporations, alumni and well-wishers provided handsome gifts to the institution. The federal government, at least for a time, gave more money per capita to Maryland for higher education than to any state in the Union except Massachusetts.[17] From the state legislature came most. Even considering that the University had far to go in catching up with other state institutions when Byrd took over, his spectacular successes left admiring friends and horrified critics in common breathless dismay.

According to one typical story, a conservative finance committee once cut the University's request with the logical explanation about an empty treasury. To this tactical maneuver Byrd answered smoothly, "If the money isn't available, naturally you can't provide it. If you did have it, of course you'd be happy to vote for such a necessary purpose, wouldn't you?" "Of course," the committee replied complaisantly. Next day Byrd reappeared armed with data supplied by his own Bureau of Business and Economic Research. "Gentlemen, you told me yesterday that if unallocated money were to turn up, you'd be glad to vote the full amount," he purred. "Well, I've been checking some figures and I know you'll be happy to learn that the state receipts from wine and whiskey taxes have exceeded the estimates by more than half a million dollars." According to the story, he got the money.[18]

Office, College Park. Hereafter cited Middle States Association, *Evaluation Report;* American Council on Education, *Higher Education in Maryland;* Stewart, "Administrative Problems."

[16]For a defense against the charge of autocracy see *Baltimore Sun,* 12 October 1954; *Diamondback,* 29 October 1954.

[17]United States Department of Interior, *Biennial Survey of Education, 1934-1936,* 2 vols. (Washington, 1939), II, 32.

[18]This story related by Shalett, "Maryland's Busiest Byrd," 33, 85. The maneuver can also be followed in the *Baltimore Sun,* February-March 1937 and February 1939.

With all of his maneuvering and bargaining, Byrd considered candor his greatest quality. He mused frankly about political success:

> I say to those fellows at Annapolis, "Do you want us to do a good job?" And I prove to them that anything short of what I'm asking will reflect discredit on the state. I appeal to pride. Sure, it's hard work. Sometimes I'm not sure whether the presidency is a promotion or demotion from my coaching job.
>
> Ah, but it's all a game. You outguess a fellow in this end of college work just as you outguess him in the sports end. Running a school is pretty much like deciding on a football system. You make sure you've got something that's right, and readily understood by the men you're aiming at. And then nothing can stop you! All I ask for at Annapolis is that they give me a good hearing. Then I show them that I've got something solid to talk about.[19]

The strategist of the gridiron and the campus was born in 1889 in the tiny Eastern Shore fishing village of Crisfield. The Byrds had been oystermen there since the seventeenth century and were many times removed, genealogically and socially, from the aristocratic Byrds of Virginia. His father, who left the fishing boats to sell oysters, was elected county commissioner and then delegate to the general assembly, but died at an early age leaving a large family. In the local school "Curley" did well with his mind and his fists, and on the advice of his principal went to the Maryland Agricultural College to study engineering. Like many bright boys, he qualified as a sophomore when he entered. He graduated in 1908, nineteen years old, second in his class and noted for his popularity with girls.

In college, athletics quickly became the center of his life. He was not an all-American and did not invent the forward pass as legend later had it, but he was a first-rate halfback and team captain. Even more noted as a baseball pitcher and track star, he established statewide intercollegiate records which lasted until long after he became president. For three years after graduation Byrd became what was known as a "ringer," playing football for whatever college would make it worth his while. The practice, more or less legal then, enabled him to obtain a smattering of graduate training in law and journalism, as well as numerous athletic letters from Georgetown, George Washington and Western Maryland. In the spring of each year he played professional baseball for teams like Hagerstown and Cambridge and, in 1910, signed with the Chicago White Sox who

[19]Cited by Considine, "Curley Byrd," 48; similar quotations in interviews with Byrd, 5 November 1959 and 16 November 1960.

farmed him out to the San Francisco Seals. There he met the famous gambler and promoter, Tex Rickard, who felt the boy was too smart for baseball and urged him to find a better career. Back in Washington Byrd obtained a $50 a week job as a playground director, using his evenings to write sports stories for the *Washington Star* and his spare afternoons to coach for Western High School. According to legend he especially liked to take his high school boys out to drub the Agricultural College in practice scrimmages.[20]

By the fall of 1912 Byrd had persuaded President Silvester to hire him as an instructor of English and athletics. Maryland teams suddenly began to win and students idolized him. At last he had found his career, not simply as a coach, for his ambition was far larger than that. His new career was the institution itself. Promoting himself and the University of Maryland were identical, and probably even he could not have separated his personal ambition from his sense of service. As a coach he was noted for fine sportsmanship as well as for victories. He created an outstanding intramural program, assisted the alumni to organize an athletic board to support the teams financially and in 1921 helped to found the Southern Conference which became a national model for the control of intercollegiate sports. On campus he became a sort of unofficial dean of men, a friend to almost every student and the moving spirit behind almost every organization. In 1921 he gave the *Diamondback* its name. When in 1923 a new football stadium was completed across the boulevard on the present fraternity circle, the students and alumni petitioned that it be named "Curley Byrd Stadium," but most people simply called it "The Byrd Cage." He never lost his attention to details of University life. In 1933 he adopted a mascot for the University, the Terrapin or Terp, sometimes called "Testudo." When the Chapel was dedicated in 1952 and no hymn seemed suitably nondenominational, he promptly wrote the words for one himself.[21]

Meanwhile the coach was making himself known outside the athletic realm. In the tiny, struggling institution of the 1910's when each professor also served as promoter and lobbyist, Byrd was espe-

[20]For details of career, Personal Files and Biographical File, Byrd Papers; *Reveille, 1906,* 48; *Reveille, 1907,* 172; *Reveille, 1908,* 31, 123-125, 139; *Reveille, 1913,* 112-113; *Diamondback,* 12 January 1922; 19 November 1934; 16 September 1935; Minutes of the Board of Regents, 21 February 1936; *Baltimore Sun,* 5 December 1937; Morris A. Bealle, *Kings of American Football . . .* (Washington, 1952), 56-74 and ff.

[21]Bealle, *Kings of American Football,* 68-99; see student annuals and student newspaper, *passim; Diamondback,* 15 May 1923; 13 June 1923; *Maryland Alumni Magazine,* XVIII (September, 1947), 30-31; interview, Alfred H. Danneger, 29 October 1965.

cially effective with his alumni contacts and his political acumen. Sometimes as errand boy for the president and sometimes on his own, he went about attracting prospective students, buttonholing legislators, speaking to every civic group that would give him a hearing and charming everyone within earshot. In 1918 Woods named him "assistant to the president." When Byrd became a leading spokesman for unification with the Baltimore schools, wags claimed that "Curley" was building a University his teams could be proud of. The unpopular, indecisive and often-vacationing Pearson became the perfect foil for the ambitious assistant whose role expanded rapidly from publicist to spokesman. Pearson was jealous of his popular rival and objected when the regents named him vice-president in 1932, but at the same time the president leaned increasingly upon him. By then there were more jokes about Byrd's future than about his past accomplishments; friends called him "the governor."[22]

The same methods that brought success also brought enemies and near-disasters to the rapidly rising football coach. The Amateur Athletic Union castigated his semi-professional status as a student, and when he was first employed at Maryland several professors expressed doubt about his qualifications for faculty status. Soon after his appointment as the president's assistant, one of the regents complained that he "has more or less butted in and assumed a semi-dictation under his title."[23] In 1924 Governor Ritchie took offense at one of Byrd's speeches and was ready to force his dismissal from the University, but Byrd's apologies were so artful that within a month he had parlayed the episode into a first-name-basis friendship and a seat in the governor's box at the Kentucky Derby.[24] A few years later he obtained $20,000 from the tight-fisted Ritchie for a field house by promising that the athletic board would raise the remainder. When the board failed, the state had to appropriate the rest or forfeit the completed building. Although the *Baltimore Sun* howled that Byrd had planned it that way all along, Ritchie reluctantly approved the additional appropriation, and Byrd turned it all into a triumph by graciously naming the building for the governor.[25] Political sleight of hand, gossip about women, investigation

[22]Minutes of the Board of Regents, 13 May 1927; 14 September 1928; 15 February 1929; 23 January 1931; 27 May 1932; *Baltimore Sun,* 7 February 1926; 7 May 1935.

[23]Charles C. Gelden to A. F. Woods, 3 June 1922, Woods Papers, McKeldin Library.

[24]See Ritchie-Byrd Correspondence, especially Ritchie to Byrd, 3 June 1922, in "Governor's Correspondence, University of Maryland, 1920-1930," Albert C. Ritchie Papers, Hall of Records, Annapolis; *Baltimore Sun,* 31 May-4 June 1922.

[25]*Baltimore Sun,* 21 January 1932; 10-11 February 1933; Ritchie to Byrd, 16 May 1932,

into his various salaries, accusations of cabal when Pearson resigned: Byrd always seemed to be one step ahead, turning calamity into greater triumphs.

From July, 1935, when he took over as acting president, until February, 1936, when he became president in his own right, the controversy over Byrd's qualifications was public and frank. Hundreds of enthusiastic followers pointed to his acknowledged achievements, and a smaller number of critics pointed to his near-disasters. A student petition with 1700 signatures urged his permanent appointment, alumni deluged the regents and the newspapers with letters of support and a large majority of the faculty supported the appointment with the general observation that he had "broadened enormously" since his days as a coach. On the other side was the *Baltimore Sun* and the quiet opposition of faculty members who did not care to speak publicly. When his permanent appointment finally came, two of the nine regents requested that their names be recorded in opposition. By that time, however, the changes on the campus were already so far-reaching that the appointment was a foregone conclusion.[26]

The New Deal and Money

As if a dam had burst, the acting president's incredible luck and masterful maneuvering began to pay off from the moment he took over. Behind all of Pearson's difficulties lay economic stringency, but within three months of his resignation money seemed almost plentiful. Frequently Byrd was simply lucky. While the hapless Pearson prepared his resignation, the regents discovered that an unknown Baltimore philanthropist, Frank C. Bressler, had left the institution over $1,000,000. Almost simultaneously Governor Nice agreed to dip into his contingency fund to restore most of the cuts which the legislature had ordered in Maryland's annual budget. A few weeks later came word that Congress had approved the Bankhead-Jones Act which gave the University $100,000 annually. Then

Governor's Correspondence, Box 8006 (15), 1931-1935, Ritchie Papers, Hall of Records, Annapolis; Minutes of the Regents, 13 February 1931; 11 December 1931.

[26]Minutes of the Regents, 20 September 1935; 15 November 1935; 21 February 1936; *Diamondback*, 23 September 1935; 2 December 1935; *Baltimore Sun*, 4, 6, 11 July 1935; 5-6, 21-22 February 1936.

Byrd announced that Roosevelt's Public Works Administration had approved a large grant for campus buildings. Much of the extra money, perhaps most of it, would have come to any university president, for the economy was finally improving, the New Deal was reaching high gear and universities everywhere were looking up. Even though people realized that Pearson was unlucky and Byrd lucky, they were inclined to give the new man credit for providing the institution with a new sign under the zodiac.

Although Byrd had nothing to do with acquiring the Bressler grant, he used the funds brilliantly to revitalize the medical school. Frank C. Bressler had spent a quiet life as a Baltimore physician and had invested his inheritance wisely. A graduate of the old College of Physicians and Surgeons which merged with the University, he was keenly aware of the plight of medical education and particularly of the fact that specialized graduate training demanded vastly expensive research apparatus. Since the days of Cordell the medical school had been the only branch of the University actively seeking endowment and numerous gifts ranging up to $10,000 had come to the school and hospital, but Bressler's gift was by far the largest. Taking only one-fourth of the bequest, Byrd obtained matching funds from the state and federal governments so that, by 1940, the medical schools had a fine, six-story laboratory and research building across from the hospital, with the Bressler capital still largely intact for maintenance, research projects and faculty salaries.[27]

Actively the president pursued other private funds, acquiring some $100,000 each year from individual and corporation gifts, foundation grants and private research contracts. In addition, a year after he became president he obtained $150,000 from a New York industrialist friend, Charles E. McManus. Three years later he acquired the splendid Clarence J. Grieves library of dental science. Most spectacular of all, after several years of giving special courses to train aircraft workers, in 1944 the University acquired $1,700,000, later raised to $4,900,000, from a Baltimore aircraft manufacturer, Glenn L. Martin.[28]

More important than gifts was the money from federal grants.

[27]*Bulletin of the School of Medicine, University of Maryland,* XX (July, 1935), 25; XXII (July, 1937), 42-43; XXIV (January, 1940), 139-141; XXV (July, 1940), 1-4; *Baltimore Sun,* 23 May 1935; Medical Building File, Bressler File, Byrd Papers.
[28]Gifts File, McManus File, Grieves File, Martin File, Byrd Papers; Minutes of the Regents, 21 January 1938; 22 September 1938; 23 June 1938; 18 December 1942; 15 December 1944; 18 January 1946; 26 January 1956.

Although nearly every institution benefited from the burgeoning New Deal expenditures, great leeway remained for a politically astute university administration to cash in on the wide range of opportunities. As one of the land-grant colleges, Maryland obtained over $100,000 annually from the Bankhead-Jones Act of 1935 which was designed to rescue the faltering farm economy by strengthening work in agricultural education, extension and experimentation. Other New Deal acts gave Byrd greater opportunity to use his political skill for special benefits. When the Civilian Conservation Corps was organized, he not only channeled about $2,000,000 in conservation work through the Board of Forestry which was then under the University, but also made the University a regional headquarters for CCC instructors. The CCC, in turn, provided the University with an unusual $50,000 in campus landscaping. When the National Youth Administration was created to keep students in school, Byrd not only obtained a generous share for Maryland students, approximately $40,000 annually, but during the war he managed to make the University a depository for great quantities of special NYA training equipment. For a time almost a quarter of Maryland's students received NYA wages for part-time work in the libraries, laboratories or dining hall, or as clerical help in professors' offices. Without such financial assistance hundreds of students would not have obtained an education and, incidentally, the University greatly benefited from their labor.[29]

By persistence, by political pressure and by charming everyone in Washington who would give him a hearing, Byrd helped the University to profit especially from the New Deal's two great construction agencies, the Public Works Administration and the Works Progress Administration. Although it is almost impossible to determine exact figures, the University's appropriation of approximately $3,000,000 was one of the largest made to any educational institution. The first grant came within weeks of Byrd's temporary appointment, and within a year had grown to almost $1,000,000. As he pressed for a second $1,000,000 late in 1937, the politically conservative Byrd published a fifty-page defense of New Deal spending policies. With a Congressional election in the near future, political advisor James M. Farley wrote to President Roosevelt: "It would be an excellent idea if you would see President Byrd. . . . He comes nearer having a

[29]Minutes of the Regents, 11 October 1935; 7 May 1937; Budget—1935 File, Civilian Conservation Corps File, United States—N.Y.A. File, Byrd Papers.

'machine' in Maryland than anyone else and is decidedly friendly."[30] A few days later Byrd was seen emerging from a back door of the White House, and soon came word that the University's full request, plus a little more, had been approved. As if to seal a bargain Mrs. Roosevelt appeared on the campus for a major address.[31]

But Roosevelt was also a shrewd trader and, in August, 1938, observers believed they saw the other side of the bargain when Byrd announced his opposition to the re-election to the senate of the anti-New Dealer, Millard E. Tydings. Speaking as if the words hurt him, Byrd invited Roosevelt to join him at Crisfield to launch a "purge" of his old friend and classmate who had been one of the University's firmest supporters. Many alumni were disturbed for the first time at Byrd's maneuvers. Many questioned whether the money was worth the methods employed, and in the alumni organization a motion to censure him was barely defeated. Two weeks later Roosevelt's yacht docked at Crisfield where Byrd welcomed him ashore as inconspicuously as possible. When Tydings won the election, the University president quickly sent him a letter of congratulations. During the next few years Byrd continued to use Tydings' support, along with Roosevelt's friendship, to obtain a third $1,000,000 in PWA and WPA funds for campus construction.[32] In addition, the University supervised the spending of still another $1,000,000 in WPA funds for recreation facilities, fine arts projects, concerts and historical restorations throughout the state.[33]

Besides receiving outright grants from the federal government, Byrd attracted large federal agencies to College Park in hopes of coordinating them with University courses. Soon after taking over, he announced that the Bureau of Mines had accepted twenty acres of campus land on which to build a research center for nonmetallic minerals. A few months later Maryland provided land for a national fisheries and wildlife research laboratory. For a time both agencies cooperated with the University by providing fellowships and allowing graduate students to work in their laboratories, but the planned schools of mining and ichthyology never developed at Maryland.[34]

[30]Farley to Roosevelt, 27 December 1937, Roosevelt Papers, Hyde Park. Photostats of material in the Roosevelt Papers relating to this incident are located in the Maryland Room, McKeldin Library, College Park.

[31]*Baltimore Sun,* 7 January 1938; 6 April 1938; 14 April 1938; 25-26 August 1938.

[32]*Ibid.,* 27, 30 August 1938; 1, 5-6 September 1938; Byrd to Tydings, 3 November 1938 and ff., Tydings File; United States—W.P.A. File, Byrd Papers.

[33]United States—W.P.A. File, Byrd Papers; *Baltimore Sun,* 1 September 1939; Minutes of the Regents, 15 September 1939; 15 May 1942.

[34]Bureau of Mines File, Bureau of Fisheries File; Byrd Papers.

Byrd chortled at his triumph in getting the agencies to the campus:

> Wow! Did Massachusetts and Colorado raise Cain! But why should
> they? Plain horse sense will tell you that these research bureaus
> belonged here rather than where they were. I told them in Washing-
> ton that the stations could be more centrally located and close to
> Washington, so that visiting experts could see them. Horse sense.[35]

Of all sources of money the state legislature offered Byrd the greatest opportunity and the greatest ultimate triumphs, even though
obtaining the money required educating the state in the basic facts
of university finance. Lacking a long heritage of a state-supported
university, and long under the influence of Governor Ritchie, the
general assembly had never fully assumed its responsibility to the
institution, and neither Woods' scholarly logic nor Pearson's compromises had forced it to face that responsibility. Byrd was prepared for a more drastic approach.

Opposition to adequate state support stemmed not so much from
any political faction as from the powerful *Sunpapers* of Baltimore,
the heirs of the Ritchie philosophy and the rallying point for almost
every conservative cause in the state. One of the finest newspaper
organizations in the country, its integrity was equalled only by its
tenacity and once opposed to Byrd it never let go. Legislators inclined to support the University winced at the thought, "What are
the newspapers going to say?"[36] In part the *Sun's* opposition stemmed
from its loyalty to the John Hopkins University, in part from a
jealous regard for the state treasury and in part from a fundamental
suspicion of higher education for the masses. Above all, however, the
newspaper disliked Byrd personally and politically, ridiculing his
lack of scholarly ideals and direfully predicting that his ambition
would lead to the governorship. In its opposition the *Sun* more than
any other factor created an aura of invincibility around its villain,
for its talk of a "political machine" only helped to build that machine. Never admitting that Byrd's victories might confirm the logic
of his views, the *Sun* preferred to explain his triumphs as a spell of
magic.[37]

Convicing Governor Nice, a Republican, to restore $78,000 of the
$90,000 in budget cuts within weeks after Byrd took over seemed

[35]Cited in Considine, "Curley Byrd," 48.
[36]Quoted in *Baltimore Sun*, 30 January 1941.
[37]For example, *Baltimore Sun* editorials, 20-29 March 1924; 29 February 1936; 3 September 1937; 7 April 1938; 5, 22-23 May 1938; 25 August 1938; 12 September 1939; 20
January 1941; 26 January 1946; 18 July 1948; 12-23 January 1949; 25 February 1950;
31 October 1954.

wizardry enough, but the sorcerer's masterpiece came in the 1937 legislature. Calmly he asked for a 65 percent rise in the University's operating expenses, to about $1,250,000, plus another $1,250,000 for construction. After obtaining Nice's support for part of the increase, Byrd descended upon the legislature to wheedle the rest. With charts and a pointer he lectured finance committees by the hour, until they realized that he probably knew more about state finances than any legislator in Annapolis, and that he had prepared an entire state budget around the University bill. Using the argument that one large appropriation "will be ample for many years to come," Byrd brilliantly isolated critics, tied his own bills to popular riders, bargained for special unbudgeted funds and deluged legislators with telegrams at the proper psychological moment. When the Commissioner of Motor Vehicles agreed to a reduction in funds, even the *Sunpapers* failed to notice the apparent payoff a few months later when the University opened a special school for highway patrolmen. And when, at the last moment, the Byrd forces came up with a long-range retirement system for all state employees, reporters debated whether Byrd was giving something more to recalcitrant legislators or obtaining something more for University employees. As the session ended incredulous observers calculated that the University had probably obtained more than it had asked. No one could be certain as to the exact total.[38]

When the assembly met in 1939, 1941 and 1943, it was sometimes hard for Byrd to make the legislators forget that their earlier appropiration was to have been "ample for many years to come." Although his later triumphs were less spectacular than his first, each year's total budget rose significantly above the preceding one. When Herbert R. O'Conor, a Democrat, replaced Nice in 1941, the friendly relations between the governor and the University continued unbroken, and even the *Baltimore Sun* began to take the rising appropriation for granted. The state still assumed only 30 percent of the total cost of operating the institution, one of the lowest percentages for any state university in the country.[39]

When Byrd attempted to reorganize certain state agencies more

[38]Nice File, Retirement Bill File, General Assembly—1937 File, Byrd Papers; Minutes of the Regents, 11 October 1935; 16 April 1937; 28 July 1937; 29 September 1937; 18 February 1938; *Baltimore Sun*, 31 January 1937; 11 February 1937; 5-25 March 1937; 14 April 1937; 21 September 1937.

[39]O'Conor File, General Assembly Files for 1939, 1941, 1943, Byrd Papers; United States Office of Education, *Biennial Summary of Education in the United States, 1944-1946* (Washington, 1947), Chap. IV, 20-36.

firmly under University control, the opposition proved more substantial. Eager to cash in on the rising sentiment for conservation, convinced that any agency ran more smoothly under his control and certain that almost any agency could be coordinated with the University for the benefit of higher education, Byrd demanded that the State Board of Forestry and the State Economic and Geological Survey be moved from Baltimore to College Park. Both were already officially supervised by the University, but over the years they had grown apart with their own never-questioned budgets and their own independent-minded supervisors. When those supervisors objected to Byrd's attempt to seize control, the Baltimore newspapers promptly magnified the episode. With some justice the editors accused Byrd of empire building, and with some demagoguery they accused him of reaching out to control "all State employees" in order to build his "political machine." From late 1938 to early 1941 the battle raged fiercely as Nice and O'Conor supported first one side and then the other. Finally the legislature settled the matter, establishing the two agencies under a Conservation Council, entirely independent of the University. Byrd had lost the battle, and the *Baltimore Sun* gloated, but when the University obtained another record-breaking appropriation from the 1941 legislature, some observers commented that the University president had struck a good bargain.[40]

One conspicuous display of the University's new prosperity lay in the new construction which cost approximately $4,000,000:

MAJOR CONSTRUCTION, 1935-1945[41]

1936   213 acres of land at College Park—$22,000.

1937   H. J. Patterson Hall—$321,000.
      Anne Arundel Dormitory—$200,000.

1938   Montgomery County Experiment Station Farm—$44,000.
      Barns, silos, etc.—$250,000.
      University Hospital—$2,984,000 (obtained earlier).

1939   Francis Scott Key Building, (except east wing)—$219,000.

1940   Administration Building—$234,000.
      Rossborough Inn remodeled—$70,000.
      Bressler Building, Baltimore—$472,000.

[40]Maryland-Forestry Department File, Nice File, O'Conor File, Byrd Papers; *Baltimore Sun*, 20-24 October 1939; 1-2, 29 November 1939; 3, 17, 25 May 1940; 13-14 June 1940; 13-14 October 1940; 29-30 May 1941.

[41]University of Maryland, *Financial Report for the Fiscal Year Ending June 30, 1952* (College Park, 1953), 113-122; see buildings by name in Construction File, Byrd Papers. Costs are approximations, sometimes including subsequent remodeling.

Washington and Howard Dormitories—$209,000.

Symons Hall, south wing—$196,000.

Margaret Brent Hall—$237,000.

Gymnasium and Administration Buildings, Princess Anne—$212,000.

1942 Shriver Laboratory—$116,000.

1943 Dormitory, Princess Anne—$131,000.

1944 Reckord Armory—$457,000.

Harford, Prince Georges and Kent Dormitories—$413,000.

While critics complained that the new buildings were designed more to impress travelers along the highway than to serve the occupants, the structures generally combined taste and maximum utility. Especially during Byrd's earliest years construction costs were modest compared to the growth of the academic budget, for he was careful that building did not overshadow internal developments.

The New Deal and Education

What goes on in the classrooms of a large university between hundreds of professors and thousands of students is not so much the product of an administration, however powerful, as it is the product of an age. At Maryland, and throughout the country, educational philosophy underwent fundamental transformations as faculty and students reached for new kinds of knowledge, more practical applications and more pertinent meanings in the lessons which, over the generations, had gone stale. Anyone could look about and see what philosophers had been saying for some time—that the world of Newton, John Locke and Adam Smith, even the world of Woodrow Wilson, J. P. Morgan and Herbert Hoover was in shambles. Whether or not it was great literature, every freshman English instructor knew that John Steinbeck waked up his classes while Ralph Waldo Emerson put them to sleep. Whether or not neatly organized fields of study were upset, almost every course in the universities had to make way for new concepts of men like Peirce, Planck and Picasso.

Although many professors hardly realized it, the educational outlook of John Dewey was making headway in the colleges for the first time. Pleading for a closer identity between education and experience, he urged the schools and colleges to face forthrightly the questions facing society. He was less concerned with instilling a body of information, however sacred, than in helping man face the problems of life. He called for breaking down the traditional barriers between disciplines, focusing on the applicability of knowledge, emphasizing the contextual nature of truth and the gradual rebuilding of present day society by the application of intellect to social problems. Advocates of courses in great books, in barkeeping, in life adjustment and advocates of no courses at all looked, correctly or incorrectly, to Dewey for inspiration. Although some of the concepts seemed vague in theory and were easily perverted in practice, they had highly specific application in the individual schools and departments of the University.

In the University's Baltimore schools, progressive education brought a shift from theoretical to practical courses, from education for private practice to education for public service and a shift in emphasis from teaching in the classroom to learning in the laboratory, the clinic and the courtroom. Under Dean Robert U. Patterson, the School of Medicine changed its emphasis from diagnosis to healing, back to what an earlier generation would have condemned as empiricism. The school placed new emphasis on research, public health, industrial medicine and extension work. It added departments of cardiology and psychiatry to deal specifically with two common disorders that physicians had once considered virtually beyond their care. Dentistry under Dean J. Ben Robinson raised its clinical professors to full equality with lecturers. It utilized visual aids such as slides and moving pictures, introduced its students to hospital work and placed new emphasis on research, preventive dentistry, specialties and extension work which reached to both graduate dentists and the public. Under Dean A. G. DuMez, Pharmacy stressed the business side of manufacturing and distributing drugs. Miss Annie Crighton in Nursing emphasized sociology, public health and community nurses' training. The School of Law, headed by Dean Roger Howell, extended its use of the case method, introduced a legal aid clinic and launched a student-edited law review. In legal theory, professors ceased to look upon law as a changeless body of sacred precedent and accepted the doctrine that law was a creation of society and that each generation must develop new precedents.[42]

Among the professional schools at College Park that of Education

[42]See biennial reports of individual schools in *Biennial Report of the University of Maryland . . . 1934-1936; Biennial Report . . . 1936-1938; Biennial Report . . . 1938-1940; Biennial Report . . . 1940-1942, passim;* also, *Catalogues, passim.*

was one of the fastest growing and certainly the most consciously im-
bued with the Dewey influence. Although critics claimed, even then,
that the courses multiplied unreasonably and that the new emphasis
sacrificed thoroughness and discipline, the two Deans of Education,
W. S. Small and Harold Benjamin, were respected as two of the
strongest men on the campus. Much of the work in Home Economics,
Physical Education, Agriculture and Engineering came under the
supervision of the School of Education. Dean Marie Mount in Home
Economics, Deans H. J. Patterson, Thomas B. Symons and Harold
F. Cotterman in Agriculture, and Dean S. Sidney Steinberg in Engineering all helped their schools to add a multitude of practical
courses which frequently overlapped those of other schools. All
attempted to provide a firm base in general education, but to guide
advanced courses away from the ivory tower into closer association
with industrial and government agencies.[43]

President Byrd, boldly embracing many of the new educational
concepts, eagerly supported the movement for applied courses and
was particularly fascinated with the prospect of combining disciplines. In 1938 the College of Commerce reappeared under Dean
W. Mackenzie Stevens. Four years later—convinced that political
science, economics and geography provided a common base for both
commercial and government administration—Byrd merged these
departments with commerce, reorganizing it under Dean J. Freeman
Pyle as the College of Business and Public Administration. Some of
the president's schemes never developed, such as the much publicized
Institute of Transport, the Institute of Geo-Politics, and the Institute of the Problems of Democracy. Even in the area of University
administration, Byrd crossed the lines dividing colleges by creating
five overlapping "divisions"—for humanities, social sciences, physical
sciences, natural sciences and lower division studies. Although
critics claimed the divisions complicated administration and needlessly weakened the colleges, the catalogue used the most up-to-date
language, about "related departments of study who are faced with
common problems and need for an exchange of experience in refer-
ence to progress underway."[44]

The College of Arts and Sciences also felt the powerful new curriculum influences. In the humanities professors emphasized social

[43]*Ibid.*
[44]S. M. Wedeberg and Dudley Dillard, "History of the College of Business and Public
Administration . . ." (Pamphlet, Maryland Room, McKeldin Library), 18-25; Files
for various institutes by name, Byrd Papers; *Catalogue, 1949-1950,* 45.

criticism. In English and foreign language courses, for example, the biographies of "great" writers and the memorization of "great" poems became less important than the appreciation of ideas which had special pertinence to the present. The social sciences enjoyed particular prestige, doubling and tripling their faculty and enrollment. Historians discovered that truth was relative to each generation, and many decided that social and economic interpretations were most meaningful to their own. Political scientists, transferred from Arts and Sciences to the more practical business school, talked less about such abstractions as "sovereignty" and more about specific matters that could be analyzed statistically, such as political power and pressure groups. Economists, also connected with the business school, discovered John Maynard Keynes and stressed new courses, such as "Comparative Economic Systems" and "Social Control of Business." In mathematics and the sciences, where the old absolutes had first begun to crumble, professors talked increasingly of probabilities.

The College of Arts and Sciences, headed successively from 1935 to 1945 by Thomas Hardy Taliaferro, L. B. Broughton, and J. Freeman Pyle, received the particular attention of the new University president. Aware of the criticism against his predecessor, Byrd, especially during his earlier years, took pains to emphasize the purely academic functions of the institution. The greatest increase in the large 1938 budget went to Arts and Sciences for expanding faculty, course offerings, standards, laboratory and library facilities. "Our first thought," said Byrd in his first interview as president, "is to improve greatly our work in the humanities." Anxious to improve teaching quality, he requested the arts and science department heads to submit reports on what they were doing to improve pedagogical procedures. For a time one of the president's greatest enthusiasms was the library. Declaring "we shall pay whatever is necessary," he sought "the very best" librarian in the country, and from DePauw University he secured Carl W. Hintz who briefly obtained an almost unlimited acquisitions budget.[45]

To secure and retain the best possible faculty for its money, the University avoided fixed salary scales and across-the-board raises but let it be known that it would compete with almost any salary scale.

[45]*Biennial Reports . . ., passim; Financial Report . . . 1938*, 17; *Catalogues, passim; Baltimore Sun*, 7 July 1935; Arts and Sciences File, Publicity—1935 File, Teaching Improvements File, Library File, Byrd Papers.

While some full professors received $3,100 annually, others received as much as $7,000.[46] During Byrd's first three years the University employed 48 new men with the Ph.D. degree. While the total number of full-time faculty members at College Park increased from 130 in 1934, to 263 in 1941, the number of doctorates on the staff increased from 44 to 119. A few years later an outside evaluating committee expressed frank surprise that the University ranked "in the highest 5 percent of . . . accredited institutions" in the amount of graduate training possessed by its faculty members. The same report noted that the amount of scholarly publication by the faculty ranked it among the top 15 percent of accredited institutions, averaging .364 books and 2.87 articles for each faculty member every four years.[47] Among the outstanding research scholars were Tobias Danzig and Monroe H. Martin who served successively as head of mathematics; John E. Younger, head of mechanical engineering; George F. Corcoran, head of electrical engineering; Nathan L. Drake, head of chemistry; and Morley A. Jull, head of poultry. Many outstanding men, of course, were not administrators. Far down in the ranks was the sociologist, C. Wright Mills. The history department alone included briefly such famous names as Frank Freidel, Kenneth Stampp and Richard Hofstadter.

For the first time in its history the University was under no pressure to coax students to the institution by publicity and easy standards. With jobs scarce and the NYA helping to keep students in school, more wanted to attend than could be accommodated, and the University used this pressure to raise quality. While students clamored especially for admission to medicine, dentistry, pharmacy and law, Byrd encouraged these schools in their desire to reduce the number of young men entering the professions. Admission standards and tuition fees so increased that the total Baltimore enrollment actually declined from about 1,400 in 1935 to about 1,200 in 1940. A similar tightening of standards came at College Park as the University adopted a new rule requiring students to pass 50 percent of their work each semester or be expelled. The president upbraided professors, departments and entire colleges if their grades ran consistently above a normal grade curve. Still, the pressure pushed enrollment from 2,000 in 1935 to 3,500 in 1940 to almost 4,000 dur-

[46]Personnel File, Faculty File, Arts and Sciences File, Promotions File, Byrd Papers; University of Maryland, Budget for 1934-35, Budget for 1938-1939, Budget for 1944-1945, in Comptroller's Office, College Park.
[47]American Council on Education, *Higher Education in Maryland*, 169-175.

ing the war. The fastest growth came in the Graduate School which was turning out well over a dozen Ph.D.'s and a score of M.A.'s each year.[48]

Although there was no necessary correlation between scholastic standards and winning football teams, Byrd took care to quiet the fears about his coaching background. He held intercollegiate athletics within rigid bounds, and Maryland's football record from 1935 to 1946—51 wins, 56 losses and 6 ties—was the poorest since he arrived on the campus as a student.[49]

Just as the University was surging ahead in so many areas and as the depression was giving way to prosperity, World War II required that education be mobilized for the national cause. As late as December, 1939, a poll showed that ten percent of the College Park students hoped that Germany would win the war, and another ten percent had no preference. By the following winter, however, America was beginning to face reality, the University was adjusting to new conditions and students were worrying about the draft. Byrd persuaded the Civil Aeronautics Authority to locate one of its training schools at College Park for students who wished to take government-financed courses in their spare time. The University, fully up to date with its spirit of progressive education, launched new courses in explosives, fire control, aircraft design, modern languages and geography, as well as a special summer course for Martin Aircraft Company foremen. The ROTC staff increased from six to thirteen. "Military Day," replete with mock battles, became a featured spring festival.[50]

When Pearl Harbor came in December, 1941, the University was ready for more drastic change. Immediately the regents announced that the institution would operate for the duration on a three-semester, year-round basis and that faculty members would be required to remain at their posts throughout the summer for a nominal salary of about $150. Since year-round teaching constituted a wartime service, the raises "should be considered more in the nature

[48]*Baltimore Sun*, 7, 16 July 1935; 23 February 1936; *Biennial Report of the University of Maryland . . . 1934-1936* (College Park, 1937) , 7-9; *Bulletin of the School of Medicine*, XXI (July, 1936) , 36-37; XXV (April, 1941) , 249-250; Medical School File, Dental School File, Law School File, General Advisory Council File, General Administrative Board File, Byrd Papers; for annual enrollments by Colleges, see last pages of the University's annual *Catalogues*.

[49]Athletic File—1935-1942, Byrd Papers; Bealle, *Kings of American Football*, 132-169.

[50]*Diamondback*, 8 December 1939; 15 November 1940; 2 May 1941; Minues of the Regents, 15 December 1939; *Baltimore Sun*, 26 June 1941; 8 September 1941; 6 October 1941.

of bonuses than as permanent increases." With students regularly being called off to war, academic standards seemed less important. Students were admitted to college with less than a high school diploma and were graduated in slightly more than two years. Teaching loads mounted, students practiced air raid drills and to save time the University abandoned final examinations. The ROTC, presumably for training purposes, posted a twenty-four-hour guard around the administration building. From the faculty and alumni of the Schools of Medicine, Dentistry, Pharmacy and Nursing, two 1,000-bed hospital units were organized and departed for the Pacific. With standards lowered and the faculty depleted by war, in the spring of 1942 Phi Beta Kappa refused for a second time to establish a chapter at Maryland.[51]

As the NYA diverted its funds from aid to needy students to aid for the war effort, Byrd became so enthusiastic about war training that some claimed he was responsible for destroying the NYA. Just as the war broke he persuaded the agency to locate a substantial workshop, now Shriver laboratory, on the campus and supply it with about $60,000 worth of metal working tools and machinery. For some months the needed war equipment remained idle and criticism mounted. Then, in February, 1943, to justify keeping the material and to provide students with needed skills, Byrd suddenly announced that every senior, man or woman, must spend eight hours weekly in the shop, studying welding and sheet metal work. Students made beer mugs and ash trays and complained that the course was worthless, while businessmen were eager to obtain the government equipment. In April, 1943, the *Baltimore Sun* launched a major "expose" of the workshop to discredit both Byrd and the agency. That same month when Congress ordered the NYA liquidated, the *Sun* boasted that its articles about "the College Park scandal" were primarily responsible for its demise.[52]

Campus mobilization reached its peak in 1943-1944 as the War Department picked Maryland as a center for the Army Specialized Training Program. Most dormitories became military barracks as

[51]Minutes of the Regents, 16 January 1942; 20 March 1942; 19 June 1942; 30 September 1942; 18 December 1942; 19 February 1943; "New Plan of Admissions Being Considered," *Education Victory*, I (16 August 1943), 11-12; *Bulletin of the School of Medicine*, XXX (August, 1946), 155-158; *Diamondback*, 12, 16, 19 December 1941; 13 May 1942; 23 October 1942.

[52]N.Y.A. File, Byrd Papers; *Diamonback*, 17 September 1942; 12 February 1942; 12 March 1943; 16, 20 April 1943; *Baltimore Sun*, 14-17 April 1943; 15-16 June 1943; Aubrey W. Williams [Director of N.Y.A.] to George H. Callcott, 6 May 1962.

some 1,400 men, fresh from basic training, descended on the campus for the most arduous college program ever given. The army crammed two years of college work into nine months. Each week the students faced 24 hours of classes, 24 hours of supervised study, 6 hours of calisthenics and 5 hours of drill. Similar Navy V-12 and Service Command Programs appeared in the Baltimore professional schools. Although the military students attended some classes with civilian students, their curriculum, chiefly in engineering and languages, was ironclad. They marched to their classes and academic failure or the slightest breach of military discipline meant immediate assignment overseas. Even their recreation was regimented, since they were ordered to attend the University's biweekly dances. Students found little joy in this type of education. The men at Maryland, like ASTP students everywhere, usually disliked the college to which they were assigned, but because the institution was no longer itself, few resented the soldier attitude.[53]

The ASTP ended in 1944, chiefly because the army had greater need for its men elsewhere. During the last year of the war, University enrollment dropped sharply for the first time in decades. People in the University felt a sense of letdown, of things suspended as they waited for the skies to clear, and as they planned, sometimes too grandly, for the dawn of peace.

Perils of Success

In some ways the University's postwar success far surpassed expectations as its physical plant quadrupled, its vast adult education program spread over Europe and its football team basked in publicity as the nation's greatest. And yet people whispered that success was blinding the University to its purpose. President Byrd seemed to be impressing the world instead of pleasing the faculty and students as he had before the war. Postwar problems seemed to fester instead of to turn magically into triumphs. Ignoring the criticism and confidently predicting that the forthcoming evaluation report by the Middle States Association of Colleges and Secondary Schools would provide "the crowning achievement of all," Byrd announced his

[53]*Diamondback,* 21 May 1943; 13 August 1943; 25 February 1944; 14 April 1944 and *passim; Terrapin* [Student Annual], *1942, 1943, 1944; Baltimore Sun,* 27 November 1943; ASTP File, Byrd Papers.

candidacy for governor.[54] When the report exploded just as the 1954 campaign reached fever pitch, it proved bewildering and tragic for the University and especially for the man who had done so much to build it.

Underlying all of the University's postwar problems was the tidal wave of enrollment which engulfed the campus as the veterans returned. From a previous all-time peak of 6,080 students in June, 1946, the total enrollment in September, 1946, reached a staggering 11,050. In a single week of registration, the University had almost doubled in size. With a four-year backlog of students, with the GI Bill providing free tuition for veterans and with postwar prosperity all coinciding, the crush was similar all over the country. During that fall coeds at Maryland lived four in a room or barracks-fashion in the dormitory basements, while 700 men camped in double decker bunks in the armory. Students waited in line for an hour to get into the dining hall, and until six o'clock in the afternoons, Saturdays included, they rushed into classrooms in hopes of finding seats.[55]

The fastest growing fields were the Graduate School, Engineering, Business and Public Administration, Arts and Sciences, Education and Law. Certain professional schools, especially Medicine and Dentistry remained close to their prewar levels:

ENROLLMENT[56]

	1934-5	1945-6	1946-7	1953-4
College Park				
Arts and Sciences	865	1364	2578	2111
Education	314	1000	1500	787
Engineering	305	651	1680	1009
Graduate School	196	773	1545	2576
Agriculture	194	263	570	546
Home Economics	126	313	369	485
Business & Public Adm.		533	1550	1569
Physical Education				257
	2000	4897	9792	9340

[54]Cited in *Diamondback,* 11 December 1953.

[55]Minutes of the Regents, 29 May 1946; *Baltimore Sun,* 24, 27 Augut 1946; 30 September 1946; *Diamondback,* 20 September 1946; 23 May 1947; *Biennial Report . . . 1946-1948* (College Park, 1949) , 6-7, 101-107.

[56]Figures for June of each year available in biennial reports and in catalogues. All graduate school enrollment is cited under College Park, although some classes were in Baltimore; no off-campus enrollment is included.

Baltimore

Medicine	444	383	348	478
Dentistry	352	244	301	430
Pharmacy	285	103	247	237
Law	220	209	399	394
Nursing	119	244	188	247
	1420	1183	1483	1786
Total	3420	6080	11275	11126

Suddenly it became more important to acquire a competent faculty than an outstanding one. With unseasoned instructors in some departments outnumbering full professors by ten to one, teaching conditions were frequently desperate. One young instructor with more than 500 students mysteriously disappeared in November, 1946, leaving a pitiful note, "I see no other way out. My student cards are in my top desk drawer." Early fears of his suicide were relieved only when the University received his endorsed salary check from a distant bank. The poor man's successor, who learned to escape each day by racing from the rear door of his auditorium-like classroom, fared no better. At the end of the semester he too quietly disappeared.[57]

The last seven years of Byrd's administration, from 1946 to 1953, witnessed a continuing struggle to adjust to the flood. While he exhorted the legislature for emergency building funds, he persuaded the army to sell scores of temporary wooden structures which appeared ubiquitously over the campus. Exhilarated by expansion, Byrd modified the old adage and boasted of "not only quality but also quantity." To maintain enrollment even after veteran registration fell off, the University held tuition and standards close to their 1946 levels. While enrollment in all state universities declined twenty-two percent from 1946 to 1953, that at Maryland remained steady.[58]

Contributing to the crowded, disjointed atmosphere of the campus after the war was the spread of ugly urbanization reaching out, octopus-like, from Washington. Nearby Bladensburg blossomed into

[57]Minutes of the Regents, 15 February 1945; 22 February 1946; University of Maryland Budget for 1946-1947, Comptroller's Office; Wedeberg and Dillard, "History of the College of Business and Public Administration," 26-27.

[58]Baltimore Sun, 21 April 1946; 27, 30 August 1946; 17 July 1948; 18 December 1953; Biennial Report . . . 1946-1948, 101-105, 128-132; The World Almanac . . . 1948 (New York, 1948), 337-346, 354; The World Almanac . . . 1955 (New York, 1955), 451-461, 478.

a notorious gambling and prostitution center, factories and automobile agencies spread into the once-fashionable suburban villages
of Riverdale and College Park and woodlands turned into barren ex-
panses of housing projects. The boulevard which linked the campus
to the outside world became a neon jungle of truck stops and filling
stations. Desperately and vainly the University petitioned to save
the charm of the once-isolated town, but frequently its faculty and
students were only too eager to find quarters in the jerry-built houses
nearby. Indeed, the University's huge construction program only
added to the rawness.[59]

As usual the American college campus was reflecting in intense
degree the mood of the nation, now peevish and fretful in reaction
from its wartime sacrifices. While the country reviled the Truman
administration, students on a hundred campuses burned their college presidents and coaches in effigy. Even the once beloved "Curley"
became the distant "Dr. Byrd." Student talk was marked by
shoulder-shrugging, half-sarcastic remarks like "big deal," "no
sweat" and "stay loose." Even campus fashions reflected the unsettled
atmosphere. Fraternity men wore loud ties and checkered sports
jackets with wide lapels while others attended classes in anything
from double breasted suits to army fatigue jackets. Coeds wore
bobby socks, short skirts and long hair. Almost everyone boasted
dirty brown and white saddle oxfords.

With commuters and veterans in an overwhelming majority at
Maryland, the grand old alma mater became for many students
simply a place to go to school. Before the war when three-fourths of
the students lived on campus the weekends rang with parties, but
after the war when over three-fourths lived away, Saturday nights
hung in heavy stillness. Veterans wanted to catch up on the gay
times they had missed, but at the same time they were too serious,
too old, too self-conscious for frivolity. Instead of hip-hurrah or
ivory towers they found inanity, grind and letdown. For 500 veteran
student families living across the boulevard in war surplus housing,
early morning diaper changes became more important than late evening proms. Such extracurricular organizations as the Veterans
Association and the Day-Dodger Club were designed less for collegiate companionship than for the protection of group interests.

[59]Jack Lait and Lee Mortimer, *Washington Confidential* (New York, 1951), 63-68;
Minutes of the Regents, 21 May 1949.

Except for athletics, most extracurricular activities were less important than they had been before the war when the enrollment was half as large.

It was the age of gripes on the college campus. Students complained about the crowding, the dining hall, the professors and the football team; they fumed about the inadequate stadium, the unsatisfactory student union, the insufficient library and the lack of cultural events on campus; they protested compulsory class attendance and restoration of final examinations. President Byrd, once the symbol for everything good on the campus, was now attacked as the "autocratic administration," the symbol of everything frustrating.[60]

The loudest outburst came in the spring of 1945, just before the veteran flood reached its peak, when a group of students inspired by an angry sociology instructor, Thomas P. Monahan, began distribution of an anonymous mimeographed sheet, "The Challenger."[61] The dissidents spoke mainly for higher academic standards and greater democracy for both students and faculty in the operation of the University. With encouragement from the *Baltimore Sun*, the students grew bolder, circulating petitions and "demanding" conferences with Byrd and the regents. The students discredited their cause by their own excesses, but the passionate Monahan, dismissed from his job, made a full-length book of the episode. Although too biased to be persuasive, it provided ammunition for Byrd's enemies during the remainder of his administration and also during his campaign for governor.[62]

Less violent outbursts occurred almost every year. Sometimes they were simply overenthusiastic football rallies which blocked traffic on the boulevard, sometimes they were springtime panty raids which were fashionable over the country, but occasionally the students demanded higher academic standards or football de-emphasis. Early in 1947 they circulated an angry petition calling for the establishment of a philosophy department which existed in the catalogue but offered no courses. Administrators who had begun their terms before the war were unable to understand the new

[60]See, *Diamondback*, 16 March 1945; 11, 25 May 1945; 8, 15 June 1945; 18 January 1946; 10 January 1947; 2 May 1947; 19 March 1948; 21 May 1954 and *passim; The Old Line, 1945-1954, passim.*

[61]Partial files of "The Challenger" in Stamp Papers, McKeldin Library.

[62]Thomas Patrick Monohan, *"Bossism" in Education* (n.p., 1946) ; see, Student Controversy-1945 File, Monahan File, Byrd Papers; *Baltimore Sun,* 24-25 May 1945; 6-16 June 1945.

generation of students who demanded higher standards and philosophy courses as vehemently as they did a football victory.[63]

Although Byrd cited enrollment pressure and student unrest as arguments for larger appropriations, his relations with the legislature also assumed a disturbing pattern. He often seemed to fight against the assembly instead of working with it to build the University. Instead of trying to overcome its members with charm as he had before the war, he seemed to rely increasingly on power. Local politicians stood in awe of "the Byrd machine," and even those on the national level kept an eye on him.[64]

As evidence of his machine, observers pointed out that the University provided free education for one appointee by each member of the House of Delegates and for two appointees by each state senator; that the University Hospital annually served thousands of patients free of charge; and that the University's agricultural agents regularly visited almost every farmer in the state. In 1948 opponents assailed Byrd's "special session" of the assembly when a full quorum of legislators appeared at College Park for a luncheon and football game, with their meals and tickets paid for by the University and thus indirectly by the state treasury. At least twice, in the elections of 1950 and 1952, the University lent its alumni and farm extension mailing lists to Democratic candidates for office. At least once, in 1953, the general assembly appeared unable to organize itself and select committee chairmen until Byrd arrived in Annapolis to express his will. When the governor of the state, William P. Lane, threatened to block a University request in 1950, Byrd announced pointedly that "if some people don't watch out" they would be turned out of office. Many people snickered about a telephone poll conducted anonymously in Baltimore that year in which a caller asked "Would you rather have a politician for governor, or a university president like Dr. Byrd?" But whatever the methods, the result was the same as before the war. The University's operating budget rose from $4,800,000 in 1945, to $9,900,000 in 1948, to $21,000,000 in 1954. In addition, in 1944, 1947 and 1949, Byrd obtained construction funds totaling about $13,000,000.[65]

[63]*Diamondback*, 16 January 1946; 15 March 1946; 7, 11, 21 March 1947; 18 November 1947; 2 April 1948; 19 March 1948; 4 October 1949; 15 November 1949; 22 May 1952; 7 October 1952; 15 March 1954; 21 May 1954.

[64]Shalett, "Maryland's Busiest Byrd," 33 ff.; *Baltimore Sun,* 21 January 1949; 25 February 1950.

[65]Entertainment of Legislature at College Park-1948 File, Byrd Papers; *Baltimore Sun,* 16, 25 November 1948; 25 August 1950; 29 October 1952; 7 January 1953; 24 February 1950; 23 May 1950; Minutes of the Regents, 31 October 1952; 19 December

The Centennial of 1907

Alumni Reunion, 1921

May Day, 1929

Richard W. Silvester
1892-1912

Albert F. Woods
1917-1926

Raymond A. Pearson
1926-1935

The campus in 1922

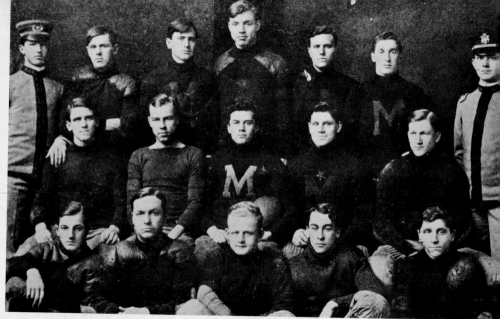

Captain H. C. Byrd, center, and the team of 1908

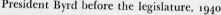

President Byrd before the legislature, 1940

President Byrd, 1953

Memorial Chapel

President Wilson Homer Elkins

McKeldin Library

An English Honors Class

The College Park campus in 1965 had 35 parking lots and 26,200 registered automobiles.

University Hospital with the School of Law in the background, 1965

College Park campus in the fall of 1965, enrollment 26,265

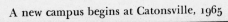

A new campus begins at Catonsville, 1965

Despite the University's success in obtaining money, each year the methods employed seemed to grow more questionable and resentment mounted. For example, the Government Auditing Office stumbled on facts indicating that the United States Veterans Administration was being charged not only out-of-state fees for Maryland veterans on the GI Bill, but extra fees beyond that—a total of about $2,000,000. No one understood the University's bookkeeping, and the government decided that the institution was technically within legal bounds, but the episode left an unpleasant memory.[66] More frustrating to the general assembly was the fact that the University was consistently receiving almost a million dollars annually beyond legislative intent by underestimating its revenue from tuitions, fees and hospital income. Each year the non-appropriated funds were larger than estimated, giving the institution extra money which sometimes was used for projects specifically rejected by the legislature in its direct appropriation.[67]

University power and legislative resentment finally reached a climax in the 1952 session with the simultaneous passage of a sweeping "Autonomy Bill" and the ejection of Byrd from the assembly floor. The bill gave the University the power to make its purchases, control its employees or alter its curriculum without supervision or checks by any state agency or by any elected official. Actually many state universities operated with similar autonomy to be free from political controls, but with Byrd as president people wondered if this were getting the University out of politics or getting it further in. In any case, after a turbulent session, on March 4, 1952, Byrd forced the bill through a resentful legislature over Governor Theodore McKeldin's veto. The next day, however, he went too far. The tired and edgy legislators worked past midnight in hopes of adjournment, and still Byrd was on the house floor, interrupting the speakers and whispering in representatives' ears, hoping to get through yet another half-million dollars attached to the appropriations bill for the University. As the clock approached 3:00 A.M. one of the legislators pointed at Byrd and exploded in anger. Suddenly the chamber was in pandemonium as everyone seemed to be

1952; Maryland-Governor's Office-Lane File, Byrd Papers; University of Maryland, *Financial Report . . . 1945*, 3; *Financial Report . . . 1949*, 3; *Financial Report . . . 1954*, 4.

[66]United States-Veterans Administration File, Byrd Papers; *Baltimore Sun*, 24-26 September 1947; 2-4 October 1947.

[67]*Baltimore Sun*, 23 February 1949; 23 March 1949; 17 February 1950; 11-12, 15, 17, 24 January 1951; Maryland-Governor's Office-Lane File, Maryland-Governor's Office McKeldin File, Byrd Papers.

shouting at the University president, demanding his ejection. As he retreated his last-minute amendment was shouted down without a dissenting voice, and the assembly adjourned for the year. Noting that Byrd had almost never been defeated by the assembly and certainly had never before been insulted by it, one reporter wondered if this marked the turning point in his incredible career.[68]

As student and legislative unrest grew the faculty also chafed under the firm control of its head. Forced to teach twelve months on a ten-month salary as a wartime sacrifice and then crushed under veteran enrollment, the faculty waited two full years after the war ended before vacation periods and salaries could be adjusted. Even then, as inflation and taxes spiraled upward, the real income of faculty members, especially relative to other occupations, probably reached the lowest point in the institution's history. In 1945 instructors began at $1,800 for ten months while the salary of full professors normally went to $4,200. Even by 1954 instructors usually began at $4,000 and most senior professors made $6,200, although two or three "name" professors received up to $10,000. The fact that salaries were no better at many other institutions hardly helped matters. The faculty turnover rate mounted alarmingly, reaching a peak of fifty-nine resignations during the single year of 1953. Whether or not the departing professors improved their lot, they frequently left with ill will toward the University, and occasionally with angry letters to the newspapers.[69]

The faculty began to feel that the president was interested only in driving the sharpest bargains he could with them. Professors quoted Byrd, perhaps erroneously, as boasting that "Ph.D.'s are a dime a dozen." On several occasions he observed that "the old law of supply and demand has set in and the salaries you have to pay a teacher varies according to the relative scarcity." This meant that professors in some fields, especially the sciences, received almost double the salary of other professors, especially those in the humanities. Byrd and the businesslike regents announced as a definite "policy" that they would grant "only those [salary] increases that might seem necessary to hold a member of the staff when that member might be offered a better or more lucrative position elsewhere." A protest

[68]Minutes of the Regents, 26 October 1951; 25 January 1952; 22 May 1952; 13 February 1953; *Baltimore Sun*, 22 March 1951; 6 May 1951; 9 January 1952; 5-7 March 1952.

[69]Minutes of the Regents, 29 June 1945; 22 February 1946; 9 November 1946; 15 June 1948; University of Maryland, *Budget for . . . 1945; Budget for . . . 1954;* Joslyn File, Kitchin File, Byrd Papers; *Baltimore Sun,* 16 June 1945; 10 March 1946, 12 June 1946.

letter from the campus chapter of the American Association of University Professors received a brusque and noncommittal reply from the president. To match a rival offer one professor received an increase from $4,800 to $8,000 at a single stroke. In the long run the policy only tended further to weaken faculty morale. Instead of being the faculty's champion and fighting the cause of its members, the president had become their employer; somehow faculty welfare had become different from, and even opposed to, University welfare.[70]

Even more alarming than low salaries was the absence of a definite tenure policy and the frightening authority of the president. "Regarding salary and promotion increases," said Byrd, "I do not usually consult with department heads at all."[71] Except for the General Advisory Board composed of deans and the American Association of University Professors, there was no faculty organization, no general faculty meetings and no way for professors to feel they had a part in policy making. Byrd always appeared eager to explain any decision he made, probably dismissed no one without adequate reason, and certainly kept his door open and was ready to listen to every complaint; but whether he intended it or not, something remained in the atmosphere that made professors a little afraid. In the American Council on Education Report of 1947, the Phi Beta Kappa Report of 1948, the privately instigated report of 1949 and the Middle States Association Report of 1953, the centralized authority of the administration and the resulting low morale of the faculty received more emphasis than any other other criticism.[72]

Maryland First

Whatever the long-run problems which lasted through the postwar years, the imaginative president never bogged down in them or lost the grand vision. As soon as the war was over, the University

[70]Minutes of the Regents, 16, 23 June 1944; 7 June 1949; 30 November 1951; 25 January 1952; 27 March 1952; 25 April 1952; 13 February 1953; *Baltimore Sun*, 15 November 1946; American Association of University Professors File, Zucker File, Byrd Papers; American Association of University Professors File, Stamp Papers, McKeldin Library; University of Maryland, *Budget for . . . 1954*.

[71]Byrd to Carl S. Joslyn [Head of Department of Sociology], 16 March 1944, Joslyn File, Byrd Papers.

[72]American Council on Education, *Higher Education in Maryland*, 346; Carl Billman [Officer of Phi Beta Kappa] to Byrd, 30 July 1948, Phi Beta Kappa File, Byrd Papers; Stewart, "Administrative Problems," 2-3; Middle States Association, *Evaluation Report*, 8-9 and *passim*.

launched a series of new educational programs which placed it in the national limelight. Its extension program expanded into a system of adult education that eventually became worldwide, and its American civilization program initiated debate in educational circles throughout the country. It was the first state university in the South to accept Negroes, its football program produced some of the most powerful collegiate teams ever known, its construction program soared, and new research bureaus multiplied. Each project became the work of many men, but it was the president's enthusiasm which propelled it to the forefront of American higher education. If a new idea excited him it would not languish in committees or wait for experimentation by bolder institutions. Byrd wanted Maryland to be first.

The most unplanned but the most far-reaching and successful program was the spread of extension work into what eventually became University College. All of the land-grant colleges had a heritage of education beyond the classroom as professors offered noncredit lectures, usually in the summer, for farm women, 4-H Clubs, special groups such as apple growers or poultry breeders and, occasionally, for non-farm groups such as fire wardens and traffic policemen. After the war, possibly inspired by the prominence of the "brain-trust" of the Roosevelt administration, specialized groups gravitated increasingly around the universities, looking to professors as sources of expert advice. At College Park the formal conferences or "courses" for such groups increased from thirteen in 1940, to sixty-eight in 1953. Some, such as the Fluid Dynamic Conference or the Supersonic Conference, were highly scholarly while others appeared remote from traditional academic subjects—such as the Golf Greenkeepers' School, the Cosmetology Institute or the Ice Cream Course.[73]

Off-campus work was developing in another direction, meanwhile, as Maryland launched a program of study abroad that led to the degree of Master of Foreign Study. Inspired by Edmund E. Miller, a professor of foreign languages and formerly instigator of the junior-year-abroad for the University of Delaware, the program took advantage of the GI Bill which paid tuition almost anywhere in the world. Working with Byrd, Miller arranged for Maryland students to take courses at the Sorbonne and later at the Universities of Zurich and Munich. The students were supervised by Maryland and

[73]University of Maryland, Combined Catalogues, 1954-1955, 1079-1080.

returned to College Park to write their theses and take their examinations. Miller led the first group to Paris in 1946, and during the next four years almost a hundred students participated, including a number of undergraduates. As the GI Bill began to peter out, however, the program lost popularity. Anyway, the president had begun to envisage far larger possibilities for an overseas empire.[74]

The noncredit conferences and the graduate-year-abroad program were only precursors for the vast extension work of University College. Continuing in the progressive education tradition and eager to extend higher education to adults, Dean Harold Benjamin and Professor George J. Kabat, both of the College of Education, presented Byrd with a broad plan for night classes which would offer full-credit courses to working people throughout the state in much the same manner that professors had long been offering noncredit lectures. Benjamin and Kabat requested a separate college within the University for their project. Far more pleased with large plans than with small ones, Byrd was fascinated. Not only would such a college extend educational opportunities, it might coordinate all of the disjointed extension work, allay demands by Negroes to enter the University proper, and it might offer a probationary period for poorly qualified students.

In 1947 the regents officially approved the new school, awkwardly known at first as the College of Special and Continuation Studies, but later simplified to University College. Under Kabat, its first director, classes met that fall at Hagerstown, Westminster, at the Calvert Distillery, The Glenn L. Martin Company and the School of Medicine in Baltimore. Although the College never took over all the miscellaneous activities that Byrd had intended, the public's response exceeded expectations. Within a year over two hundred faculty members, usually from the College Park campus, had covered almost the full range of the University's regular offerings. The night classes spread to nearby Fort Meade and to military establishments in Virginia and Washington, such as Bolling Field and the Pentagon. With draftees hungry for intellectual activity and with ambitious officers eager for a college degree, response at the military centers was especially enthusiastic.[75]

[74]Graduate School File, Miller File, Byrd Papers; interview, William R. Quynn, 26 October 1963; interview, William F. Falls, 26 October 1963; *Washington Post* 24 July 1949.

[75]College of Special and Continuation Studies File, Kabat File, Byrd Papers, *Biennial Report . . . 1946-1948*, 77-79.

The most significant step came in the fall of 1949 when the University arranged with the army and air force to send seven Maryland instructors to bases in Germany. For the University it was a financially self-sustaining public service, closely related to a flourishing extension program and also to a successful experiment in overseas education. For the military officials the courses provided a use of off-duty time which raised both the educational level and the morale of their men. In Europe the response was even greater than at home. More than 1,800 students—triple the expected enrollment—crowded into the first group of after-hours classes and each term the enrollment multiplied. Joseph Ray replaced Kabat as dean in 1950, and in 1952 the energetic Ray Ehrensberger took over.

From the overseas headquarters in Heidelberg classes pursued the troops from frigid Thule in Greenland to burning Dhahran on the Persian Gulf. The University developed an eight-week term which allowed courses to be rotated frequently from base to base, and developed a special military science curriculum which allowed certain aspects of military training to be transferred into college credits. Usually the army or air force paid about three-fourths of the students' tuition, and increasingly they allowed their men to understand that the courses had a certain official standing. Officers without a college degree suspected that work in the Maryland program was essential for promotion. Although most students accumulated credits for transfer to stateside colleges, some completed their entire college education abroad. In May, 1954, amidst grand medieval pomp, twenty-one students received University of Maryland degrees in the venerable halls of Heidelberg University. By then the overseas faculty numbered 140, the overseas enrollment was approximately 10,000 students annually and back home about 4,000 others attended University College. It was the largest division within the University.[76]

University College was a contribution to the entire nation. The average age of overseas graduates was thirty-seven, but almost every instructor was ready to testify that they were among the most highly motivated and frankly appreciative students in the world. Despite their heterogeneous backgrounds and despite the scattered faculty, the academic quality of the program, to almost everybody's surprise, remained sound. The stern Middle States Evaluation Report of 1953

[76]Edward F. James, "Serving America around the World," Maryland Alumni Magazine, XXVIII (March-April, 1957), 12-19; Newsweek, XXXV (12 June 1950), 86-87; XLIII (10 May 1954), 84.

declared that "standards of instruction and student performance in overseas classes would be at least as high, and very probably higher, than the standards achieved in the same classes on campus." The College altered the lives of thousands of men who launched or continued an education they would never have obtained elsewhere. Financially the program actually contributed about a half-million dollars by 1955 for College Park construction. Although most adult education programs have been disappointments in America, Maryland's extension work, especially its overseas project, may actually rank as the most successful such experiment since the nineteenth century lyceum movement.[77]

Another major development at Maryland, and one closer to President Byrd's personal interest, was the program in American studies or, as people at Maryland came to call it, American civilization. Early in the war Byrd had been impressed with a series of articles by Benjamin Fine in the *New York Times* revealing college students' widespread ignorance of American history. According to nationwide tests, 25 percent of the country's college freshmen could not name the United States president during the Civil War, 50 percent failed to identify Andrew Jackson or Thomas Jefferson and 94 percent failed to name the thirteen colonies. Byrd became acquainted with Fine and appointed a faculty committee to find ways for Maryland to step into the breach. With customary decisiveness, Byrd moved to the forefront of one of the most talked about curriculum changes in higher education.[78]

American studies recognized the long-standing demand for greater emphasis on national institutions and culture but, more important, it gave impetus to the movement for interdisciplinary study. For years educators had criticized the rigid lines dividing departments, and for years men like Vernon L. Parrington and Henry Steele Commager had been half-consciously breaking down those lines in their studies of American society. The depression and the world war added to the nation's self-consciousness and to its desire to know itself. Once launched the program spread rapidly. Maryland went further, obtained more publicity and probably did more to solidify the movement than any institution had done previously.[79]

[77]Middle States Association, *Evaluation Report*, 116; College of Speciaal and Continuation Studies-1955 File, Ehrensberger File, W. H. Elkins Papers, Administration Building, College Park.

[78]*New York Times*, 21 June 1942; Fine File, American Civilization File, Byrd Papers.

[79]Robert H. Walker, *American Studies in the United States* . . . (Baton Rouge, 1958), 156-163.

The program, which began in the fall of 1945, contained three parts. First, every student was required to take at least eighteen semester hours of work in American history, literature, government and sociology, and men took twelve hours of military training. Second, students could obtain an interdisciplinary major in American civilization and, third, students could pursue the program for an M.A. or Ph.D. degree. The University's experiment delighted educators and patriots throughout the country. The *New York Times* gave it a front page story, and Byrd collected some 2,000 other newspaper stories almost unanimously favorable. "This," said Byrd, "has given us more favorable publicity than anything we have ever done."[80]

While Maryland foreshadowed the rise of American studies, it also signaled its dangers and decline. Some complained that the distinction between American and foreign civilizations was as arbitrary as the old division between history and English; qualified teachers were hard to find; established departments were reluctant to be torn apart; and efforts to coordinate courses often ended in duplication. More damaging than opponents of the plan were its friends. When the William Randolph Hearst newspapers gave $37,500 to Maryland in 1945 to endow two American studies fellowships, the program immediately fell under the shadow of anti-intellectual chauvinism. Byrd himself referred to the "Americanization" program. University publicity was marred by cliché and provincialism in promising to "inculcate students in the American way of life," and to "innoculate" them against "the various foreign isms." Rightly or wrongly, many students and faculty members were hostile because of a conviction that the program was associated with the rapidly expanding College of Military Science. Although eighteen semester hours of American civilization remained in the curriculum, the interdisciplinary cooperation never really developed. Under the firm control of Professor Carl Bode, many majors and a number of graduate students worked out degree requirements among departments, but the more ambitious plans for a new curriculum were generally a disappointment the nation over.[81]

[80]American Civilization File, Byrd Papers; University of Maryland, *General Catalogue, 1946-1947*, 26, 78, 201; *New York Times*, 7 February 1945; Minutes of the Regents, 15 February 1945.

[81]"Hearst Gift of $50,000 [*sic*] Establishes Scholarship," *Alumni News*, XVII (May, 1945), 2; "A Program in American Civilization," *Maryland Alumni Magazine*, XVIII (April, 1947), 7-10; *Diamondback*, 16 February 1945; 11, 18 May 1945; 22 June 1945; 15 March 1946; 21, 28 March 1947; 4 April 1947; 18 April 1950; Monahan, *"Bossism" in*

The same chauvinism that some feared in American studies appeared in other forms on the campus. As McCarthyism reached its peak in the early 1950's, as the traditional postwar nationalism blended with cold war frustrations, and as conservatism blended with perverse anti-intellectualism, the public looked with particular suspicion on the universities. The Maryland legislature passed the Ober Law, one of the most sweeping of its kind in the country, which required all University professors, along with other state employees, to sign an oath of loyalty. Byrd enthusiastically supported the law, and his public speeches increasingly seemed to reflect the anti-liberal sentiment behind it. Long an ardent nationalist, a particuarly outspoken anglophobe, he seemed more eager to promote loyalty on the campus than academic freedom. Communist speakers were forbidden to appear at Maryland, and the faculty was scrutinized for past associations. While there is no evidence that anyone was fired because of his political views, some professors were fearful and some may have violated professional canons by withholding their opinions. With professors through the country outspoken in defense of academic freedom, possibly the very weakness of the protest at Maryland was significant. The faculty contented itself with a mildly worded resolution against the Ober Law passed by voice vote in the local chapter of the American Association of University Professors. Although most professors were doubtless happy with the fact, many were disturbed at the implications when Byrd boasted as one of his greatest "achievements" that "the F.B.I. has found fewer un-American influences at Maryland" than at any other institution of higher learning.[82]

As the state and the University slowly developed a policy for Negro education, again President Byrd stood in the limelight. Although he displayed more vision than most people in the state and did much for the higher education of Negroes, many believed that he acted for the wrong reasons. During the 1930's Byrd worked earnestly to build the University's Negro branch with the argument, "If we don't do something about Princess Anne we're going to have to accept Negroes at College Park, where our girls are."[83] The

---

Education, 29-31 and *passim;* American Civilization File, Byrd Papers; American Civilization Program File, Elkins Papers.

[82]"The Ober Law," *Maryland Alumni Magazine,* XXII (January-February, 1951), 8-9; *Baltimore Sun,* 10 March 1946; 8 April 1950; 9 August 1950; 10-11 June 1951; 13 July 1952; 10 December 1953; *Biennial Report . . . 1946-1948,* 110.

[83]Quoted in *Baltimore Sun,* 5 February 1937.

Legislature in 1935 acquired from Morgan College full title to Princess Anne and made it a part of the University which had long been supplying most of the smaller school's inadequate budget. For the first time the University assumed real control. Since Negro pressure was insignificant, however, the legislature ignored Byrd's pleas and refused to pour large sums into Princess Anne. Instead of building the first-rate Negro college he demanded, the legislature followed a narrow, contradictory policy designed merely to appease the Negroes. It gave a pittance to the University for Princess Anne; it agreed in 1939 to assume control of Morgan State College for Negroes in Baltimore; and all the while it continued to provide scholarships for Negroes who wished to attend colleges outside the state. By the end of the war the total appropriation to Princess Anne, Morgan State and the scholarships was substantial, but there was little to show for it. Morgan State was weak, Princess Anne was weaker and the demands of the Negroes were growing.

Stimulated by postwar prosperity and the growing demand for integration, Negroes began pressing for admission to the University. Powerful delegations appeared before the board of regents and the legislature threatening court action to force the opening of the University to all citizens of the state. Suddenly alarmed, the legislature appointed a commission in 1947 and another in 1949 to review the entire question of Negro higher education. To Byrd's consternation, both commissions recommended that Princess Anne be abandoned and that the state's efforts be concentrated at Morgan State. Whether because of concern for the Negro or of concern at the threat to his empire, Byrd was furious. Immediately he made Negro education his "first priority." He changed the name of Princess Anne Academy to Maryland State College in 1948, and quadrupled the state's investment in the institution before the legislature quite realized what was happening. To attract students to the college full-page advertisements appeared in Negro newspapers as far away as Philadelphia. Then, assuming full initiative, Byrd turned the tables on the commission reports by demanding that Morgan State be abandoned, or at least absorbed, by Princess Anne and the University.

While the furor raged, the courts were changing the issue from one of expanded Negro colleges to one of integration. As early as 1935, following the case of Pearson versus Murray, the University accepted Negroes into its Law School, regularly graduating one or two in each class. After another court suit in 1950, McCready versus Byrd, the first Negro entered the Baltimore Nursing School. The following year, without court action, the University accepted its first Negro graduate student at College Park. Finally, one month after the famous Supreme Court decision of 1954 ordering integration in the public schools "with all deliberate speed," the University regents spoke out forthrightly. Although they could have delayed the matter, they seemed almost eager to have it settled, and declared that henceforth every branch of the University was open to all residents of Maryland without regard to race. That fall the first two Negro undergraduates entered the University without incident.

Although the initiative had come from the courts, the University of Maryland, a southern institution in much of its heritage and outlook, had acted in good faith. In 1935 it had been the first state university in the South during the twentieth century to accept Negroes in any branch, and in 1954 it was the first to accept Negro undergraduates. The University kept no statistics on students as Negroes, and during the next decade observers doubted that the total Negro enrollment exceeded one or two percent; but dormitory housemothers and University officials could report not a single incident involving racial feelings. As Negro demand for higher education grew, it appeared that in addition to integration at the University, both Morgan State and Maryland State were necessary. In the University's effort to establish a policy only President Byrd seemed to be seriously hurt. Attacked on one hand as a segregationist and on the other as an integrationist, and under fire by Negroes for his effort to destroy Morgan State, he may have owed the margin of defeat in his 1954 bid for the governorship to the issue.[84]

Of all the University's postwar projects the most spectacular, and

[84]On this complex issue see, Minutes of the Regents, 15, 28 February 1947; 30 June 1948; 24 September 1948; 22 October 1948; 1, 7 June 1950; 20 December 1950; 31 January 1951; 20 April 1951; 25 June 1954; *Diamondback,* 13 December 1949; *Baltimore Sun,* 27 April 1945; 7-8 February 1946; 26 March 1946; 12 March 1947; 5, 17-18 July 1947; 25 September 1948; 23, 27 October 1948; 3, 14, 26 November 1948; 2, 4 December 1948; 19-20 January 1949; 29 July 1949; 16 November 1949; 15-16 April 1950; 28-29 September 1950; 25 July 1950 [Weglein Commission Report]; 16 August 1950; 28-29 September 1950; 10 October 1950; 27 November 1950; 12, 15, 24 January 1951; 2, 6 February 1951; 27 April 1951; 28 April 1952; 5 March 1953; 26-28 June 1954; 20, 31 October 1954; American Council on Education, *Higher Education in Maryland,* 339-384 [Marbury Commission Report]; University versus Murray, 169 *Maryland Reports,* 478; McCready versus Byrd, 195 *Maryland Reports,* 131; Princess Anne File, Byrd Papers; Middle States Association, *Evaluation Report,* 151-163; Disciplinary records, Dean of Students' Office, College Park.

possibly the one nearest Byrd's heart, was building the nation's greatest football team. The new platoon squads, the wide open split-T formation, expanded bands, student card sections and tight-sweatered coed cheerleaders brought college football to its zenith in the early 1950's, with Maryland standing proudly at the top. Some people were skeptical of Byrd's claim that football promoted the all-American values of sportsmanship and manliness, but everyone acknowledged that winning teams lifted campus morale and even those professors who depreciated the teams felt a new national status. The Gator Bowl of '49, the Sugar Bowl of '51, the Orange Bowl of '53 and '55—these were heady days for Maryland. If the faculty were short of Nobel prize winners, schoolboys everywhere acknowledged the pre-eminence of Maryland's coach, "Big Jim" Tatum. From school playgrounds to fashionable cocktail parties knowledgeable people talked of the University's greatest all-Americans—Dick Scarbath, Bernie Faloney, Bob Ward, Ray Krouse, Stan Jones, and the two brothers, "Big Mo" and "Little Mo" Modzelewski.

Byrd deliberately played down athletics during the 1930's, and experienced trial and error in finding the proper coach after the war. In 1947, however, he found his man in James M. Tatum, the handsome 220-pound coach at Oklahoma whom he brought to Maryland at an undisclosed salary. His first two years were mediocre with 13 wins, 6 losses and 2 ties. Tatum recruited his players and added to the schedule the greatest powerhouse teams in the nation—Michigan State, Miami, Tennessee, U.C.L.A. and Alabama. In 1949 Tatum had a 9-1 record, and swept to a rousing victory over Missouri in the Gator Bowl. The following year Maryland lost two games, but in 1951 it enjoyed a perfect 10-0 record and a trip to the Sugar Bowl. The upset 28-13 victory over Tennessee, called by sportswriters the greatest college football game ever played, was the kind that lives in legend. Tennessee's Senator Estes Kefauver lost his famed coonskin cap to Maryland's Senator Millard Tydings, and Maryland was the undisputed top team in the nation.[85]

After 17 straight victories, the following year Maryland cracked in its last two games; but in 1953 Tatum rebounded with another perfect record and an invitation to meet Oklahoma in the Orange Bowl. Byrd was already an avowed candidate for governor, with his resignation dated December 31, 1953, but the regents extended

[85]Bealle, *Kings of American Football*, 169-208; Harvey L. Miller, "Maryland Wins National Title," *Maryland Alumni Magazine*, XXIII (March-April, 1952), 7-11.

his term for forty-eight hours so that, as president, he could sit with his boys on the bench during the New Year's Day game. If he were superstitious he might have regarded the game as an omen. The team that so often had won upsets was an easy favorite, but that day it lost to Oklahoma by a heartbreaking 7-0.[86]

The University's athletic program was far larger than the Saturday football game. Maryland won national and regional championships and turned out a generous sprinkling of all-American players in lacrosse, soccer, cross-country, track, baseball, boxing, wrestling, riflery, golf and tennis. A large intramural program flourished. In 1950 Physical Education, Recreation and Health became a separate college within the University under its own dean. The following year the 35,000-seat Byrd Stadium was completed, and by 1954 Maryland could boast one of the finest athletic plants in the country. The College of Physical Education had thirty-two instructors, in addition to the coaching staff, who offered over one hundred courses leading to the B.S., M.A., and Ph.D. degrees. Some people were disturbed that the University provided eight courses in dancing, seven in swimming, five in camping and nature lore and not a single course in Latin or Greek.[87]

When critics scrutinized Maryland's athletic program they sometimes made alarming discoveries. Investigators found that physical education students consistently ranked lowest on freshman entrance tests, that they devoted less than 30 percent of their class time to general education subjects, but that in some of their special courses they received up to thirty-eight times as many A and B grades as they received grades of D and F. Athletes received 179 scholarships each year, and while nonathletic scholarships averaged $105, those for football averaged $944 plus well-paying jobs that looked suspiciously like sinecures. Seventy-three percent of the 1953 football team came from outside the state. One all-American player, repeating four of his five courses, still ranked as a sophomore after more than five years of college. All students were charged $15 a year to support athletics, plus an additional $40 used chiefly for amortizing the debt on the physical education facilities. Otherwise athletics just

[86]Minutes of the Regents, 16 December 1953. For all sports events see Clippings File, containing some 100 scrapbooks from over 40 newspapers during 1935-1953, in Administration Building, College Park; also Student Annual, *Terrapin*.

[87]*Terrapin*, 1945-1955; Athletics File, Athletic Board File, College of Physical Education File, Byrd Papers; Middle States Association, *Evaluation Report*, 43-61, 110-112; University of Maryland, *Combined Catalogues, 1953-1954*.

about broke even with gate receipts and expenditures balancing at about $500,000 annually.[88]

Perhaps more discouraging to the administration than outside criticism was the attitude of many students toward the winning teams. While students were vaguely proud of the football team as New Yorkers were proud of the Yankees, it had ceased to be their own. Even during the most successful seasons almost half of the students failed to attend the home games. Football enthusiasts complained in the *Diamondback* about student apathy, while opponents expressed themselves freely in favor of de-emphasis. Frequently students were more cynical than the facts warranted about the "hired Hessians" on the teams. The players, who ate at special "training" tables apart from other students, were often looked upon with more curiosity than envy. Like the raccoon coats of the 1920's, big-time football was in large part a movement of the alumni trying to recapture their own palmy days rather than a movement of the students. Just as the administrators never quite understood the students who petitioned for higher standards, many of them failed to comprehend the indifference or hostility of the students toward the winning football teams which the University built for them.[89]

Maryland's athletic emphasis was certainly no greater than at many other fine institutions, and if the cost of football victories were too great, that was an indictment of the values of higher education almost everywhere. Indeed, as a relatively new University in need of publicity, and as a semiurban University needing a focus for student life, Maryland had more to gain and less to lose from athletics than most other institutions. Only once did Byrd knowingly violate accepted procedures and that was in allowing Maryland to play in the Sugar Bowl in 1951 in defiance of an anti-bowl resolution of the Southern Conference. The resolution was passed at the last moment and was revoked the following year when another team wished to attend.[90] For all of the criticism that Byrd and Tatum received from academic quarters, it remained difficult for

[88]Middle States Association, *Evaluation Report,* 48-57, 110-111; Minutes of the Regents, 30 November 1951, 26 June 1953; *Baltimore Sun,* 20 November-1 December 1951; Tim Cohane, "How Maryland Became a Football Power," *Look,* XVIII (2 November 1954), 50-58; "How To Get Big Time Football," *U. S. News and World Report,* XXXVIII (28 January 1955), 54-58.

[89]*Diamondback,* 18 January 1946; 19 March 1948; 7 December 1951; 21 May 1954, and *passim;* interviews, six members of the faculty, 22-29 October 1963.

[90]Athletics-Southern Conference File, Byrd Papers; Minutes of the Regents, 21 December 1951; 22 May 1952; Bealle, *Kings of American Football,* 195-199.

anyone to break out of the established pattern. For Byrd the irony appeared again: whatever his shortcomings before the war he only seemed to win new friends; and whatever his successes after the war he only seemed to win new enemies.

Even Byrd's most visible achievement, a spectacular expansion of the physical plant, had its critics. Like many university presidents he seemed to turn increasingly to bricks and mortar during the later years of his administration. His office was filled with blueprints, and from early morning until late evening students often glimpsed him clambering over construction sites, advising foremen or proudly explaining developments to visiting officials. Although some complained that they could not understand where the money came from—a tangle of appropriations, loans, student fees and endowments—or where it went—an equally complex system of bids, cost-plus and direct employment—most conceded that the president displayed genius in obtaining the most for a dollar. Other critics spoke of the overemphasis on construction and a tendency toward ostentatious display, but they found it difficult to name a single superfluous building or unseemly luxury. For the three campuses at College Park, Baltimore and Princess Anne the University obtained approximately 700 acres of land, about 60 new structures and added over $25,000,000 in capital improvements:

Major Construction, 1946-1954[91]

1947 33 temporary buildings—approximately $1,200,000.
Fire Service Building—$170,000.
1948 Addition to Symons Hall—$660,000.
Woods Hall—$283,000.
Frederick, Talbot, Garrett Dormitories—$610,000.
1949 Glenn L. Martin Engineering Building—$1,423,000.
Engineering Laboratories—$1,036,000.
Chemical Engineering Building—$591,000.
Wind Tunnel—$1,240,000.
Somerset, Queen Anne Dormitories—$855,000.
Dormitories at Princess Anne—$520,000.
1950 428 acres, College Park—$378,000.
Livestock Sanitary Buildings and barns—$171,000.
Dormitories and heating plant at Princess Anne—$500,000.
1951 Chemistry Building—$1,780,000.
Byrd Stadium—$618,000.

[91]University of Maryland, *Financial Report . . . 1955*, 139-151; Construction Files, Byrd Papers; Minutes of the Regents, 1945-1954, *passim*.

1952   Physics Building—$986,000.
        Memorial Chapel—$627,000.
        Harrison Laboratory and Greenhouses—$242,000.
1953   Land and Psychiatric Institute in Baltimore—$3,184,000.
        Kelley Memorial in Baltimore—$92,000.
1954   Mathematics Building—$908,000.
        10 houses on Fraternity Row—$890,000.
        Student Union—$760,000.
        Allegany, Charles, Montgomery, Caroline, Carroll, Wicomico
           Dormitories—$1,312,000.
        Jull Laboratory—$370,000.
        J. M. Patterson Hall—$310,000.
        Agricultural Building in Princess Anne—$348,000.
        Laboratory at Crisfield—$144,000.
        Cole Activities Building—$3,300,000.

In the long run the University's greatest postwar accomplishments were the least publicized and the least spectacular. Amidst all the fury over new programs, it was quietly broadening its services and its offerings without controversy and almost without notice. One of the outside investigating committees caught a basic truth about the Byrd administration: "It holds the limelight to such a degree that the glare tends to make us unable to see how great have been the accomplishments."[92]

Every college within the University pointed proudly to significant developments. In Agriculture, Dean Gordon M. Cairns was enriching the courses, the research facilities and especially the number of Ph.D.'s on the faculty. The Dean of Arts and Sciences, Leon P. Smith, established full-scale programs in art, music and philosophy, while the science departments attained nationwide recognition for outstanding work. Under Dean J. Freeman Pyle the College of Business and Public Administration added work in journalism, geography and office management as well as new research bureaus in Business and Economic Research, and Governmental Research. In Education, Dean Harold Benjamin expanded the offerings, played an active part in launching the adult education program and established an experimental Nursery School and an Institute for Child Care. The continuing leadership of Dean S. Sidney Steinberg, along with the magnificent gifts from Glenn L. Martin, made Engineering particularly strong. Its special new features included its work in aeronautical engineering, its wind tunnel and its Institute for Fluid

[92]American Council on Education, *Higher Education in Maryland*, 345.

Dynamics and Applied Mathematics. One of Byrd's greatest disappointments was his failure to obtain an airport for experimental research. Military Science became a separate college in 1951, one of the few such colleges in any state university. Home Economics continued to expand its work under Dean M. Marie Mount. The Graduate School under Dean Ronald Bamford, the fastest growing school in the University, was producing about fifty Ph.D.'s and two hundred M.A.'s each year.

In the Baltimore professional schools similar developments outshone the headline controversies. The greatest progress in medical history was taking place in the development of the sulfa drugs, cortisone, antihistamines, tranquilizers, penicillin and the antibiotics. Although the School of Medicine found it difficult to keep up with the soaring costs of faculty, facilities and research, and thus found itself in serious trouble during the accreditation examination of 1953, many devoted physicians played their part in the medical revolution. These included men like Arthur M. Shipley, Julius Friedenwald, John C. Krantz, Louis H. Douglass, Edward Uhlenhuth, Hugh R. Spencer and Maurice C. Pincoffs. In 1950 the Psychiatric Institute was established under Jacob E. Finesinger, and three years later the $3,000,000 Psychiatric Hospital was completed. The School of Dentistry regained past renown under J. Ben Robinson and Myron S. Aisenberg; the School of Law prospered under Dean Roger Howell; Pharmacy developed a broad graduate program under Dean Noel Foss; and in 1952 the School of Nursing under Dean Florence M. Gipe launched a full four-year degree program. In every field the record of Maryland students on state board examinations was well above the national average.[93]

The Race For Governor

President Byrd had been close to every governor of Maryland from 1924 until the election of Governor Theodore McKeldin in 1950, but despite the efforts of both men Byrd and McKeldin could never become friends. Each instinctively viewed the other as a rival. In each political campaign after 1932 Byrd had been discussed as

[93]For departmental developments before 1949, *Biennial Reports;* after that see *Maryland Alumni Magazine.* Also see *Catalogues,* and departments by name in Byrd Papers.

a probable Democratic candidate for governor. Each time, at the last moment, he had stepped aside content with the power that came from offering his support to the man in office. In 1950, however, the articulate McKeldin attained an upset victory over Byrd's candidate, William Preston Lane, and the new governor's first promise in his inaugural address was "to turn a skeptical eye" on the rapidly expanding University.[94] From then on the two men battled ceaselessly over the University appropriations, the autonomy bill and the control of Morgan State College so that, by 1953, Byrd was convinced that for the sake of the University and the state McKeldin would have to be defeated. This time Byrd determined to lead the fight in person. Long before the formal announcement, political seers anticipated the clash.[95]

In June, 1953, more than a year before the general election, Byrd addressed a public letter to the board of regents suggesting they begin looking for a successor. Almost everyone looked upon the letter as an announcement of candidacy. Immediately his enemies attacked the egotism it displayed while his friends cheered its sense of devotion and sacrifice. Said Byrd:

> It will be a pleasure, in fact, a personally satisfying procedure to me, to remain with the University under another title, possibly President Emeritus, or Chancellor, or with any other title, for such time as may seem to be required to orient the new President in his position and the duties relating thereto. . . .
>
> I can see nothing more horrible than to wait for the time of legal retirement and then find it too late to enter some new field, and, consequently, have to spend the rest of my life doing nothing. It is not my intention to retire in the sense of discontinuing work.
>
> Therefore, it seems absolutely essential to me, even considering my worth to the University of Maryland, to take up some other endeavor and go into a field in which retirement is not compulsory. . . .
>
> This letter has been written after long consideration. The University of Maryland has been my life and to think of leaving it seems to be one of those things that simply do not happen. However, the University will have me available whenever needed.[96]

The board of regents requested Dr. Thomas B. Symons, recently retired as Dean of Agriculture and Director of Extension, to become

[94]*Baltimore Sun*, 11 January 1951.

[95]*Ibid.*, 28 January 1953.

[96]Byrd to William P. Cole [Chairman of the Regents], 26 June 1953, filed in Minutes of the Regents, 26 June 1953.

acting president in January, 1954, when Byrd's resignation took effect.

With almost every Democratic leader supporting Byrd, the primary election of July, 1954, looked easy at first, but difficulties soon erupted as a foretaste of others ahead. George P. Mahoney, a Baltimore contractor and a perennial candidate for office, crashed into the race charging that Byrd had tried to bribe him to stay out, that Byrd represented "boss rule" and that his administration of the, University was a "disgrace." Campaigning furiously, Mahoney attacked Byrd for getting the University into politics, and for his policies on athletics and Negro education. Concentrating on imputations of personal dishonesty, the contractor accused Byrd of "squandering" the taxpayers' money on the University and of profiting personally from land sold to it. Although fair-minded people were offended by the charges of scandal, and even the Byrd hating *Baltimore Sun* expressed dismay at such tactics, Mahoney was confirming an image of Byrd as authoritarian and secretive. Instead of an easy victory for the former University president, the election count stood 159,230 for Mahoney and 163,324 for Byrd. Even then the angry contractor refused to accept defeat and kept the Democratic nomination tied up in recounts and court litigation almost until the eve of the general election with McKeldin. Normally the Democratic Party in Maryland was heavily favored in a general election, but now it was split, its candidate smeared and it faced a popular Republican incumbent.[97]

The general election campaign which culminated in November was more dignified and the central issues were far more substantial than in the primary. McKeldin simply asked for the evaluation report which the Middle State Association of Colleges and Secondary Schools had made to the board of regents prior to Byrd's departure. Such reports were always made in the strictest confidence to guarantee the evaluating committee complete frankness. In the Maryland report, for example, was mention of specific athletes whose academic standing was doubtful and certainly it would have been unfair to spread their names over the newspapers. Nevertheless, McKeldin was asking for the report not only as a candidate, but as the governor who was ultimately responsible for the University. Consulting lawyers on their rights and anxious to keep the Uni-

[97]Personal (1954) File, Publicity (1954) File, Byrd Papers; the campaign can be followed in *Baltimore Sun*, especially, 27 June 1953; 14 October 1953; 20 December 1953; 19 April 1954; 17-30 June 1954; 13 July 1954; 26 August 1954.

versity out of the campaign, the regents took it upon themselves to refuse the governor.[98]

McKeldin seemed willing to let the matter drop, but with the existence of the report made public and with Byrd's University record a major issue, the political tempo quickened. When a candidate for a minor office made headlines with the charge—probably a guess—that the School of Medicine was on probation, Byrd was prodded to mention the report. Lifting certain direct quotations, such as one which referred to himself as "a skillful administrator who has made few mistakes," he cited the report to prove that any University shortcomings actually stemmed from McKeldin who had refused to grant money for essential facilities.[99] Probably for the first time in twenty years the regents were deeply troubled by an action of Byrd's for his quotations did not provide a comprehensive view of the report and more than ever they made the University the central campaign issue. In emergency session the regents hammered out their own painfully honest six-page summary of the report. Along with statements praising Byrd's administration they listed briefly the five "critical areas" cited by the evaluators:

1. The highly centralized nature of the administration;
2. The lack of proper status of the faculty and the deans in the organization and operation of the institution, and particularly the lack of faculty participation in the formulation of educational policy;
3. Library;
4. Status of the School of Medicine; and
5. Intercollegiate athletics.[100]

Concerning the "probation" of the School of Medicine and of the whole University, the regents explained that every school was fully accredited; however, instead of renewing accreditation for the indefinite future, the Middle State Association had voted to "reconsider" the University after two years. The election betting odds shifted to McKeldin. The report played directly into the governor's hands as he developed the old Mahoney charge of Byrd as a "dictatorial and devious" administrator. At least two prominent Maryland professors made public statements attacking their former president on similar grounds and, for the first time since 1895,

[98]*Baltimore Sun*, 1 October 1954 and ff.; Minutes of the Regents, 14 October 1954; 29 October 1954.

[99]*Baltimore Sun*, 10 October 1954; 12 October 1954; 16 October 1954.

[100]Press Release, Minutes of the Regents, 14 October 1954; see also Middle States Association, *Evaluation Report*.

the *Baltimore Sun* announced its support of a Republican for governor. While the Democratic Party swept most offices in the election, the gubernatorial count stood at 319,033 for Byrd and 381,451 for McKeldin.[101]

Although Byrd retained the honorary title of president emeritus, the board of regents believed that a fresh start by a new administration was more valuable than advice from the former president.[102] For a short time Byrd worked for a Baltimore construction company, supervising the building of a race track in Puerto Rico. Briefly he toyed with the idea of running again for governor, but when he withdrew and J. Millard Tawes was elected in 1958, he was named chairman of the Maryland Tidewater Fisheries Commission. Soon after Byrd left the University his son, William, graduated in the vast Cole Field House which his father had planned and which his father's successors, Acting President Thomas B. Symons and President Wilson H. Elkins, had seen to completion. President Elkins and Governor McKeldin both spoke at the commencement exercises without mentioning the former administration, but assuring the crowd that permanent accreditation had been secured and that the University was moving ahead as never before. The former president had refused an invitation to sit on the platform. Almost no one noticed him restlessly pacing along the upper balcony of the Field House, alone.[103]

Few at the huge commencement remembered what the University of Maryland had been when "Curley" Byrd arrived as a student in 1905, or when he became football coach in 1912, or president in 1935. In large measure its growth had come because of him. The evaluation report recognized this fact, pointed to the progress with respect and called the entire institution his "lengthened shadow."[104] Perhaps no other man could have brought it so far and so fast against so many difficult obstacles. Although the evaluation report also pointed sharply to certain weaknesses, it would not have required much time to organize a faculty assembly, to establish closer supervision over athletics or to enlarge the library and the medical laboratories. Byrd's bitterest foes were no longer opponents of the University, but those who wished to make it worthy in every

[101]*Baltimore Sun*, 17 October-3 November 1954; Morris L. Radoff, *Maryland Manual, 1955-1956* (Annapolis, 1955), 275, 289.

[102]Minutes of the Regents, 18 May 1955.

[103]Byrd File, Maryland Room, McKeldin Library; Interview, Adele Stamp, 14 May 1962.

[104]Middle States Association, *Evaluation Report*, 9 and *passim*.

respect of the high-ranking status to which the president had guided it.

In a larger sense Byrd represented more than a series of achievements in building an institution. He represented the democratization of higher education—the democracy of increased enrollment, of progressive education, of equality of occupations, of expanded community services and of concern for well-rounded students. During his administration the population of Maryland increased 60 percent, but University enrollment increased over 300 percent. The University gave free reign to the experimental concepts of John Dewey, concepts which emphasized practical courses, new fields of study and service to the entire community. It represented the new emphasis on the "whole student," not only his intelligence but his character, not only his specialized knowledge but his potential as a citizen. The emphasis resulted in expanded athletics, fraternities, student unions, chapels, counseling and even job placement services. The Byrd administration had roughly paralleled the national administrations of Franklin D. Roosevelt and Harry S. Truman.[105]

Byrd's administration had also come to represent the authoritarianism, the business corporation efficiency, the cold impersonality which plagued so many huge state universities and which paradoxically seemed to accompany democratization. In European universities and in the professional schools of Maryland before 1920, the faculties largely governed themselves, sometimes inefficiently, but with a spirit of freedom and mutual participation. In an institution supported by taxpayers, however, and particularly in one so vast and complex, absolute power resided in a board of regents appointed by the governor. The regents at Maryland were distinguished citizens who volunteered their services and worked conscientiously for the University, but of necessity they delegated their enormous power to a president and a bureaucracy which ran the institution like a factory. A president invariably plays a decisive role, either to make an institution great or set it back for many years. The son of an oysterman, Byrd's personality reflected the vigorous initiative, the vision, the egalitarianism, and sometimes

---

[105]William Manchester, *The Long Gainer* (Boston, 1961) is a fictionalized biography of a university president who bears more than coincidental resemblance to Byrd. The novel's hero is motivated by a passion for democracy, a passion which explains his achievements and schortcomings as university president. Manchester was formerly a reporter for the *Baltimore Sun*.

the authoritarian ruthlessness that built the University of Maryland and also built the nation.

The problems of the University of Maryland in 1954 stemmed from the achievements, not the failures, of the past. A huge and powerful plant employing a thousand scholars and providing training for tens of thousands of students each year, it represented democracy and power. Now it needed to develop excellence within democracy, it had to find a place for the individual in the world of size and power and it had to nourish academic freedom, humanism and a sense of dedication within its efficient operation. College Park, like the whole world, needed values which were not diluted or drowned out by the rushing traffic on the boulevard. These were the real problems when Byrd left, and they were more vague and more difficult than those of an earlier generation. Maryland was ready for the new era. Byrd had seen to that. But it was a different era now.

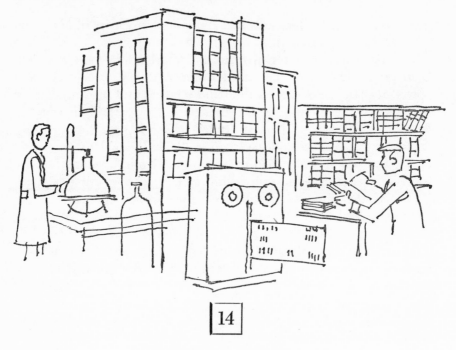

14

Quantity and Quality

As the Russian sputnik beeped aloft during the mid-1950's, saddle oxfords gave way to the Ivy League look on American campuses and a serious purposefulness came over education. The colleges and universities seemed to reflect a national yearning for consensus and responsibility. Experimental institutions of an earlier day began to emphasize traditional values and conservative institutions permitted change; exclusive schools began to cultivate democratic ideals and vast public institutions cultivated quality. No longer little empires unto themselves, the colleges and universities became accepted into the mainstream of society as a part of almost every family's life and the hope of a nation's future.

Just as President Byrd had personified the expansive years before and after World War II, so President Wilson Homer Elkins personified the concern for purpose and quality that came in the 1950's. His administration was characterized by moderation, and he used such old-fashioned words as individualism, discipline and excellence. Although people never felt themselves to be in the midst of radical change as Byrd had made them feel, the difference in mood and in conditions was fully as revolutionary.

The Climate of Learning

The transition at Maryland began during the first eight months of 1954 when Thomas B. Symons served as acting president with the simple acknowledgement, "My primary job [is] to conduct what might be called 'a good housekeeping job'."[1] With all of its modesty the statement contained a radical implication, for Byrd had generally taken an imperial, outward view. For the University to turn inward and clean house marked a departure. For the first time in many years the faculty felt a comfortable familiarity with the administration. The easygoing Dr. Symons had spent a lifetime at Maryland, beginning as a freshman in 1898, and rising to professor of entomology, director of extension and dean of agriculture. Quickly he approved a staff proposal to transfer the remodeled Rossborough Inn to the long dormant faculty club. Under such professors as Ronald Bamford, Russell W. Allen and Peter P. Lejins, the club became an important focus of campus life and even seemed to mark a resurgence of the academic values which the faculty represented.[2]

Dr. Symons' modesty stimulated harmonious feelings outside the University, a harmony immediately evident in the ease with which the University's budget sailed through the 1954 legislature. While Byrd had seen to it that University requests were moderate just before he ran for office, and while legislators were inclined to respect requests drawn up largely by the man likely to be their next governor, they also admired Symons' forthright presentation. In July, as the primary between Byrd and Mahoney grew torrid, observers approved the way Symons kept the University on the sidelines. When the acting president stepped down in September some thought that he might have won the office in Annapolis that his predecessor craved.[3]

Meanwhile the board of regents looked for a permanent appointment, a man who could confirm the new found harmony and guide the institution to the front of the obvious trend toward quality.

---

[1] Regents Minutes, 29 January 1954.

[2] *Ibid.*, 24 September 1954; T. B. Symons, "Report of Progress, University of Maryland, during the Incumbency of T. B. Symons . . ." (Pamphlet, McKeldin Library); Faculty Club Papers, in possession of Professor Peter P. Lejins.

[3] *Baltimore Sun*, 17 December 1953; 2 September 1954; 6 September 1954.

Although the regents smarted under Mahoney's unfounded charges that they were holding the post open for Byrd in case of his defeat, they took their time in considering almost three hundred men. According to the newspapers the regents considered Harry Truman and Adlai Stevenson among others, and certainly they considered the presidents of some of the nation's foremost universities. But the available man who best filled their needs was the soft-spoken president of Texas Western College in El Paso, Wilson Homer Elkins. As a product of public education and an outstanding athlete he fitted a tradition of which Maryland was proud; as a humanist and a Rhodes scholar he assured a new emphasis for the future.[4]

Even in personality the new president seemed to reflect the changed ideals of higher education. Calm rather than flamboyant, formal rather than familiar, direct rather than scheming, and inspiring trust rather than love, he appealed to people on an intellectual level with words which were usually qualified but never evasive. Elkins seldom talked about himself, and it was significant that the first Maryland reporters to interview him wrote their stories without discovering many of the greatest honors of his career. One of the few public references he made to himself came when he was asked to deliver a keynote address at a nurses' convention. Expressing his "abhorrence of the shout and shock" approach, he explained with characteristic qualification:

> I am not by nature the keynote type. I am inclinded to associate the "keynoter" with political conventions where emotion is given a much higher priority than reason, and, while recognizing the place of emotion in our lives, I question the need to encourage more than is naturally present.[5]

His career, like his personality, was quietly spectacular, at once too commonplace and too extraordinary for a novel. Born on a west Texas farm in 1908, the year Byrd finished college, he grew up in San Antonio where his parents ran a grocery. After public school he attended nearby Schreiner Institute, a junior college, where he broke his leg playing football. In 1929 he entered the University of Texas, paying his expenses with a part-time job and an athletic scholarship. There he became famous as "Bull"

---

[4]Regents Minutes, 30 April 1954; *Baltimore Sun,* 13 August 1953; 2 October 1953; 1 May 1954.

[5]Elkins, "The Advancement of Professional Nursing" (1 March 1959) Speeches and Statements File, Elkins Papers, President's Office, College Park.

Elkins, one of the greatest quarterbacks in Texas football history. Aside from earning eight varsity letters in football, basketball and track, he served as president of the student body, was elected to Phi Beta Kappa and four years after entering Texas he simultaneously received his A.B. and M.A. degrees. On a Rhodes scholarship to Oxford University, he completed his doctorate with a dissertation on British-American commercial relations and returned to Texas for two years as an instructor of history. From 1938 to 1948 he served in San Angelo as president of a municipal junior college which during his administration expanded from 200 to 1,000 students. In 1948 he became president of the Texas College of Mines and Metallurgy which had an enrollment of 1,800, and he left it six years later as Texas Western College with 3,800 students. The University of Maryland was a big step upward for the forty-five-year-old college president, but he was used to taking big steps calmly.[6]

In his early speeches as Maryland's president Elkins spoke incisively about emotionally laden concepts of democracy and high standards. Emphasizing quality, he asked whether college education had been "oversold" in America, and whether, perhaps, some people might not be better off in terminal junior college programs or in vocational trade schools than in a university. Far from curtailing democratic opportunity, he would extend it by elevating the social respectability of junior college education and by guaranteeing everyone the fullest opportunity to develop his talents. A university, however, was the place for truly "higher" education, for men and women of outstanding capacity and ambition; it must not reduce its standards to the lowest common denominator; it must battle mediocrity rather than produce it. Stung by the Maryland evaluation report, most people were delighted with the president's stern emphasis on "basic" subjects like English and mathematics and with his polite jabs at any "progressive" education which promised an easy road to learning. Maryland was ready for such ideas, especially if applied in the moderate, straightforward way Elkins explained them.[7]

The president also struck a responsive chord in his concern for

[6]See *Baltimore Sun,* 10 October 1954; *Washington Post,* 20 January 1955.

[7]Elkins, "The Individual in a Complex Society" (Address at Johns Hopkins University, 22 February 1955) Speeches and Statements File, Elkins Papers; Elkins, "The State and the University" (Inaugural Address, 20 January 1955) Speeches and Statements File, Elkins Papers; *Baltimore Evening Sun,* 23 September 1954; *Baltimore Sun,* 24 November 1954; 23 February 1955; 16 December 1955; *Philadelphia Evening Bulletin,* 15 March 1958.

the old-fashioned virtues of individualism and self-discipline. Frightened by the growing standardization of society with its faceless organization men, many Americans blamed the welfare state while others, such as Admiral Hyman Rickover, blamed the life-adjustment curriculum of the public schools. Elkins attacked nothing, but spoke up eloquently in favor of individual differences rather than conformity and of the intellectual rather than the social function of higher education. The University must be a place to learn and not a place to be taught. In practice this meant an emphasis on individual study, on the humanities, on the recognition and reward of outstanding work, on classroom rather than extracurricular activity and on individual freedom and responsibility. Indeed, throughout Elkins' career and throughout his speeches ran an almost Victorian emphasis on self-sufficiency, responsibility, character and drive. Such virtues were beginning to sound modern again.[8]

Quite naturally the students expressed the new climate of learning even better than the administration. In the early years of the twentieth century the student mood was characterized by hazing and juvenile pranks; in the 1920's students were exuberant and pleasure bent; and in the 1930's they were worried and searching. After World War II came a disjointed and dissatisfied mood, and by the late 1950's the characteristic attitude was one of determined self-improvement. When the serious mood first appeared, about 1955, journalists talked about the apathy of college students who seemed uncommitted to causes or revolts, but on closer examination they appeared to be more moderate and cautious than indifferent. Unlike the students before them, they seemed to be keenly aware of the expense of college, of the honor of being there and of the eagerness of others to take their places.

Probably the main reason for the changed mood was the growing necessity for an academic degree in obtaining a job. The campus had become a recognized training ground for life, and the college transcript with its A's and B's, or with its D's and F's, was almost as essential in applying for employment as a clean shirt had been a few decades earlier. A new figure on the campus was the corporation personnel recruiter. Long before graduation the better students

[8]Elkins, "The Individual in a Complex Society," Elkins, "A Community of Quality" (Convocation, 27 February 1957) Speeches and Statements File, Elkins Papers; Elkins, "The Challenge to Democracy" (Convocation, 28 January 1958) Speeches and Statements File, Elkins Papers; Diamondback, 15 October 1954.

were signed up or accepted in graduate school, while the poorer students reported—a little too loudly—that they had not made up their minds which of several offers to accept. Students knew that the once gentlemanly C grade had become a stigma of mediocrity. The growing number of graduate students, the increasing pressure for admission, the conservative mood of the country, the uncertainty of life in a world with the mushroom cloud, all contributed to the restrained and serious attitude. "Academic performance," observed Elkins "is becoming socially acceptable."[9]

Although extracurricular life remained important, it seemed to assume a self-improvement quality for students eager to take advantage of the entire scope of college life. To enjoy themselves and to acquire the well-rounded background that the job recruiters desired, students almost dutifully attended dances and athletic events, joined fraternities and took part in intramural activities, student government, publication efforts, drama groups, professional clubs and honoraries. Like self-conscious suburbanites, they briefly took the initiative in channeling off excess springtime energy in a "Greek Week" tradition of chariot races and songfests, but like most contrived suburbanite activity it gradually expired. The stereotype of fraternities with their excessive social life and snobbery began to fade as the University and the fraternities themselves imposed restrictions, and as dormitory units organized almost to the point of being fraternities. Not that the groups were dying, as their enemies continued to predict, for many students wanted the close social contacts they provided; but the old controversy surrounding them slowly faded as joining them became more a matter of individual choice than of wealth or social pressure.[10]

Student publications reflected the changed atmosphere. The humor magazine, *Old Line*, gave way to the highly serious literary periodical, *Expression*, which later changed its name to the *Calvert Review*. The *Diamondback* extended its coverage of world events, educational trends and broad University policies. Sports were relegated to the back pages, and social columns disappeared almost entirely. The more dedicated students, particularly in the profes-

[9]Elkins, "The Climate of the University" (Convocation, 17 March 1961) Speeches and Statements File, Elkins Papers; Elkins, "Decisive Issues in Higher Education" (Convocation, 17 February 1960) Speeches and Statements File, Elkins Papers.

[10]See Elkins, "The Campus Greeks, Their Opportunities and Responsibilities" (National Convention Sigma Kappa, 1 July 1962) Speeches and Statements File, Elkins Papers; *Baltimore Sun*, 18 March 1961.

sional schools, joined their professors on research projects, some of which were evaluated in articles in scholarly journals. Even the *Maryland Alumni Magazine* evolved from accounts of reunion banquets to serious articles, frequently written by faculty members, about important questions of the day.

Campus dress reflected the climate of moderation. Men were as conscious and more circumscribed in fashion attire than women, limiting themselves to the conservative understatement of the Ivy League look. For classroom wear the ideal attire was dirty white bucks—they could be purchased pre-dirtied—khaki trousers and a slightly frayed button-down-collar Oxford weave blue shirt; the ideal dress for dates was a charcoal suit, oxblood cordovans and a hand-blocked challis tie. So long as the attire was subdued there were many variations. Strangely, the fashion existed in the name of individualism rather than conformity, for students imagined they were asserting themselves against the styles of the business world and especially of Madison Avenue. For coeds the Ivy League look was less well-defined, but it required short hair, subdued colors and a tailored trimness.

Although student attitudes remained infinitely varied, those who established the mood of the campus set a narrow course between individualism and conformity. On the one hand, the student who played chess while his friends played tennis was admired. On the other hand, the true believer, the self-pitying esthete, the party drunk, the once admired eccentric of any sort was likely to be advised matter-of-factly by his fraternity brothers to visit the campus counseling-psychiatric center. Unlike the students of the 1930's, those of the 1950's held political opinions which reflected the editorials of staid daily newspapers rather than excitement over such ideas as Marxism or postivism. For almost a decade, from the early 1950's to the early 1960's, they were neither particularly enthusiastic about, nor especially angry at, whatever political party was in power.[11]

Only twice during the decade did students rebel against authority, and perhaps there was as much maturity as juvenile delinquency in both protests. The first revolt occurred in 1955 when the administration determined to enforce the state law and the old University ban against campus drinking. Students howled that they were being

[11]See David Boroff, *Campus U. S. A.* (New York, 1961), 190-204 and *passim;* see also University student publications, *passim.*

treated as children and that the rule would drive them to off-campus cabarets. Although discontent smoldered and violations continued, the ban stuck. Soon *Diamondback* editorials were pointing to the "fairness" and the "necessity" for the rule.[12]

The second ouburst grew out of the first with the appearance of the mysteriously named and clandestinely circulated "TTTT" newspaper. Attacking the drinking ban, the housemothers whom they deemed too strict, the professors who were too lax, the ROTC, big-time football and the opponents of higher faculty salaries and academic standards, the paper destroyed its possible effectiveness by vulgarity and exaggeration which antagonized both the administration and the students. By basing their case on student freedom and academic quality, however, even the campus radicals seemed to reflect more maturity than the Chi Omegas of the 1920's, the political extremists of the 1930's or "The Challenger" of the 1940's.[13]

While the administration and the student body reflected the new climate of learning, the change rested fundamentally in the attitude of the general public which had begun to worry about the pall of mediocrity that seemed to hang over the schools. Especially after the Russian achievements in space, everyone seemed to be asking why Johnny could not read and why the universities had allowed American science to lag. Such words as "intellectual" and even "egghead" began to have a favorable connotation. Beginning in 1947, when a Truman-appointed commission produced a six-volume report on the defects of American education, investigations multiplied until educators soon spoke of "the age of the report." Within Maryland, the evaluation report of 1953 seemed to mark the turning point in the public's attitude toward the University. It was as if at the very end of his administration Byrd had regained his capacity for turning disaster into triumph, for the report's criticism of the University, along with Elkins' straightforward talk, evoked only sympathy and affection for the institution.

The state's changed attitude was especially evident in the editorials of the *Baltimore Sun*. For some years the editors had shown signs of making peace with the University, and instead of exulting that the evaluation report had proved many of their suspicions to be correct, they displayed only concern for improving the institution. When Elkins arrived they greeted him effusively, and almost every inter-

---

[12]*Diamondback*, 7-18 November 1955; also, 19, 21 February 1957; 5 March 1957.
[13]Incomplete files of "TTTT" in Public Relations Office, College Park, and in Maryland Room, McKeldin Library.

view or speech inspired them to more enthusiastic praise. No longer did the editors treat the University as a rival of Johns Hopkins; it had become their own, an important part of the state they loved. Once the University's sharpest enemy, the *Sun* had become one of its warmest friends, proud of its accomplishments and eager to help make it great.[14] Elkins' formal inaugural in January, 1955, was impressive. Distinguished scholars from the nation over paid their respects; Governor McKeldin promised assistance in grandiloquent terms; and the following month Johns Hopkins University awarded its first honorary degree to a University of Maryland president.[15]

Even the general assembly appeared positively eager to aid the University. After Elkins' first appearance before a legislative committee, the senate unanimously passed an unprecedented resolution acclaiming his "quiet, unhurried, and unruffled" demeanor and his deep "ability and sincerity."[16] Instead of the University's scheming to obtain every possible penny, and instead of the assembly's maneuvering to save every cent, the two worked together with mutual respect to build the best possible University with the funds available. With the University genuinely uninterested in expanding beyond its normal sphere of teaching and research, there was a note of irony in 1961 when the assembly requested the institution to accept supervision of the Maryland Department of Research and Education, a state agency for conservation and fisheries research which Byrd had once fought so fiercely to obtain. During Elkins' administration the governor's budget commission imposed some cuts in requests for buildings, but the legislature never rejected a single major item, and neither the governor's commission nor the legislature made a substantial change in requests for the operating budget. Occasionally the governor's commission actually added a minor item which it believed necessary.[17]

During Elkins' first year the assembly approved almost $3,000,000 for a new library and an addition to the hospital, both of which Byrd had pleaded for in vain. In addition, the legislature approved a

[14]*Baltimore Sun,* 1 May 1954; 21 July 1954; 2 September 1954; 24 November 1954; 19 January 1955; 16 December 1955; 26 July 1956; 26 February 1957; 28 March 1959; Regents Minutes, 13 June 1958.

[15]University of Maryland, *The Inauguration of Wilson Homer Elkins . . .* (College Park, 1955).

[16]*Journal of Proceedings of the Senate of Maryland . . . 1955* (Baltimore, 1955), 113-114.

[17]*Baltimore Sun,* 15 March 1961; 23 May 1961; Regents Minutes, 13 May 1959; 18 May 1960; For comparisons of budget requests and appropriations, Regents Minutes, *passim.*

$2,000,000 increase in the operational budget, primarily for improving faculty salaries and laboratory equipment. From 1953 to 1965 the plant value soared from $65,000,000 to $120,000,000; the operating budget more than doubled, to approximately $70,000,000 annually. An astonishing explosion of growth, it was the quietest, most orderly expansion in the University's history.

The public attitude toward higher education was also evident in the increased attention which the federal government, foundations and private industry gave to the universities. The National Defense Education Act of 1958 provided large loan funds for students, and in 1965 came substantial direct appropriations for scholarships, library and classroom construction and medical education. Foundations such as Ford, Guggenheim and Rockefeller gave increasingly large sums to academic pursuits. Most important, government and industry were looking to the universities for their own purposes, especially for research. Each year they signed millions of dollars worth of contracts with universities, agreeing to pay the salaries of research professors and graduate students in exchange for the investigation of particular problems. In 1953 Maryland received about $2,000,000 annually for research, primarily in agriculture, but by 1965 the sum had increased to more than $14,000,000, primarily for research in the physical and health sciences. This expenditure, larger than the entire University budget before World War II, ranked Maryland among the twenty largest research universities in the nation. Not only did research mark a rise in public confidence, but it also served to elevate the entire intellectual atmosphere of the institution.[18]

Inevitably there was a testing of the new academic climate at Maryland. Some critics detected an undemocratic note in the emphasis on quality, a few alumni imagined the University was lessening the value of earlier degrees and others were frankly disappointed by the apparent decline of football. The protest was triggered by two national magazine articles which overpraised the University's progress by making unfair comparisons with the past. Late in 1956 Harper's Magazine featured a story titled "The Fall and Rise of the University of Maryland" which specifically contrasted the Byrd and Elkins administrations, and soon after Newsweek published a similar article entitled "Losers Are Winners" which related the University's rising standards to its losing football teams. Certainly any implica-

[18]Regents Minutes, 16 March 1962; 15 June 1962; 14 June 1963; Industrial Research Magazine (April, 1963), 19-25.

tion that the University had "fallen" under Byrd was absurd, and many alumni disliked the slurs both articles cast on the former president.[19]

The protest was led by a Prince George's County legislator, Hervey Machen, and a weekly Prince George's County tabloid, the *Free State News*. The politician and the tabloid attacked the University for "allowing" the articles to be published, demanded alumni control of the board of regents and called for a legislative investigation of "unrest" on the campus. It was soon apparent, however, that Machen had misjudged the public temper. Newspapers throughout the state saw the proposed investigation as an attack on high standards and released a barrage against the Prince George's County politician. Citizens' groups sprang to the defense of the University, Byrd publicly disassociated himself from the call for an investigation and faculty and students drew up petitions expressing near-unanimous support of the administration. Calmest in the excitement was Elkins who met with Machen to assure him the University had not sponsored the magazine articles and that it followed a policy of avoiding comparisons with the past. After quiet study the general assembly tabled Machen's demands, assuaging him by reducing the regents' terms from nine to seven years with a maximum of one reappointment.[20]

Actually this protest, like that of the "TTTT," only confirmed the great majority of students, alumni and people of the state in their eagerness to elevate the University into a larger realm. The episode cleared the air and defined the new direction of the University better than any number of philosophical speeches. Within a bracing new climate of learning the University set out to harness the new enthusiasm.

Ingredients of Quality

Although many changes took place simultaneously, in general the University turned first to internal reform—to a broad extension of

[19]*Harper's Magazine*, CCXIII (October, 1965), 64-68; *Newsweek*, LII (November 24, 1958), 68-70; *Diamondback*, 16 October 1958; 21 November 1958.

[20]*Free State News*, 15, 29 January 1959; *Baltimore Sun*, 25 January 1959; 16, 20, 28 March 1959; 2 March 1960; *Washington Post*, 24-28 January 1959; 1, 6 February 1959; 27-29 March 1959; 2 April 1959; *Washington Star*, 26 January 1959; Faculty Senate Minutes, 5 February 1959; *Diamondback*, 5, 10 February 1959; Regents Minutes, 9 March 1959; *Maryland Alumni Magazine*, XXX (January-February, 1959), 5; XXX (March-April, 1959), 9.

Dr. Symons' good housekeeping policy and to a quiet reorganization and strengthening of its faculty, its departments and its administrative operations. Some of the early changes were suggested by the evaluation report, but from the beginning the University was interested in attaining far more than minimum standards. With its house in order, the University next turned its attention to the improvement of its students.

Faculty morale and self-government seemed to be the two things which Elkins was in something of a hurry to improve. Almost immediately after he assumed office and two weeks after classes began in September, 1954, the president called the first general faculty meeting that most of its members could recall. The professors caught a note of respect in his voice as he called them the "backbone" of the University. Not only did he speak of higher salaries to attract able men on a supply and demand basis, but also of a university's duty in elevating the status of the scholar. He emphasized the importance of winning faculty loyalty to the institution and of closing the gap between administration and faculty by giving professors a major voice in shaping educational policy. Specifically, he suggested that the faculty take the initiative in organizing a governing body. Taken aback, the professors could only request him to appoint a committee, and promptly he named sixteen professors and five deans to serve under the chairmanship of Professor Carroll E. Cox. All winter the committee deliberated, not making its report until the following spring. The faculty as well as the regents debated every sentence, but by September, 1955, the new government went into operation substantially as proposed.[21]

The new University government provided, first, for the faculty in each college to meet at least once each semester to establish policies for that college and to refer broader questions upward to the University assembly and senate. Second, it provided for an assembly of the entire faculty once a semester to discuss University policies and to refer questions to the senate. Finally, the government provided for a senate which was to meet at least twice each semester and was to be the real core of faculty government. It included twenty-seven ex-officio members from the administration and sixty-eight members

[21]Elkins, "The State and the University"; *Washington Star*, 1 May 1954; *Baltimore Evening Sun*, 23 September 1954; Minutes of the General Administrative Board (Registrar's Office, College Park), 10 September 1954; Faculty Assembly Minutes (Registrar's Office, College Park), 27 September 1954; 6, 9, 26 April 1955; 23 September 1955; 25 October 1955; *Diamondback*, 29 September 1954; 5 November 1954; Regents Minutes, 23 September 1955; 27 September 1956.

elected from the faculty on the basis of one representative for each eleven members of the teaching staff. The senate named twenty-one standing committees which dealt with every phase of University life. Although the exact composition of the senate and the number of committees changed with time, the basic structure remained. Faculty government was emerging in a similar way all over the country. As late as 1939 only 25 percent of America's 177 largest universities had a working faculty government, but by 1955 the figure had risen to more than 60 percent.[22]

Faculty government gave the appearance, at least, of solving one of the most persistent problems in higher education. From the very institution of American universities, and certainly from Maryland's beginning as a medical college, the concept of an independent community of scholars had clashed with the need for efficient centralization and with the determination of taxpayers to control an institution which they helped to support. On one hand, power radiated down from a board of regents to a president, and on to the deans and department heads. Whether this authority appeared through authoritarian leadership or through an amorphous professional bureaucracy, the faculty often found it alien and intimidating. On the other hand, as power radiated up through the faculty, professional self-seeking, intrigue and stagnation were often apparent.

While the problem of the exact balance between central authority and faculty remained, the equilibrium which Maryland achieved in 1955 seemed typical of the new era of good feelings in higher education. The senate established a point of contact in which faculty and administration sensed that they might be allies in a common cause. The administration began to appear as a spokesman rather than an employer, as an assistant rather than a usurper of power. During the next decade the faculty took the initiative in suggesting important changes within the University, and what they did was sometimes different and sometimes more effective than what the administration could have accomplished alone. More important, perhaps, faculty morale rose as professors increasingly felt responsibility and loyalty to their institution as well as to their specialties. Calling faculty government "the most important single development since the beginning of my administration," President Elkins ob-

[22]Faculty Assembly Minutes, 23 September 1955 and ff.; Faculty Senate Minutes, 24 October 1955 and ff.; John S. Brubacher and Willis Rudy, *Higher Education in Transition* . . . (New York, 1958), 358-359.

served that "the voice of the faculty is heard again in the land of the terrapin."[23]

Faculty conditions improved in a multitude of other ways. The administration and regents accepted a tenure policy drafted by the senate which specified that after a given number of years—usually six at the rank of assistant professor or upon promotion—a professor could not be dismissed except for "immorality, misconduct in office, incompetency, or willful neglect of duty." This insured a security and academic freedom unknown for many years at Maryland. A redefined sabbatical policy, vague in the past, guaranteed professors freedom from classroom duties for at least half a year of every seven. A liberalized patent policy guaranteed professors a portion of the royalties on inventions or copyrights resulting from work done on the campus. Professors assumed full control over absences and examinations, and had a major voice in determining promotions, schedules and teaching loads.[24]

One of the greatest boosts to faculty morale and to the internal structure of the University came in 1957 when the administration adopted a faculty senate recommendation for the creation of a General Research Board which provided summer salaries, equipment and even publication costs for men engaged in independent research. Designed largely to promote research in the humanities and social sciences—which did not share proportionately in the vast research contracts from government and industry—the board sought to encourage promising young faculty members as well as established scholars. Although other universities had similar programs, the plan at Maryland placed the University in the forefront of one of the most progressive developments in higher education. In actual practice it meant that promising and productive members of the faculty received a summer salary beyond their base pay. By 1965 the board was awarding over sixty grants a year, averaging approximately $1,800 each.[25]

The largest program for improving the faculty came through salary increases. From 1940 to 1954 academic salaries over the coun-

[23]Regents Minutes, 25 January 1957; 11 June 1957; University of Maryland, *Your State University Reports* (College Park, 1956), 1; Elkins, "The Age of Education" (Convocation, 28 February 1958) Speeches and Statements File, Elkins Papers.

[24]Faculty Senate Minutes, 29 October 1956; 26 May 1958; 28 January 1960; Regents Minutes, 25 January 1957; 11 June 1957; 25 November 1958; 29 January 1960; 21 June 1960.

[25]Faculty Senate Minutes, 15 May 1956; Regents Minutes, 21 June 1960; General Research Board File, Graduate School, College Park.

try reached their lowest ebb; while the real income of the American people had risen 42 percent, the income of ordinary laborers had risen 48 percent, and that of many professions had increased over 80 percent, yet the college professor lagged behind every major occupational group with an actual 5 percent decline in real income. At Maryland salaries lagged even behind the national average. Instructors averaged $4,163 for the regular ten-month year, while full professors averaged only $6,487. The *Diamondback* published pictures contrasting the fine new automobiles in student parking lots with the run-down jalopies in the faculty areas. With the increasing concern over education, however, the rise of salaries after 1954 was as significant as their earlier decline. Just eleven years later, in 1964-1965, the average faculty compensation at Maryland was $9,510 with some full professors making double that figure. Although efforts to obtain faculty housing and special insurance coverage had still not materialized, the faculty obtained social security coverage in 1956 and slightly improved retirement benefits in 1960. In addition, the University launched an endowment drive to supplement salaries for distinguished professors. Faculty conditions were improving with almost equal rapidity everywhere and, even though professors still ranked below their nonacademic friends, they were confident that their future was bright. Faculty turnover at Maryland was sharply reduced, and observers noted dramatic improvement in the professor's attitude toward his profession and his institution.[26]

Within the administration there were both personnel and basic structural changes. The regents created the new positions of Executive Vice President, to which they named Albin O. Kuhn, and Academic Vice President, to which they named R. Lee Hornbake. The president and the two vice-presidents formed a sort of top administration triumvirate. In other new positions were B. James Borreson as Executive Dean of Student Life, Alvin E. Cormeny as Director of Endowment and Development, and Robert J. McCartney as Director of University Relations. As older men retired, many new men appeared as deans of the various colleges, including William S.

[26]Charles P. McCormick, "What's Happened to Faculty Salaries," *Maryland Alumni Magazine*, XXVIII (January-February, 1957), 7-9; *Diamondback*, 28 September 1956; University of Maryland, "Budget for . . . 1954" (Comptroller's Office, College Park); "Budget for . . . 1963"; Records from the Office of the Vice President for Academic Affairs, College Park; Faculty Senate Minutes, 25 January 1956; 5 March 1957; 7 November 1960; Regents Minutes, 3 February 1961; 15 June 1961; University of Maryland, *Prospectus for New Development of the Distinguished Professor Program* . . . (College Park, 1961). Salary averages omit the School of Medicine.

Stone (Medicine), Vernon E. Anderson (Education), Frederic T. Mavis (Engineering), Selma F. Lippeatt (Home Economics), Verl S. Lewis (Social Work), Donald W. O'Connell (Business and Public Administration), William P. Cunningham (Law), John J. Salley (Dentistry), Charles Manning (Arts and Sciences), and Paul Wasserman (Library Science). Professors noted with approval that both vice-presidents came from faculty ranks and also approved the tendency to fill other major vacancies with able outsiders. Of the first thirty-one new department heads, twenty came from the outside.

With the emphasis on strengthening existing offerings rather than on launching into different areas, new educational programs developed slowly out of sustained demand and usually out of established work. A long-promised classics department appeared in 1955 to enrich the humanities. Six years later, after prolonged dispute over its location, a School of Social Work was established in Baltimore with a two-year program leading to a master's degree. Assuming an important role in various programs associated with President Johnsons' war on poverty, the new school prepared to move into the remodeled old law school building. Probably the most significant new program came at College Park where the established science departments demanded vast computers. The multi-million dollar Computer Science Center began operation in 1962, moved into a new building the following year and quickly emerged as one of the strongest such departments in the nation. Many people predicted that the computer centers would one day be as important as libraries to the work of a university. Statewide demand required creation of a Graduate School of Library Science which in 1965 accepted its first students. An Institute of Applied Agriculture appeared the same year, offering a two-year vocational program. Plans slowly developed for a new School of Architecture.[27]

Traditional departments expanded and deepened their offerings. Engineering added significant work in aeronautical, chemical and civil engineering; Agriculture added work in animal sciences and agricultural engineering; Arts and Sciences expanded most with important new work in anthropology, fine arts, mathematical theory, microbiology and music. An interdepartmental program of comparative literature appeared which launched a widely acclaimed scholarly journal, *Comparative Literature Studies*. Far-reaching de-

[27]Regents Minutes, 28 January 1955; 25 February 1955; 27 September 1957; 13 June 1958; 15 June 1961; 3 May 1963.

velopments came in physics with new fields of astronomy, astrophysics, cosmic ray and space physics, high-energy and molecular physics, nuclear and plasma physics and general relativity. Government and foundation awards of over $6,000,000 gave University physicists one of the largest cyclotrons in the world. With some of the most renowned scholars in the country and approximately 300 full-time graduate students each year, many observers considered physics to be the strongest department in the University and one of the strongest in the nation.[28]

The University strove especially to strengthen basic undergraduate work. The administration constantly stressed good teaching and instructed deans and department heads "to appraise the teaching of each faculty member and to consider carefully classroom performance when recommending new appointments." The board of regents created a number of $1,000 awards for excellence in teaching to be given annually to effective teachers. Most departments assigned their top men to elementary as well as graduate courses. With the huge influx of graduate students, some departments, such as history, used their outstanding professors for lectures to large groups which broke up once a week into small discussion sections directed by graduate students. Many believed that this system provided undergraduates with better lectures and closer supervision and also provided graduate students with valuable teaching experience. Zoology, mathematics and sociology transferred much of their basic work to television. Foreign languages, placing new stress on the spoken word, introduced electronic teaching machines. Education experimented with reading machines. Better equipped offices and classrooms, often air-conditioned, aided almost every department.[29]

The long delayed McKeldin Library was finally completed in 1958, and two years later the Health Sciences Library was finished in Baltimore. The University made major efforts to acquire standard works for undergraduate use, and the increase in the library budget was impressive. Attempting to keep pace with the enormously increasing flow of current materials for graduate student use while simultaneously striving to supply past deficiencies remained major

[28]Regents Minutes, 18 June 1959; 4 May 1962; Records of the Department of Physics, College Park.

[29]Faculty Senate Minutes, 29 October 1956; 19 November 1963; "The Tidewater Conference," *Maryland Alumni Magazine*, XXX (May-June, 1959) , 6-8; *Baltimore News-Post*, 15 September 1959; 2 October 1959; Regents Minutes, 14 June 1963; *Diamondback*, 8 November 1963; 20 November 1963; Wilson H. Elkins, *A Decade of Progress and Promise, 1954-1964* (College Park, 1964) , 9.

problems. A faculty study in 1965 urged that the library facilities be approximately doubled and that total book holdings be more than tripled within the next decade.[30]

Among the various colleges in the University, the most sweeping changes came in medicine. Stimulated by the evaluation report and by active faculty committees, the board of regents took the initiative even before Elkins arrived by naming William S. Stone, formerly a colonel in the United States Medical Corps and Commandant of the Graduate School at Walter Reed Medical Center, as Director of Medical Education and Research to coordinate the School of Medicine, the School of Nursing, and the hospital. A few months later, to further integrate these branches, Dr. Stone was also made Dean of the School of Medicine.

Within the next few years outstanding new department heads were acquired for the medical school. Clinical professors were shifted from a part-time to a full-time basis comparable with the regular lecturing professors, the curriculum was revised to emphasize clinical work in the junior and senior years, and both the lecture and the clinical departments were affiliated more closely with the administration. New work came in preventive medicine, physical therapy and biophysics. In 1957 the general assembly approved a 56 percent increase in operating expenses for the medical school, and early in the following year the Council on Medical Education of the American Medical Association acknowledged unqualified accreditation of the school with special praise for its vigorous administration.

From eminent respectability the medical school moved into professional leadership. It pioneered in the use of a core laboratory to serve students for all of their pre-clinical training. To stimulate student morale and to encourage self-education, it also pioneered in a program allowing students time off from their regular work to pursue research under a particular professor. Slowly the medical classes were expanded from 100, to 128 and then to 150. Medical research increased in spectacular fashion. A government-financed International Center for Medical Research and Training appeared at Maryland with a branch in Pakistan to stimulate the study of medicine on a worldwide basis. Maryland obtained the most powerful betatron in the world for medical use. A million-dollar Shock Trauma Center was established. By 1965 the faculty could boast that

[30]David S. Sparks, et al., "Report of a Committee For a Study of Library Needs," Faculty Senate Minutes, 11 May 1965.

there was nothing happening in medical science that was not also happening at Maryland.[31]

The law school also underwent its greatest internal changes in a half-century, adopting a revised curriculum which was at once more applicable to daily practice and better grounded in legal theory. To emphasize the practical aspects, new courses appeared in trial tactics, business planning, government contracts and international trans- actions. The courses stressed such daily matters as cross-examination, legal writing, obtaining legislation and approaching government agencies. The old case method of instruction often gave way to a problems approach in which, for example, a student might deal with the sale of a suburban home from financing, through title search and preparation of a deed, to settlement and problems of default on financing. To provide perspective, meanwhile, new theoretical courses and seminars appeared in comparative law, constitutional law, legal history and jurisprudence. Between the practical and the theoretical, students obtained a wide range of electives in which to develop their own specialities. The school term was lengthened and, beginning in 1966, a college degree was finally required for admis- sion. New faculty members came increasingly from other states. Faculty research increased. A continuing legal education program was established to keep graduates abreast of changes in the law. Many believed that the night school, with its part-time approach to legal training, would soon disappear.[32]

One program in the University actually declined as military sci- ence was reduced from a college to a department. The ROTC requirements were slowly relaxed, first for conscientious objectors and then for certain transfer students; in 1962 the requirement was cut from two years to one, and in 1965 the course was finally dropped as compulsory. Professors were generally pleased that the military fanfare at student assemblies and commencements was being re- placed, at least in part, by an atmosphere more harmonious with the intellectual functions of a university. Perhaps it was entirely un-

[31]Regents Minutes, 18 November 1953; 30 April 1954; 2 November 1954; 29 April 1955; 18 May 1955; 24 February 1956; 23 January 1959; *Bulletin of the School of Medicine*, XXXIX (April, 1954), xix-xxi; XXIX (July, 1954), iii-vii; XXIX (October, 1954), xxv-xxcii; XL (April, 1955), lxviii-lxix; XL (October, 1955), 97-98, i-ii; XL (July, 1955), i; XLII (July, 1957), xxii-xxiii; XLIII (December, 1958), 3-23; XLVIII (January, 1963), 1-4; xlix (July, 1964), li "Arlie House Seminar on Medical Education, June 1963" (Pamphlet, Medical School archives).

[32]Lawrence M. Jones, *et al.*, "Final Report of the Curriculum Committee . . . March 19, 1964" (Pamphlet, Law School archives); also, see *Catalogues*.

related, but the administration announced that student political activity, discouraged since about 1948, would again be permitted on the campus. Although certain "social action" groups such as CORE were still apparently unwelcome, student Democratic and Republican clubs flourished.[33]

Through all of the changes, the public watched most eagerly for modifications in athletic policies. From the start of his administration President Elkins made it plain that, while Maryland would follow scrupulously honest procedures, it would continue to strive for superior performance in athletics as in everything else. He declared that athletics added a "wholesome tone" to college life, and that losing teams did not in themselves raise academic standards. Instead of reducing the number of athletic scholarships, which were well within Atlantic Coast Conference limits, the University increased the number of academic scholarships. Instead of cutting back on facilities for football players, it broadened sports facilities for all students. In 1959 it opened an 18-hole golf course, one of the finest on any college campus, paid for largely by receipts from football bowl games. Scrutinizing every detail of football policy, the president promised that every athletic grant would pass through an appropriate committee and that he would be personally informed of its deliberations and actions.

While the examination of procedures went on, the football teams, which had largely been recruited during earlier years, continued their spectacular performance. In 1954 Maryland won seven games, lost two and tied one. Then, in 1955 Bob Pellegrini, Mike Sandusky, Ed Vereb and Frank Tamburello led the team to a perfect 10-0 record and another trip to the Orange Bowl, the fifth bowl game in nine years. There, Maryland lost again to Oklahoma. A few days later came an even greater blow when Coach Jim Tatum announced that for personal reasons and through no disagreement with the administration, he was leaving for a position at North Carolina.

Tatum's departure and the disastrous seasons which followed did far more than investigations to silence charges that Maryland was primarily a football school with a hired team. During the next three years under Coach Tommy Mont, Maryland won eleven games, lost eighteen and tied one. Since Tatum and Mont operated under almost the same system, skeptics began to admit that Tatum's genius rather than Maryland's excesses must have been chiefly responsible for the victorious record of the past. As suspicions faded and as professional football increased during the late 1950's to relieve the pressures on college teams, the old collegiate spirit began to return to campus games. Players who could be defeated began to be accepted as students again.[34]

On one occasion, in October, 1957, when Queen Elizabeth II and Prince Philip of England spent a Saturday afternoon at Byrd Stadium, athletic glory shone brighter than ever before. The entire nation was thrilled by the thought of royalty at a football game, and the Queen later called it the high point of her American visit. No longer was Maryland the great powerhouse team and perhaps for that very reason the autumn spectacle—with bands and cheerleaders, capacity crowd and the upset 21-7 victory over North Carolina— seemed to represent the finest in American college life.[35]

The University continued to seek victories in every phase of its athletic program. In 1959 Coach Mont was replaced by Coach Tom Nugent, according to the cruel but well understood procedure of sports. During the next seven years Nugent won thirty-six and lost thirty-four games. In all sports from the fall of 1959 to the fall of 1965 the University won or tied for forty of a possible sixty-nine conference titles, by far the finest record in the league. The College of Physical Education under Dean Lester M. Fraley came to be accepted as an outstanding school of its type rather than a perversion of things academic.[36]

Improved physical facilities, which had once seemed opposed to academic values, emerged as another important ingredient of quality. Although growing enrollment accounted for much construction, the new buildings also provided finer libraries and research facilities and better working conditions for students and faculty as well as expansion of the University services to the state. At various centers some sixty major buildings appeared:

[34]Wilson H. Elkins, "Football Has Place on Campus," *Maryland Alumni Magazine,* XXVIII (January-February, 1957), 13; Regents Minutes, 29 October 1954; 24 March 1955; 14 May 1955; 24 June 1955; 6 April 1965; 16 April 1958; 23 January 1959; 30 September 1959; *Baltimore Sun,* 4-13 January 1956; *Baltimore Evening Sun,* 6-9, 13, 18 January 1956; *Washington Star,* 18 January 1956; Terrapin (Student Annual), 1955-1962.

[35]Queen's Game Scrapboook, Maryland Room, McKeldin Library.

[36]*Washington Star,* 2 December 1959; Regents Minutes, 21 June 1960; 15 June 1961; 15 June 1962; 14 June 1963.

Major Construction, 1955-1967[37]

1955   Engines Research Laboratory—approximately $500,000.
      Asphalt Institute—$200,000.
      Stores Building, Baltimore—$700,000
1956   Journalism Building—$400,000.
      Swimming Pool—$400,000.
      Heating Plant—$1,000,000.
      Golf Course—$200,000.
      Garrett County Farm—$200,000.
      President's House—$80,000.
1957   Howard County Farm—$400,000.
1958   McKeldin Library—$2,600,000.
      North Administration Building—$500,000.
      Whitehurst Hall, Baltimore—$500,000.
      Dunning Hall, Baltimore—$600,000.
      Two fraternity houses—$200,000.
1959   Cecil, Frederick, Dorchester, Worcester Dormitories—$1,400,000.
      Faculty apartments, Princess Anne—$200,000.
      Parking Garage, Baltimore—$500,000.
      John E. Howard Hall, Baltimore—$1,300,000.
      Fraternity house—$100,000.
1960   Health Sciences Library, Baltimore—$1,200,000.
      Student Union, Baltimore—$1,900,000.
      Nathan L. Drake Lecture Hall—300,000.
      Nuclear Research Laboratory—$200,000.
1961   Business and Public Administration Building—$1,500,000.
      Foreign Languages Building—$500,00.
      Cambridge, Antietam, Belvedere, Catoctin Dormitories—
        $1,300,000.
      Two fraternity houses—$200,000.
1962   Taliaferro Hall, addition—$500,000.
      Student Union, addition—$2,000,000.
      Physics and Mathematics, addition—$400,000.
      Cumberland, Bel Air, Chestertown, Centreville Dormitories—
        $4,800,000.
      Fire Service Building, addition—$300,000.
1963   Denton Dormitory and Dining Hall—$2,800,000.
      Infirmary—$500,000.
      Five fraternity houses—$500,000.
      Calvert Apartments—$1,200,000.
      Computer Science Center—$200,000.

[37]University of Maryland, *Financial Report for . . . 1964* (College Park, 1964), 137-153; Records of the Assistant to the President, College Park; University of Maryland, "Educational Facility Needs: The Next Ten Years," Office of the Assistant to the President. All costs are approximations.

1964   Howard Hall, remodeling, Baltimore—$2,000,000.
        Physics, addition—$2,700,000.
        Easton Hall Dormitory—$2,100,000.
        University College, Adult Education Center—$2,500,000.
        Dairy Research Laboratory—$200,000.
1965   Law School Building, Baltimore—$1,900,000.
        J. Millard Tawes Fine Arts Building—$2,800,000.
        Education Building—$1,800,000.
        Physical Education and Student Union, Princess Anne—$600,000.
        Elkton Hall Dormitory—$2,100,000.
        Computer Science, addition—$200,000.
1966   H. J. Patterson Hall, addition—$1,600,000.
        Dormitory, Princess Anne—$400,000.
        McKeldin Library, air conditioning—$240,000.
        Ellicott City Hall Dormitory and Dining Hall—$2,900,000.
        Space Sciences Building—$1,500,000.
        Utilities, roads, etc.—$800,000.
        Academic Building, Baltimore County—$2,400,000.
        Cyclotron—$6,500,000.
1967ff Physical Sciences, addition—$3,300,000.
        Library, Princess Anne—$600,000.
        Library, Baltimore County—$3,000,000.
        Hospital, addition—$12,000,000.
        Dentistry Building, planned—$10,000,000.

The academic quality of the Baltimore professional schools especially depended upon improved facilities. While enrollment in the city remained relatively stable, severe crowding was relieved by new quarters for Nursing and Pharmacy, by additions to the hospital and by a huge new laboratory building. Perhaps even more important, the Health Sciences Library and the new Student Union with dormitory facilities for 198 students provided the beginning of a campus atmosphere. As urban renewal got underway with city and federal funds, open spaces and even a few shrubs began to appear. The handsome new Law School Building added a touch of elegance. By 1965 the University had spent over $15,000,000 in Baltimore for new professional school facilities, with another $25,000,000 appropriated or expected in the immediate future. Architecturally more modern than College Park, the brick facades maintained a relationship to the home campus. Observers noted that student pride in Baltimore, which had sometimes been lacking in recent decades, was beginning to rise.

In College Park at least $45,000,000 went for new library facilities, student activity centers and science laboratories; for filling out the mall with classroom buildings and the beginning of a new one in front of the president's house; and for spectacular eight-story dormitory centers along the northern perimeter of the campus. Although some complained about the slavish dedication to the brick Georgian style, at least it gave the campus unusual architectural homogeneity. During all of the new construction there were enough older buildings to prevent the rawness which had scarred the campus during the late 1940's. No one suggested that the construction was hasty, luxurious or overemphasized. It seemed to reflect the essential growth of a dynamic institution and to be intimately related to academic quality.

The University and the Student

Once internal reforms at Maryland were underway, the administration and faculty set out on a sweeping program to encourage excellence in their students. The University moved slowly, for the exclusion of taxpayers from a state institution was a delicate matter. For almost two years in advance President Elkins prepared public opinion, explaining the basic fact that quality education was incompatible with the maintenance of a social center for any one with tuition to spend. Meanwhile, a faculty committee under Professor Charles Manning drafted proposals which would gradually raise academic standards to equal those of the best state universities in the nation. The first step, the Academic Probation Plan, was announced in the spring of 1957 and took effect in the fall.

Although complex in its details the plan provided generally that if a student's average fell below C, or if he failed 35 percent of his work in a semester, or if he failed to make junior standing after five semesters, then he was placed on academic probation under special supervision; and if he failed to better his standing after one semester on probation he was dismissed. At the end of the first year under the plan even the officials were astonished at the result. Falling upon accumulated generations of academic deadwood, the regulations made 1,550 students, about 18 percent of the total undergraduate enrollment, subject to dismissal. Interpreting the rules generously, the administration reinstated some students and modified some details of the plan; still almost 14 percent of the undergraduates were permanently eliminated.[38]

The second phase of the program for higher standards came in 1961 with the introduction of the precollege summer session. High school graduates with less than a C average were, with minor exceptions, required to attend a special University summer school. There, along with certain orientation work, they took two courses, including the traditionally difficult freshman English. Students had to pass both courses with certain minimum grades in order to be admitted to the freshman class. With the program first went into operation about 450 low-ranking students withdrew their applications rather than attend the school, 188 failed the summer classes and 132 were allowed to register as freshmen. It was the first time in Maryland history that high school graduates were refused admission to the state university. Out-of-state students had to present a high school average of C to be considered for admission, and in practice almost all of those admitted had at least a B average.[39]

The faculty pushed still further for quality education with the revision, in 1965, of the basic undergraduate curriculum. In general the new program increased the number of required courses from eight to twelve, with additional work in mathematics, science, social science and fine arts or philosophy. The physical education requirement was reduced from two years to one. To supervise the basic work, Professor Gayle Smith was appointed to the new position of Director of General Education. The faculty also urged four years of high-school foreign languages for admission to the University but, when public school officials protested, it agreed that for the time being the four years of languages would remain a recommendation rather than a requirement.[40]

While eliminating the weak students the University, in 1962, launched a special honors program to provide extra stimulation for those who were outstanding. Pioneered at Swarthmore and elsewhere in the 1920's as a means of encouraging specialization, the programs caught on during the 1950's, especially at large public universities, as a means of providing select students with the enriched curriculum and tutorial attention they might receive at the most exclusive insti-

[38]Elkins, "A Quantity of Quality"; Faculty Senate Minutes, 25 March 1957; 19 January 1959; Regents Minutes, 11 April 1957; 27 September 1958.

[39]Faculty Senate Minutes, 19 April 1961; Regents Minutes, 15 June 1961; 19 June 1964; *Baltimore Sun,* 31 August 1961.

[40]Regents Minutes, 13 March 1964; 22 January 1965; *Baltimore Sun,* 14 March 1964.

tutions. Far more rigorous than the regular program, the honors program was designed for the unusual students to whom education was more important than an easy diploma, for those who wished to learn instead of those who had to be taught, for intellectual leaders instead of followers.

Limited at first to less than fifty students, the honors candidates were selected not only on the basis of their grades, since one purpose was to escape the tyranny of statistics, but also on the basis of their interests. Some departments, such as mathematics, began their honors program by articulating their work with high schools and frankly recruiting able students. Other departments, such as English and history, created prehonors sections of their basic courses in which selected teachers worked with promising students. During their junior and senior years the students invited to continue in the program devoted about twelve semester hours of their major subject to guided reading, personal discussion with professors and directed research. The program culminated with special oral and written examinations which entitled the student to graduate with "honors" or, in exceptional cases, with "high honors." The University also established a number of honors scholarships and a special honors dormitory where outstanding students were invited to live together. Probably the most fashionable lodging on the campus, it seemed to indicate that the day had passed when the outstanding student was considered peculiar.[41]

The effect of raising standards appeared with startling clarity by the 1960's. In 1950 about 65 percent of the entering freshmen had graduated in the top half of their high school classes, but by 1964 the figure had risen to 82 percent. Since University grades remained the same, or were even slightly lower than before, it appeared that the professors' expectations were also rising. Many students, of course, were unable or unwilling to approach the mark of excellence, but they were no longer proud of their shortcomings.[42]

A portrait of the College Park student in the mid-1960's was probably fairly typical of his counterpart throughout the country. About 79 percent of the total were undergraduates and about 66 percent were men. Of the undergraduates, 44 percent lived in dormitories, 9 percent lived in fraternity or sorority houses and the rest lived with

[41]Faculty Senate Minutes, 31 January 1961; 30 January 1962; Regents Minutes, 15 June 1962; 19 June 1964; *Diamondback;* 19 November 1963.
[42]Regents Minutes, 14 June 1963; 19 June 1964.

parents, relatives or in nearby apartments. About 10 percent of the undergraduates were married. Coming chiefly from middle class backgrounds, about 18 percent of the students estimated their parents' incomes at less than $6,000, and only 7 percent estimated that income to be over $15,000. Only 2 percent came from the farm to the University once designed for farmers' sons. Less than 30 percent of their parents had completed college, but 90 percent expected their children to finish. About 35 percent of the undergraduates held part-time jobs, usually on the campus, but 60 percent owned or regularly used a car. For all of the emphasis on standards, the study load hardly appeared crushing. Less than 40 percent of the undergraduates reported studying as much as 20 hours a week outside of class, although over 40 percent expected to continue with graduate study. About 75 percent of the students considered C work poor, or only fair, for themselves. About 70 percent valued the character traits of stability, responsibility and industry above intellectual curiosity, independence or cultural appreciation.[43]

Most of the graduates since 1920 had not yet reached the peak of their careers, but already their achievements pointed in diverse directions. Many had succeeded in business. James F. Dingman (Engineering '21) was vice-president of American Telephone and Telegraph, John W. Smith (Engineering '21) became president of Seaboard Air Lines Railroad, Wilbur G. Malcolm (Agriculture '22) became president of American Cyanamid, Carlisle Humelsine (Education '37) was director of Colonial Williamsburg. Joseph C. Burger (Arts and Sciences '25) became a lieutenant general in the Marine Corps, and Elwood Quesada (Arts and Sciences '27) became a lieutenant general in the Air Force. A foreign student, Galo Plaza (Agriculture '29) became president of Ecuador. In the field of literature and education, Munroe Leaf (Arts and Sciences '27) was a famous author of childrens' books, and John T. Fey (Law '40) became president of the University of Vermont. Such names, of course, were only examples of scores of other successful alumni.[44]

Confirmation of the University's academic progress came late in 1964 with the establishment of a chapter of Phi Beta Kappa. By far the oldest and most famous undergraduate scholarship society, it served the academic world as a kind of super accreditation agency, accepting as members only those institutions judged to have the soundest undergraduate programs. In the past, because of inade-

[43] From answers to questionnaires distributed to students at registration, fall 1961 and 1963, Counseling Center, College Park.
[44] Records, Alumni Office, College Park.

quate standards and partly, perhaps, because of bad luck, Maryland had been rejected for membership more times than people liked to remember. President Elkins had made membership a goal of his administration, and the goal was reached almost ten years to the day from his arrival. The University basked in acclaim. "The Brains at Maryland Are Beginning to Show," headlined the *Washington Post.* Many people inside the University felt that the rejoicing was in celebration of a milestone which the institution had, in fact, long passed.[45]

The Education Explosion

Enrollment rose steadily after 1954, and the growth contributed to the affluence and achievements of the University; but by the mid-1960's the increase was reaching landslide proportions which seemed to be altering the mood and structure of the institution. As officials planned for the future, soaring numbers was the acknowledged problem that seemed to hang strangely ominous.

Growing enrollment, the impersonality of a huge institution, the tyranny of statistics in a mass society, these were the best answers people could find for the new climate of restlessness which seemed to come over the campus during the mid '60's. They were not full answers, for social unrest and political extremism was a national phenomena. Civil rights, Barry Goldwater and Vietnam incited passions everywhere but, as is often the case, the national passions seemed to be intensified on the campuses—as symbolized by the student rebellion at Berkeley—and reflected at most large universities, including Maryland. Instead of the universities providing a haven for self-discovery and idiosyncrasy, personal identity became as difficult to discover on the campuses as anywhere else. Attending college had once been a mark of distinction and identity in itself, but with almost everyone attending it no longer offered a sense of achievement. Students complained that they were only holes in the punch cards that registrars used, that each individual was assigned a place in a system where he desperately struggled to keep up or get ahead. The efforts to personalize the system—the orientation lectures, the careful classification of students according to interest and ability, the antiseptic luxury of student lounges and the professionally sympathetic counsellors—only seemed to close the avenues of escape.

[45]*Washington Post,* 3 September 1964; 23 May 1965.

At Maryland, as elsewhere, enrollment pressures required more professors than existed to give students the personal attention they really wanted. The University had been unusually successful in maintaining its old seventeen to one student-faculty ratio, but it had succeeded only by increasing its number of graduate assistants. Such assistants, along with improved methods of teaching, probably provided more efficient instruction than ever before; but the warmth of personal relationships was undoubtedly lacking. Regretfully, English professors instructed freshmen how to obtain personal attention: "To see a reader, the student must sign a conference chart two days in advance. . . . He should indicate the time (at fifteen minute intervals), his name, and his section number. . . . Before coming to a conference the student should prepare for it by. . . . having specific questions to ask about his problems."[46] Theoretically it was possible for a student to graduate without having spoken to a professor in his major field. Increasingly these were the realities of the education explosion, and inevitably students looked for means of self-expression. Inevitably, too, the self-expression sometimes became protest.

The first wave of protest seemed associated with the civil rights movement. When a faculty committee rejected the establishment of a CORE chapter on campus and when the administration appeared to discourage an appearance of Martin Luther King, student interest in the civil rights movement only increased. During the 1964 presidential primary, when Governor George C. Wallace of Alabama appeared on the campus appealing for segregationist support, over 8,000 students turned out, perhaps the largest student crowd in the University's history. The emotional intensity of the crowd exceeded that of a football game, and perhaps exceeded that of the issues involved. A large majority jeered the governor. Perhaps in an effort to quiet the turmoil over civil rights the Dean of Student Life, B. James Borreson, instructed the chaplains associated with the University not to participate in civil rights rallies. The resulting storm of abuse lasted almost a year until the dean resigned.[47]

Student self-assertion, often shared by the faculty, generally seized upon the catchword "freedom." Student conservatives deepened their commitment to freedom from government controls and liberals deepened their commitment to freedom from the rich and powerful. Great protests about academic freedom erupted when President Elkins and the board of regents rebuked the Presbyterian chaplain,

[46]Syllabus, English I, 1963-1964, English Department Office.

[47]*Washington Star,* 14 January 1962; *Baltimore Sun,* 13 October 1963; *Diamondback,* 12-14 November 1963; 12 February 1964; 6 May 1964; 16 September 1964.

Reverend Jesse W. Myers, for advising incoming freshmen to shun fraternities. Students rallied to each side. The campus chapter of the American Association of University Professors met three times in an effort to censure someone, but each meeting bogged down in the semantics of freedom and responsibility. In 1965 the administration felt pressures from the opposite direction. When University officials, after some hesitation, allowed the civil rights leader Bayard Ruskin to appear on campus, the general assembly passed a resolution of censure.[48]

The changing mood appeared with the coming of a modified "beatnik" look to the campus. Few went to the extremes of sandals and beards, but most students let their hair grow longer, men's attire became less formal and coeds wore less make-up. For most students freedom and democracy meant their right to establish dress regulations in the dining halls; for a vocal minority freedom meant the right to wear whatever clothes they wished. When theologian Paul Tillich appeared on campus, two sets of student protesters marched outside with opposite theological objections. Campus "teach-ins" over Vietnam reflected the search for answers and also for self-expression. One group of students, calling for departure from Asia, set up headquarters in the Student Union to fast for peace; a rival group appeared opposite them urging a larger war in Asia and munching candy bars under the slogan "Eat for Peace." By threatening a library sit-in to protest limited library hours, students probably hastened an extension of closing time from 10 P.M. to midnight. Other students protested poor teaching by preparing a publication to rank different courses. Perhaps the ultimate protest came in 1965 with the organization of CAPOG—the Collegiate Anti-Protest Organization Group.[49]

No one could be sure whether the mood was healthy or irresponsible. Generally the best students were involved, but the objects of their protests seemed interchangeable, their goals unfocused. Censure by the administration only seemed to stimulate them. The problem of facelessness in a mass society and the need for personal identity was, after all, the dilemma of the twentieth century.

The University of Maryland was an educational collosus by 1965— one of the ten largest universities in the nation, one of the five largest

[48]*Baltimore Sun,* 19 October 1963; *Diamondback,* 18 October 1963; 13 February 1964; *Washington Post,* 29 January 1964; Regents Minutes, 29 January 1964; 13 March 1964; Minutes of Maryland Chapter, American Association of University Professors, 14 March 1964; 18 March 1964; 26 March 1964; *Baltimore Sun,* 14 October 1965.

[49]*Diamondback,* 16, 23-24, 30 April 1964; 17-20 February 1965; 14-19 May 1965; *Washington Post,* 13, 15 September 1965.

if its off-campus enrollment were counted, and one of the fastest growing. A few older men still remembered when the president of the struggling little Maryland Agricultural College had been willing to cross the state to persuade a single prospect to come to College Park and when ten new students gave the institution cause for general rejoicing. Now the statistics were awesome:

ENROLLMENT, 1953-1965[50]

	1953-1954	1959-1960	1965-1966
Agriculture	546	457	532
Arts and Sciences	2,111	3,497	8,455
Business & Public Administration	1,568	1,939	3,156
Education	787	2,044	4,202
Engineering	1,009	2,024	2,556
Graduate School	2,139	2,584	4,758
Home Economics	485	356	655
Physical Education	257	411	576
Library Science			81
Undetermined	101	780	1,294
Total College Park	9,003	14,092	26,265
Dentistry	430	384	391
Law	394	481	575
Medicine	478	371	480
Nursing	146	165	180
Pharmacy	237	231	103
Social Work			138
Graduate	80	116	245
Total Baltimore	1,765	1,748	2,121
University College, Stateside	4,434	8,729	12,657
Europe and Atlantic	9,895	19,396	22,488
Far East		9,584	8,231
Total University College	14,329	37,709	43,376

The growth of certain colleges within the University altered the composition of the student body. Undergraduates increasingly shifted from technical to general education, especially into Arts and

[50]From Registrar's Office, College Park. Figures for 1953-1954 and 1959-1960 are year-end figures; those for 1965-1966 are slightly smaller beginning-year figures. University College figures are for course registrations, not individuals, during the course of the year. University College figures in last column are registrations during 1964-1965.

Sciences. The Schools of Engineering and of Education also grew, reflecting their expanded role in society, but other professional schools both at College Park and Baltimore, remained relatively stable. The student body was shifting dramatically into graduate work. The development of the Graduate School reflected the increased stature of the University, and the growing number of older students contributed to the serious and intense atmosphere of the campus. The fastest growing division, and the most difficult for conservative educators to adjust to, was University College. Its students usually attended at night or in off-campus centers, but they were too numerous to be dismissed as outside the mainstream. An accurate representation of the University student had to account for servicemen, businessmen and housewives as well as the boys along fraternity row.

Explanations for the enrollment increase lay in the growing population, the continued prosperity and the rising demands of employers for highly trained personnel. Only slightly less obvious were the challenge and fears of the space age, the glamour of science and the growing complexity of modern society. Politicians cited the need to keep ahead of the Russians, humanists cited the need for values and social scientists theorized that higher education was a cause rather than a result of social and economic well-being. Finally, there was a circle effect. As demand created stronger colleges, colleges became all the more fashionably essential for the middle class respectability to which almost everyone aspired.

At the University of Maryland unusual area population increase combined with the institution's reputation for rising standards to keep the growth rate well above the national average. Administrators continued to express surprise that restricting the admission of unqualified students usually increased the number of applications from the qualified. While enrollments over the country increased about 4 percent each year after 1954, the students at Maryland grew at the rate of about 8 percent annually. Generally the growth was anticipated and orderly, creating little of the dislocation of the postwar flood. The University continued to accept about 15 percent of its students from other states and about 2 percent from foreign countries.[51]

With all of the growth, however, the jarring fact remained that the

[51]For comparative statistics, see January issues of *School and Society;* Commission for the Expansion of Higher Education in Maryland (John N. Curlett, Chairman),

enrollment increase had just begun. Statisticians predicted that total college enrollment in the state would double during the 1960's and more than triple during the 1970's. In one way or another, the University would have to assume the chief responsibility of serving that increase. Even assuming the rapid development of other campuses, officials predicted the enrollment of 35,000 students at College Park by 1975. The University had scheduled the erection of a new 500-student dormitory building annually for the indefinite future, but that construction would provide for less than half of the predicted annual increase. State and University officials found it necessary to re-examine the structure of higher education throughout Maryland.[52]

The first major examination, ordered by the governor and legislature, was the Maryland Commission to Study the Needs of Higher Education, the so-called Pullen Commission of 1955, which called attention to the forthcoming explosion in education and called upon the University and the five state teachers' colleges—Bowie, Coppin, Frostburg, Salisbury and Towson—to prepare for it. The commission noted approvingly the tendency in Maryland and throughout the country for local leaders to take the initiative in creating community junior colleges. Supported largely from county appropriations, such colleges usually began without a campus, holding evening classes in a local high school and attracting students unable to leave home or to gain admission to the University. Sometimes the academic standing of the colleges was doubtful, but with adequate guidance and support they offered a promise of relieving the enrollment pressure on the University and also of providing an education for students who would not receive it otherwise. The commission recommended, and the legislature approved, substantial aid to these institutions, so that the five community colleges of 1955 had tripled in number and quadrupled their enrollment by 1965. The commission was vague about over-all regulation of the state's burgeoning college system.[53]

The second survey came in 1961, the Commission to Study the Problem of Expansion of the University of Maryland—generally

Public Higher Education in Maryland, 1961-1975 (Baltimore, 1962). Hereafter cited as Curlett Commission Report. Regents Minutes, 30 September 1959; 19 November 1959; 29 September 1961; 15 June 1962; 13 September 1963; 25 September 1964.

[52]University of Maryland, Division of Institutional Research, "Long Range Projections For Planning Purposes, University of Maryland . . ." (January, 1965).

[53]Maryland Commission to Study the Needs of Higher Education (Thomas G. Pullen, Jr., Chairman), *The Needs of Higher Education in Maryland* (n.p., 1955); Junior College File, Maryland Room, College Park.

called the Warfield Commission—which aroused a furor of controversy by its frank approach to the problem of administration. The
commission urged that the three largest teachers' colleges—Frostburg,
Salisbury and Towson—be converted into regional centers of the
University of Maryland. They would become liberal arts colleges,
their students could transfer to College Park for special work and
their control would be transferred from the State Board of Education
to the University. To the Board of Education, however, and especially to its powerful superintendent, Dr. Thomas G. Pullen, the
entire scheme was a power grab by the University, a means of down-
grading teacher training, a seizure of the strong teachers' colleges and
a refusal to accept responsibility for the weaker ones. When Governor Tawes wavered in supporting the commission's recommendation, the 1961 general assembly tabled the report and ordered a
third study.[54]

The third report, destined to set the educational future for the
state, came in 1962 from the Commission for the Expansion of
Public Higher Education in Maryland, the so-called Curlett Commission. Basing its proposals on the highly successful California plan,
the commission recommended that the community colleges be recognized as one system directed by the State Board of Education; that
the five teachers' colleges be converted into liberal arts colleges and
recognized as a second system directed by a state-appointed board of
trustees; and that the University remain a third system as constituted.
Morgan State, despite its objections, would be combined in the
second system under the state board. The entire structure would be
"coordinated" by an Advisory Council for Higher Education representing each of the various institutions. Eager for action after so
many delays, the legislature in March, 1963, enacted the Curlett
Commission recommendations into law. As if this were not enough,
the legislature simultaneously instructed the University to proceed
with the establishment of four additional campuses—in the Baltimore
area, in Western Maryland, in Southern Maryland and on the Eastern Shore.[55]

From the start, the Advisory Council had trouble controlling the

[54]Commission to Study the Problem of Expansion of the University of Maryland
(Edwin Warfield, III, Chairman), *A Plan for Expanding the University of Maryland*
(n.p., 1960); *Baltimore Sun*, 25-27 February 1960; 5, 14, 19, 23 March 1960; 19 April
1960; 19, 26 May 1960; 10-14 September 1960; 30 October 1960; 5, 14, 16 February 1961;
8, 19, 22 March 1961; 13 June 1961. See Expansion of University File, Regents Office.
[55]Curlett Commission Report; *Baltimore Evening Sun*, 22 June 1962; 4 July 1962;
Washington Post, 26 August 1962; *Baltimore Sun*, 2, 22 June 1962; 7-8 February 1963;
7-27, March 1963.

system. University officials were frankly fearful that it might be dominated by the smaller state institutions, and the small institutions feared competition from the University's branches. As the University pushed for development of a Baltimore branch, the area that supplied one-third its total enrollment, friction in the council intensified. University officials wanted the branch in the suburbs, probably the northern suburbs which would supply the most students. Towson College officials, on the other hand, fearing a nearby University branch, rallied support among other small colleges. The Mayor of Baltimore, Theodore R. McKeldin, eager for a downtown college, joined in opposing the University's suburban choice. Torn by controversy and too paralyzed even to elect an executive officer, the council did nothing. Citing the authority of the legislature, University officials proceeded with a compromise of their own and announced a suburban location near Catonsville, almost as far as possible from Towson.[56]

The Baltimore branch developed rapidly. People called it the Catonsville campus, or more officially UMBC—University of Maryland in Baltimore County. In the preceeding century academic builders usually had planned too grandly, especially in the matters of finances and enrollment, and often they had to curtail plans as they went along; but in the twentieth century planners had to keep raising their sights. The legislature appropriated $2,500,000 in 1964 for the first academic building, $3,000,000 the next year for a library, and these were only beginnings. As if symbolic of the change, the new architecture was modern. The regents named Albin O. Kuhn as Vice-President for the Baltimore City and County Campuses. Homer W. Schamp, Professor of Molecular Physics at College Park, became Dean of the Faculty for the Catonsville campus. The first 500 freshmen were expected in the fall of 1966, with a new class to be added each year. At first officials predicted 3,000 students by 1975, then they said 10,000 and then they talked of the not-distant day when the branch would have more undergraduates than College Park. Times had changed since the little Maryland Agricultural College struggled into existence.[57]

[56]Baltimore Sun, 27-31 March 1963; 15-20 September 1963; 15 October 1963; 14 January 1964; 22 February 1964; Baltimore, Department of Planning, "A Third Campus, A Statement of the Need For An Undergraduate Branch of the University of Maryland in Downtown, Baltimore . . . (January 1964).

[57]Regents Minutes, 12 March 1965; 14 May 1965; 11 June 1965; Baltimore Sun, 26 January 1964; 18 June 1965.

The University of Maryland, if only to save itself from numbers, was providing real leadership where leadership was needed. The legislature approved its initiative with suggestions for other branches. Still looking for overall coordination, the legislature reorganized the Advisory Council under nine members, independent of any institution and appointed by the governor. The new council appointed Dr. Wesley N. Dorn as executive director and went to work on another report. In whatever manner the system evolved, the University of Maryland was developing as part of the total needs of society, not as an ivory tower, but according to a larger scale which some people called the "multiversity."[58]

Evolution toward the multiversity of the future meant infinitely more than larger enrollments and proliferating campuses. It meant that the institution that once nourished ancient truths must become an institution that actively guided society. The University of Maryland traditionally defined its goals in terms of education, service and research. These categories could stand, but their meaning broadened. Education no longer meant serving those who happened to enroll and no longer meant presenting programs which appealed to a president or a committee; education for the multiversity meant guaranteeing fair opportunities for all and inspiring the ablest to leadership. Service no longer meant promoting the special interests of the farmer or physician, but promoting the balanced social, economic and political well-being of the entire community. Research no longer meant the opportunity for professors to pursue truth unfettered, but it meant assuming the direction and guaranteeing the balance of society's search for knowledge.

In the area of education the University was becoming increasingly concerned with statewide needs, was reaching out through scholarships and counseling to attract able students who were missing opportunities, and was increasingly seeking to maintain a reasonable balance between the number of graduates who entered various professions. No longer concerned with a single program for brilliant or average students, for liberal arts or vocational students, or for rich or poor students, the University was establishing different programs for different students in which no one compromised the others. No longer measuring its success by expansion, the University carefully studied the state's need for such programs as a School of Library

[58] *Washington Post,* 7 March 1964; *Baltimore Sun,* 3 July 1964; 3 October 1964; 9 January 1965; Clark Kerr, *The Uses of the University* (Cambridge, Mass., 1963).

Science or of Architecture. Committees searchingly examined University shortcomings, such as inadequate libraries, while other committees considered educational "extras," such as endowed chairs, more flexible curriculum requirements, a junior-year-abroad program, campus beautification and a better atmosphere for study. With all of the broadening aims the philosophical basis of educational planning seemed more practical than ever before. No longer did professors talk of remaking human nature or even of increasing human happiness, but of providing education as a normal function of life and an essential element in civilization.

In the area of service the agricultural agencies were shifting their emphasis from increased production to marketing and consumer protection and to the broader problems of agricultural economics and sociology. New University agencies slowly entered the vast area of urban services, providing coordination and guidance for city planning, urban renewal, urban sociology and for the financing and structure of township government. The medical sciences added to their numerous services in keeping the alumni abreast of recent developments, in expanding the dissemination of information to the public and by increasingly entering the broad area of psychology and sociology. The University more and more became a meeting place and a source of counsel for business and professional groups of almost every type—bankers, physicists, florists or stamp collectors. The Adult Education Center served these groups handsomely with its 150-room hotel and its abundant conference facilities. All such services, which once had seemed to threaten purely academic functions, became increasingly complementary to them, a natural facet of University leadership.

The area of research, finally, became the most rapidly expanding of all the University's functions. Millions of dollars poured into universities from government and industry, transforming the investigations of the scholar into what economists called the "knowledge industry," one of the mainsprings of national growth. University officials planned new research institutes, additional research professorships and rapidly multiplying graduate assistantships. As outside money poured into scientific research, Maryland worked to maintain the balance in the social sciences and humanities.[59]

The public was coming to understand the University of Maryland,

[59]Reports of the Committee on The Future of the University, Faculty Senate Minutes, 16 March 1963; 30 March 1965.

as it integrated itself into society, better than ever before. The people of a proud state in the most prosperous era of all history recognized a responsibility to nourish the institution which helped men to learn, to serve, to reach toward the unknown. Combining a noble heritage with a fresh promise for the future, the University provided a fitting capstone to society. It was, of course, impossible to prove the absolute value of the institution, or of knowledge, or for that matter of civilization or life itself. But if life did have meaning, then civilization was worthwhile, and so was knowledge, and so was the struggle for a finer University of Maryland.

Bibliographical Note

Although specific references have appeared in footnotes, this story rests primarily upon certain large bodies of material scattered over the University's campuses and over the state. Before about 1912 those records are generally sparse, so that the historian eagerly seizes upon every available detail from which to construct his account. After about 1912, and especially after about 1935, the historian's problem, even for a single institution like the University of Maryland, becomes one of overabundance, of discovering the underlying themes of history amidst the vast accumulation of detail.

For the University as it emerged in Baltimore, the basic body of material consists of a number of leather bound manuscript volumes located in the archives of the School of Medicine. This includes three large volumes comprising the regents' minutes from 1813 to 1920, one volume comprising the trustees' minutes from 1826 to 1839, and five volumes comprising the medical faculty minutes from 1812 to 1839, and from 1857 to 1923. Other volumes there include the records of the stillborn School of Divinity, the long-struggling College of Arts and Sciences in Baltimore, and the numerous nineteenth century medical schools which eventually merged with the University. The School of Dentistry, rightly proud of its history, carefully preserves a large body of material dating from the 1840's. The School of Law, the School of Pharmacy, and the School of Nursing have smaller collections of material dating from their founding. In the Health Sciences Library is a fascinating collection of notebooks, compiled by students attending the School of Medicine during the nineteenth century. Small collections of the unpublished papers of individual professors, of alumni, and of state officials concerned with the University are located in the Maryland Historical Society, the Maryland Medical and Chirurgical Society, the Peabody Library and the Hall of Records. Particularly important, both for Baltimore and College Park, are the Albert C. Ritchie Papers in the Hall of Records.

Of published material on the early University of Maryland, the catalogues of the various schools, published regularly after 1837, provide important material. The *Laws of Maryland,* the *Proceedings of the General Assembly,* and the *Documents of the General Assembly* yield a surprising amount of material, including the messages of the successive governors, irregular reports and petitions from the University and occasional committee investigations on higher education in the state. From the faculty has come an unending stream of articles, published lectures, study guides, textbooks and memoirs. John R. Quinan's *Medical Annals of Baltimore* . . . (Baltimore, 1884) provides a full bibliography of early medical faculty publications. Professional journals, some of which were edited or sponsored by members of the University faculty, contain important material for the entire span of the University's existence. *Old Maryland* (1905-1914), The *University Gazette* (1914-1917), the *Hospital Bulletin* (1906-1916) and the *School of Medicine Bulletin* (1916 to date) are among the most important twentieth century publications from the professional schools.

Valuable histories of the Baltimore schools have come from men intimately associated with the events they recount. Nathaniel Potter, a medical professor from 1807 to 1843, published *An Account of the Rise and Progress of the University of Maryland* (Baltimore, 1838), an inaccurate and opinionated book, but a first-hand account containing much information not available elsewhere. Bernard C. Steiner, a prolific Maryland historian, compiled *Education in Maryland* (Washington, 1894), a book which includes both historical accounts and contemporary descriptions of the institutions of the state written by men closely associated with those institutions. Eugene Fauntleroy Cordell, a graduate of the School of Medicine in 1868 and subsequently professor and librarian, devoted much of his life to collecting material for his *University of Maryland, 1807-1907* . . . 2 vols. (New York, 1907), a detailed and accurate work which provides a point of departure for any subsequent historian.

The early records of the Maryland Agricultural College are even more sparse than those of the Baltimore schools. Except for a few bound manuscript volumes of matriculation records, stock transfer registers and financial accounts, the other documents relating to the institution burned in the fire which swept the College in 1912. Two excellent agricultural periodicals in the state, the *American Farmer* (1818-1897) and the *Maryland Farmer* (1864-1887), maintained such bitter rivalry that when one championed the College the other was inclined to view it as a major source of all the farmer's ills so that together they provide a remarkably board coverage of the institution. The College published its catalogues and biennial reports, with minor interruptions, from its founding. Beginning in 1888 a stream of published agricultural reports were issued from the institution. Student annuals began at College Park, as they did in Baltimore, during the 1890's. A number of these, particularly the College Park annual of 1920, contain interesting historical articles and reminiscences. The student newspaper began to appear early in the twentieth century.

After the Maryland Agricultural College trustees became the state board of agriculture in 1916 and after they, in turn, became the board of regents of the combined University of Maryland in 1920, the records multiply rapidly. The regents' minutes, located in the regents' office in Baltimore, now fill twenty-nine closely typed volumes and are supplemented by six four-drawer filing cabinets of reports and correspondence. For the historian they represent the dawn of the age of the filing cabinet. In the president's office in College Park the papers relating to President Woods' administration (1917-1926) fill two tightly packed cabinets; those of President Pearson's administration (1926-1935) fill about five cabinets; the papers relating to President Byrd's administration (1935-1954) fill forty-odd cabinets; and those relating to President Elkins' administration (1954 to date) are outpacing all his predecessors combined. This material can be supplemented, especially for the recent years, by records in the comptroller's office, the registrar's office, the public relations' office, the alumni office, and the vice presidents' offices. Particularly important are the minutes of the University senate since 1954. In recent years every college and department maintains records which become abundant. There are valuable collections of papers in the McKeldin Library and in the possession of individuals who have been associated with the University. Many people, of course, simply remember interesting material about the institution's past, material which cannot be found at all in the filing cabinets and which sometimes should probably not be put in such written form as could be found there.

Good newspapers in Annapolis and Baltimore contain useful material on the social and political background for the development of higher education, on the emergence of the professions and on the specific schools. In this study systematic use has been made of the *Maryland Gazette* (Annapolis) from 1745 to 1813, the *Federal Gazette* (Baltimore) from 1802 to 1838, the *Baltimore American* from 1817 to 1877, and especially the *Baltimore Sun* from 1837 to the present. During much of the twentieth century the *Sunpapers* cast a mercilessly critical eye on the University emerging in College Park and Baltimore, and especially on its politically oriented president, Harry Clifton Byrd. Although the *Sunpapers* judged harshly the accomplishments and motives of President Byrd, they provided unequalled coverage of the institution. Clipping files of these and other newspapers, including those from the counties of Maryland and from Washington, D. C., are maintained in the regents' office, the president's office and the McKeldin Library.

Index